Endgames and New Times

The Final Years of British Communism 1964-1991

GEOFF ANDREWS

Lawrence & Wishart
LONDON 2004

Lawrence and Wishart Limited
99a Wallis Road
London
E9 5LN

First published 2004

Copyright © Lawrence and Wishart 2004

The author has asserted his rights under the Copyright, Design and Patents Act, 1998 to be identified as the author of this work.

All rights reserved. Apart from fair dealing for the purpose of private study, research, criticism or review, no part of this publication may be reproduced, stored in a retrieval system, or transmitted, in any form or by any means, electronic, electrical, chemical, mechanical, optical, photocopying, recording or otherwise, without the prior permission of the copyright owner.

British Library Cataloguing in Publication Data.
A catalogue record for this book is available from the British Library

ISBN 0 85315 991 2

Text setting E-type, Liverpool
Printed by Biddles, Kings Lynn

Contents

Preface — 10
Introduction — 12

Part One: Class, Culture, Communism and the Challenge of the New Social Movements: 1964-1974

1. Communist Identity and the Impact of the YCL — 20
   The Context of the 1960s
   Class as the Organising Principle of Communist Identity
   The Contradictions of Class: Emancipation or Cultural Conservatism?
   Working-class Unity
   The Communist Party in the early 1960s
   The YCL and the Cultural Explosion
   The Trend is Communism
   Anticipating Gramsci?

2. Unlikely Allies: Feminists, Students and the Party — 50
   The Politics of the New Social Movements
   The CP and the New Student Movement
   Left Behind: Communist Students in Crisis 1968-1972
   Broad Left and Organic Intellectuals; the Communist Student Breakthrough: 1972-1974
   The Origins of the Feminist Critique
   The Impact of *Red Rag*
   Feminism comes in from the Cold

Part Two: Renewing the Party: 1964-1974

3. Ideological and Strategic Renewal in the CPGB 1964-1968 — 73
   The Break with Leninism: The British Road to Socialism and the New Political Strategy
   The Return of Socialist Humanism
   Questions of Ideology and Culture
   The Communist-Christian Dialogue

The Contours of Militant Labourism
   The Critique of Monopoly Capitalism
   Organising For Struggle: The Principle of Left Unity
   The Prague Spring and After
   In Search of a Strategy?

4. **The Communist Party's Industrial Strategy 1968-1974**   105
   Militant Labourism and the Consolidation of the New Militancy
   Situating the Party within the New Militancy
   The CP and Free Collective Bargaining
   Assessing the Party's Impact
   Extending the Party's Influence in the Unions
   The Limits of Pragmatism: The Party's Influence in the Trade
      Union Broad Lefts
   The Consolidation of Militant Labourism: Industrial Strategy
      Meets Political Strategy
   The Conservatism of Militant Labourism
   The CP, the Labour Left and the Alternative Economic Strategy
   Battles From Within: Divisions over Economic and Industrial
      Strategy Emerge
   Battles From Without: The Split over the Social Contract

Part Three: The Rise and Fall of an Alternative Strategy: 1975-1979

5. **From Gramscism to Eurocommunism 1975-1977**   140
   The Emergence of British Gramscism
   British Gramscism and the New Left
   The Influence of Gramsci in the CP
   The Critique of Economism
   The Feminist Critique
   The Cultural Critique
   Political Agency and the Limits of Economism
   Redefining Class Politics
   Class and the Politics of Liberation
   Gramscism Meets Eurocommunism: A New Political Strategy?
   Eurocommunism and the Centrality of Democracy
   The Revolutionary Democrats and the New British Road to
      Socialism
   The Return of the Soviet Mantra
   A Hollow Victory?

6. **The CP in Decline 1977-1979**   178
   Gramscism Put On Hold
   From Renewal to Inertia: The Leadership Fights Back
   The Forward March of Labour Halted

The Debate Opens Up
The Consolidation of Division
The Decline of the Party's Industrial Base
The YCL's Downturn
The Student Demise
Another Exodus of Intellectuals?

Part Four: The Final Battle

7. **The Death of Militant Labourism and the Crisis of Class Politics** — 201
   The Battle Commences
   The Soviet Mantra Lives On
   Divided We Stand
   No Private Drama
   Class Crisis; the Wider Context
   Feminism and the Crisis of Class
   From Class Politics to New Times.

8. **New Times and After** — 224
   The Evolution of the New Times Project
   Marxism Today's New Times
   From British Gramscism to New Times: A New Political Trajectory
   The Manifesto For New Times
   The Philosophy of the Manifesto
   New Times and the New Left
   New Times and New Labour

Bibliography — 247

Index — 260

Acronyms

ACTT	Association of Cinematograph, Television and Allied Technicians
AES	Alternative Economic Strategy
AEU	Amalgamated Engineering Union
APEX	Association of Professional Executive, Clerical and Computer Staff
ASLEF	Associated Society of Locomotive Engineers and Firemen
AUEW	Amalgamated Union of Engineering Workers
BDA	Broad Democratic Alliance
BBC	British Broadcasting Corporation
BRS	British Road to Socialism
CBI	Confederation of British Industry
CND	Campaign for Nuclear Disarmament
COHSE	Confederation of Health Service Employees
CP	Communist Party
CPGB	Communist Party of Great Britain
CPSA	Civil and Public Services Association
CUL	Communist University of London
DC	Democratic Centralism
EC	Executive Committee (Communist Party)
EEC	European Economic Community
EETPU	Electrical, Electronic, Telecommunications and Plumbing Union
ETU	Electrical Trades Union
FBU	Fire Brigades Union
GMWU	General and Municipal Workers Union
ILP	Independent Labour Party
IMG	International Marxist Group
IRA	Industrial Relations Act
IS	International Socialists
IWC	Institute for Workers Control
LCDTU	Liaison Committee for the Defence of Trades Unions
NALGO	National and Local Government Officers' Organisation
NEC	National Executive Committee (Labour Party)
NLR	New Left Review
NSO	National Student Organiser (Communist Party)

NSC	National Student Committee (Communist Party)
NUPE	National Union of Public Employees
NUS	National Union of Seamen/National Union of Students
NUT	National Union of Teachers
PC	Political Committee (Communist Party)
PCE	Spanish Communist Party
PCF	French Communist Party
PCI	Italian Communist Party
RSA	Radical Student Alliance
RSSF	Revolutionary Socialist Student Federation
SOGAT	Society of Graphical and Allied Trades
SWP	Socialist Workers Party
QIC	Questions of Ideology and Culture
TASS	Technical and Supervisory Section of AUEW
TGWU	Transport and General Workers Union
TIC	Theory and Ideology Committee
TUC	Trades Union Congress
UCATT	Union of Construction, Allied Trades and Technicians
UCS	Upper Clyde Shipbuilders
USDAW	Union of Shop, Distributive and Allied Workers
WEA	Workers Educational Association
WLM	Women's Liberation Movement
YCL	Young Communist League

Preface and Acknowledgements

This book started out as a PhD in late 1992, a short time after the Communist Party of Great Britain turned itself into the Democratic Left. The Communist Party archives also became available to researchers at this time and I benefited considerably from access to previously unavailable material and from the advice and helpfulness of George Matthews and Francis King, custodians of the archive, which was originally housed in an old warehouse in Hackney, east London. The archive was subsequently moved to the National Museum of Labour History in Manchester, where it was collated and supervised by Andy Flinn and colleagues, and I am grateful for the help I received from them. Having a range of primary sources available to me meant that I was able to overcome the difficulties faced by many previous researchers, while my own membership of the CPGB from 1985-1991 allowed me to use personal contacts.

Research into the most recent period of the party's history means that many of the protagonists, intellectuals and activists are still around, and I'm grateful to the generosity of the following for giving up their time to talk about the past in interviews and informal discussions: Sam Aaronovitch, Joe Ball, Sarah Benton, Jon Bloomfield, Jude Bloomfield, Doug Bourne, George Bridges, Genia Browning, Trevor Carter, Pat Devine, Reuben Falber, Joanna de Groot, Jackie Heywood, Sally Hibbin, Steve Iliffe, Martin Jacques, Steve Jeffereys, Monty Johnstone, Gordon McLennan, Alan McDougall, George Matthews, Chris Myant, Chris Nawrat, Mark Perryman, Gerry Pocock, Mike Power, Mike Prior, Dave Purdy, Geoff Roberts, Sue Slipman, Ken Spours, Graham Taylor, Nina Temple, Willie Thompson, Angela Weir and Elizabeth Wilson.

I'm also grateful to Mike Prior, Mike Power, Joe Ball and Willie Thompson for giving me access to private papers and correspondence. I would also like to record my thanks to Raphael Samuel and Michael Stephen, who in different ways provided me with important insight, but who died during the course of my research.

Professor Anne Showstack Sassoon supervised my research and I am very grateful to her for her insight, encouragement and friendship over these years, though she may disagree with the book's political conclusions. I am also grateful to Kevin Morgan, Nina Fishman, Philip Spencer, Professor David Howell and Professor Willie Thompson for reading and commenting on draft chapters at different stages of my research. I am very grateful to Ethlyn Boothe for helping me with various technical issues along the way. Sally Davison at Lawrence and Wishart has been a constant source of advice and encouragement. I shared many interesting conversations with Herbert Pimlott as a contemporary researcher and friend. David Selbourne, my old tutor at Ruskin, has continued to provide invaluable insight on the predicaments of the British left.

The politics department at the Open University, under Professors Grahame Thompson and Mike Saward has been a very friendly and conducive place to work, and I'm grateful for the sabbatical which enabled me to complete the book. I'm also grateful to the Barry Amiel and Norman Melburn Trust for providing a grant for the latter stages of my research and to Kingston University for funding a trip to Montreal to give a paper on the Communist University of London in 1995. The book was completed in Bologna, a beautifully preserved medieval city which, through its enlightened local government in the 1970s, became the symbol of an alternative idea of communism, one shared by many of the people discussed in these pages.

Introduction: the Legacy of British Communism

Since the defeat of the communist regimes in Eastern Europe in 1989 there has been renewed interest in the history of communism. The scope of this research has been broad and includes overviews of communism in the 'short twentieth century', insight into the failures of communist ideology and comparative studies on the fortunes of former communist parties after 1989. Much of the research has considered the role of the Soviet Union, helped to a substantial degree by the opening of the Moscow archives.[1] As far as the British Communist Party is concerned, most of the research has focused on its earliest years, with the later period receiving less attention, or featuring mainly as a minor part of more general accounts of its history. This has meant that the hopes, aspirations and illusions of the most recent generation of communists have either been obscured, or have been the subject or anecdotal references in the wider history of the New Left.

One much discussed example of the latter was Martin Amis's *Koba The Dread*. The difference between Amis's account and the line of argument that has been growing since 1989 that has reduced the communist experience to that of the Soviet Union and Stalin's legacy is that his target is his own generation.[2] He focuses on the '60s' cohort of 'New Left' activists, those who came to socialism with fewer illusions about the Soviet Union than earlier generations and had been inspired by the events of 1968. His most obvious oversight in what is largely an intemperate attack is the failure to acknowledge that the New Left was born from anti-Stalinism.[3] The dissident intellectuals who resigned or were expelled from Communist Parties in the wake of Khrushchev's revelations about Stalin in 1956, and in protest at the Soviet invasion of Hungary in the same year, made important contributions to the various movements and ideas of the subsequent decade. In Britain, where the CPGB lost a quarter of its membership in the aftermath, notable intellectuals such as Edward Thompson, John Saville and Raphael Samuel responded by establishing an extremely imaginative, original, intellectually rigorous and indigenous dissident Marxist tradition – the 'first New Left' as it has been described – with pioneering work in areas of culture and social history.

Accounts such as Amis's not only make simplistic assertions; they also miss the opportunity to look at distinctive and underlying features of the 'communist experience' in Britain. Antonio Gramsci's view that to write a history of a party is also in effect to write the history of a country has much relevance in this respect.

As far as Britain is concerned, members of the small but at times quite influential Communist Party did share illusions about the Soviet Union, notably in the party's early period and during the war, and this remained true for a declining number in the aftermath of 1956 and its later years.[4] But the events of 1956 did much to undermine this position.

Indeed the impact of 1956 for the party, as many have shown, was almost catastrophic. Alison Macleod, in her insider's account, has shown the personal as well as political dilemmas many faced on the party's paper *The Daily Worker*, as they attempted to comprehend the seriousness of the events. She also describes the cold and calculating demeanour of Rajani Palme Dutt, as well as the hopeless illusions and doublespeak of many other party leaders, the censorship of journalists and the dismay and depression of those who learned the worst.[5] Communist Parties across the world staggered and attempted to renew themselves in the wake of these events. Some barely managed it, others retained loyalty to the Stalinist legacy.

For many, it was the Italian Communist Party (PCI), rooted as it was in the anti-fascist moment of resistance and reconstruction (and co-author of Italy's post-war constitution), that set out the most comprehensive attempt to find another road. Its mass support, strong cultural presence, big workers' movement and innovative local government (in its later years) brought admiration from those beyond the communist tradition as well as strong electoral performances at home. Thus the Italian Communist Party became for many a symbol of an alternative road to socialism. Of course the British Communist Party was much smaller, and presented no electoral threat – it was always tiny in comparison to the Labour Party – and furthermore it was not as reformist as the PCI. It lost many impressive intellectuals in 1956, and often presented, in the late 1950s and early 1960s, a grey image of workmanlike pragmatism.

That the party was able to survive and – for further brief moments – prosper, suggests there is another history; or at least that there are different, often contending communist histories of its later period that need attention. The opening up of the party archives and a growing and significant attention to a 'history from below' have already contributed to a recognition of the diversity in the communist experience in earlier moments. Research in this area has raised questions in relation to the party's identity, culture and political strategy that are discussed in the first part of this book.[6]

The 'history from below' approaches are revealing, and when

applied to the CPGB in its later years point to a party of contradictions. While funding from Moscow continued in one form or another until 1979, and the Soviet Union remained for some a positive example of what an alternative society could be like, the 1956 humanist spirit of dissent returned in later years in the development of a British Gramscian perspective. In spite of the anti-intellectualism which was evident in the attack on the party's intellectuals in 1956, in later years a more prominent role was given to a formidable array of intellectuals, as those humanists who remained in the party made alliances with a new cohort shaped by the ideas and movements of the 1960s. For them, 1968 was the defining moment. Dubcek's attempts at reform in the Prague Spring, and the widespread student protests in the West, as well as other new forms of militancy, represented a turning-point in the politics of many party members and intellectuals; the British party leadership's criticism of the Soviet action in Prague was thus crucial in sustaining their commitment.

There were also contradictions in the culture of the CPGB. A party that was conservative in its attitudes to culture and society was also the site of innovation, promiscuity and change. A patriarchal party whose activities often depended on a sexual division of labour which mirrored that of wider society was also able to produce a notable cohort of feminists: while their politics was often troubling (and at times incomprehensible) to party leaders, many feminists found in the party a rather unlikely space for their agendas for a few brief years. In the account that follows we will find that those who joined the Communist Party in the 1970s were as likely to be working on a feminist collective or a student newspaper as in a trade union, and their influences were more likely to come from Lennon than Lenin. Some, like Amis and his contemporaries at the *New Statesman*, may have spent their time over long lunches comparing notes on the merits of the Soviet Union as compared to the USA. But this was not found to be a major preoccupation amongst the cohort of intellectuals I interviewed. 'I plead guilty to innocence, naivety and enthusiasm', one communist activist admitted to me, recalling his earlier commitment.[7]

If any one figure symbolised the optimism of this communist generation it would have to be Dave Cook. Trained as a communist organiser, he first came to prominence in the party when he was parachuted in by the leadership as National Student Organiser in the early 1970s (much to the initial annoyance of the National Student Committee). He brought to this work creativity, organisational nous, and an attitude to life which seemed to reflect the more libertarian era. As a party organiser for most of the 1960s and 1970s he enjoyed an increasingly fractious relationship with the leadership, particularly its more traditionalist sections, as he grew into his key role of seeking to articulate the Gramscian politics of the new social movements. Formed by the party, his identity as a communist – one which he retained until his premature death during a round the world bike ride – seemed to be one of competing, if not contradictory, allegiances, both to the party of which he was a leading member and to the ideas and movements which continually questioned its strategy.

The most important 'domestic' feature of British communism remained its commitment to working-class struggle, and this was evident in the high proportion of skilled workers amongst its members, and its influence in the trade unions; and its strength in this area was vigorously renewed from the mid-1960s under the leadership of Bert Ramelson. This ability to immerse itself in the culture and organisational practices of the labour movement gave the party its most effective indigenous identity, and the high regard in which communist organisation was held, and the breadth of solidarity it was capable of generating, went some way to providing an alternative image of communist identity to the one associated with the Soviet Union. It was also crucial in the development and consolidation of its industrial strategy, and meant that the party was to play a big organisational role in the major period of industrial militancy of the 1970s.

Indeed the party was so strongly embedded in the British labour movement tradition that its demise was fundamentally linked to the crisis of labourism in face of the major social and economic changes of the late 1960s and early 1970s. Its reliance on the Labour Party and the labourist assumptions that went with it, and its inability to find a distinctive independent political role, played a crucial role in the party's downfall. The CPGB shared many of the conservative aspects of labourism, notably economism and sectionalism, while it had misplaced faith in the ability of the skilled working class, located as it was in declining industries, to organise wholesale political change.

The developments in the Soviet Union precipitated the swiftness of the end and meant there was no possibility of reviving a communist dream in whatever form. However they cannot be seen as the root cause of the party's demise: the party cannot be understood solely in terms of the history of the Soviet Union. It had long since embarked upon a reformist direction, and had always drawn on local British and – in its last years – other Western European political traditions.

This, essentially, is the argument in this book. It is the British context that is crucial in understanding the CPGB's ideology, cultural influences and strategic options. This is not to ignore the party's wider relationship to the international communist movement. But even here it needs to be understood that, though the 'Soviet Mantra' – the cause of significant faith and loyalty for many members of the CPGB – remained important in debates and events at certain moments, there were other equally important international links. The 'Eurocommunist' movement in the mid-1970s provided a vital external context for understanding some of the strategic dilemmas facing the party, as its more prominent peer parties, the Italian PCI, the French

PCF and the Spanish PCE, came to enjoy a degree of electoral and political success. In the case of the former, cultural as much as political factors were a constant source of inspiration, as young communists, intellectuals, feminists and students attempted to modernise the image of communist identity.

This argument frames the following parts and chapters of the book. Part One assesses the impact of social and cultural changes on the party's communist identity, and the ways in which the rise of the new social movements critically questioned the party's strategy, firstly the youth movement, through the Young Communist League (YCL) in the 1960s, and then the women's and the students' movements in the 1970s. As well as generational shifts, there were significant cultural challenges to the party's identity. The YCL sought to root their politics in popular-cultural initiatives, which reflected the musical, sexual and generational milieus of British society at the time. As such they received rebukes from party leaders that were similar to those handed out by other parental figures. These social and cultural challenges had long-term implications for the party. The traditional working-class ethos which sustained traditional communist commitment and activity was challenged, while culture as a site of political struggle was a feature of later Gramscian-Eurocommunist politics.

Similarly, there was a profound feminist influence on the party, firstly through the journal *Red Rag*, the dissemination of which was contrary to party rules, then through the involvement of feminist activists on the party's National Women's Advisory Committee, and ultimately through the theoretical critique feminists made of labourism. This brought conflict as well as much creativity and energy; hostility, but also attempts to accommodate and understand the demands of a new generation of women who were not prepared for the politics of gender or sexuality to be subordinate to class as a secondary political concern.

Communist students, left behind as a conservative force in the upheavals of student protest of 1968, benefited from the development of a new political generation in the 1970s; they were influential in the Broad Left group which dominated student politics at this time. In addition to their organisational capabilities and sense for political strategy, they provided crucial intellectual input – through the Communist University of London and other forums – in which Gramscian ideas were discussed and dispersed within and beyond the party. Together with feminists, young communists and the older earlier generation of intellectuals and activists who responded to their call, they were crucial to the renewal of the party and to the construction of an alternative political strategy.

This attempt to renew the party is the central theme of Part Two, which describes how the ideology of militant labourism shaped the political direction of the party's industrial strategy under Bert Ramelson. This resulted in the party having a closer relationship than before to the Labour Party and trade union mainstream, which it managed to sustain while mobilising support from the grassroots, in a very intense period of militancy in British industrial politics. The somewhat paradoxical relationship to the Labour Party – as both left critic and supporter – was evident as the party's major strategic dilemma. *The British Road to Socialism* (*BRS*), the party's programme, continued to commit itself throughout the period to the election of a Labour Government of a 'new type', while attempting to maintain a distinctive communist position.

The other dimension of ideological renewal was the rediscovery of a socialist humanist tradition; William Morris was identified as a key antecedent of this tradition, as were the anti-fascists of the 1930s. Indeed this tradition had been formative for the generation of intellectuals who came to politics in the 1930s. Socialist humanism was committed to an ethical dimension to politics, and attributed a greater role to personal agency. This in turn facilitated an important 'Communist-Christian' dialogue, the consolidation of a more autonomous role for culture in the party's programme, the growth of more critical attitudes towards the Soviet Union and, above all, a productive alliance with the younger cohort of party intellectuals. Crucially, this humanism resonated with positions adopted elsewhere on the 'New Left', allowing in some cases common platforms, and greater respect, between differing positions that had developed in the aftermath of 1956.

My argument here is that from the mid-1960s onwards, militant labourism and socialist humanism, and subsequently 'British Gramscism', provided the decisive ideological contours within which the party formed its communist identity. As such it is my contention that the more common distinctions, notably that between 'Stalinist' or 'Leninist' on the one hand and 'Eurocommunist' on the other, while useful in many ways, are inadequate terms which do not enable us to understand in any coherent or clear way the dynamics which shaped British communist experience. In the last years of its existence this traditional terminology is even less appropriate. It might be argued that the British Communist Party's loyalty to the Soviet Union is a sufficient reason to describe its position as 'Stalinist'. However this not only obscures the impact of other experiences, influences and contradictions, but fails to distinguish in any significant way the different relationship between Moscow and national parties before and after 1956 and then post-1968. The adoption of the parliamentary road set out in the *BRS* in 1951 abandoned any Leninist pretence (despite the term remaining in communist jargon), and while the party officially organised itself on the basis of democratic centralism, it did not operate as a tightly-knit organisational group and tolerated significant breaches of party rules (by young communists, feminists and also industrial organisers, not to mention the activities of dissident factions in the last years).

Thus the disagreements that focused the party's attention as it debated its strategy were shaped by influences closer to home. In the third part of the book, I discuss the development of the British Gramscian perspective and how this position grew – despite uneven and specific articulations by feminists, students and assorted intellectuals – into the main ideological and strategic challenge to militant labourism, the governing philosophy of the British Communist Party during these years. The links between Gramscism and Eurocommunism are discussed, with the 'British Eurocommunist' high tide being the re-writing of the *BRS* in 1977, a time when other communist parties in Europe made big electoral gains. However the 'victory' of 1977 when the Gramscians had many of their proposals accepted was only partial and short-lived. Further attempts to reform the party's structures were defeated when the Inner Party Democracy proposals were rejected in 1979, leading to further conservative responses by the party leadership.

This became a signal for decline, and for the intensification of division between rival positions in the party. In Part Four of the book I argue that the main cause of the party's decline was the crisis of labourism, and the crisis of 'class politics' that went with it. This was a crisis that had become deeply rooted in the culture and practices of the British left, and the party reflected this wider inertia, and the widespread backward-looking culture of decline. Thus the pulling down of the Berlin Wall and the fall of the Soviet Union, while decisive in confirming the realisation that communism could not be 'reapplied' – a conclusion already drawn by many on the party's reforming wing – only accelerated processes which had been underway in the party for some time. The irony of 'New Times' being the last will and testament of the British Communist Party is a poignant one. However, as I argue in the final chapter, the Gramscian influence which connected with earlier New Left traditions, and inspired the last generation of party activists, did not die completely with the party. It lived to fight another day in an assorted group of intellectuals and networks who continued to believe that a viable, radical and modern left was possible.

NOTES

1. See E. Hobsbawm, *Age of Extremes: The Short Twentieth Century*, Michael Joseph 1994; R. Skidelsky, *The World After Communism: A Polemic For Our Times*, Macmillan 1995; D. Selbourne, *Death of the Dark Hero*, Jonathan Cape 1990; F. Mount, *Communism*, Harvill 1992.
2. See amongst others F. Furet, *The Passing of an Illusion: The Idea of Communism in the Twentieth Century*, University of Chicago Press 1999.
3. 'In the days when the New Left dawned, the argument was about whether Bolshevik Russia was better than America'. M. Amis, *Koba The Dread*, Jonathan Cape 2002, p25.
4. The term 'party' will be the usual description of the activities of the CPGB in this book, following a similar usage in other research, including N.

Fishman, *The Communist Party and the Trade Unions 1933-1945*, Scolar Press 1995; W. Thompson, *The Good Old Cause*, Pluto Press 1995; and F. Beckett, *Enemy Within*, John Murray 1995. On some occasions CP or CPGB will be used to distinguish it from other political parties.
5. A. Macleod, *The Death of Uncle Joe*, Merlin Press 1997.
6. The 'history from below' research on the CPGB includes: H. Adi, *West Africans in Britain*, Lawrence and Wishart 1998; H. Srebrnik, *London Jews and British Communism*, Vallentine Mitchell 1994; A. Croft (ed), *Weapon in the Struggle: the Cultural History of the Communist Party in Britain*, Pluto Press 1998; P. Cohen, *Children of the Revolution*, Lawrence and Wishart 1997.
7. Chris Nawrat, interview with author.

PART ONE

Class, Culture, Communism and the Challenge of the New Social Movements: 1964–1974

1. Communist Identity and the Impact of the YCL

THE CONTEXT OF THE 1960s
The purpose of Chapter One is to explore the impact of the social and cultural changes associated with the 1960s on the Communist Party of Great Britain, and the consequent implications these carried for its overall politics. It will assess the ways in which class as the organising principle of communist identity – evident in the dominant aspects of the party's social composition and in the culture and ethos it espoused, as well as in the core role attributed to it in delivering political change – started to be eroded and challenged by the rise of a new young communist cohort. This cohort, in its political activities, both reflected the emerging social and generational changes in British society, and sought to articulate a new political direction embedded in the radical social movements that were beginning to emerge in Britain at the time.

This chapter is divided broadly into two parts. Firstly, it will explain the CPGB's class culture, namely the way in which a particular set of social values associated with the skilled working class became an overriding ethos around which the party organised its political identity. This will include a discussion of the contradictions and paradoxes of this class culture, which reflected a tension between educative strategies of emancipation and the perceived need to reflect, in aspects of party life and culture, what it saw as the morality of the mainstream. This will then be followed by a discussion of the way in which the party's class culture was held to be the unifying core around which its different social constituencies could be incorporated. This in turn will include an assessment of the way in which class as the organising principle of British communist identity was prioritised over other social categories such as gender and 'race'.

Secondly, the chapter will show how the cultural transformations in the Young Communist League, notably in the period between 1964-1967, disrupted the assumptions upon which this unifying core depended, with the assertion of more strident and autonomous political voices, ones which reflected wider socio-cultural changes. Finally, the implications of these challenges for the party's subsequent political strategy will be assessed, including an indication of how subsequent chapters will build on the arguments presented here.

The argument developed here will focus on the way in which the wider changes of the 1960s impinged on, and re-shaped, the particular political community that made up the CPGB. Much has been written about the political significance of the 1960s as a watershed decade; this period saw the rise of the new left and new social movements that coalesced around the events of 1968, and proved crucial in articulating new ideas of emancipation. Writers have disagreed over the precise significance of the decade; some, like Jameson and Marwick, have stressed the cultural transformations of the decade as having the most decisive effect;[1] while Cockett has argued that where the left benefited most from the long-term cultural effects, the libertarian right has drawn more on the political legacy.[2] Recent research has pointed to the paradoxes of the decade; at different times, the political and social movements asserted anti-Americanism, or pro-Americanism; at times asserting pro-materialist values, with the references to fashion, pop icons and glamour; at other times, anti-materialist, in the 'opting out' stance of the hippies.[3] Most accounts however point to the effect of social changes on lifestyles, though there has also been disagreement over which social groups benefited most from the 1960s. Some, like Jonathan Green, have seen the 1960s as an essentially middle-class affair, where the development of a student vanguard was a relatively short-term protest, after which 'those primarily middle-class activists would for the most part fade back into the conventional world of work'.[4] Stuart Hall sees the decade as formative in the erosion of class as the 'master identity' that shaped people's perceptions of who they were, and their belief systems and aspirations, and in the shift towards multiple differences. In this sense, he argues, the birth of 'identity politics' can be traced to the black civil rights movement, and the beginnings of the student, feminist and gay liberation movements during this decade.[5] Moreover, others have seen the 1960s as the decade in which these 'new social movements' challenged the institution of the political party as one no longer able to represent or contain their different political expressions.[6]

The CPGB during this period can be seen at one level as a microcosm of the wider society, and therefore strongly affected by these changes. It too was faced with a cultural challenge to its existing conservative ethos; the newer cultures of feminism, sexual freedom and generational tensions called into question the traditional skilled working-class culture which had exuded particular moral attitudes, cultural orthodoxies and social behaviour. The party was also challenged by groups seeking new forms of autonomy which threatened to undermine the party's own organisational structure based on democratic centralism. These general dilemmas, which the party shared with the wider traditional cultures, were supplemented by the party's own specific predicaments. It will be argued that the cultural changes of the 1960s both challenged *and* redefined what it meant to be a communist. In other words the impact of the wider changes, while serious for the party's own future, also helped *maintain* a critical political perspective, by bringing previously latent groups to the fore of the party's profile, as the forces most likely to renew its appeal.

In assessing the 1960s many commentators have referred to the 'long sixties' – a cultural and political watershed that outgrew the decade itself, lasting into the early 1970s.[7] This periodisation will be adopted here to emphasise the extent of cultural and political shifts that took place within the party. The year 1963, which many have seen as the onset of the 'sixties', was also a defining moment in the new influence of the Young Communist League, through its identification with rock culture, hedonistic aspirations and the commitment to popular culture as a political form of protest. As well as serving to undermine the party's existing cultural outlook, these developments, I will argue, were crucial in influencing the subsequent development of a Gramscian politics, and thus helping to delineate later points of conflict and strategy.

CLASS AS THE ORGANISING PRINCIPLE OF COMMUNIST IDENTITY

As argued in the introduction, recent research on the history of the CPGB has warned of the dangers of reducing its influence to that of the fortunes of the Soviet Union. However crucial its relationship was to the Soviet Union and the experience of the socialist countries at particular moments in its history, these do not provide an adequate explanation for the levels of commitment, loyalty and identity amongst those who joined the party. This is particularly the case from the 1960s and into the 1970s, when there were disagreements over the invasion of Czechoslovakia and the denial of civil liberties and political pluralism in the Soviet Union. Not only were these increasingly tense areas of contestation, but in general terms the Soviet Union was less likely to be a prime source of identity. Indeed, from interviews of the generation of communists who joined after 1968, it is clear that the party's criticism of Soviet action in Czechoslovakia was a pre-requisite for their decision to join.[8]

Moreover, even in the earlier cold war period of the 1950s it can be argued that allegiance to the Soviet Union, though often an important source of faith and symbol of an alternative society, is a very inadequate way of explaining the identity of British communists.[9] Many historians have therefore found other explanations for the dynamics which have provided the raison d'être for being a communist. The most common explanation has been the class basis of the party, characterised both by its particular social composition and in its wider cultural practices and sources of political identity. Politically, it is of course hardly surprising that class should be a defining feature of communist politics, as all communist parties, through their Marxist doctrines, have embodied a class analysis as central to their ideology. The CPGB was no different from this, and subsequent chapters will show the ways in which its ideological outlook was shaped by Marxist approaches, often in revised and contested forms. However the significance of class for the CPGB went deeper than its ideological emphasis in justifying the need for social transformation. There was also a strong class *ethos* which was crucial in shaping the party's political identity, and which pervaded different aspects of the party's life. Nina Fishman, for example, has argued that it was the strength of this class ethos which gave the party the ability to engage with what she calls 'Life Itself'. By this she means the way in which the party was able to enmesh itself successfully – albeit in particular occupational groupings – in the day to day realities of industrial struggles in the 1930s.[10] Raphael Samuel, writing about a similar period of mass politics, has argued that this 'class feeling' of the CPGB was reflected in a whole set of moral, organisational and behavioural practices, whereupon a 'class lead', a 'class position' and 'proletarian morality' were crucial to its 'sense of corporate identity and to its idealised self-image'.[11] Geoff Eley has also pointed to the 'binding power' of the party's class approach, throughout its history, one which provided 'the integration and directionality (for) ... a politics of radical change to cohere more persuasively together'.[12] In the only major sociological survey of the CPGB's membership, conducted in the early 1960s, Kenneth Newton found the party's class appeal to be the principal point of attraction for those who joined the party.[13] Hobsbawm has noted the distinctive class cohesion of left-wing movements in Britain, in comparison to other countries. For Hobsbawm, 'the massive sense of class solidarity and class unity of the British working class' was a feature of both the Labour Party and the Communist Party; class identity was the crucial point of appeal for the left parties in Britain.[14] It will be argued here that these similarities between the two parties in their class culture continued into the 1960s and 1970s, and enabled them to find common political ground; a commonality that was to have both positive and negative implications for the party's overall strategy.

The party's social composition showed a decisive working-class orientation from the beginning, though it recruited from very specific occupational categories. From its foundation in 1920, the party recruited disproportionately from core skilled and semi-skilled occupations, notably engineering, mining, docking and transport. It also recruited heavily from the industrial heartlands of Scotland, South Wales, the West Riding of Yorkshire and the North East, as well as the East End of London. This domination of the skilled working class was crucial, as will be argued below, for providing the party with its cultural ethos.[15]

It is also important to recognise that the party's social composition, while heavily dependent on the skilled working class, was also influenced by very specific regional factors at different moments in its history. In the 1920s for example, as a small agitational party, a large proportion of its 5000 members were concentrated in the 'Little Moscows', notably the Rhondda Valley in South Wales and the Vale of Leven outside Glasgow, while membership extended into other mining communities in support of the Miners Strike of 1926. From the late 1920s and into the 1930s the party recruited heavily amongst the unemployed, so that 60 per cent of its membership was unemployed by 1932.[16] During the 1930s and 1940s the party's membership broadened and increased substantially; it drew on a further range of skilled workers and professionals, including many teachers,[17] while it attracted a considerable intellectual following as a result of humanitarian opposition to fascism, support for the republican side in the Spanish Civil War, the readership of the Left Book Club and a range of worker-cultural initiatives.[18] In the 1930s it found deep roots, as Srebrnik has shown, amongst the Jewish community in the East End of London in the wake of the fascist threat.[19] During the war, when membership reached its peak of 56,000 in 1942, it recruited from a wider range of workers, attracted to its broader popular front image. In the 1950s, the party recruited substantially amongst West Africans because of its opposition to colonialism;[20] but it lost a quarter of its membership, amongst them many intellectual figures, in the aftermath of the events of 1956.[21]

These specificities illustrate the breadth of the party's appeal to different social groups. Only in the unusual context of the 'class against class' period (approximately 1928-1935) did the party adhere to a very narrow concept of class, and from the 1930s it maintained a strong appeal to what it perceived as the 'progressive' sections of the middle class, valuing the importance of 'cultural' and artistic endeavours; it was also in the foreground of struggles for women's emancipation, and its work in the colonial period won many converts.[22] The party was an early supporter, at various times, of the legal rights of women, access to birth control and equal rights at work, and it consistently initiated campaigns to recruit more women to the party; in 1931-32, as Bruley has documented, there was a major investigation into the party's 'failings' in involving women, and between 1941-43 the Women's Parliament was set up, out of which emerged the National Women's Advisory meetings.[23] In the period of its peak support, namely the time of the Popular Front, in which it helped mobilise broad cross-party opposition to fascism, it was the party's commitment to 'democratic patriotism' that helped sustain its appeal, leading many to argue that it was always at its strongest when it was part of a wider social coalition.[24]

Moreover, what the above points suggest is that the party was able to maintain an appeal to different segments of the population at different times, one that often reflected itself in broad popular alliances, but, equally, it often found it difficult to resolve these different 'identities' with its cultural ethos and political strategy. Recent research by Adi, Carter and Srebrnik into the party's ethnic composition has revealed how many of these cultural differences were ignored or obscured, through the complex interplay between class and ethnic identity.[25]

THE CONTRADICTIONS OF CLASS: EMANCIPATION OR CULTURAL CONSERVATISM?

Nevertheless, the centrality of class remained pivotal for the CPGB, in the period before the early 1960s, not only in terms of composition – in that it maintained a skilled working-class base – but, equally importantly, through the formation of a class identity as both the cement which held the party together and the key to the alternative future society. Raphael Samuel has given a definition of this class identity as he found it in the period of mass politics and culture in the 1930s: 'Political parties were thought of by communists as concentrated expressions of class being. They were judged not in terms of programme or policy but whether they helped a class to discover its true destiny'.[26]

In establishing the way in which this class identity was maintained, however, we need to be aware of the differences as well as similarities between the party's representation of class values and the realities as they existed. While the CPGB mirrored quite closely, at a very general level, major aspects of the class composition of British society as a whole, this should not obscure the very real differences between the party's class *ethos* and those of the wider population. To quote Thompson, while the party's fortunes 'have in a very rough fashion shadowed those of the industrial workforce, relatively flourishing when it was politically and culturally strong, declining when it was on the defensive or suffering defeat ... the party has never even remotely mirrored the prevailing attitudes and perceptions of the British working class'.[27] There is a paradox here which needs to be grasped in order to understand the centrality of class in British communism, and the amplification of such contradictions in the period under current investigation. This is that the party, by rooting itself inside the industrial culture of the British working class, both sought to *transcend* the ethos of this class, by means of educational, intellectual and moral reform, as a precondition to delivering an alternative society, and to *imbibe* or take on board the cultural values of that class, in order to avoid being seen as remote from mainstream working-class culture.[28] This helps to explain why the party targeted the skilled working class: they were seen as more 'advanced' and 'mature', the first to establish trade unions, and generally less apathetic and deferential about politics; furthermore they evinced stronger expressions of class solidarity and militant activity, more widespread take-up of forms of self-education, firmer resistance to populist shifts in political allegiance, and greater geographical and occupational stability.[29]

This commitment to self-education was crucial to the way in which the party sought to transcend existing working-class culture, in the hope that it would help to facilitate the maturity of the working class. Stuart MacIntyre has discussed at length the development of an autodidactic, proletarian political culture in the party's earliest years, with its roots in the Plebs League and the National Council For Labour Colleges. This helped shape the party's educational work as well as encouraging the dissemination of Marxist ideas within the working class.[30] Close connections between the Communist Party and adult education have been found by other researchers.[31] MacIntyre identified an 'earnest minority', (a term he borrowed from Richard Hoggart),[32] whom he saw as crucial in mediating the party's values to the working class through their own self-education and development of Marxist ideas. This made them both 'at once representatives of, and strangers in, their own society', reflecting further the paradoxical aspect of the party's attitude towards the wider mass culture.[33] This tension was formalised after 1922, when the party standardised its education materials to reflect more official Comintern priorities, while from 1929 the bureaucratisation and professionalisation of the party structures also provided more rigid layers between the mainstream culture and the party's own culture. Nevertheless, one of the effects of the success of the communist commitment to self-education was to introduce and sustain a working-class leadership (termed by Hobsbawm 'a first-rate group of native proletarians'[34]) earlier than other parties of the left. This included in its early years Arthur Horner, Harry Pollitt, J.R. Campbell and Willie Gallacher. The long succession of self-educated party General Secretaries, including John Gollan and Gordon McLennan, who continued to graduate from the ranks of the skilled working class, reinforced this tradition.

A further indication of the party's commitment to develop working-class culture was the importance given to the role of intellectuals, who began to join in larger numbers in the 1930s, in humanitarian opposition to fascism and support for the republican side in the Spanish Civil War.[35] During the 1930s the party exerted a strong hegemony over left-wing intellectuals, and began to develop a range of party journals and cultural organisations. The influx of intellectuals, notably a cohort of Marxist historians such as Hobsbawm, Saville and Thompson, and the breadth of the party's cultural interests, which ranged from classical music and graphic art to more popular cultural forms such as mass pageants and an extensive commitment to radical film initiatives, combined to broaden the scope of the party's appeal.[36] Art and culture, as Croft argues, was 'one of the ways in which communist ideas entered the mainstream of British life and through which the party was able to identify itself as the defender of native popular traditions and as the bearer of the new, and therefore of the future'.[37]

Some of the more extreme examples of the party's attempt to impose an alternative morality as the precondition to emancipation have been discussed by Raphael Samuel. Samuel, reflecting on the 1930s, described communist morality in the period of mass politics as 'even more class-defined than communist politics'.[38] In this he was referring not only to the values of loyalty, self-sacrifice, and a desire for class solidarity over private, individualistic aspirations, but also to an adherence to a narrow set of moral principles. These included unofficial (and sometimes, through disciplinary action, official) guidelines for conduct, such as how party members should conduct their private lives, how they should spend their leisure time and even how they should dress. Cafés were preferred to pubs, 'clean living' (such as walking, reading and community work) to 'foul language' or 'excessive drinking', while 'working men's clubs' were regarded as 'foreign territory'.[39]

This alternative morality was shaped not only by puritanical instincts but, notably in the Cold War era, by strong doses of Anti-Americanism, whereby the party condemned the importation of what it considered to be decadent and commercialised art, and cultural forms of 'American Imperialism'.[40] At its 1952 Congress it rejected what it saw as 'the Americanisation of Britain's cultural life', and America's 'reactionary films and debased literature and comics',[41] while American dance routines of the same era, such as jitterbugging, were regarded even by Young Communist League members as 'decadent yankee be-bop'.[42]

It is important not to over-generalise from Samuel's emphasis, in what was to a degree a personal reflection based on his own experiences of Jewish communist identity and local activities in the St Pancras district of London. His experiences could be countered by other biographies which found drinking to be an important part of communist culture and the pub to be an important communist meeting place.[43] At the other extreme, moreover, if Douglas Hyde's biography is taken as representative, there were strong bohemian influences within the higher echelons of the party, particularly at party centre, where a more relaxed attitude towards conventional morality was evident. By the end of his first week's work on the *Daily Worker*, where he was news editor, Hyde became aware of various 'amorous entanglements which existed throughout the building'. It was, he revealed, 'a very loose moral atmosphere, supercharged with sex'.[44]

Mostly, however, the party attempted to appropriate what it perceived as the moral traits of the skilled working class. It is here that many of the contradictions become apparent; identifying with the mainstream often meant endorsing a conservative culture which was frequently at odds with its emancipatory ideals. Thus the party may have made an important contribution to the early development of feminist ideas, but this did not preclude its acceptance of the traditional family structure, traditional attitudes towards sex, and a subservient role for women in its own ranks. One insight into the way in which the party was concerned to reflect mainstream working-class culture in this respect has been provided by Kevin Morgan in his study of the *Daily Worker*, the party's newspaper between 1930-1956. He argues that the paper provides a revealing indication of 'how the CP conceived of its public'.[45] In addition to the relentless coverage of workers' struggles, it was felt by Harry Pollitt, the party's General Secretary, that it should, from its foundation, become a 'popular mass newspaper', closely linked to the 'needs' and 'desires' of the masses, and focusing on news, sport, fiction and general interest articles. These popular features included racing tips, knitting patterns and film reviews, with a 'worker's notebook' providing an item of humour. While providing a science page and other educational material, it was also concerned to appeal to traditional forms of working-class culture. These cultural matters invariably reflected the priorities of the male breadwinning trade unionist, making its primary appeal that of 'Dad's Paper', with sports features, gambling and other recreational forms of escapism in tune with mainstream patriarchal values.[46] Such assumptions were also prevalent in the Young Communist League's paper *Challenge* in the 1950s, which regularly featured beauty contests of YCL women, while similar 'cheesecake' pictures remained a feature in the *Morning Star* after it succeeded the *Daily Worker* in 1966.[47]

Finally, although the party could claim to have enjoyed a strong influence amongst left-wing intellectuals – certainly until 1956, when many of them left over Hungary and the Khrushchev revelations – they had a somewhat ambivalent role within the party. Respected for their contributions, at times they were also distrusted, expected to defer to industrial leaders and not given a clear role in the party. Either they became incorporated into the party structure as full-timers (such as Rajani Palme Dutt and James Klugmann), or they carried on their own field of work and remained detached from the party's strategy and ideology. At its worst, and in the wake of 1956, either they would lead a 'life of compromise' and 'surrender to party values', as Neal Wood put it, or they would leave the party altogether.[48]

WORKING-CLASS UNITY
There were significant contradictions therefore in the party's identity. The reasons the party did not perceive them as contradictory was the faith it maintained in working-class unity as the cement which would hold its different constituencies together. This was made easier by the period of mass politics, and the links between the 'Fordist' work cultures of the 1930s and 1940s and the growth of modern political parties in these years.[49]

Others have commented on the links between the ethos and culture of Fordism and the governing ethos of communist parties. For the British party during this time, according to Samuel, it was the nature of organisation itself; its 'bureaucratic collectivism' was apparent in the everyday intensity of party work, the 'mania for reports', and the 'drives' to meet 'targets' and 'quotas'.[50] Moreover, these social, cultural and political links cannot be solely reduced to the theory of democratic centralism which – since Lenin's theorisation and the Comintern's endorsement of it – has largely constituted the organisational structure of the communist party in different countries.[51] As Samuel has shown, the importance of this theory should not obscure the way in which people's day-to-day experiences became assimilated into the culture of the party, including the discipline on street marches, the 'solemnity of meetings', the 'fetishising of organisational matters', and the 'untroubled faith' in leadership; these provided the party's momentum or 'will to unity'.[52] This is supported by Waller's research, which has found diversity in the way in which democratic centralism has been practised in different communist parties. This suggests that specific cultural contexts provided at least part of the justification for party unity and discipline.[53]

The nature of the British Communist Party as an organisation was thus derived to a significant degree from wider social and cultural trends. However it is important to recognise that its class approach to politics did not prevent the party from maintaining a broad enough appeal to avoid the charge of class reductionism; although this could be occasionally found in party texts, it was less apparent in the party's everyday activities.[54] But the specific grievances of particular groups, while treated seriously by the party, were nevertheless linked to the bigger question of how to organise to change society. Class was prioritised *before* other forms of stratification. This was derived from Marxist doctrine, but became the legitimation for organisational activity in less theoretical and more practical ways. The party's feminism, for example, was often limited by its industrial priorities, and not only because it rejected the label feminist as 'bourgeois', but because it did not perceive the need for autonomous forms of organisation. Its literature put the emphasis on recruitment amongst women industrial workers and, as Bruley argues, women were seen essentially as part of the working class: their conditions would be resolved through the 'socialisation of labour, rather than the sexual division of labour'.[55] This class perspective meant that the party's position prior to the 1960s did not lend itself easily to a specifically feminist agenda.

Likewise, the party's recruitment amongst black people was heavily constrained by the priority given to class. Hakim Adi's research into the West African branch in the 1950s has found that the party's anti-colonial work was a source of inspiration to many black people who joined from colonised countries.[56] Yet this did not expand into a recognition of the particular experiences of its black membership, despite the presence of separate Robeson, West African and Indian branches, as well as a West Indies Committee (later the West Indian Advisory Committee), an advisory committee to the EC. The major committees were staffed by white party full-timers, with anti-racism seen largely in terms of anti-colonialism; and 'chauvinistic' and 'patronising' attitudes went unchallenged, with some negative effects on the work of leading black communist activists, including Claudia Jones, a black communist leader who came to Britain from the USA in 1955.[57] The belief that primary attention should be given to colonialism often meant that addressing the interests of its own black membership went ignored. According to Trevor Carter, one of the party's leading black activists, this was the main reason the party failed to recruit amongst black British people, and in particular the reason why a thriving West Indian branch set up in the early 1950s did not last.[58]

For young communists there was a greater measure of autonomy, with the YCL enjoying separate status from the party. But evidence from the main study available shows that, with the exception of some generational differences in attitudes to sex and relationships, there were few occasions of difference between the YCL and the party prior to the 1960s, with the composition and ethos of YCL mirroring that of the party. Those differences that did exist, moreover, were mild and insignificant compared to the schisms that were to occur in the 1960s.[59]

THE COMMUNIST PARTY IN THE EARLY 1960s

In order to understand the subsequent differences over moral values and cultural attitudes that emerged within the CPGB in the 1960s, some discussion of the political context of the early 1960s is necessary. The CPGB in the early 1960s was beginning a long road to recovery from its crisis in 1956 when it had lost a quarter of its membership in the wake of Khrushchev's Stalin revelations and the Soviet action in Hungary. Its membership rose substantially from 28,000 in 1961 to 34,000 in 1963, in spite of the ETU scandal in 1962, when communists were found to have been involved in ballot-rigging in the Electricians Union.[60] According to Thompson there were three reasons for this rise in membership. Firstly, after initially opposing the unilateralism of the Campaign for Nuclear Disarmament (CND) when it was formed in 1958, the party had thrown its weight behind it from 1960. This brought major dividends, as party activists were able to extend their broad campaigning work in the areas of peace and anti-militarism. Secondly, the relative improvement of the Soviet economy and its advances in science had, for some, re-established a degree of faith in the socialist system. Thirdly, anti-colonialism had reached its climax, with the beginnings of independence for many third world countries. The role of communists in these struggles had been important and was a key influence in maintaining the internationalist character of the party.[61] On top of this the left turn in the Labour Party, which endorsed unilateralism at the Labour Party Conference of 1960, defeating the Labour leadership in the process, gave some grounds for optimism and the prospect of new alliances.[62]

Despite the splits in 1956 and the bad publicity surrounding the ETU scandal, the party had the appearance of a strongly cohesive organisation. This cohesion was to a large degree shaped by its class composition. According to Newton's research into the composition of the party conducted at this time, the party remained an overwhelmingly working-class party with 75 per cent membership from skilled or semi-skilled working-class occupations, a figure which closely mirrored Britain's occupational structure as a whole. The key occupational groups remained the engineers, miners, builders and teachers.[63] This evidence is confirmed by the 1962 membership survey, the most detailed of this period.[64] The cohesiveness of the party could also be seen as a narrowing of the party's social base. While membership amongst professional workers such as teachers had continued to rise from the 1950s, and the Young Communist League had shown a gradual rise under the leadership of shipbuilding worker Jimmy Reid, the party's intellectual base had been severely hit by the exodus of 1956; with a student membership of less than one per cent, and facing challenges from the New Left, the party was no longer perceived as the natural constituency of left-wing intellectuals. Nor had there been any significant shift in the status of women in the party; and, while the party continued its extensive work in anti-colonial movements, there was no evidence of the party recruiting extensively amongst black people – as might have been expected, for example, in a response to the outbreaks of racism in Britain in the late 1950s.[65] These factors give some indication as to the challenge the social movements would present to the party during the subsequent decade.

Moreover the party's apparent cohesiveness appears all the more surprising when we consider the wider social changes of the period. Debates over the impact of the 'affluent society' on working-class aspirations were becoming intense within the Labour Party, notably in the aftermath of its third successive electoral defeat in 1959. Major disputes had arisen over the reasons for this defeat and, for the 'revisionists' around the Gaitskell leadership, the reasons were clear: the changing nature of class alignment, new social aspirations and a modernised capitalism meant that the Labour Party should change its programme and ultimately its class identity.[66] Moreover there was a wider debate going on about the changing nature of class alignment within mainstream sociology; in particular the working class was seen as far less homogeneous than previously, with, for example, rather greater delineations between different types of working-class alignments noted in Lockwood's research,[67] and evidence of more differentiated class values forming the basis of other research work.[68]

It was the more affluent groups to whom Labour revisionists were seeking to appeal in shedding Labour's traditional working-class image. The Communist Party on the other hand continued to appeal to its core working-class groups, denying that major changes in the conditions of the working class had occurred, and reaffirming a commitment to traditional politics in its Congress resolutions, in its programme *The British Road to Socialism* and in its wider language and culture. There was no corresponding enthusiasm in the Communist Party for the debate about the political ramifications of the changing nature of class (which was taking place on the wider 'New Left' as well as in the Labour Party[69]) – presumably because the party did not believe there were any. The nearest it got to any recognition of these changes was the dispute over the name of its newspaper in 1966, when some feared that the change of name from the *Daily Worker* to the *Morning Star* indicated a weakening of its class image.[70] The major debate in the party over questions of class occurred much later – in the mid-1970s following initiatives by the party's Sociology Group, and in the late 1970s in response to Eric Hobsbawm's article 'The Forward March of Labour Halted?', published at a time when the party's own industrial base was disintegrating.[71] Moreover, the party showed little initial interest in the debates about the changing cultural manifestations of class, despite the fact that the leading proponents of the new thinking were recent party intellectuals. The party was therefore ill-prepared for the cultural critique, audacious rebellions and intellectual energy of the new era, particularly when it was from sources within its own ranks.

THE YCL AND THE CULTURAL EXPLOSION

The origins of the cultural explosion in British society in the 1960s are often dated from 1963, when the Beatles were becoming a major force in popular culture, and a more promiscuous youth culture was beginning to emerge.[72] For the Young Communist League, these events had their own particular importance. There was a change in the leadership of the YCL during 1963-65; Jimmy Reid, a young communist engineer and shop-steward, from within the traditional ranks of party culture, was replaced by Barney Davies as National Secretary, and this was the signal for a major shift in the outlook of the YCL.[73] Prior to the 1960s differences between the party and the YCL were few, and not in essence of a 'generational' nature; rather, prior to the 1960s, the faultlines that did occur – as Waite argues – 'ran *through* the league and the party rather than *between* the party and the league'.[74] John Gollan, the party's General Secretary from 1956, was widely quoted as being proud that he had 'never had to discipline the YCL'.[75]

The tensions between the YCL and the party in the 1960s were therefore very different in intensity and scope from anything that had gone before. Not only were they generational; they were sharply delineated by the YCL's engagement with a popular culture that was more

1. Communist Identity and the Impact of the YCL

audacious than in the past, and which deeply challenged the party's own ethos and cultural outlook. Increasingly from 1964 the YCL sought to develop a new politics derived from the shifts in popular culture. An early indication of this can be found in the YCL's more positive attitude (in comparison to that of the party as a whole) towards the Campaign for Nuclear Disarmament after it was set up in 1958. While the Communist Party remained opposed to unilateralism until 1960, on the grounds of pro-Soviet loyalty, YCL members were quick to endorse the movement, in some cases holding dual membership in Young CND and the YCL. To some extent this difference may have arisen out of an earlier difference over the merits of National Service – with YCLers critical of the party's support for conscription.[76]

However, the divergences were not confined to the crucial area of arguing for peace, but also included taking part in newer forms of protests such as sit-ins, and in broad alliances that went beyond the labour movement; these indicated a more autonomous approach, both in moving beyond pro-Soviet loyalty, and in the lack of deference to the party leadership's positions. The Aldermaston marches, organised by CND and the Committee of 100, were also occasions for a broader 'loss of innocence' for some YCLers.[77] In CND, YCL members also came into contact with members of the first New Left, many of whom had left the party in 1956.[78] An engagement with popular culture was, of course, one of the defining characteristics of the New Left, and while it is important not to assume a direct linkage between the YCL and the New Left,[79] some similarities can be seen in terms of their interest in cultural politics and other areas; it was to be some time before the party itself was prepared to give attention to such cultural developments.

The leading YCL activists at this time were overwhelmingly working-class in background. Many were from parents of the skilled working class, and they shared the same 'class approach to life' as their parents.[80] Many had been to secondary modern schools, leaving school at 15 or 16, some with spells of unemployment, others serving apprenticeships. Thus they shared with earlier generations of YCL members a predominantly working-class background and formative personal experiences of deprivation and social injustice. This also distinguished their backgrounds from many of those in the communist student movement who were to become influential in the 1970s, though one area of similarity was that leading activists in both came from communist families. Indeed, as research by Kaplan and Shapiro has shown with regard to the US, parental influence was important for the generation of communists who grew up in the 1960s, both in providing a stronger political awareness than in children from non-communist families, and in stimulating generational tensions within the families over the communist tradition.[81]

The wider experiences and peer group influences of the YCL and student activists were, however, clearly different. Where the later student activists developed their politics around Marxist reading groups, the communist universities and other intellectual forums, the YCL activists were directly engaged with popular culture; in this respect they were 'mods' as well as communists, seeking to ground their politics in the popular movements of the period, particularly those around rock music, which soon replaced more traditional communist pursuits such as folk music as a radical cultural symbol – the Beatles appeared on the front cover of the YCL paper *Challenge* in December 1963.[82] Moreover the relative success of young communists in immersing themselves in popular culture – which was at its peak from 1964 to 1968 – was all the more surprising when the Labour Party's failed attempts at a similar venture are taken into account. As Peter Thompson has shown, Labour's attempts to attract the young did not go beyond lowering the voting age to 18; the evidence suggests that, while support from the new white-collar and professional groups was crucial to Labour's electoral success in 1964, this was a result not of any engagement with the alternative morality of the young, but of processes of industrial modernisation.[83] The YCL's activities at this time seem to challenge existing research into youth subcultures of the period, which tended to find that young people were increasingly turned off any form of political organisation.[84]

In the Wembley YCL branch, for example, the dividends started to pay off, with membership rising from a handful of 6 or 7 members to over one hundred between 1963-64. This was largely the result of the Rhythm and Blues Club that the branch had set up, whose visiting bands included the yet-to-be-established Who, booked for £13 before they became internationally famous.[85] Pete Townshend, the Who's lead singer, was a member of both the YCL and CND (and known to play his banjo on Aldermaston Marches); though his YCL membership was kept quiet by Who managers, it is no coincidence that the YCL should find a particular liking for his brand of music.[86] Like Townshend, the YCL activists 'sought a new relationship with modernity', by projecting their radical 'hedonistic', 'irreverent' and 'democratic popular' politics as being more suitable to the needs of urban working-class youth; and in doing so they went well beyond the cultural constraints of the past.

THE TREND IS COMMUNISM
The most significant attempt to give political expression to these cultural energies occurred with the development of the 'Trend is Communism' campaign, which the YCL leadership initiated in 1967.[87] Encouraged by membership figures that had risen from 1796 in 1960 to a peak of approximately 6000 by 1967, at a time when the party's own membership was in decline, the YCL sought to take advantage of a new mood of optimism and what they perceived of as the beginnings of a new radicalism. 'The Trend ...' was a mass campaign, with 10,000

1. Communist Identity and the Impact of the YCL

leaflets published that outlined how communist ideals would meet young people's aspirations. Communism, it was argued, was the 'new trend in the world'. Linking 'ban the bombers', Oxfam, anti-racialists, protesters and others, 'The Trend ...' set out its modernist and progressive visions of the future. Communism represented the young, emerging new world, while 'the capitalist, colonialist and racialist governments represent the old, the past'. With its imagery of computers, space, the 'revolution in science' and 'the eradication of disease', the communist goals were to 'join the stream of progress in the world'. 'The Trend ...' ended its appeal to the youth of Britain with the invitation to 'help set the trend – the communist way'. The culmination of this campaign was an international youth festival organised by the YCL between May and June 1967, to which the Kinks and other leading bands were invited.[88] This coincided with the 26th YCL Congress, at which there was a major disagreement over the political direction of the YCL, defined by its cultural agenda. The leadership of the YCL won this dispute, with their argument for the need to develop a new mass cultural politics; they defeated those who sought a more orthodox route – the maintenance of a tighter vanguard organisation, geared to produce labour movement cadres.

The 'Trend' campaign explicitly identified culture as an essential part of the political terrain, and by so doing helped to 'problematise' the meaning of politics itself, a trajectory that it shared with the New Left, but which set it apart both from mainstream Labour politics and the existing traditions of its own party. At the same time, the YCL was able to use the organisational framework provided by the CPGB, an asset that was beyond the reach of new left activists. It continued to maintain a strong commitment to class politics, but its approach was more libertarian and popular-democratic than that of the mainstream party, as exemplified in its attitude to 'sex, drugs and rock and roll' – one which it shared with the wider culture of urban working-class youth. This more libertarian and irreverent class perspective also adopted elements of American 'hippy' culture; this was an enormous deviation from the traditional anti-American positions of the party, and became an issue of concern for those already disturbed by what was seen as the substitution of the traditional working-class image by the more 'garish' persona of the 'The Trend ... '.[89] Indeed the identification with hippy culture for a while dominated discussion in the pages of *Challenge*, with traditionalists seeing it as a decadent diversion from the main issues, while the YCL leadership continued to promote popular hippy images, notably in the February 1968 edition, where a hippy girl requested the readership to 'make me happy', by sending a contribution to the *Challenge* Development Fund.[90]

The positive identification with hippy culture was indicative of a new attitude to sex, and had significant, if complex, effects on the YCL and the way its relationship with the party was mediated. The peak period of the YCL, from 1964 to 1968, when these activities were strongest and its membership was expanding, predated the feminism movement of the later 1960s and 1970s, and some of the positions adopted reflected an open though ambiguous attitude towards sexual liberation. While YCL culture had previously mirrored mainstream party morality on the role of women, albeit with some moments of bohemianism and promiscuity, there was a significant shift in attitude towards sex and the role of women in the YCL from the early 1960s. The pill allowed greater sexual freedom and promiscuity, and this was a development which the YCL welcomed in the pages of *Challenge*, where it started to carry regular features on sex education, and critiques of what it perceived as moral policing and forms of puritanism, as well as more explicit images of nude women. Criticisms from both within and beyond the YCL on the 'commercialisation of sex' were rebuffed from the editorial board on the grounds that: 'Sex is a natural, healthy desire. There is no earthly reason why a revolutionary youth magazine should not use it to help project our ideas in an attractive way ... we want better sex, not less sex, with socialism ...'.[91] The more explicit use of sex as a political topic had mixed reactions from within the YCL, with both increases and decreases reported from *Challenge* sellers, while the party press recorded some criticisms, though without any sign of prospective disciplinary action. For women in the YCL there were also some reservations about the contradictions between a developing feminism and the commercialisation of sex that was taking place within the wider culture. Some women YCLers found more freedom in their relationships, which were becoming less confined by the expectations of taking a secondary role to the men (though some were constrained because of childcare arrangements). They were nevertheless critical of the way in which the celebration of sex and pornography often reinforced the image of women as sexual objects. Men in the YCL also found contradictions in making the most of their greater sexual freedom in endorsing the mainly male hippy culture, while simultaneously maintaining a critique of the way in which women were generally portrayed. The YCL remained a male dominated institution in many respects, in its editorial board and most of its leadership, though exhibiting a 'softer' rather than 'harder' masculinity.

The divergences between the YCL and the party leadership became more marked from 1967-68, when the cultural politics of the YCL started to impinge more directly on the party's strategic and ideological agendas. This reflected a new generational and cultural schism between the YCL and the party leadership.[92] As Waite argues: 'cultural conflicts (between the YCL and party leadership) ... for the first time ... became the predominant and defining aspects of some disputes, rather than being a secondary expression of some other generationally rooted tensions over political or organisational questions'.[93] Political conflicts, derived from the cultural turn represented by 'The Trend ...'

began to emerge, as the party continued to condemn the decadence of the 1960s, while also downplaying wider cultural issues in favour of the big economic questions of the day.

The party was not unaware of the cultural and social changes taking place, and at times sought a pragmatic engagement with them; in the case of TV, for example, it went to some lengths to secure adequate coverage, and the best presentation of its image, as a revised way of projecting the party through modern media.[94] Tensions occurred when the party's core values and political strategy were thought to be threatened. Although YCL leaders regarded themselves as 'quite autonomous',[95] there were occasions when the party leadership found their activities and ideas too much, and YCL leaders were occasionally called in for an explanation. One notable incidence of this was when Pete Carter, George Bridges and Barney Davies were asked to explain themselves by General Secretary John Gollan in 1968, after they had called a meeting on the legalisation of drugs; the YCL leaders responded by making a mock salute of agreement.[96] The dispute over drugs had similar characteristics to that over sex. To some, including sceptics in the YCL itself, the drug culture was a further capitulation to bourgeois decadence. Drug culture was thought to be particularly offensive, as it was perceived to legitimise 'dropping-out', in place of educating and changing society through activism. Thus the following was indicative of a commonly held view within mainstream party culture:

> I would think that the proportion of pill-takers and potsmokers is less among YCLers, young socialists, Young Liberals and others playing an active part in changing society than it is among average cross-section of young people ... it seems to me that a weekend at the YCL's recent festival of socialism is more likely to patch up any personality defects than an LSD trip.[97]

The meeting on drugs went ahead, despite the threat of disciplinary action. The party leadership hesitated to take action against these more troublesome sections, since it felt bound to support areas of growth in the party, but it fell short of openly encouraging their behaviour for fear of serious political ramifications for its other constituencies. This meant that the leadership sat on the fence on the question of the legalisation of drugs. This reluctance to discipline newer voices was to be repeated five years later, when it backed down from taking action against *Red Rag*, the non-party feminist journal. For their part, the YCL leaders were not willing to defer to party authority as in the past: 'We were aggressively into our politics ...We weren't intimidated ... They knew we were different from them'.[98] There were many battles over the editorial direction of the YCL papers – *Challenge* and the theoretical journal *Cogito* – and as editor of the latter Jackie Heywood remembers frequent conflicts over content.[99]

The cultural turn of the YCL leadership developed into mainstream disagreements over the party's politics and strategy. The first indication of this was the different responses of the YCL and the party leadership to the Soviet invasion of Czechoslovakia. The CPGB leadership wavered and deliberated over how to respond to the arrival of Soviet tanks in Prague, its uncertainty prompted both by a more ingrained loyalty to the Soviet Union and by a pragmatic judgement on the need to keep its more Stalinist members.[100] But for the YCL it was a formative moment. The 'Prague Spring' – a term that was not used in the official party statements or journals – had been enthusiastically taken up by the YCL, and they saw 'socialism with a human face' as one which 'really did fit in with what we wanted'.[101] As Heywood remembered: 'there was never any ambiguity in our minds about Czechoslovakia whatsoever'.[102] Leading YCLers' recollections of the invasion, described as such by the YCL at its Congress of 1969 (as distinct from the party's term 'intervention'), suggest that 1968 was a fundamental turning-point. For some it signified the end of the orthodox Marxist-Leninist political tradition, while the weak position of the leadership gave grounds for pessimism over the prospect of changing a deeply divided party.

The YCL leadership showed at their Congress of 1969, and in their journals, the extent of their difference with the leadership over Czechoslovakia. An unsigned *Cogito* article, for example, argued that the:

> ... Soviet invasion has emphasised and widened the theoretical gulf between the monolithic conception of socialist society held by the Soviet, East German, Polish and other Communist countries on the one hand and the pluralist model on the other of Western communist parties like the Italian, Austrian, Swedish, British, Spanish and more recently and less pronouncedly the French ...[103]

Political pluralism and independence were the principles underpinning the critique, with a clear indication that the British party needed to strengthen its loyalty to the latter group:

> Czechoslovakia in 1968 gave the world the first glimpse of a democratic, just and human form of socialism in an advanced industrial country ... in contrast to the monopoly capitalist 'mixed economies' of right-wing social democracy and the bureaucratic paternalism of Stalinism.[104]

Another hippy girl, meanwhile, appeared on the front cover of *Challenge*, in September 1968, this time with the message: 'If you think communism means that the tanks can roll in at any time you're bloody wrong'.[105]

ANTICIPATING GRAMSCI?

This image reflected the mix of culture and politics that dominated the YCL at this time. The discussion period before the 1969 Congress indicated that the cultural spheres were largely shaping the contours of political debate.[106] The attempt to articulate a new cultural politics by the YCL was a significant development that, in the long-term, had more effect on the ideological and strategic debates in the CPGB than it did on the immediate future of the YCL; this can be seen in the 'graduation' of YCL leaders – notably Pete Carter, George Bridges and Jackie Heywood – into more influential positions in the main party by the late 1960s or early 1970s. This helped provide a distinctive component of the later Eurocommunist generation in the 1970s. Following its peak years of 1964-1968, however, the YCL did not extend its influence either numerically or through the development of its political critique; it entered a period of long-term decline, at a time when other critical sections of the party were growing stronger.

In spite of this later decline, the legacy of the YCL's cultural politics should not be ignored in the party's subsequent development. By emphasising the cultural terrain, the YCL had put on the agenda an alternative vision of how the party should relate to mass culture. Moreover the impact of the YCL in the 1960s challenges the view that radical cultural politics originated from middle-class groups. The experience of the YCL provides the basis for an alternative interpretation to the phenomenon described as 'middle-class radicalism', as found in Parkin's research into CND membership in the early 1960s, and to Newton's distinction between 'middle-class idealists' and 'working-class pragmatists' in his study of the social composition of the CPGB during the same period – contemporaneous with the YCL cohort under investigation here.[107]

Though the YCL started to fragment following the elevation of its 1964-1968 cadre into the party, even succumbing to a traditionalist backlash from 1971-72, the cultural turn continued to have an impact, notably through the person of Dave Cook, who assumed an organisational role in the YCL before taking up key positions as National Student Organiser in 1972, and the party's National Organiser from 1975-79. In these positions Cook first developed his 'cultural is political' approach, as well as developing his organisational and political skills. The politics of the YCL, he argued at its Congress in Scarborough in 1971, must become embedded in wider cultural concerns:

> Branches and Districts that run football teams, dances, sponsored swims and poster workshops also seem to run the biggest demos, sell most *Challenge* and get a lot of delegates to youth workers conferences. Why? Because politics does not end at one point and social, sporting and recreational activity start at another ...[108]

In a wider context, the YCL's cultural politics prefigured later party debates in which the concept of the political was extended to include not only popular culture but also the private sphere – identified by feminists – and the crucial terrain of civil society, where informal networks organise outside 'official' politics. The Communist Party had a long history of organising in broad coalitions, and the importance of these traditions for the YCL should not be underestimated. However, the YCL emphasis on culture, particularly the extent of its critical interrogation of mainstream cultural forms, mores and lifestyles (including some of those found in the party itself), not only chimed with aspects of the counterculture of the 1960s, but also resonated with the ways in which the later 'Gramscian' approach took hold in these areas within the party over the subsequent decade. Yet the works of Gramsci had not been published at length in English at this time, and YCL activists have acknowledged that they didn't have access to his work; nor was there serious discussion of Gramsci within the CPGB before the first publication of the *Prison Notebooks* in 1971, which was only made possible after a major financial contribution from a leading party intellectual.[109] Despite this, the YCL's cultural turn helped create favourable long-term conditions for the development of the political alternative within the party, based on a renewed humanism, Gramscian critique and Eurocommunist strategy. Many of the YCL cadre which helped shape its cultural turn, notably Dave Cook, George Bridges and Pete Carter, were to become key figures in this political alternative. It also meant that when Gramsci's work became available, these former YCLers took to him 'like ducks to water'.[110]

Notes

1. Frederic Jameson argues that the main legacy of the 'sixties' was the cultural challenge to the West from the civil rights movements in the US and third world liberation movements. See F. Jameson, 'Periodising the 60s', in S. Sayres (ed), *The Sixties Without Apology*, University of Minnesota Press 1984. For Arthur Marwick in *The Sixties*, Oxford University Press 1998, it was the liberalisation of the social and cultural and political institutions that was decisive.
2. See R. Cockett, 'The New Right and the 1960s: the Dialectics of Liberation' in G. Andrews et al (eds), *New Left, New Right and Beyond*, Macmillan 1999, pp85-105.
3. See for example Donald Sassoon, *One Hundred Years of Socialism*, I. B. Tauris, London 1996, p406.
4. J. Green, *All Dressed Up: The Sixties and the Counterculture*, Jonathan Cape, London 1998, p445.
5. S. Hall, 'Cultural Identity' in B. Gieben and S. Hall (eds), *Modernity and its Futures*, Sage/OU 1992.
6. The work of Alain Touraine, in particular *The Return of the Actor*, University of Minnesota Press 1988, is important in this respect.
7. This term is used variously by A. Marwick, *The Sixties*, op cit; A. Hooper,

'A Politics Adequate to the Age: the New Left and the Long Sixties', in G. Andrews et al (eds), *New Left, New Right and Beyond ...* op cit; J. Green, *All Dressed Up* op cit.
8. M. Jacques, J. De Groot, S. Slipman interviews with author.
9. There is a large sociological literature initially developed during the 1950s in America which attributed communist identity to 'alienated' and 'disconnected' anomic individuals, who had become divorced from the mainstream 'mass society'. See for example G. Almond, *The Appeals of Communism* Princeton University Press 1954, W. Kornhauser, *The Politics of Mass Society*, Routledge Kegan Paul 1960. This approach has been challenged by subsequent research which has stressed the different conditions and experiences within which communist parties have existed. Newton, for example, who was partly constrained by the same orthodoxy, found British communists to be relatively down to earth individuals who 'are not recruited from "isolated masses"' in his *Sociology of British Communism*, Allen Lane, 1969, p105.
10. N. Fishman, *The British Communist Party and the Trade Unions, 1933-1945*, Scolar Press 1995.
11. R. Samuel, 'The Lost World of British Communism: Part III, "Class Politics"', in *New Left Review* 165 Sept-Oct 1987 p59-60.
12. G. Eley, 'From Cultures of Militancy to the Politics of Culture: Writing the History of British Communism', *Science and Society* Vol 61, No 1, Spring 1997, p129.
13. K. Newton *The Sociology of British Communism*, op cit, p55.
14. E. Hobsbawm, *Labouring Men*, Weidenfeld and Nicholson, 1964, p332.
15. In addition to Newton's *The Sociology of British Communism*, op cit, other indications of the party's social composition can be derived from the delegates' credentials in bi-annual Congress Reports published in the party's weekly paper, *Comment*. In the CPGB archive in the National Museum of Labour History details of membership are held in CP/CENT/ORG including, for those attending party education schools up to 1965, short biographies. See K. Morgan, 'Archival Report: The Archives of the British Communist Party' in *Twentieth Century British History* op cit. For discussion of the party's industrial roots see A. Campbell, 'The Communist Party in the Scots Coalfields in the Inter-War Period' in G. Andrews et al (eds) *Opening the Books* op cit, pp44-63; I. MacDougall, Militant Miners, Polygon 1981; J. Hinton, *The First Shop Stewards Movement*, Allen and Unwin 1973; W. Kendall, *The Revolutionary Left in Britain*, Weidenfeld and Nicholson 1969; L. J. Macfarlane, *The British Communist Party; Its Origins and Development Until 1929*, MacGibbon and Kee 1966.
16. See S. MacIntyre, *Little Moscows: Communism and Working Class Militancy in Inter-War Britain*, Croom Helm 1980, p3; K. Newton, *The Sociology of British Communism*, op cit, p32. See also R. Croucher, 'Divisions in the Movement: the National Unemployed Workers Movement' in G. Andrews et al (eds), *Opening the Books*, op cit, pp23-43 and R. Croucher, *We Refuse to Starve in Silence*, Lawrence and Wishart 1987, for discussions of the CPGB's work amongst the unemployed.
17. See S. Parsons, 'British Communist Party School Teachers in the 1940s and 1950s' in *Science and Society*, Vol 61, No 1 Spring 1997. His extended

analysis of professional workers as a whole can be found in 'Communism in the Professions; the Organisation of the British Communist Party Among Professional Workers 1933-1956' PhD Thesis, University of Warwick, June 1990.
18. See M. Heinemann, 'Left Review, New Writing and the Broad Alliance Against Fascism', in E. Timms and P. Collier (eds), *Visions and Blueprints: Avant-Garde Culture and Radical Politics in Early Twentieth Century Europe*, Manchester University Press 1988.
19. H. Srebrnik, *London Jews and British Communism*, Vallentine Mitchell 1994.
20. H. Adi, 'West Africans and the Communist Party in the 1950s', in G. Andrews et al (eds), *Opening the Books*, op cit, pp176-194.
21. For discussion of the implications of the conflicts in 1956 see A. Macleod, *The Death of Uncle Joe*, 1997; the special edition of *Socialist Register*, The Merlin Press 1976; W. Thompson, *The Good Old Cause*, Pluto Press 1992 pp100-113.
22. For further discussion of these issues see J. Clark, M. Heinemann, D. Margolies and C. Snee, *Culture and Crisis in Britain in the Thirties*, Lawrence and Wishart 1979; M. Heinemann and N. Branson, *Britain in the 1930s*, Weidenfeld and Nicholson 1971; D. Margolies, *Writing the Revolution*, Pluto Press 1998.
23. S. Bruley, 'Women and Communism: A Case Study of the Lancashire Weavers', in G. Andrews et al (eds), *Opening the Books*, op cit; N. Branson, *History of the Communist Party of Great Britain 1941-1951*, Lawrence and Wishart 1997, p45-47.
24. G. Eley, 'From Cultures of Militancy . . . ', op cit, p120. For an account of the 'Popular Front' see J. Fyrth, *Fascism and the Popular Front*, Lawrence and Wishart 1985.
25. H. Adi, *West Africans and the Communist Party in the 1950s . . .*, op cit; T. Carter, *Shattering Illusions*, Lawrence and Wishart 1986; H. Srebrnik, *London Jews and British Communism*, op cit.
26. R. Samuel, 'The Lost World of British Communism: Part III . . . ', op cit, p56.
27. W. Thompson, *The Good Old Cause*, op cit, p12.
28. K. Newton, *The Sociology of British Communism*, op cit, pp62-64.
29. W. Thompson, *The Good Old Cause*, op cit, p152.
30. S. MacIntyre, *A Proletarian Science*, Lawrence and Wishart 1986.
31. See M. Kenny, *The First New Left*, Lawrence and Wishart, 1995; T. Steele, *The Emergence of Cultural Studies*, Lawrence and Wishart 1997; R. Fieldhouse, 'The 1908 Report: Antidote to Class Struggle?' in G. Andrews et al (eds), *Ruskin College: Contesting Knowledge, Dissenting Politics*, Lawrence and Wishart 1999, pp35-57.
32. Hoggart uses this term widely in *The Uses of Literacy*, Chatto and Windus 1957.
33. S. MacIntyre, *A Proletarian Science*, op cit, p39.
34. E. Hobsbawm, *Labouring Men*, op cit, p237.
35. For a discussion of the party's appeal amongst intellectuals at this time see C. Day Lewis, *The Mind in Chains: Socialism and the Cultural Revolution*, Frederick Muller 1937; A. Croft, *Red Letter Days*, Lawrence and Wishart 1990; M. Heinemann, 'The People's Front and the

1. Communist Identity and the Impact of the YCL

Intellectuals', in J. Fyrth (ed) *Fascism and the Popular Front*, op cit; J. Lewis, *The Left Book Club: An Historical Record*, Victor Gollancz 1970.
36. E. Hobsbawm, 'The Historians Group of the Communist Party', in M. Cornforth (ed), *Rebels and Their Causes: Essays in Honour of A. L. Morton*, Lawrence and Wishart 1978. For a good recent discussion of the party's links with culture see A. Croft (ed), *A Weapon in the Struggle*, Pluto Press 1998. For the party's links with early radical film see B. Hogenkamp, *Deadly Parallels: Film and the Left in Britain 1929-39*, Lawrence and Wishart 1986.
37. Introduction to A. Croft (ed), *A Weapon in the Struggle*, op cit, p4.
38. R. Samuel, 'The Lost World of British Communism: Part III ...', op cit, p61.
39. Ibid, p71. Samuel's reflections drew on personal autobiographies of party members, including Ernie Trory's *Between the Wars; Recollections of a Communist Organiser*, Crabtree Press 1974, which revealed that the author himself requested he be disciplined by the party for attending the Empire Club (regarded by the party as a place of ill-repute). He was subsequently put on probation for 6 months. See also Arthur Exell, 'Morris Motors in the 1940s', in *History Workshop Journal* 9, Spring 1980, pp103-104.
40. See J. Woddis, 'Another American Export For Britain', in *World News and Views* No 22, 5 June 1948; S. Aaronovitch, 'The Communist Party and the Battle of Ideas' in *Communist Review* May 1948, pp148-157; B. Hogenkamp, *Film, Television and the Left 1950-1970*, Lawrence and Wishart 2000, pp1-31.
41. See A. Croft (ed), *A Weapon in the Struggle*, pp1-2.
42. 'Jitterbugging is really the lowest to which anyone can sink. To turn oneself into a slobbering savage, a drooling psychopathic horror, a jerking bundle of sensual emotions ... ', quoted in K. Morgan, 'King Street Blues', in A. Croft (ed), *Weapon in the Struggle ...*, op cit, pp137-138. This was originally reported in the Young Communist League weekly paper *Challenge* from the 21 February, 20 March, 10 April, 1 and 22 May, 1948 edition.
43. See for example Kevin Morgan's *Harry Pollitt*, Manchester University Press, 1993.
44. D. Hyde, *I Believed*, William Heinemann Ltd, 1950, p80.
45. K. Morgan, 'The Communist Party and the Daily Worker 1930-1956', in G. Andrews et al (ed), *Opening the Books*, op cit, p142.
46. Ibid, pp155-156. This perception was based on readers' surveys by the *Daily Worker* during the 1950s, available in the Allen Hutt papers in the Communist Party archives at CP/IND/HUTT/2/7.
47. Mike Waite records this in his unpublished M. Phil thesis, Young People and Formal Political Activity: A Case Study: Young People and Communist Politics in Britain 1920-1991, Lancaster University 1992, p275.
48. N. Wood, *Communism and British Intellectuals*, Gollancz 1959, p218. The dilemmas of intellectuals in the CPGB in 1956 are discussed further in M. Kenny, *The First New Left*, op cit; L. Chun, *The British New Left*, Edinburgh University Press 1993; and *Socialist Register*, Merlin 1976.
49. These links were discussed by Antonio Gramsci who, writing during this

period, developed his concept of the 'modern prince'. This term, adapted from Machiavelli, was used to explain the role of the political party in the modern period. He argued that political parties operated as a 'school of state life ... organisations which would have a positive benefit in providing 'character' (resistance to the pressures of surpassed cultures), honour (fearless will in maintaining the new type of culture and life), dignity (awareness of operating for a higher end)'. The 'discipline' and 'structure' of Fordism provided the basis for what Gramsci called *organicità* – what he perceived as the organisational dynamism of a revolutionary party. Gramsci uses the term *organicità* to explain his particular meaning of democratic centralism, notably how the unity and cohesion of the revolutionary party is maintained through a 'matching of thrusts from below with orders from above, a continuous insertion of elements thrown up from the depths of the rank and file into the solid framework of the leadership apparatus which ensures continuity and the regular accumulation of experience', (*Selections From Prison Notebooks*, Lawrence and Wishart 1971, p189). His analysis of the links between the nature of work, the role of the party and the relationship between the state and civil society took him beyond Lenin's interpretation of democratic centralism found in *What is to be Done?* Many of Gramsci's arguments were influenced by his debates with Bordiga, who favoured a more tightly organised party, in the leadership of the Italian Communist Party. They were also informed by his criticism of Robert Michels' work and that of the two Italian elite theorists, Pareto and Mosca.

50. R. Samuel, 'The Lost World of British Communism: Part II: Unity, Discipline, Organisation', *New Left Review* 156 March/April 1986, pp63-107. Sarah Benton also saw mass political parties as 'organisers of communities' and a focal point of 'self-sacrifice, loyalty and identity'. See S. Benton, 'The Decline of the Party' in S. Hall/M. Jacques, *New Times* Lawrence and Wishart 1989, pp334-346.

51. Lenin first theorised this concept in *What is to be Done?* in 1902, but his understanding was also influenced by Kautsky's view that socialist consciousness could only be brought to the working class from 'without', a position that was deliberated at the Second Congress of the RSDLP in 1903, in which rival Bolshevik and Menshevik positions were developed. For a discussion of the development of Lenin's thought in this context see N. Harding, *Lenin's Political Thought*, Macmillan 1983; R. Service, *Lenin; A Political Life Volume 1*, Macmillan 1985; and A. Westoby, *The Evolution of Communism*, Polity Press 1989. Westoby also points out that an early influence on Lenin's idea of party organisation was the Webb's History of Trade Unionism, first published in 1899, where he found that British trade union culture had important lessons for organisational structure (op cit, pp22-23).

52. R. Samuel, 'The Lost World of British Communism: Part II ... ', op cit. C. Shore in his social anthropological study of the PCI in more recent years also found an 'ideology of unity' based on a range of cultural factors including 'linguistic rituals' and 'formalised codes', which helped sustain the authority of the leadership; *Italian Communism, The Retreat From Leninism*, Pluto Press 1990, p133. See also J. Jensen and G. Ross, *The View From the Inside*, 1980, University of California Press 1984, p98, for a simi-

lar significance attached to *la bonne parole* (the good word) in the PCF. Both studies also stress the deference by the membership to full-timers (*les permanents* in the case of the PCF) in consolidating the structure and cohesion of the party.
53. For a discussion of the vagaries of democratic centralism see M. Waller, *Democratic Centralism*, Manchester University Press 1981, and R. Tiersky, *Ordinary Stalinism: Democratic Centralism and the Question of Communist Political Development*, George Allen and Unwin, London 1985.
54. For example, R. Palme Dutt's assertion that 'The subordination of women, and the forcible compulsion of the majority of women to economic dependence on marriage as their sole means of livelihood, are bound up with the existence of private property society, and can only be ended with communist social organisation', in *Fascism and Social Revolution*, 1934, p218, quoted in N. Branson, *History of the Communist Party of Great Britain 1941-1951*, Lawrence and Wishart 1997. Branson discusses the range of work on the position of women during the war, culminating in the 'Women's Parliaments' and the decision to set up the National Women's Advisory, a sub-committee of the EC, in 1943.
55. S. Bruley, 'Women and Communism', in G. Andrews et al (eds), *Opening the Books*, op cit, p65. Much of the Party's activity amongst women was couched in terms of class before gender: 'Wake Up Mrs Worker' was the title of one of its pamphlets in the 1920s – cited in K. Morgan, 'The Communist Party and the Daily Worker ... ' op cit.
56. H. Adi, *West Africans in Britain 1900-1960*, Lawrence and Wishart 1998; H. Adi, 'West Africans and the Communist Party in the 1950s', in G. Andrews et al (eds), *Opening the Books*, op cit, pp176-194.
57. According to Marika Sherwood in her recent biography, Claudia Jones had a much more uneasy relationship with the CPGB, who mistrusted her, than with the CPUSA. See M. Sherwood, *Claudia Jones, A Life in Exile*, Lawrence and Wishart 2000, pp62-88. Jones herself noted the more limited awareness of British communist members to the pervasiveness of 'imperialist and racist' ideas (speech to CPGB Congress 1957, reported in Sherwood op cit, p76). Sherwood also cites the following recollections in interviews with former black communist activists: Dorothy Kuya, 'the Party was not willing to debate the race issue - they just didn't understand race issues'; Avtar Jouhl, 'the communists were no different from the population in general regarding racial issues' (Sherwood, op cit, p71).
58. According to Carter in *Shattering Illusions* (Lawrence and Wishart, 1986, p56), the West Indian branch 'was set up in response to the difficulties faced by many black members in working within the ordinary party framework'. Carter points out that the existence of the branches was not part of a strategy by the party leadership and records that the branch had petered out by 1956, and was succeeded by the West Indian Advisory (dominated by party functionaries like Palme Dutt and white communists from the leadership). He argues that 'Had there been a proper analysis at the time, which recognised that racial oppression cannot just be neatly packaged up in subordination to class oppression, then the West Indian branch might have survived and the allegiance of those comrades preserved'.
59. M. Waite, 'Young People and Politics', M. Phil thesis, op cit.
60. CP/CENT/ORG.

61. See Willie Thompson's discussion in *The Good Old Cause*, op cit, pp116-121.
62. The decision was reversed however at the 1961 Conference. It is also difficult to gauge the extent of this shift as conference decisions depend to a significant degree on behind the scenes manoeuvres between trade union leaders over where to cast block votes. For a further discussion of this period in Labour politics see F. Parkin, *Middle Class Radicalism*, Manchester University Press 1968, and L. Minkin, *The Labour Party Conference*, 2nd edition, Manchester University Press 1980, pp279-289.
63. K. Newton, *The Sociology of British Communism*, Allen Lane 1969, p55.
64. CP/CENT/ORG
65. Indeed the party was losing its black members at this point. CP/CENT/ORG shows declining membership figures in particular districts.
66. In addition to the classic revisionist text, C. A. R. Crosland's *The Future of Socialism*, Cape 1956, see also M. Abrams, R. Rose and R. Hinden, *Must Labour Lose?* Penguin 1960, and S. Haseler, *The Gaitskellites*, Macmillan 1969.
67. David Lockwood claimed three distinct types of working-class identities were now evident: the 'proletarian' identity, mainly found amongst traditional manufacturing industries, characterised by strong class loyalties of 'fraternity' and 'comradeship', a pride in 'male work' and a 'distinctive occupational culture', and solidarity derived from highly concentrated mass industries, leading to strong class consciousness. He also found a 'deferential' worker, who accepted hierarchy, the role of elites and the status divisions characteristic of British society – values mainly found in women or agricultural workers. Finally, Lockwood noted a third 'newer' variant, the 'privatised worker', a type that had grown in the era of affluence and defined by greater material 'instrumental' and 'consumerist' values, where work was a 'means to an end' and where weakening class solidarity was replaced by more individualistic values. See D. Lockwood, 'Sources of Variation in Working-Class Images of Society', in *Sociological Review*, Vol 14 No 3 November 1966, pp249-267.
68. See also J. Goldthorpe and D. Lockwood, 'Affluence and the British Working Class', in *Sociological Review* 11 1963. This provided preliminary research material for the four-volume *Affluent Worker* (J. Goldthorpe et al), published later by Cambridge University Press between 1968-69. See also M. Abrams, 'Class and Politics', in *Encounter* 17 pp39-44, 1961; R. Samuel, 'The Deference Voter', in *New Left Review* 1 9-13 1960.
69. See S. Hall, 'A Sense of Classlessness', in *Universities and Left Review* 5 1958, pp26-32, which stimulated a debate amongst the first new left; M. Kenny, *The First New Left*, op cit, pp57-68.
70. As well as debates in the party press, Allen Hutt, a previous editor, was not happy about the name change. See his correspondence with John Gollan in Hutt papers in CP Archive CP/IND/HUTT/2/7; George Matthews, interview with author.
71. See Chapter Six for a discussion of Hobsbawm's work. The earlier debate on class had been in *Marxism Today* during 1973-74; these debates were taken further in a conference organised by the party's Sociology group in 1976 which led to A. Hunt (ed) *Class and Class Structure*, Lawrence and Wishart 1977.

1. Communist Identity and the Impact of the YCL   47

72. For a discussion of the rise of youth cultures in the 1960s see S. Hall and T. Jefferson, *Resistance Through Rituals: Youth Subcultures in Post-War Britain*, Hutchinson 1977.
73. George Bridges' emergence as London Organiser of the YCL was another indication of a shift in generations.
74. His emphasis. M. Waite, 'Sex, Drugs and Rock'n'Roll (and Communism)', in G. Andrews et al (eds), *Opening the Books*, op cit, p211. For the early years of the YCL see M. Waite, 'Young People and Politics', op cit.
75. W. Thompson, *The Good Old Cause*, op cit, p124.
76. M. Johnstone interview.
77. M. Jacques interview.
78. The YCL lost half its members in 1956. CP/CENT/ORG.
79. The classic texts are: R. Williams, *Culture and Society*, Penguin 1958 and *The Long Revolution*, Pelican 1961; R. Hoggart, *The Uses of Literacy*, 1957 Chatto and Windus 1957.
80. J. Heywood interview.
81. Some similarities can be found with the 'Red Diaper' babes in the US who influenced the radical 'Students For A Democratic Society' in the 1960s. See M. Isserman, *If I had a Hammer; The Death of the Old Left and the Birth of the New Left*, Basic Books, New York 1987, pp206-207; J. Kaplan and L. Shapiro (eds) *Red Diapers: Growing Up in the Communist Left*, Urbana and Chicago, University of Illinois Press 1998; for a similar generation in Britain see also P. Cohen, *Children of the Revolution: Communist Childhood in Cold War Britain*, Lawrence and Wishart 1997.
82. W. Thompson, *The Good Old Cause* op cit, p153
83. P. Thompson, 'Labour's Gannex Conscience?: Politics and Popular Attitudes in the Permissive Society' in R. Coopey, S. Fielding and N. Tiratsoo, *The Wilson Governments 1964-1970*, Pinter 1993, p139. The evidence of attitudes amongst Labour's new professionals comes from D. Butler and A. King, *The British General Election of 1964*, Macmillan 1964. The evidence of the attitudes of Labour's youth wing cited by Thompson is from *Focus*, the Labour Party's youth newspaper. He quotes an edition from 1966 (vol 1 No. 2) where a member complains that there was a lack of politics. 'If the paper is to be political I suggest we have more of it. The only article was on drugs, not very political'. P. Thompson, 'Labour's Gannex Conscience?' op cit, p148.
84. See for example G. Mungham and G. Pearson, *Working Class Youth Cultures*, Routledge and Kegan Paul 1976; S. Hall and J. Jefferson, (eds) *Resistance through Rituals*, Hutchinson/CCCS 1976; M. Brake, *The Sociology of Youth Culture and Subcultures*, Routledge and Kegan Paul 1980; D. Hebdige, *Subculture: The Meaning of Style*, Methuen and co 1979.
85. George Bridges and Jackie Heywood interviews with author. According to Doug Bain, a YCL activist in Glasgow, the Mandela Club was the site for rival communist rock (the Jay Hawks) and folk bands, an example of a more direct cultural clash within the party. See D. Bain, interview with M. Waite, 'Young People and Politics'.
86. According to Kevin Davey, as rock's 'premier rock theorist and moralist' and 'one of the New Left's most prominent contacts in the music industry', Townshend tried to epitomise in his music the claims of the growing urban

working-class youth culture of the Mods, through a 'softer' masculinity and an 'ambiguous' relationship with anglo-white Britishness'; K. Davey, *English Imaginaries*, Lawrence and Wishart 1999, pp81-82.
87. CP/CENT/ORG.
88. CP/CENT/ORG *The Trend is Communism*, YCL leaflet, 1967.
89. W. Thompson, *The Good Old Cause*, op cit, p153.
90. M. Waite, 'Sex'n'Drugs'n'Rock'n'Roll (and Communism)', op cit, p216.
91. The range of critical and supportive views can be found in M. Waite, *Young People and Politics*, op cit, p279. Waite's in-depth study is by far the most comprehensive account of the YCL, based on questionnaires of 83 respondents across generations. While other evidence exists, this is more of a general or anecdotal nature, and therefore in addition to interviews with YCL activists by the current author, Waite's research has been used extensively.
92. 'What is a boutique?', Bert Ramelson, the party's Industrial Organiser, is reported to have asked a member of the YCL leadership in the late 1960s. M. Power interview with author.
93. M. Waite, 'Sex, Drugs and Rock'n'Roll (and Communism)', op cit, pp212-213.
94. See the discussion on the party's attempts to secure TV election coverage for the 1964 and 1966 General Elections in B. Hogenkamp, *Film, Television and the Left, 1950-1970*, Lawrence and Wishart 2000, pp91-95.
95. George Bridges interview with author.
96. This was recalled by Jude Bloomfield, a YCL member at the time. Jude Bloomfield interview.
97. J. Moss, 'Should Marijuana be Legalised?' *Comment* 3/6/1967. Betty Reid of the party's Organisational Department sat on the fence over legalisation. See article in *Comment*, 7/2/1970.
98. Jackie Heywood interview.
99. Ibid.
100. The party press was concerned to project a 'balanced' view of party opinion. The *Morning Star* (according to George Matthews, its then editor) ensured equal space in the letters column for both viewpoints, while *Comment* and *Marxism Today* published extracts from the official Czechoslovak party publications as well as those supporting Dubcek. George Matthews interview.
101. Genia Browning interview.
102. Jackie Heywood interview.
103. *Cogito*, September 1969. *Cogito* was the theoretical journal of the YCL.
104. Ibid.
105. Noted in M. Waite, 'Sex Drugs and Rock'n'Roll (and Communism)', op cit, p221.
106. For example, Pre-Congress Discussion No. 2 February 1969, pp12-14, carried 'Two Views' on 'Social Life'. Firstly Val Watson, writing about 'communist morality': 'Let us replace the drugs, drink and the pent up frustrations of the young with something constructive, more social amenities and a meaning, a goal in life. I feel that the YCL has not come out forcefully enough on these issues, drugs, drink, violence and sex. I would like very much to see this Congress lay out a clear code of morality ... '. On the other hand, George Silverman was concerned that the YCL was

too far removed from mainstream culture and morality: ' ... most young people think of a communist as some sort of nutter who wants nothing out of life but revolution and demonstrations and who has no time or interest in doing the sort of things that most young people do'.
107. F. Parkin, *Middle-Class Radicals*, Manchester University Press 1968; K. Newton, *The Sociology of British Communism*, op cit.
108. Report of YCL National Congress, held in Scarborough 24-26 April 1971. YCL Files CP Archive. His optimism of the cultural terrain even extended to the football pitch: 'The ruling class certainly does not tremble at Red Star (the YCL's successful football team) but they would begin to worry about their influence on working-class youth if there were YCL teams in every local league'.
109. Roger Simon, interview with Kevin Morgan. Simon was the leading Gramscian exponent amongst the older generation of intellectuals. His *An Introduction to Gramsci's Political Thought*, Lawrence and Wishart 1978, was to have an important role in disseminating Gramsci's ideas within the party.
110. Genia Browning interview with author. The most sophisticated 'Gramscian' discussion of youth culture within the party took place in *Marxism Today* between 1973 and 1975, when the YCL was already in decline. See M. Jacques, 'Trends in Youth Culture', in *Marxism Today* September 1973, and subsequent discussion contributions.

2. Unlikely Allies: Students, Feminists and the Party

THE POLITICS OF THE NEW SOCIAL MOVEMENTS
Recognising the rise of what have commonly been called 'new social movements' during the 1960s in Western societies is crucial to an understanding of the major political events that took place during this period. These included opposition to the Vietnam War, the May 1968 events in Paris, what has been called the 'hot autumn' of industrial and political unrest in Italy in 1969, the black consciousness movement in the US, and the early campaigns of second wave feminism. Historians and sociologists have explained the significance of the new social movements in different ways. Some, like Marcuse, saw them as a new revolutionary force, by virtue of their being on the margins of 'one-dimensional' industrial societies, the traditional working class having become incorporated into the dominant value systems and structures.[1] Touraine has suggested that the outbreak of student activities was brought about by the crisis in the nature of industrial societies, which led to expectations and aspirations that could not be fulfilled other than by radically changing society.[2] Undoubtedly there was a global context, with students in many different countries taking action from the mid-1960s in movements that were distinctive from traditional political parties and trade unions. Indeed the new social movements drew their strength from opposing the traditional form of politics, preferring for example the 'sit-in', the 'demo' and occasionally the 'teach-in', while, as Tarrow suggests in the case of Italy, their demands were of a different nature, seeking more rights rather than increasing the extent of economic redistribution.[3]

The disparate social movements had a particular significance for the left, as many of their demands diverged from those of orthodox left strategies. As many have pointed out, the nature of their demands – such as the acceptance of new sexual freedoms, respect for difference, or new forms of participatory democracy – while aimed at the 'Establishment' or the capitalist state, were also a critique of the forms and practices of the left. These included the party system and culture itself: traditional parties were regarded as part of the problem for many of the movements during that time. This raised important questions for the left, including the British Communist Party. Could the demands of these groups be accommodated by the party or would they remain outside as separate autonomous organisations? What changes in culture and ethos as well as political strategy were needed by the parties if they were to win over these new generations?

The previous chapter explained how the CPGB was confronted at an early stage of these changes by the radical outlook of the YCL. It went on to assess the ways in which the YCL challenged the party's very specific political culture and identity. It suggested that the party's ethos, its prioritising of class over other forms of stratification, and its organisational structure, would make it difficult to accommodate the new movements. However the previous chapter also indicated that the party did become aware of the need to encourage the new generation and adapt, albeit in limited ways. This chapter will explain how the new social movements that were attracted to the CPGB – notably feminists and students – provided a further challenge to the party. It will also assess the attempt by the party to accommodate these groups, and the significance the resulting conflicts held for the party's future political direction. It will argue that the tensions between the party leadership and the student and feminist groups were often creative, for example in the development of the CUL, the transmission of new Marxist ideas, most notably, those of Gramsci and Althusser, and a more advanced cultural politics. Above all it will show how the new movements contributed fundamentally to the party's political strategy, especially through the development of a new generation of intellectuals and party activists.

THE CP AND THE NEW STUDENT MOVEMENT

Party students were left behind by the events of 1968, mainly remaining in the background of disputes at the London School of Economics and other campuses. The leadership of the students under Fergus Nicholson was critical of much of the activism and tactics adopted, and preferred to maintain the more traditional route of working through the National Union of Students (NUS), while for intellectual inspiration they relied on the orthodox texts of Marx, Engels and Lenin. It was not until the early 1970s under the leadership of Dave Cook that party students became a strong force both in the organised politics of the NUS and in their broader cultural and ideological activities, a decade or so after the YCL, in 'street' rather than 'seminar' politics, had embarked on a similar path. It was in these spheres of student politics that much of the Gramscian analysis was first applied in a strategic way to politics by communists, as the CPGB played a pivotal role in directing the political and democratic alliances that made up the Broad Left that dominated student politics in the 1970s. The activities of the student cohort in the CPGB were to have long-term implications for the ideological direction of the party, as they provided the initial intellectual spaces for the dissemination and discussion of Gramscian and Eurocommunist ideas, an analysis of the importance of new social movements, and a shift in intellectual emphasis towards cultural agendas. However, while it will be shown that the 1970s saw the CPGB eventually reap the benefits of the changes associated with the politics of the student generation of 1968 – such as a more libertarian socialism, the growth of a national student *movement*, the proliferation of new revolutionary perspectives – in the early years of the student movement the party was left behind events; it was isolated to a large extent from both the activism associated with 1968, and the ideas that were espoused.[4] Moreover, there was a marked distinction between the slow response of the CPGB student leadership, which, under Fergus Nicholson's direction since 1962 had remained aligned to communist tradition and orthodoxy, and that of the YCL, with its appropriation of often heretical directions. Where the YCL leadership therefore sought to widen the sphere of politics through 'cultural struggle', and a positive endorsement of the shift in moral, political and social values of the decade, the student leadership in the same period (1964-1968) was dominated by conservatism and Marxist orthodoxy, regarding the new student movement with suspicion, in particular its demands for autonomy as a specific social group.[5] The challenge to this conservatism and orthodoxy in the leadership of the communist students did not have a major impact until the 1970s. In 1968 communist students were isolated from the important political events. Indeed it will be argued here, in contrast to other accounts which have interpreted the 1968 peak of student activity as having favourable impact on communist students, that the communist student leadership was in crisis between 1967-1972, no longer able to offer leadership and direction to the student movement and unable to develop the enthusiasm of local communist student branches.[6] This situation would only be reversed by the replacement of Fergus Nicholson by Dave Cook as student organiser in 1972, and the subsequent 'high tide' of communist student politics in Britain between 1972-74, when CP student influence was strongest in the organising role it established in Broad Left and the intellectual role that communist students played in the renaissance of Marxist ideas, notably through the CUL and local student forums.

LEFT BEHIND: COMMUNIST STUDENTS IN CRISIS 1968-1972
Communist students were ill-prepared for the events that took place in 1968. Historically, the Communist Party had supported the extension of student rights and conditions, and the widening of access to university, in a way that mirrored its commitment to representing the interests of other groups, such as women or black people. It did this in a way that maintained the centrality of class; student activism was to be encouraged as a way of influencing and drawing people into Marxism, linking intellectuals to the working class. Communists had in earlier periods played

a leading role in representative student bodies; in the 1930s, for example, national student leaders included Brian Simon and George Matthews, both leading influences within the party during the 1960s and 1970s.[7]

A similar concern to be in the forefront of student politics resulted in a strong communist input into the first broad student organisation of the 1960s, the Radical Student Alliance (RSA), formed in the autumn of 1966, and drawing 400 students from 108 universities and colleges to its first national convention of that year. The leading communists in the RSA were Martin Jacques and Alan Hunt, who would both later become key players in the development of the Gramscian and Eurocommunist currents within the party. But at that time they were in the minority on the National Student Committee of the Communist Party. The RSA's declared objectives in its founding manifesto were for a 'programme necessary for the interests of students, for the removal of barriers to a full and democratic education, and for the greatest contribution of students to society and social progress'. On wider issues it talked of the need to build a students' movement, one which 'must be able to take collective action on matters of general social concern'. It noted that 'lack of militancy and perspective have so far prevented student organisations achieving these aims', and proposed structures and organisational forms to encourage activity and participation.[8]

The RSA, which included Labour and Liberal as well as communist students, was an early example of the broad left alliances that were to dominate student politics in the 1970s, with the objectives of building a mass student movement. Nevertheless the scale and depth of student radicalism went much beyond the objectives of the RSA, suggesting a whole new meaning of student power.[9] Though Jacques, Hunt and other communist students were profoundly affected by the events of 1968, the communist student leadership remained in the hands of more traditional custodians, who had been absent from the RSA and were reluctant to recognise the autonomy of the student movement. Fergus Nicholson, the National Student Organiser (NSO), along with allies Brian Filling and Phil Goodwin, remained unreceptive, at times hostile, to the new movements that were emerging and the ideas of liberation they espoused, preferring to concentrate their activities on the more limited agendas of improving conditions of students through the traditional politics of the NUS. Goodwin, for example, rejected the view that students were an autonomous group, separate from the working class. On the contrary, he argued, they were destined to 'acquire a body of knowledge and skills which will subsequently be used either for the production of profit as skilled labour power, or for employment by the state as teachers, doctors and so on'.[10] He therefore rejected the view that students should be seen as 'intellectuals'; they should not be given special status; the labour movement would throw up its own intellectuals without the need for them to 'come from without'.[11]

This view of the new student movement led inevitably to the notion that student initiatives should be secondary to those of the labour movement, reaffirming the more traditional perspective that class should remain at the core of the party's outlook. However it also meant that the party was unable to adapt to the new situations that were occurring within the student movement.

There were criticisms of this position, however. Indeed, to others on the National Student Committee, the events of 1968 represented a defining turning-point. Martin Jacques had been profoundly influenced by the Soviet invasion of Czechoslovakia and the events in Paris in May, the culmination of which he later described as his 'political birth'.[12] Jacques had been elected to the Communist Party's EC in 1967 (where he was to remain until 1991), on the back of what he saw as 'patronage', in effect headhunted by the leadership as a promising young member of the new generation. It was his organisational as much as intellectual contribution that impressed; it was his role in the RSA and as a student activist at Manchester University that first drew him to the attention of the leadership.[13]

There were many other communist students who identified positively with the events of 1968. For many the Communist Party's decision to condemn the Soviet 'intervention' in Czechoslovakia was a crucial factor in remaining in, or deciding to join, paralleling in many ways similar decisions by feminists.[14] It was the scale of the other major development of 1968, the May events in Paris, that transformed student politics in Britain, as elsewhere, with the emergence of new organisations such as the Revolutionary Socialist Students Federation (RSSF); and the general growth of Trotskyist groups, notably the International Socialists, provided new focal points of radical identification which challenged the hitherto leading role communists had enjoyed in the student body. The 'Red Bases' strategy was denounced by the CPGB leadership, though they allowed individual communists to affiliate to the RSSF if they so wished, as long as they did not promote the ideals of that organisation.[15] The mistrust of Trotskyist student groups had led to a special party committee, set up as early as 1964 but at its most active in the late 1960s.[16] The extent of the party's isolation from the dynamics of the moment of 1968 has been confirmed by leading communist activists at the time. According to Digby Jacks, a member of the NSC and later communist NUS President in 1971: 'In 1968 it became suddenly harder to be a communist in student politics. I had the feeling that things were passing the party by'.[17] To Mike Prior, a communist student active at Essex in 1968, 'Being a communist was just about on the edge of left-wing respectability'.[18]

This failure to be at the heart of student politics in 1968 led to growing divisions within the NSC and regular disputes between the factions around Fergus Nicholson and Martin Jacques. The CPGB leadership for its part was also concerned that the party remained in touch with the fast-moving events in the wider student world, which included the

2. Unlikely Allies: Students, Feminists and the Party

new enthusiasm for Marxism, albeit in new forms. The intellectuals in the leadership, such as Brian Simon, thought that a new generation of intellectuals was needed if the party was to remain in touch.[19]

One major outcome of this need to increase the communist influence amongst students was the decision to start the Communist University of London (CUL) in 1969, to provide an intellectual forum whereby students could effectively be socialised into the political positions of the CPGB. It was motivated by the need to try and wrest the initiative from the rising Trotskyist groups and to give some political leadership to the student movement. The first CUL was held at University College London in the summer of 1969, advertised as 'a series of intensive courses in Marxism-Leninism'.[20] It was a traditional Marxist forum of study which, despite appealing beyond the party, closely followed a traditional curriculum, and depended on a select group of tutors, comprising of party organisers – such as Jack Woddis, Bert Pearce and Ron Bellamy – and party intellectuals – notably James Klugmann, editor of *Marxism Today*, Andrew Rothstein, Brian Simon, Chair of the party's Cultural Committee, and Maurice Dobb, the party's leading economist. The attendance at the first CUL, of 159, was a tenth of that of the peak years of 1977-78 (though it was twice the estimated figure), and was made up overwhelmingly of party members, who chose from ten specialist courses on offer, ranging from Imperialism and National Liberation, Student Movement and Socialist Revolution, to Philosophy and Art and Revolution. The simple format perhaps reflected the party's political priorities, in discussing key political issues in the morning, followed by a theoretical underpinning, through the texts of Marx, Engels and Lenin, in the afternoon. The organisers' reports confirm the political pragmatism of the approach, which attempted to link theory and practice in an unproblematic way, rather than seeking out new Marxist thinkers, or the New Left influences; the tone and emphasis of the reports remained convinced of the party's theoretical superiority in providing intellectual leadership to the student movement, through the classical thinkers. The aims of the first CUL were to make inroads into student politics by offering 'revolutionary theory' in order to challenge the 'reactionary ideology which holds sway' in the universities. The cultural events which took place in the evenings stood in stark contrast to those of the YCL, or wider counter-cultural initiatives of the period, and included a visit to the *Morning Star* Film Show and a 'student-worker talk-in'.[21]

The CPGB leadership launched the CUL initiative as part of its wider commitment to intellectual renewal, reflected in its earlier *Questions of Ideology and Culture* statement in 1967,[22] and in two other conferences in 1969, one on the role of intellectuals and the other the 'socialist scholars conference'. At the same time there was continued unease with the ineffectiveness of the student leadership, which was also drawing criticism from within the student and university sections of the party. This reached a climax in May 1970, when the EC decided to dispense with a full-time National Student Organiser (NSO), a position which it had maintained since 1945, officially, according to Reuben Falber, because of the party's 'serious financial difficulties'.[23] Correspondence between the EC and NSC members indicates that there was a lot of opposition from the NSC to the decision to relinquish a full-time student organiser.[24] Digby Jacks, the communist President of the NUS, regarded the decision as 'one of the utmost seriousness to the party and to the student movement generally'. Without a National Student Organiser, Jacks argued, 'the quality and quantity of our work in relation to the new overall situation, a bigger and wider movement with more struggles to be fought, will degenerate'. He concluded his letter to John Gollan, CPGB General Secretary, with the warning: 'I fear for the future of the party in the student movement. I would further fear for my own position in the National Union'.[25]

Despite the support of communist students in raising the necessary finance to keep the NSO on a part-time basis, events continued to confirm the inability of the party to make inroads into the student movement. Increasing communist influence in the labour movement in the same period, the subject of a following chapter, was not reflected in student work. The student membership had not expanded in any significant way, nor did the party seem to exert much intellectual influence amongst students. The CUL, though showing a gradual increase for its second meeting in 1970, encountered further problems in attracting participants in 1971; its courses retained the image of a 'party finishing school', isolated from new Marxist works or the new ideas associated with feminism. Fergus Nicholson himself acknowledged the weaknesses of the party's student work, noting in March 1971 'the very real weakness in our ability to speak directly to students, to move them politically, to evoke a response to our policy, our meetings or our publications'.[26] This was also the view of the Executive Committee, which authorised a statement on 'Further and Higher Education for the 1970s', recommending a series of radical changes such as mass expansion; the abolition of the binary system; grants for Open University students; the opening up of Oxford and Cambridge; the lengthening of degree courses; and the expansion of research funding.[27] This crisis reached its climax in 1972, with the replacement of Fergus Nicholson by Dave Cook as National Student Organiser.

THE BROAD LEFT AND ORGANIC INTELLECTUALS: THE COMMUNIST STUDENT BREAKTHROUGH 1972-1974

In 1972 the CPGB's student organisation remained peripheral to the party's machine. Individual communist students who wanted a more innovative strategic and ideological politics had not succeeded in wresting control away from Nicholson and his supporters. It was the EC in fact which precipitated the rejuvenation of the student organisation, by its decision to appoint Dave Cook as full-time student organiser. It was now felt by the party leadership that the NSC was not functioning very effectively; officially, Nicholson left by 'mutual consent',[28] but his attempts to nominate his successor failed and he was clearly unhappy at the decision.[29] At the same time the decision to appoint Cook was initially met with almost unanimous opposition from existing NSC members, on the basis that the latter was not a recent student, and had been appointed without consultation with the NSC.[30] An NSC motion was passed rejecting Cook's nomination, but the EC reaffirmed its decision on the grounds that 'the most essential qualities for the leadership of our student work are political understanding and capacity, all round political experience and the ability to organise and fight for our policy'.[31] Cook had already shown these qualities in his work in the YCL. According to the leadership he had helped to 'unify the YCL', by leading 'an exemplary fight for the party's policy'. Therefore Cook, like his subsequent close ally Martin Jacques, was appointed to a leading position in the party through forms of patronage. This suggests that there was concern in the leadership to select and develop a new generation of communist political leaders.

Cook's role as National Student Organiser was instrumental in revitalising the party student organisation. It became, under his leadership, the fastest growing section of the party between 1973 and 1974, and he helped re-shape its direction in two fundamental, related ways. Firstly, it won and consolidated political successes as the leading group within Broad Left, and secondly it strengthened its growing intellectual and cultural presence, which was to help transform the Communist University of London. Under his leadership the student membership reached a peak of nearly a thousand members in February 1973, increasing from 619 in November 1972.[32] The qualitative shift in the political profile of communist students, however, was even more far-reaching.

The first area of revival was in the role communist students began to play in the Broad Left, set up officially at a conference in Leeds in 1972. The Broad Left consisted of Communists, Labour students and the non-aligned left. Rejecting both what it saw as the 'revolutionary vanguardism' of the Trotskyist left and the narrow electoralism represented by Labour students, it called for the 'active involvement of the mass of students in campaigns and activities ... as the only basis for politicisation to a socialist perspective on a wide scale'.[33] Its purpose was to go beyond the narrow work of NUS politics, something which party students under Fergus Nicholson had never sought, and to help extend democratic and participatory power to the student body, a strategy which included alliances with feminist and anti-racist movements, with some active feminists such as Sue Slipman being among leading Broad Left activists. The strategy of communist students from this time on became merged with the Broad Left as a whole, and thus removed both their pretence of 'theoretical superiority' and the subordination to working-class agendas. Broad Left meetings were advertised at communist student gatherings and communist students stood on Broad Left platforms and as Broad Left candidates. Dave Cook's pamphlet *Students* (1973) was similar in tone and emphasis to the Broad Left in stressing the need for alliances between sections of the left and new social movements. It was also significant in identifying students as a new distinctive mass grouping, whose position had been transformed by the social changes associated with contemporary societies and the economic constraints of monopoly capitalism. 'The experiences of mass action', wrote Cook, 'lay the basis for shifts in their consciousness and assist in developing a correct relationship with the working class'.[34] Cook envisaged a new ideological role for students, as intellectuals who would challenge bourgeois ideology and attempt to foster intellectual leadership in the working class.

Though Cook did not refer to Gramsci in his pamphlet (and indeed may not have encountered Gramsci's work in depth at this time), the writings, forums and articles of communist students active at the time referred increasingly to Gramsci's work, giving a theoretical justification to politics, notably in the strategic areas of alliances.[35] The pursuit of broad alliances was not new to communist politics – indeed this was evident, for example, in the popular front and Broad Left groupings that had been up and running in the trade unions since the mid-1960s. What was different about this approach – and this was a consequence of the renaissance of Marxism in the politics of the left – was the application of Gramsci's ideas in a strategic way. Notably, this included the need to develop a prefigurative politics whereby broad alliances would go beyond tactical positions to constitute in embryo the alternative hegemonic bloc. Great emphasis was placed on democracy as providing a common thread in order to unite all progressive movements. The wider availability of Gramsci's work in English from 1971 helped provide the intellectual underpinning of the Broad Left strategy of extending democracy to areas of higher education, while it also provided a theoretical justification for different kinds of alliances between the working class and new social movements. As one of the new political forces that were being created beyond the traditional class profile of the party, students were no longer prepared to defer to the organised working class, even though communists maintained a commitment to forming alliances with the wider labour movement. As one leading communist student put it later, the key role for the CPGB within the Broad Left was to be 'an innovator of strategy and theory, unifier of democratic forces and the transforming agent of political forces'.[36] Significantly, the CP students had moved towards a pluralist politics of broad alliances some years before the party's own adoption of a 'broad democratic alliance' at its 1977 Congress.

The second major development amongst communist students was their capacity to engage with and help facilitate the intellectual renaissance of Marxism. There was great interest in the newly available writings on Gramsci, and these, together with a number of other writers, notably

Althusser, became the basis for a range of critical forums and reading groups, the most important of which was the transformation of the CUL from an orthodox party education school to a heretical site of intellectual ferment. Not only was there an increase in numbers of students attending from 1972 (with a resulting rise in expectation and publicity), but also there was a qualitative change, with a broader range and scope in the topics being discussed – which even extended to Archery and Archaeology – as well as a stronger focus on political strategy, including more critical examinations of the party's own history. It became a forum for both party and non-party intellectuals, including such thinkers as Stuart Hall, Raphael Samuel and the younger Althusserians Paul Hirst and Barry Hindess, as well as Gramsci scholars like Anne Showstack Sassoon; and it raised the possibility of some reconciliation between the lost generation of communist intellectuals who had left in 1956 and the younger post-1968 generation. The CUL reflected, to many of the participants, the unlimited creative possibilities of the new interest in Marxism. As Ken Spours, one of the CUL organisers, put it:

> When you can stuff a university with 1500 people and more professors per square inch than anywhere else ... When you can put on courses with a Marxist interpretation of virtually every living thing, then what you've got is a theoretical perspective which has shown a lot of confidence; it's saying 'actually we have an alternative way of understanding the world'.[37]

The CUL helped to put intellectual work at the centre of the party's concerns, reflected not only in the increase in enthusiasm and greater publicity for the party, but also in a new role for the intellectual, no longer conceived of as a specialist in a particular academic or cultural area, but as someone who sought a more political, strategic and public role: in Gramsci's terms an 'organic intellectual'.[38] This was apparent in the intentions of the CUL leaders themselves, who sought 'to create a different type of intellectual, not a detached and aloof professional, but one who is organically linked to the working-class struggle for socialism'.[39] The new role was also indicative of the strategic importance intellectuals started to assume in the party from the mid-1970s. This new importance was not one the party had tried to instigate directly; rather it had endorsed it pragmatically, and in this it was indirectly helped, as will be shown in following chapters, by the renewed input from older party intellectuals.

THE ORIGINS OF THE FEMINIST CRITIQUE
In the previous chapter it was argued that there was a contradiction between the party's cultural ethos, which reflected in some measure the patriarchal family structure of wider society, and its early commitment to improving the position of women, as evidenced by its support for

birth control, the extension of women's rights on pay and conditions, and a greater involvement by women in trade unions. By committing itself to a 'class before gender' position, the party saw the interests of women as bound up with the interests of the working class as a whole; women's oppression was a feature of capitalist societies and would ultimately be resolved with socio-economic transformation. This analysis did not, as we have seen, prevent communists calling for an improvement in women's position within the existing society. It was rather that there was no extended analysis into the pervasiveness of women's oppression beyond the workplace and the 'public sphere' generally, or within the institutions of the labour movement.

These omissions included a failure to be critical of the role of women in the Communist Party itself, where their status was usually some way below that of their husbands. A generation of communists who grew up in the 1960s have testified to the unspoken sexual division of labour in the party. There was an inherent contradiction in this division. On the one hand, party women were recognised as having an important role in the party as branch activists, with the party maintaining in its pamphlets that the position of women in society needed to be changed. On the other hand, women took responsibility for specific supporting roles – organising socials and *Morning Star* bazaar committee work, for example, while the men often took on more significant time-consuming activities. This led to an 'absent father' problem, with its own particular communist meaning.[40] Long meetings and time spent away from the family (particularly for full-timers) was justified on the grounds of political importance, in much the same way as sacrifices in other forms of work were justified. As one communist child growing up in the 1960s recalls: 'If that (i.e. party) work is going to improve the whole world in their eyes then letting their families down has some justification'.[41] Men, for their part, in commending the supportive role of their partners, often managed to combine it with condescension and cultural conservatism.[42]

The emergence of second-wave feminism in the 1960s, and the development of the Women's Liberation Movement, following its founding British conference in 1970, brought new challenges to the Communist Party, as it did to other traditional forms of left politics. What was distinctive about second-wave feminism was the extent of the ideological interrogation of 'patriarchy', including the public-private axis of power, and the search for more autonomous ways of organising and the transformation of left-wing practice.[43] It is also necessary to stress that in the two dominant strands within second-wave feminism – socialist feminism and radical feminism – it was the former that took on most significance in Britain, becoming part of the debates over the future of left politics, while radical feminism was the most influential aspect of the movement in the United States.[44] One of the features of the way in which feminism influenced the political direction of the CPGB was its gradual movement beyond the Marxist tradition, to encompass a wider theoretical underpinning, which included not only the works of neo-Marxists like Althusser but also, for example, psychoanalytical theory. This was made easier because of the alliances formed within the Women's Liberation Movement between radical, Marxist and other feminists. It will be shown that a cumulative result for the party of these developments was a challenge both to its political ways of organising among women, and to its overall political strategy.

It is also necessary to distinguish between the 1960s, which saw the publication of some of the key feminist texts, as well as formative moments of transformation in the role of women – including the increase in women's paid employment, and the arrival of contraception on a wide-scale, and the legalisation of abortion – and the 1970s, which saw the development of the Women's Liberation Movement. This distinction is important in understanding the nature of the impact of feminism on the CPGB. Like other sections of the left and society generally, the Communist Party in the 1960s remained relatively unaffected by feminism. The *May Day Manifesto*, a rallying call issued by the key thinkers of the first New Left, first written in 1967, omits any reference to feminism, despite feminists being involved in the discussions that led to the publication of the document.[45] Many feminists have also testified to the low priority given to the role of women by the movements in the forefront of the events of 1968, despite the creative, grassroots and anti-hierarchical values that were espoused by the new movements. For many of the Trotskyist movements, feminism was a diversion from the class struggle – a form of class reductionism that actually exceeded the CPGB's own cultural conservatism.[46] The party at one level reflected other left groups in being slow to take on board the demands made by new feminist thinking. However, another reason for its conservatism was its dependence on traditional assumptions about the nature of work, notably the deference to the industrial skilled (male) workforce. A survey of the minutes of the National Women's Advisory meetings throughout the 1960s shows a very traditional analysis of women's oppression, and a commitment to traditional forms of work amongst women, as well as a highly gendered approach to targeting women as potential recruits to the party. In January 1966, for example, there is a report of an education school for party women ('Women and the Fight For Socialism'), at which serious reading of classical works of Marx and Engels was encouraged, around such questions as 'What are the differences between socialist and communist society', and 'How can we win more Women for the Fight For Peace?'.[47] In the same year, the National Women's Advisory's recommendation to the Editorial Board of the new *Morning Star*, when it succeeded the *Daily Worker*, was that in addition to establishing a regular 'Women's Page', party women might like 'to arrange supper or tea parties' to help raise the profile of the paper.[48] In the activities expected of communist women, there is little sign throughout the 1960s of any fundamental change in the sexual division of labour; women were allocated what were definitely supporting roles – such as organising amongst housewives, on issues to do with the cost of living. A pragmatic feminism co-existed with an uncritical or implicit acceptance of traditional roles of women in the party. The *Morning Star* itself seemed to maintain the cultural baggage of the *Daily Worker*, and continued to reflect this contradiction; at one level there was a campaigning tone on improving the lives of women; at another there was a reassertion of the role of the male trade union activist.

Nevertheless, the long-standing commitment by the Communist Party to improving the conditions of women, together with the fact that the party had maintained a National Women's Advisory Committee and a National Women's Committee, provided some potential spaces for discussion amongst feminists. The feminist impact on the party began in 1968-1970. The dates are important in two fundamental respects. Firstly, evidence from interviews suggests that many of the women who joined the party after 1968, and who went on to become leading feminists, did so for a distinctive set of critical reasons in respect of the party's traditions; these included its more critical stance towards the Soviet 'intervention' in Czechoslovakia,[49] its more critical intellectual work, related to student activity, and its other less dogmatic perspectives as compared to Trotskyist groups. According to one feminist who joined the party in the early 1970s, in comparison to other sections of the left there was a higher 'degree of honest debate': 'My respect for the CP was increased not because it was saying the right things but because it was so honest in its difficulty with changing from a traditional male dominated gender-blind left party'.[50]

As discussed above, this turning-point was also responsible for the decision of many students to join the party at this time. This should not imply that a new generation of feminists all converged on the party after 1968, however. Some leading activists, like Beatrix Campbell, came from party families and saw their political development evolve out of a more traditional acceptance of Marxism-Leninism; others had encountered some of the issues – such as sexual liberation, autonomy and the politics of personal lives – in the YCL in the preceding decade. Others such as Mikki Doyle, who wrote the women's column in the *Morning Star*, asserted a more class-based feminism, which put at the forefront the experiences of women in the workplace.[51] It is also the case that some older women who had been in the party for many years, like Gladys Brooks and Florence Keyworth, found a strong identification with the younger generation; therefore simple generational conflicts cannot be assumed, though there was a distinctive current of feminism amongst younger feminists, often derived from prior involvement with the Women's Liberation Movement before joining the party. The important point to note in these developments was that

2. Unlikely Allies: Students, Feminists and the Party

the commitment to feminism became a priority for the new generation; it was not relegated by, or subordinate to some higher goal; it was a crucial part of redefining socialism.

Donald Sassoon's description of the wider impact on the left of second-wave feminism holds good for the CPGB. Feminism, he writes

> ... invited the organised left fundamentally to recast its own ideological framework, abandoning the unspoken axioms that the socialist movement was a movement of men which women could join on men's terms and, in exchange, receive men's support ... This new movement of universal emancipation required a demasculinised politics, a socialism for women and men.[52]

Secondly, the feminist input was given a very specific strategic impetus by the work of a dissident clandestine group of young party intellectuals, known initially as the Smith Group and subsequently re-named the Party Group. This was set up in 1970 by university lecturer Bill Warren, and based in London. The group circulated clandestine discussion documents and focused on what it perceived of as weaknesses in the party's theory and strategy. The wider significance of the group will be discussed in later chapters, but one primary objective was the need to pursue a feminist agenda. One of the group's leading members was Beatrix Campbell, a journalist on the *Morning Star*, who was to play a leading role in the attempt to transform the party's relationship to women, and in arguing for the necessity of it adopting a feminist agenda. Campbell, in documents circulated within the group, described the position of a feminist within the CPGB as akin to 'an oppositional fifth column', in terms of raising issues about women's oppression, including those of women party members. 'The politics of sexual oppression has been significant only for its absence in Communist Party women's work. It has taken disaffected radical women and feminists in the Women's Liberation Movement to document the politics of sexism for us'. She also noted the 'curious reaction among some leading comrades to the Women's Liberation Movement'; it received 'almost overwhelming opposition from the National Women's Advisory, which seemed to hope that if the new movement was ignored it might go away'. She was particularly critical of the way women's issues were considered as 'the smaller things of life', unconnected to 'real politics', and ignored as 'special' 'sectarian' issues, while those concerning men were seen as 'universal' and 'human', a distinction she attributed to the work of the radical feminist Shulamith Firestone. While she acknowledged that the party had been involved historically in important struggles of particular interest to women, such as the fight for child care and equal pay, she argued that it was the wider issues that remained to be confronted.[53]

The height of the Party Group's attempt to influence the party's strategy culminated in an alternative motion to the one presented by the National Women's Advisory at the party congress of 1971. The official motion, moved by Rosemary Small, the National Women's Organiser, was entitled 'Women in Society', and repeated the party's traditional analysis of the role of women. It defined 'the subjugation of women' as originating from the division of society into classes ...

> ... with the class owning the means of production exploiting others. The ruling classes have always sought to divide and weaken the exploited classes. They have therefore instilled prejudices of male superiority and female inferiority which are now deeply rooted amongst people in our society.

It gave a cautious welcome to the Women's Liberation Movement, on the basis of 'the contribution of these movements to bringing women into action on some important social questions and in raising the issue of women's role in society'. However, it argued that the WLM should seek 'closer association' with the labour movement, and that the 'solution' to the problems of women was 'consistent class struggle in which both men and women participate'. The practical measures it proposed as its 'programme for action' included equal pay, removal of legal inequalities, equal opportunity for training, free nursery education and free advice on abortion and family planning. These measures were necessary 'to make inroads into the power of the monopoly capitalist interests'. With regard to the status of women in the party, the motion recommended that more women should be brought onto the leading committees, and more energy directed at 'increasing numbers won to read the *Morning Star* and become members of the Communist Party and the Young Communist League'.[54]

Though the presence of the motion in itself indicated that the party was responding to the feminist challenge to the party, there was little in its substance that differed from previous resolutions at earlier Congresses. Even on the National Women's Advisory (from where the motion had emerged), there was only muted enthusiasm. According to a report submitted to its meeting two months prior to the Congress, the proposed resolution was 'not an inspiring document ... [while there was] ... much excellent and thought provoking material in it ...it did not reflect the excitement of the movement'.[55]

For the feminists in the Party Group, the issues were much more fundamental. The alternative motion, which had been previously circulated within the group as an article for discussion, was critical both of the limited theoretical analysis offered by the party on the position of women in society, and of the party's own failure to come to terms with the extent of patriarchy in its own ranks. It read:

> The Communist Party reflects the general situation; we concede to women's equality but then do not analyse the reasons why they stand the

test so badly, why they are so passive, why they are so capable of pursuing party policy (maintaining, interpreting) but at the same time are so incapable of setting (making) it.[56]

The motion argued that the party, together with the wider labour movement, 'divorced' issues of equal pay from 'the fight for free contraception and free abortion on demand'. Indeed what the alternative motion described as the 'social aspects of women's oppression' were 'regarded with suspicion by the party', which prevented a theoretical engagement with the 'complex of social, psychological and sexual oppressions'. This reflected to some degree the wider theoretical critique the Party Group had made of the economism at the heart of the party's strategy, the focus of the later Gramscian critique and the subject of following chapters. Here it is sufficient to point to this earlier critique as one which objected to the way the party's official analysis ignored different levels of oppression, which were rooted in a range of value systems, cultures and practices. These included the party's own values and structures, and the alternative motion pointed out the need to confront 'male chauvinism, which hinders the work of the party at all levels within the party'; it operated at branch level, where 'paternalistic attitudes', lack of crèches, and the allocation of 'organisational' rather than 'political' tasks to women relegated 'women's issues' to the bottom of the agenda. The motion condemned the 'dangerous chauvinistic attitudes expressed by our top leadership', and in the pages of the *Morning Star*, and noted that there remained a 'taboo' in the party on discussions of private life. It concluded that an 'ideological battle' must be waged in the party in order to transform the party's values, a process that would only be achieved by constant discussion at national, district and branch level on the problems of women, 'with constant self-criticism and examination of our work in this area'. All members were urged to 'consider their position with relation to housework'; and it was argued that practical measures should be taken, such as the provision of crèches, 'special education for women to raise their consciousness', the setting up of a monthly women's paper, and even party medical centres to provide 'birth control and abortion facilities'.[57]

The alternative motion was rejected at the Congress and the official motion passed with only four votes against.[58] However the Party Group's alternative motion marked the start of a more assertive ideological feminism within the party, which was to become much more critical of the party's existing social and cultural practices, and to seek more independence in ways of organising, applying a feminist critique to the party's overall political strategy. Beatrix Campbell, along with some other feminists – some younger and some from an older tradition – went on to put into practice one of the recommendations of the alternative motion, by founding a monthly paper.

THE IMPACT OF RED RAG

Party feminists were not prepared to confine their energy to official publications, or to organise in a clandestine way, particularly in light of the party's previous record. The decision to set up *Red Rag* by party feminists in London, with the support of feminists outside the party, was evidence of the growing rift between the concerns and priorities of the feminists and those of the party leadership.[59] While party members were encouraged to join with other progressive forces in day to day work, such as in the Women's Liberation Movement, the party expected its members to follow the general direction of the party's policy, which was based on official Congress decisions, and to accept the decisions and organisational leadership of the National Women's Advisory Committee. Party rules, supported by democratic centralism, did not allow for the promotion or dissemination of unauthorised journals within the party. *Red Rag* was set up without any authorisation, and although it did not project itself as an official party journal, it was clearly identified with the work of party feminists, and was distributed widely within the party as a way of influencing debate over the party's policy on women. The ideological direction of the magazine, which first appeared in 1972, served to broaden the gulf between the party's official positions and that of dissident feminists.

Such developments should be seen of course in the context of the wider activities and impact of feminism, as well as the impact of new Marxist writers, notably the importance given to ideology by Althusser; these were factors which combined to provide a strong impetus for the new journal. *Red Rag* identified itself as an explicitly marxist-feminist journal, in which the oppression of women was seen in the context of the development of capitalism, and which sought the achievement of an alliance between the Women's Liberation Movement and the working class. Yet the range of subject areas covered – sexuality, lesbian politics, domestic violence – went much beyond the usual parameters of the workplace and the trade union, though these were also covered extensively. Within the journal too there was not only a dialogue at times between feminists of different left groups, but also a theoretical discussion which examined sympathetically some of the work of radical feminists. It was therefore 'first and foremost a feminist journal, because feminism is the political movement which emerges as women's response to their own oppression'.[60] This illustrated the more audacious, uncompromising stance of the new feminist generation. Furthermore, as a joint initiative of party and non-party feminists, the priority was clearly to wield an influence beyond the party – though it also sought to alter the party's priorities on feminism. According to its 'Declaration of Intent', *Red Rag*, while seeing itself as existing within the Marxist revolutionary tradition, took up an explicitly critical position of the existing practices of the labour movement, a viewpoint clearly at odds with the party's own views: 'The trade union

2. Unlikely Allies: Students, Feminists and the Party

movement is virtually silent about the discrimination which excludes women from many jobs'.[61] It also rejected the view dominant in the party's mainstream outlook, that the interests of women could be dealt with by the labour movement 'in general': '"in general", we've been getting trodden on for a very long time'.[62] 'In general', of course, was a reference to the way in which the party had used class as the organising principle for an understanding of the oppression of women – and for its likely solution – the 'class before gender' analysis; the implication being that the solution to women's oppression could not be divorced from that of the working class, and that strategies to overcome it would not succeed through independent feminist activity. In contrast to this, the *Red Rag* 'declaration of intent' continued: 'we are in no mood ... to wait for socialism to bring us liberation. We are interested in liberation now and in wrenching from capitalist society every advance we can get'.[63]

The organisational and ideological nature of *Red Rag* was of great concern to the party leadership, and the Executive Committee made the decision to call in those members of the editorial collective who belonged to the CPGB, and to instruct them not to publish further issues. Correspondence between the EC and the *Red Rag* collective illustrates the degree of difference that existed at this time. According to Reuben Falber, then Assistant General Secretary, 'no prior knowledge of intention' had been given about its publication, and, according to him, the first the EC got to hear of it was a 'letter informing us that the first issue would soon be out'. He went on: 'this is contrary to the norms of party practice where comrades who, whether in association with other party members only, or with non-party members, wish to publish a party journal first approach the party for a discussion on the matter and seek agreement'.[64]

After meeting with those party members who were on the editorial collective of *Red Rag*, it was clear to the EC members who had been delegated to deal with the matter (Reuben Falber and Gerry Cohen, London District Secretary), that the journal was not going to accede to the pressures exerted by the party leadership. Refusals to provide the names of leading members of the collective to the EC was followed by a determination to carry on the publication of *Red Rag*. Gladys Brooks, a feminist from an older generation on the *Red Rag* collective, informed the EC that *Red Rag* would continue publication despite the EC's instructions, confirmation of the extent to which feminists were prepared to go in keeping to their principles.[65]

The publication of *Red Rag* was in breach of party rules which, based on democratic centralism, required that permission be granted from the EC before the publication of any journal by party members. However, as in the case of the YCL cohort discussed above, the party fell short of disciplining the people who were challenging the party's ethos as well as its organisational structure. Instead it made a decision to go ahead with its own women's journal, *Link*, that would reflect the party's policy, and would 'of course, be produced by Marxists, the Marxists who are responsible to the party and will work on the basis of the decisions of our Congress. The new journal will, wherever necessary, take into account the decisions coming up in the Women's Liberation Movement'.[66]

FEMINISM COMES IN FROM THE COLD

Despite the growing rift between the official policy on women and the more robust approach of *Red Rag*, the decision to tolerate the unofficial magazine allowed an ongoing discussion to take place and ensured that the party remained part of the feminist debate. An important example of this debate, and illustrative of the theoretical differences between the two positions, was a discussion on 'Marxism and the Family' which took place within the pages of *Marxism Today*, initiated by an opening contribution from Rosemary Small in December 1972. Small reiterated a very standard outlook, still based on the writings of Engels, and noting positive developments in the Soviet Union. In response, *Red Rag* contributors and supporters, such as Maria Loftus, pointed out the article's theoretical limitations, notably the 'tendency to separate the economic aspect of existence from social institutions and ideologies': 'She has grossly underestimated the family as an institutional site for particular forms of social consciousness, as an institution which is itself (partially) determined and cemented by ideological pressures'.[67] Here, the Althusserian influence is evident, with the family viewed as an ideological state apparatus, rather than as merely reflecting in a more passive way the economic division of labour. Such an analysis, which was common amongst socialist-feminists beyond the CP, started to interrogate in a more direct way the nature of family life; and this included for party feminists the nature of the communist family. Sexism and chauvinism among party members also became more contested by feminists, with letters to the EC, and 'sexism in the party' becoming the main topic at one National Women's Advisory, leading to a recommendation to the EC that it addressed the matter.[68] The topics of discussion at the National Women's Advisory meetings during 1973-74 broadened in range to include sexuality, lesbianism, and a more positive attitude towards the WLM.[69] The intensification of interest in feminism, which reflected the peak years of the feminist movement in Britain, led to more '*Red Rag* feminists' writing for the party's official paper *Link*, and by 1975 (which also saw a major increase in the number of women delegates to party Congress), leading feminists such as Beatrix Campbell and Sue Slipman were influential figures at the National Women's Advisory meetings.[70] Thompson's statement that the contribution of the feminists 'was accepted virtually without public opposition as the official CP standpoint'[71] could perhaps be seen as an underestimation of the level of ideological struggle and campaigning that had taken place, but it is

2. Unlikely Allies: Students, Feminists and the Party

apparent that the party was beginning to face up to challenges from its new sections. Feminists, like the young communists and students, had established themselves as an important constituency, whose influence in the party looked likely to increase.

Notes
1. H. Marcuse, *One-Dimensional Man*, Routledge 1964.
2. A Touraine, *The Return of the Actor*, University of Minnesota Press 1988.
3. S. Tarrow, *Democracy and Disorder: Protest and Politics in Italy 1965-1975*, Clarendon Press, Oxford, 1989.
4. It was difficult to talk of a 'student movement' prior to 1967, for two reasons. Prior to the expansion of higher education in the 1960s, students were mainly middle- and upper- class. Following the Robbins Report of 1963 and the expansion of the polytechnic sector, initiated by Tony Crosland in the Labour Government of 1964-1970, the numbers of students rapidly increased mirroring similar, sometimes larger, increases in other European countries. Secondly, while there had been other periods of student political activity, notably during the 1930s over the 'humanitarian' struggles such as the Spanish Civil War, being so few in number, their narrow class background and relative isolation from the working class and labour movement prevented any cohesive 'mass' movement from developing. In the 1960s, both the expansion of higher education and the politicisation of students on a mass scale, evidenced by the rise of JF Kennedy, the issues played out at Berkeley and the civil rights movement in the US and Anti-Vietnam War Movement, provided a new focus for a student movement. Different arguments have been offered over the origins of this radicalism. Sassoon in *One Hundred Years of Socialism*, (op cit, pp383-4) has suggested that the student movement represented the renewal of ideological politics following the 'end of ideology' consensus which had prevailed in the 1950s. Hobsbawm in *Age of Extremes* (op cit, p444-446) has stressed the importance of seeing the student protests as occurring at the 'very peak of the great global boom', as much a direct global response to the nature of the materialistic consumer driven modernised society. This contrasts with Marwick in *The Sixties* who saw the student movement as symptomatic of a wider drive for modernisation. For Lacqeur the implosion of student movements had a more specific context as a protest against the lack of reforms and conservative hierarchies of higher education, a point of view at least supported by the immediate causes of much of the unrest. See W. Lacqueur, *Europe Since Hitler: The Rebirth of Europe*, Harmondsworth 1982, pp292-294.
5. Interviews with NSC EC members Willie Thompson and Martin Jacques.
6. The weakness of this analysis is implied by over-generalisations about the relationship between the communists and the wider student movement and suffers to a large degree by lack of in-depth attention; see W. Thompson, *The Good Old Cause*, op cit, and J. Callaghan, *The Far Left in British Politics*, op cit. F. Beckett's more journalistic account *Enemy Within* (op cit, pp167-168) is more accurate on this.
7. See N. Wood, *Communism and the British Intellectuals*, op cit, for an extended discussion of these issues.
8. RSA Founding Statement 1966, NSC File CP Archive.

9. The classic statement of this can be found in A. Cockburn and R. Blackburn, *Student Power*, Harmondsworth 1969.
10. P. Goodwin, 'Student Perspectives', *Comment*, October 1969.
11. Ibid.
12. M. Jacques interview.
13. M. Jacques interview.
14. Sue Slipman, M. Jacques, interviews.
15. F. Beckett, *Enemy Within*, op cit, pp167-68.
16. Under Betty Reid's direction, the 'Trotskyism Study Group' encouraged research and articles on the new phenomenon. The founding article was B. Reid, 'Trotskyism in Britain Today', *Marxism Today*, September 1964.
17. D. Jacks, interview with Francis Beckett, *Enemy Within*, op cit, p167.
18. M. Prior, interview with author.
19. A meeting was held in 1969, under the auspices of the party's Cultural Committee, on 'the role of intellectuals today': Martin Jacques presented a paper – 'Notes On Intellectuals' – a version of which was later to appear in *Marxism Today* in October 1971. Reflecting on the event, Bill Carritt, Cultural Committee member, wrote to Brian Simon (24.6.69) that ' … the party is lagging behind in the field of ideological work' and that there was a ' … need to develop a clearer approach to the intellectuals in the party' (Cultural Committee minutes, CP Archive).
20. *Comment*, 31.5.69.
21. There are extensive organisers' notes of the annual CULs, held in the two CUL boxes in the CP Archive, from which a range of information on CUL sessions and speakers can be found.
22. See following chapter for in-depth discussion of this.
23. R. Falber, explaining the reason in a letter to Brian Durrans, University College Branch, CP 11.6.70, NSC Box, CP Archive.
24. NSC Box, CP Archive.
25. Digby Jacks, letter to John Gollan, 7.7.70, NSC File, CP Archive. Jacks had been elected NUS President on the back of an alliance of communist and Labour students that pre-dated the Broad Left.
26. F. Nicholson, 'NSC Notes', March 1971, NSC Box, CP Archive.
27. NSC Box, CP Archive.
28. Letter from Reuben Falber to NSC, 16.3.72, NSC Box. More precise evidence of the reasons for his departure is not available. However there were complaints that the National Student Committee was not functioning effectively by not consulting regularly with districts, and evidence shows some branches had become moribund. See letter from John Attfield to EC, 7.3.72. In addition, according to former NSC members Willie Thompson and Martin Jacques, there were strong dissenting positions over the political direction taken by Nicholson. NSC Organiser's notes 1972, CP Archive.
29. Interviews with R. Falber and W. Thompson.
30. At the NSC meeting of 29.30 April 1972, the decision to appoint Cook was opposed by 13 out of 14 members present, with one abstention. This led to a motion asking the EC to 'rescind' its decision to appoint Cook. Reuben Falber on behalf of the EC replied reaffirming the latter's decision. R. Falber, letter to NSC, 17.5.72, NSC Organiser's notes, May 1972, CP Archive.

2. Unlikely Allies: Students, Feminists and the Party

31. R. Falber letter to NSC, 17.5.72, CP Archive.
32. Figures taken from records in NSC box, CP Archive.
33. 'What is the Broad Left?', Broad Left Student Box. No date, CP Archive.
34. D. Cook, *Students*, CPGB, 1973, p21.
35. K. Spours, Jon. Bloomfield, Jude Bloomfield, S. Hibbin; interviews with author.
36. K. Spours, 'Students, Education and the State', *Marxism Today*, November 1977.
37. K. Spours, interview with author. The transformation began with CUL 4 in 1972, where there was a 100% increase over the previous year. The party gave it greater attention by appointing a full-time organiser to work closely with the National Student Organiser; this was to have a profound effect on the party's strategy. CUL Box 1, CP Archive.
38. For Gramsci's concept of the organic intellectual see A. Gramsci, *Selections From Prison Notebooks*, Lawrence and Wishart, 1971, pp3-14; Anne Showstack Sassoon, *Gramsci's Politics*, Hutchinson, 1987, (Postscript).
39. K. Spours, 'Students, Education and the State', *Marxism Today*, November 1977, op cit.
40. This was a recurring issue in the interviews with children of communist parents conducted by Phil Cohen in his *Children of the Revolution*, Lawrence and Wishart, 1998.
41. Jackie Kay, quoted in P. Cohen, *Children of the Revolution*, op cit, p36.
42. On returning home from work each evening Frank Watters, Midlands District Secretary of the party in the 1960s, was 'comforted' by the thought that 'the door would still be open and a welcome waiting with a cup of tea and a sandwich or cheese and biscuits, or sharing a late fish and chip supper, as I poured out my inner thoughts' (*Being Frank: The Memoirs of Frank Watters*, Askew Printing, Doncaster 1992, p45). The mixture of support and condescension is evident in Frank Jackson's letter to *Comment*, 6.1.68, where commenting on the 1967 Congress he wrote: 'I was impressed by the contributions of our women comrades. No despairing note here; all proud of what they had done ... Our Party need never despair while we can attract such beauty, such lively discussions with such a political grasp of things as was shown by our women comrades who came to the rostrum'.
43. For a discussion of the rise of second-wave feminism see J. Mitchell – for example, *Women: The Longest Revolution*, Virago, 1984; A. Coote and B. Campbell, *Sweet Freedom*, Basil Blackwell, 1987; S. Firestone, *The Dialectic of Sex*, Paladin, 1971.
44. Liberal feminism was a third type; which had longer origins in the work, for example, of Mary Wollstonecraft, John Stuart Mill, and the Suffragettes.
45. D. Sassoon notes this in *One Hundred Years of Socialism*, op cit, p407.
46. See Sheila Rowbotham et al, *Beyond the Fragments*, Merlin Press, 1979, p35, for discussion of the International Socialists and the relatively pro-feminist International Marxist Group.
47. CP/CENT/WOM/1/11.
48. CP/CENT/WOM/3/4.
49. Sue Slipman, interview.

50. Joanna de Groot, interview.
51. Doyle's brand of feminism was much admired by Elizabeth Wilson and Angela Weir. Interviews with author.
52. D. Sassoon, *One Hundred Years of Socialism*, op cit, p422.
53. All the quotations here that pertain to the Party Group are from the papers of Mike Prior, a leading member of the group, who made his documents available to the author. Campbell's discussion document cited here was not dated, but its date is most likely to be 1970. Campbell's critique was also informed by a broader theoretical engagement with radical feminist writers – witness her favourable reviews of Firestone's *The Dialectic of Sex* ('quite the most radical and daring book to come out of the Women's Liberation Movement') in *Comment*, 5.6.71, and of Millett's *Sexual Politics* (*Comment*, 22.5.71) – another indication of the drift away from Marxist-feminist orthodoxy among party feminists.
54. Congress Report, *Comment*, 18 December 1971. A longer version of Small's analysis appeared in R. Small, *Women: The Road to Socialism and Equality*, CPGB, 1972.
55. CP/CENT/WOM/3/5.
56. 'Alternative Motion to Women in Society', Party Group Journal 2, Mike Prior papers, no date but 1970/71.
57. Ibid.
58. Congress Report, CPGB, 1972.
59. *Red Rag*'s collective and regular writers included non-party members Sheila Rowbotham and Audrey Wise. In addition to the younger party feminists such as Beatrix Campbell and Sue Slipman, it also featured articles from members of an older generation, such as Florence Keyworth and Gladys Brooks, with the latter doing much of the editorial work.
60. 'Declaration of Intent', *Red Rag*, No 1, no date but early 1972.
61. *Red Rag*, No 1, 1972.
62. Ibid.
63. Ibid.
64. R. Falber, letter to D. Homer (Secretary, Cheltenham branch), 14.11.72. In an interview with the author Falber denied *Red Rag* was published in breach of party rules; the documents suggest otherwise, however. EC Box, November 1972.
65. This correspondence can be found in CP/CENT/WOM.
66. R. Falber; letter to D. Homer cited above.
67. *Marxism Today*, April 1973.
68. CP/CENT/WOM/3/5.
69. Ibid.
70. CP/CENT/WOM/3/5. The minutes show that Campbell and Slipman amongst others were attempting to push the committee in the direction of the more mainstream feminist movement on questions related to patriarchy, sexuality and political autonomy.
71. W. Thompson, *The Good Old Cause*, op cit, p165.

PART TWO

Renewing the Party: 1964–1974

3. Ideological and Strategic Renewal in the CPGB 1964–1968

In the previous chapters it was argued that the young communists, feminists and students had a significant effect on the Communist Party's social composition and ethos and, in their mediation of the wider cultural changes, provided the force for a renewal of the party's political identity. Moreover, the party's eventual willingness to accommodate these 'new social forces' – albeit with important limitations – suggested that its ideological outlook was becoming more open, with some recognition of the need for renewal. The argument of this chapter is that attempts to renew the party's ideology were underway contemporaneously with the rise of the party's social movements, and were made possible by two currents; socialist humanism and militant labourism. These two doctrines, in different ways, represented a move away from Leninism, and helped create the conditions for the further development of the party's independent road, which began to take shape in particular in the aftermath of the Soviet action in Czechoslovakia in 1968. In this way militant labourism and socialist humanism helped to refine the parameters of ideological debate within the party.

They did this in two ways. Firstly the influence of socialist humanism helped trigger an important role for ideas as the basis for political action. This resulted in a higher status for intellectuals, a stronger role for intellectual forums and new dialogues between communists and christians. Socialist humanism became an important bridge between some of the party's earlier traditions which had inspired an earlier generation of intellectuals and the development of the Gramscian currents that were to develop among new generations in the party in the 1970s. Secondly, militant labourism enabled closer integration with the mainstream labour movement, allowing the party to exert an unprecedented degree of influence in industrial politics during the late 1960s and 1970s. However, in prioritising particular forms of industrial and economic ideas, it also provided the ideological basis for the 'traditionalist' strand of the party, in the process delineating areas of contention with those committed to the politics of the new social movements. Therefore the major strategic debate between what I will call Gramscians and the traditionalist leadership – the focus of later chapters – has its origins here.

THE BREAK WITH LENINISM: THE BRITISH ROAD TO SOCIALISM AND THE NEW POLITICAL STRATEGY

The publication of the first edition of the *British Road to Socialism*, the party's strategic programme, in 1951, has been acknowledged as the moment at which the party finally renounced its Leninist heritage, in favour of a democratic parliamentary road.[1] There are, however, some ambiguities within this position. Firstly, the party's independence was always compromised to some extent. It has recently been confirmed, for example, that the BRS was scrutinised and endorsed by Stalin, who welcomed the new direction.[2] Further, positive references to Lenin and Leninism remained important features of the party's vocabulary, regularly found in motions, and used to provide authority and legitimacy to elements of party strategy; and the party remained committed to the concept of democratic centralism right up until its final dissolution.[3]

On the other hand, the party's Leninist origins were never comprehensive. This is partly due to the fact that the main features of Leninism, namely a vanguardist party organisation based on democratic centralism, were conceived within a very particular situation in Russia between 1906-1917, when clandestine organisation was regarded as necessary.[4] Although the British Communist Party endorsed Leninist organisational forms from its origins – when it did have more of a clandestine party structure – it had already immersed itself in the wider labour movement by the 1920s.[5] Following the exceptional 'class against class period', the party extended its broad links during the 'popular front', with some MPs being elected on a common Communist-Labour platform, while broad campaigns between Labour and Communist Parties became a regular occurrence.[6] As Kevin Morgan found in his research on the war years, there was an underlying democratic ethos to much of the party's work at this time.[7] The BRS emphasis on the parliamentary road to socialism, its rejection of the aim of creating a 'Soviet Britain' (the title of its previous programme in 1935), and its desire to work closely with the wider labour movement, had thus all been rehearsed in earlier stages of the party's history, most intensely during the war-time 'popular front' period. These factors suggest that the commitment to a *British Road to Socialism* was a consequence of a complex range of factors, rather than merely a consolidation of previous trends, or, indeed, an imposition by Stalin.

While it may be an exaggeration therefore to describe the 1951 version of *The British Road to Socialism* as representing the 'final and complete break with Leninism',[8] it nevertheless provided a useful reference point for the party in its attempts to offer a peaceful parliamentary alternative. The rise in membership in the early 1960s gave the party the confidence to seek out a new mass base, a position it reiterated at its Congresses of 1961, 1963 and 1965.[9] The catalyst for this new optimism was provided by a significant change in the party leadership in 1965, which effectively saw a generation of leading communists that had been in leading positions since the 1920s – Peter Kerrigan, J.R. Campbell and R. Palme Dutt – replaced by a new leadership, which included Gordon McLennan and Bert Ramelson. And in the meantime a new generation of 'leading industrial comrades' were taking their places in influential trade union positions.[10] The Cultural Committee was also revitalised, under the leadership of Brian Simon and Ted Ainley – a development that was important to the renewal of socialist humanism. This generational change was also significant in broadening the party's influence within the wider labour movement. Ramelson's appointment as Industrial Organiser in 1965, as successor to Peter Kerrigan, was the most decisive catalyst of these changes. His appointment coincided with the merger of the party's industrial and economic departments into what became the Economic Committee from 1965, and this gave him greater power over economic strategy than his predecessor had enjoyed. Subsequently the Economic Committee played a pivotal role, as the sub-committee of the EC which carried the crucial debates over the party's industrial and economic strategy. Ramelson's appointment also followed a very debilitating period for the party, after the ETU 'vote-rigging' scandal of the early 1960s. Although for some contemporary party leaders there was a reluctance to admit the full implications of this scandal – they saw it as a 'side-issue as far as the general development and political advance of trade unionism are concerned'[11] – it became clear that it had, not surprisingly, reinforced the suspicion of communists and their clandestine ways of organising, something that was still part of cold war assumptions about the party. Above all the scandal had weakened the CPGB in their crucial sphere of influence: the trade unions were at that time the primary source of recruitment for party members, and provided a bridge between the party's industrial and political strategies.

Ramelson's main contribution was to strengthen the party's influence and contacts, and to open up new directions within the trade union movement. Many have pointed to his forceful, pro-active style of leadership, his 'dominating personality',[12] and his organisational abilities (for example as chair of the party's trade union advisories); all these helped him to win trade unions to communist positions,[13] and his status grew within the party as he increased the party's influence in the unions. He had excellent connections with many trade union leaders, and, following the rise of the trade union left in the late 1960s – when men like Jack Jones and Hugh Scanlon became key figures in the movement – strong broad left and party presences were established in large sections of the trade union movement.

Ramelson's organisational contribution, though relying on tightly-knit and centralised forms of control, had the effect of consolidating and extending the party's break with Leninism, through strengthening its links with the mainstream labour movement and effectively abandoning any pretence to 'exclusive' leadership. These closer labourist affiliations only served to amplify an unresolved ambivalence at the heart of the party's ideology and strategy about its attitude towards the labour movement and Labour Party. It was never clear whether it was in competition with them or was part of the same movement. This was largely derived from Lenin's advice to Communist Party members to seek affiliation to the Labour Party. Lenin had argued, in *Left Wing Communism*, that the party should participate in parliament, and should affiliate to the Labour Party, if only to expose to the workers the futility of parliamentary democracy.[14] Thus in the party's early years many members maintained dual membership of both organisations, most famously Shapurji Saklatvala, who was elected as a Labour-Communist MP in 1922.[15] The eventual Labour Party ban on Communists holding dual membership heightened this paradox, as the party remained committed to working within and through the trade unions and the Labour Party (as the mass working-class party), but now maintained an independent electoral presence, opposing Labour candidates at both national and local elections.[16] The success of its strategy was bound up with the success of the Labour Party – it aimed to elect a 'Labour Government of a new type' (as its documents often described it) – yet it remained committed in theory to Labour's defeat at the polls.

As its membership started to decline from 1964, the importance of the party's presence in the labour movement increased, and its attempts to influence the Labour government through the left intensified. As Willie Thompson notes, the 'trade union milieu formed the connecting link between the CP's industrial and political strategies as it not only represented power at the base of industrial society but also disposed of votes at Labour Party conferences and in the selection of parliamentary candidates'.[17] This process was aided by the fact that the party was now prepared to support non-party candidates for trade union elections, including cases where there were CP alternatives.[18] This more open approach to left unity resulted in weakening the priority given to the party's own candidates and policy, and placing more emphasis on mobilising, instigating and supporting action. This meant that its 'leading role' was increasingly subordinated to the broader aims of the labour movement, a position which some minority critics in the party rejected, on traditional Leninist – and Maoist – grounds.[19]

The subsequent revisions of the BRS in 1958 and 1968 consolidated this strategy of aiming for a socialist majority in Parliament, through mass struggle and unity between the CP and the Labour left. It was the job of the CP not only to form an alliance with the Labour Left but to instigate, through struggle in factories and other workplaces, the politicisation of the labour movement. The new contacts reinforced the party's belief that its strategy was paying dividends, and the status of industrial organisers and trade union networks grew, helping to consolidate militant labourist positions.

Despite these closer affiliations, and the move towards a more reformist stance, the party maintained a Marxist critique of capitalism in its theoretical outlook. The object of its critique was defined in the BRS, from the 1951 version onwards, as 'monopoly capitalism', a stage of capitalism which, it was claimed, was penetrating all forms of public life and institutions. The pervasiveness of the monopolies meant a marked increase in the number of those whose interests were in conflict with capitalism. Such groups went beyond the traditional working class to include professional groups, small shop-keepers and white-collar groups. A broad 'anti-monopoly alliance' was thus needed to represent these interests, and it was the job of the party to organise new forms of 'left unity' to coalesce these groups. In order to do this, the defeat of the right wing of the labour movement, the Labour Party and the trade union leadership was the priority; this was often described as 'breaking the right wing grip'.[20]

The critique of monopoly capitalism and the pursuit of new forms of left unity were the party's key organising principles; they dominated its strategic documents and policy statements, allowing it, in theory at least, to distinguish its programme from the Labour mainstream, while at the same time seeking common alliance on particular campaigns. The closer relationships it sought meant a softening of its critique of other left groups within the Labour Party. Where in the past it had been hostile towards Bevanism, the Independent Labour Party (ILP) and Common Wealth, in the 1960s it had a much more sympathetic attitude towards the Labour left. Indeed the Labour left newspaper *Tribune* saw 'almost nothing' in the party's programme of the 1960s that a Labour left-winger would object to.[21] This similarity between the Communist and Labour left was part of a process of erosion of the Leninist idea of an exclusive leadership role for the party; it meant that continual references to 'Marxist-Leninist ideology' and 'the vanguard party'[22] were little more than rhetoric. That these closer affiliations were detrimental to the party's independent political standing in an electoral system unfavourable to small parties was apparent in the continuing decline in the party's own electoral support, and in its membership figures, even during the more propitious climate of the industrial struggles of the late 1960s and 1970s. These costs remained an area of contestation within the party itself, and are a central theme of this book.[23]

THE RETURN OF SOCIALIST HUMANISM

Two distinctive ideological perspectives consolidated the move away from Leninism. The first of these, socialist humanism, was found mainly in the ideas of party intellectuals, such as Arnold Kettle, Maurice Cornforth, James Klugmann and Brian Simon, who found a renewed confidence and new spaces opening up in the party from the mid-1960s.[24] For this cohort of intellectuals, who had been attracted to socialist humanism in its earlier guise in the 1930s, and who had remained in the party in the aftermath of 1956, the need to rescue Marxism from its association with Stalinism became a major concern.[25] Indeed in the early 1960s the party was still recovering from the exodus of 1956, to such an extent that many later referred to a 'lost generation of intellectuals', although the Cultural Committee was beginning to show some signs of a revival of intellectual and cultural work.[26]

It should be noted here that many who left the party in 1956 carried their socialist humanism into the creation of the first New Left, where, as Michael Kenny has shown, the communist legacy was evident in much of the latter's ethos, political commitment and cultural politics.[27] Indeed one originator of this variant of socialist humanism was Edward Thompson, a leading CPGB dissident, who ultimately left the party in the post-1956 exodus. As Chun and Kenny have pointed out, Thompson's main contribution to the rediscovery of socialist humanism can be found in his work on the British communist William Morris.[28] For Thompson, the significance of Morris lay in the latter's emphasis on human agency and moral consciousness.[29] This emphasis on agency and the necessity of creative human intervention was counterposed to the 'Stalinist' orthodoxies of anti-intellectualism, dogmatism, and a 'denial of the creative agency of humanity'.[30] For Thompson, therefore, what he called the 'new rebellious humanism' ... 'must be of profoundest importance to British socialists' in their search for alternatives to Stalinism.[31] Indeed, as Chun argues, 'socialist humanism' became an 'immediately available weapon' for dissidents from the orthodox communist tradition who sought to maintain a socialist or communist identity, while it was the founding theme of the *New Reasoner*, the journal set up by Thompson and his fellow communist dissident John Saville in 1957.[32] The force and relevance of these arguments was to intensify as Western communist parties faced the aftermath of 1956.

This interest in socialist humanism was given further impetus by a new interest in Marx's early works, following the publication of his *Economic and Philosophic Manuscripts* in 1958, while the work of Jean-Paul Sartre and the earlier writings of George Lukacs also helped stimulate interest in 'existentialist', 'humanist' and other anti-determinist forms of Marxism.[33] Such work was fundamental to the direction taken by the first New Left (and remained with Thompson in subsequent theoretical battles he was to have with Louis Althusser and later *New Left Review* thinkers such as Perry Anderson).[34] For the Communist Party in the mid-1960s, a time when it was seeking to open its thinking, the ideas of socialist humanism thus provided a common thread in its attempt at a rapprochement with the New Left currents. Humanism provided a point of common purpose between what had previously been seemingly irreconcilable positions.

3. Ideological and Strategic Renewal in the CPGB

At the beginning of the 1960s there was still a considerable political breach between those intellectuals who remained in the party, such as Arnold Kettle and James Klugmann, and those who had left, such as Edward Thompson and John Saville. Thus Arnold Kettle denounced the New Left in 1960 as 'petty bourgeois', arguing that its adherents had the characteristics of the 'literary intelligentsia, with its special tendencies towards anarchic individualism, love of self-expression (to the point quite often of exhibitionism), ignorance and near contempt of science and a general preference for living in a world of "ideas" and "values" rather than practical action'.[35] By 1966-67, however, the evidence shows that the party had a warmer attitude, to the extent where party intellectuals such as Klugmann were attending May Day Manifesto Committee meetings, the forum which led to the *May Day Manifesto*.[36] The *Manifesto* itself, first published in 1967, and including Thompson among its authors, was sympathetically reviewed in the party's press (though with some reservations). Jack Cohen's review in *Comment* welcomed the 'deep humanism' with which the Manifesto was 'imbued', and the fact that it occupied much of the same ground as the Communist Party: 'the identity of outlook as far as policy is concerned is often striking'. Where the commonality in thinking broke down was in attitudes to the Soviet Union. Party intellectuals were not prepared to go as far as Thompson and his allies in contrasting socialist humanism with Stalinism; indeed their criticisms of the *May Day Manifesto* included the lack of recognition it gave to 'the positive role of the Soviet Union'.[37] However the commonality of view with the New Left was crucial in allowing the later involvement of thinkers from the British and European Left in the CUL; and ideas associated with socialist humanism were also part of a much broader range of critical Marxist thinking that developed from the later 1960s onwards.

QUESTIONS OF IDEOLOGY AND CULTURE

As confirmation of its reconnection with humanism the party started to show new forms of pluralism in its outlook towards art and culture. Its condemnation of the persecution of the writers Daniel and Sinyavsky by the Soviet Union in 1966 represented an important indication of this new found desire for artistic pluralism, particularly as it was symptomatic of a more critical attitude towards Soviet approaches to culture. This was also the occasion of the 'rehabilitation' of Monty Johnstone, an intellectual in the party who had been consistently critical of the party's relationship to the Soviet Union, and who was an expert on questions of socialist democracy. Johnstone had been part of a New Left milieu beyond the party, and from the late 1960s onwards was to play an important part in the development of a more critical Gramscian and Eurocommunist position. He appeared in the media in 1967, representing the party's criticism of the treatment of the two writers.[38]

The most significant evidence of the renewal of a humanist perspective in the party, however, was the publication of *Questions of Ideology and Culture* (QIC) by the party's Cultural Committee in 1967. The Cultural Committee, under Brian Simon's chairmanship, had become an increasingly fertile area of discussion, with its members showing signs of breaking from their more specialist fields or limited role as full-time 'functionaries'.[39] The QIC statement was evidence of a greater confidence on the part of party intellectuals in their capacity to influence the party's strategy; though its analysis was not a breakthrough on the scale of the cultural initiatives of the YCL in the mid-60s, or the later growth of the CULs, it represented an important official shift in outlook. QIC was adopted by the EC on 11 March 1967, and its publication opened a wide-ranging debate within the party, and in particular within the pages of *Marxism Today*, over the nature of art and culture and its relationship to politics. The driving force behind the document was the need to show that the party's view of culture was no longer shaped by dogma. Above all it was a rejection of the view that a 'party line' could be enforced on scientific and cultural questions. In science, for example, QIC welcomed 'the most critical, enquiring and searching spirit among scientists, whose function we recognise is to explore all aspects of phenomena and to avoid going into enquiry with a fixed notion of the result'. The party did not and would not attempt to 'lay down a line' on science.[40]

In art, there was concern to avoid a 'single standard congenial to all, or immediately comprehensible without effort and study'. The party did not see its role as 'laying down laws governing literary and artistic creation', and rejected the concept that 'art, literature or culture should reflect only one (official) school or style'; it also argued for 'complete freedom of religious worship'. The document stated that: 'We welcome the widest variety of artistic approaches, subjects and styles and encourage our members freely to express their views'.[41]

The necessity of a more pluralist approach dominated the document, and also shaped much of the debate in the party press.[42] The humanistic approach was further reflected in the perception of art, culture and science as liberating in themselves. Not only were they important spheres of life, to be rescued from 'debased' and 'perverted' capitalist cultures, but, it was claimed, they helped provide a creative field of political struggle. This emphasised the importance of human agency and the need to reassert the faith communists held 'in the future of mankind; in man's ability through struggle and effort to transform society, increasingly to gain control of nature'.[43]

The humanist turn was therefore confirmed ('we who are Marxists claim to be the most consistent humanists of our time'),[44] and was consolidated around an emphasis on human agency. The belief that 'man' should be at the centre of analysis was also indicative of the interest in the early works of Marx, in which the importance of men intervening in history, and helping to shape their (and their fellows') destiny, was paramount. Marx's famous phrases 'man makes history, but not under conditions of his own choosing', and 'mankind only sets itself such tasks as it can solve', were frequently quoted in the discussion over the QIC. This concern with human agency was epitomised above all in the contributions of James Klugmann, the editor of *Marxism Today*, who had been a compromised figure as a party intellectual, but who from the late 1960s was at the forefront of influencing the party's thinking in a humanist direction.[45] As well as an extended discussion of humanism in *Marxism Today*, Klugmann published a party pamphlet, *The Future of Man*, whose purpose he identified as 'recapturing' the humanist tradition in Marxism. *The Future of Man* was an attempt to mark out a perspective which counterposed the creative energies of humanity to the materialism of contemporary capitalism ('the drab standardised society ... super-market (sic) uniformity that haunts so many nightmares of the future').[46] It was an attempt to oppose agency to determinism, based upon the belief that 'men and women change for the better, develop their latent talents in the collective struggle against capitalism ... and that men are not just passive products of their environment and education'.[47] In his critique of determinism Klugmann included not only 'fashionable Althusserianism', but the bureaucracies of existing socialist countries, which had led not only to 'delays in the building of socialism', but to 'deterioration in the character of man'.[48]

The humanist turn that Questions of Ideology and Culture represented had a broader significance with regard to the party's ideology than the mere updating of the party's policy towards culture. It reflected a renewed confidence amongst party intellectuals that their voice could be heard and, though the QIC document may have been outpaced by the scale of cultural and political change in the 1960s, it did help prepare the party for the subsequent Gramscian agendas of the 1970s, in which the critique of economic determinism, and the importance given to culture, were crucial. Moreover the party's renewed humanist current reflected a wider interest in socialist humanism among the new left activist movements of the late 1960s.[49]

THE COMMUNIST-CHRISTIAN DIALOGUE
The return to humanism had an impact beyond the intellectual sphere; it helped to give political substance to the growing belief that the party had to forge a more independent path for itself. In this sense, as an emerging ideological theme, humanism helped to organise a distinctive element of the party's political activity and strategy. The most notable example of this was the Communist-Christian dialogue, whereby party members and church activists found common cause around a number of humanitarian themes, including poverty, peace and anti-colonialism. This alliance took the form of collaborative meetings and conferences, as well as written articles and other publications. The thawing of the cold war from the early 1960s and the replacement of the anti-commu-

nist Pope Pius XII with John XXIII provided the wider context for this alliance; the latter, in his *Mater et Magistra*, was more open towards the left, and he maintained a critical stance towards some aspects of contemporary capitalism. In Italy this dialogue was a very important part of Togliatti's attempt to broaden the appeal of the PCI, and enhance the spiritual content of socialism.[50] In Britain, the dialogue was the occasion for a renewal of links between elements of christian socialism and communism.

A starting-point for both sides was the view that the cold war had prevented areas of common humanitarian concern between communists and christians being discussed or advanced. The dialogue was therefore an attempt to debunk 'the naive belief that christianity and communism are two antagonistic and given constants'.[51] The dialogue was seen as an attempt to find important points of agreement rather than any detailed strategy, though practical steps towards a 'brotherhood of man' – which included declarations on racial equality, civil rights and for the elimination of poverty – were proposed. The leading proponent on the christian side was Canon Paul Ostreicher, who was convinced of the plausibility of such an alliance: 'Our common roots are inescapable ... Justice for man is our common objective'.[52] Furthermore, a 'radical self-examination' and mutual trust needed to be strengthened; there was confidence that the 'optimistic view of humanity' would drive the dialogue. 'All the while we need to remember that most people are neither Christians nor Marxists. They are hungry'.[53] The 'gathering pace' of the dialogue was recorded consistently by James Klugmann in the pages of *Marxism Today*, and from March 1966 a debate was launched in the pages of that journal. Public meetings took place in different parts of the country. In October 1966 700 people met in St Pancras Town Hall; in December of the same year 400 attended a student Communist-Christian dialogue conference; in February 1967 the Marx Memorial Library was 'filled to the brim' for a debate on Marxism and religion, while a 'young Communist-Christian' conference in Coventry the following month on 'How to Change the World?' was also packed. The International Youth Festival in May 1967 had as its theme 'Marxism and Christianity', while in June of the same year, the Quaker, Peace and International Relations Committee and *Marxism Today* held a '10-a-sider' weekend discussion on 'Man, Society and Moral Responsibility'.[54]

For Klugmann, the growing critique of capitalism characterised the two approaches. 'Among Christians of all denominations there is a growing questioning of the morality of capitalism and colonialism ... what was once the attitude of a small minority of Christian radicals or socialists is becoming a much more general attitude ... there is a movement for return to the ideals of early Christianity'.[55] According to Klugmann, the concern for Marxists should be to emphasise the non-violent, peaceful road to socialism, and to give attention to the 'character of revolution', the means as well as the ends; and to assert that Marxists were not 'economic determinists'. He argued that 'capitalist society, in our view, narrows man, distorts him, alienates him, limits the development of his talents ... men and women make themselves more human, change themselves ... ':[56]

> In a world where the contrast between poverty and wealth is still widening, where so many millions are hungry amongst such unfathomable resources, where the miracles of science and technique that could quickly remove all men from sordid want can, misused and abused, extinguish all humanity without any nice distinction of political or religious creed, it would be unmarxist, unchristian, unprincipled – call it what you will – not to pool our efforts, whatever our differences, to keep this earth a world of the living and not of the dead.[57]

The Communist-Christian dialogue, which took up considerable space in the party press from 1967,[58] was not confined to intellectuals; it extended to the workplace as well as branch and district levels of the party.[59] It seemed to resonate with other forms of humanist ethics, such as the commitment to self-education; and alliances with christians already existed in different forms, in some cases with deep roots, particularly in the peace and anti-colonial movements. Together with the QIC discussion, it confirmed a greater degree of openness within the party, and helped to recapture a belief in a more democratic communism – one that was able to engage with the implications of the Soviet invasion of Czechoslovakia. Above all, it helped prepare the groundwork the party needed in order to rethink its ideological priorities.

THE CONTOURS OF MILITANT LABOURISM

The concept of 'labourism' has often been used by Marxist critics to describe the dominant culture of the labour movement in Britain; such critics argue that this labourism has prevented the development of more radical or revolutionary perspectives. This kind of analysis has largely concentrated on the conceptual distinction between labourism and socialism. The labourist values of pragmatic, gradualist parliamentarism and compromise have been contrasted unfavourably with more grassroots, activist, ideologically principled and revolutionary positions. For the historian John Saville, labourism was historically 'deeply rooted' within the industrial communities of Britain, and represented the 'theory and practice of class collaboration'. It emphasised 'the unity of capital and labour, and the importance of conciliation and arbitration in industrial dispute. Those social attitudes which stressed the unity of classes found an outlet in various aspects of petty-bourgeois ideas and practice ... '.[60] For Nairn, it was 'second best socialism'.[61] And for Ralph Miliband, in *Parliamentary Socialism*, it was the 'sickness of Labourism' that was responsible for the betrayal of successive Labour leaderships as they put their faith in change through parliament.[62] For Panitch, the Wilson governments after 1964 were a prime example of how labourism operated as part of a dominant set of ethics which helped maintain the existing social order; while for Foot, labourism – 'an incoherent ideology, riddled with inconsistencies' – had nevertheless 'become so ingrained in the Labour Party that both right and left wings were constrained by its assumptions'.[63]

One problem with these definitions is that although they recognise the contradictory components of labourism – such as the need to extract concessions from capital by wage bargaining – they reduce the application of the concept to the experience of the Labour Party and that of the Labour leadership (Saville is the exception here).[64] Therefore they underestimate the breadth of reach of labourism within the wider movement and culture. An alternative interpretation of labourism has been adopted by Willie Thompson, who has argued that the failings of the wider left – including the CPGB – were due to the same 'labourist ailments'.[65] Although accepting that there have been 'bodies and tendencies within the labour movement consciously and explicitly antagonistic to the labourist ideology', Thompson goes on to argue that 'these have themselves been deeply penetrated and strictly moulded by a labourist consciousness'.[66] A prime example of this was the CPGB. Since it shared its labourist origins with the wider labour movement, and grew from the same structures and cultures of the skilled working class, the CPGB also exhibited 'hierarchical, disciplined, authoritarian organisations, with strong-minded and strong-willed leaderships, emphasising prudent management and stringent bureaucratic procedures'.[67] These values replicated the ideological priorities of labourism – to 'manipulate' rather than 'overthrow' the existing system, and to depend upon extracting concessions from capital through wage bargaining rather than offering a political challenge to the system. This shared ideological heritage directed the CPGB towards a strategy that eschewed political radicalism, favouring instead industrial militancy. And such common ideological traits were even more significant following the publication of the *British Road to Socialism* in 1951, and the need to look for more domestic sources of strength in the wake of the defections of 1956. As Thompson argues: 'British communism and British labourism in the 1950s ... were marked far more by the cultural presumptions they shared than by the politics which divided them'.[68]

These shared assumptions also marked a conceptual distinction between labourism and European social democracy. The left in Britain had not suffered to the same degree the divisions that had split social democracy and communism in other European countries, and the ideological polarities between the Labour and Communist Parties were thus less clear-cut; their pragmatic and day-to-day political and industrial alliances had encouraged closer ideological attachments than in other countries. This resulted in a greater reach for labourism across different political traditions, albeit, as some have argued, that it is less theoretically coherent than European social democracy.[69]

This labourist emphasis on pragmatism and loyalty was most marked in the Communist Party's industrial strategy. Moreover, it was the areas of convergence and common culture with the Labour Party that gave the CPGB such a decisive organising role. As Fishman has shown, the party's shared labour movement ethics not only allowed it to identify with and work alongside labour movement allies in the Labour Party; it also provided justification for its activism and ultimately its revolutionary optimism. It was, according to Fishman, a combination of 'trade union loyalism' and 'rank and fileism' – rather than Leninist doctrine – that provided the impetus for party activism in the unions.

> The successes chalked up by communist shop stewards in the economic struggle were not due to their following prescriptive formulae laid down by King Street, nor could they be ascribed to their earnest emulation of Marxist-Leninist methods of dialectical materialism. Most party activists learned to wage the economic struggle through trial and error, watching their elders and peers and generally assimilating the trade union culture of which the party centre insisted they must become an integral part.[70]

'Trade union loyalism' refers to an acceptance of the need for unity and solidarity, including working with mainstream trade union leaderships; while 'rank and fileism' refers to the militant agitation of communists on the shopfloor. These two were not as contradictory as might first appear in the practice of party industrial work. They provided on the one hand the necessary links and prestige, and on the other a revolutionary edge. They combined to produce a political strategy defined by Fishman as 'revolutionary pragmatism', a strategy which 'provided party members with a flexible guide to action and definite boundaries within which different activists made many different, sometimes opposing, decisions about how to conduct the "economic struggle"'.[71]

Revolutionary pragmatism was adopted by the party to overcome the seemingly contradictory status of communists who worked both with and against Labour Party members. In this respect it provided the necessary links and common experiences while attempting to transform the movement in a more radical direction. It was a paradoxical relationship. On the one hand the party imbibed the main tenets of labourism, while on the other it sought a critique of, and attempted to articulate an alternative to, the labour movement mainstream. The term 'militant labourism' can be used to describe this paradox. In Thompson's words, militant labourism was characterised by a posture based upon the expectation that 'if only traditional practices and forms of struggle were applied vigorously and uncompromisingly enough and adopted by other disadvantaged minorities and groupings they would mobilise the labour movement into an irresistible political force and win over, by force of example, further elements of the masses as well'.[72]

Indeed this posture became, from the mid-1960s, the dominant ideological and strategic principle around which the party organised its political agenda. However some further considerations need to be borne in mind when looking at the post-1964 period. Given its formal rejection of the Leninist road and its greater determination to distinguish itself from the Soviet Union, it is difficult to describe the CPGB after this time as 'revolutionary' in any meaningful sense; yet it is also inadequate to describe its approach as 'reformist' – a term used by many[73] – when considering the complex objectives, aspirations and internal justifications of party members who remained committed to a transformation of society. While the party's strategy at this time was a continuation of many of the long-standing and close alliances that had been formed in the 1930s, a new context can be discerned after 1964. Party leaders – and in particular industrial organiser Bert Ramelson – felt that there was now a greater possibility for shifting the Labour Party to the left. More attention was thus given to a strategy aimed at influencing the Labour Party through the trade unions, through winning left union leaders to CPGB policy. Prior to this the CPGB had always sought to maintain its distance from the Labour Left, except when it pursued united or popular fronts as strategic objectives; and this had left unresolved the problems of politicising the Labour Party, a key communist objective.[74] This closer CP-Labour Left unity was made possible, as will be shown below, by the marked development of Broad Lefts in the unions, and culminated in the development of the Alternative Economic Strategy (AES) from the late 1960s.

This militant labourist approach was characterised by greater militancy and organisational strength, and helped to produce the strikes of the late 1960s and 1970s, as well as closer ideological, political and strategic connections with the Labour Left. The doctrinal justification for militant labourism came from two sources: the critique of monopoly capitalism and the pursuit of left unity. These two doctrinal principles dominated the party's political and strategic documents at this time, including the leading resolutions at all the Congresses between 1964-1975, and the leading speeches of party leaders.

THE CRITIQUE OF MONOPOLY CAPITALISM

The British Road to Socialism, from its founding edition in 1951, identified monopoly capitalism as the systemic cause of the social and economic problems facing Britain. It claimed that the intensification of monopoly power was indicative of the development of capitalism in its imperialist phase – an analysis influenced both by Marx's views of the internationalisation of capital and Lenin's work on imperialism.[75] Their theories had been developed in the 1950s and 1960s in the work of several economists and political scientists, notably Baran and Sweezy.[76] This analysis, taken up in a modified and more limited form by the party, took as its starting-point the concentration of capital in fewer companies, through mergers and take-overs, as well as the concentration of capital in fewer countries. The rise of monopoly power meant that the monopolies were responsible for employing mass numbers of people; they took an increasing stake in overseas markets, and they were beginning to penetrate all forms of social life, from the sponsoring of sporting and educational events, to controlling the mass media and extending across the boundaries of culture, politics and the state itself. According to the CPGB, Tory and Labour governments alike had their agendas shaped by the monopolies. Right-wing Labour leaders had merely accommodated themselves to monopoly capitalism. Party documents, notably *End Monopoly Rule*, rejected the view common amongst right-wing Labour intellectuals such as Crosland that changes in the nature of contemporary capitalism, with the rise in power of managers and an extension of share-ownership, was transforming society. On the contrary, the involvement of the state, through forms of public ownership, was merely an attempt to 'manage' monopoly capitalism.[77]

End Monopoly Rule also noted the contradiction in the so-called 'technological revolution', between the 'astonishing possibilities' of general prosperity that it made realisable and the extent of the waste, inequality and concentration of wealth that it had brought, resulting in major economic and political divisions:

> The hundred largest companies have increased their share of all quoted company assets to well over half, while the number of such companies has fallen. Less than a dozen steel firms produce most of our steel. ICI dominates British chemicals as well as artificial fibres. Shell and British petroleum are the kings of petrol (in connection with the American giants). Three giants (two of them American) dominate our motor car industry. Consumer goods more and more fall into the hands of a small number of producers and multiple stores, supermarket chains and the like. An increasing number of town centres are being handed over for private development to a handful of property tycoons in alliance with the insurance companies. What we read is now determined by four press barons. What we see on television is largely for the profit of a small group of financiers and press lords.[78]

Not only was it a problem that 'the economy of Britain is in the hands of the monopolies ... a combination of financial and industrial power',[79] but there was also the 'myth', substantiated by right-wing revisionist Labour leaders (such as Crosland), that capitalism could be 'managed', which also needed to be challenged. The document argued that, 'the trade union and labour movements are not powerless in face of the monopolies',[80] and a programme for a new Labour government, prior to the 1964 election, included proposals whereby public ownership would be extended and restraints put on monopoly power, through the planning of resources.

This critique of monopoly power was sustained through the first years of the 1964 Wilson government, as the latter attempted to modernise the British economy through technological innovation. In 1966 John Gollan, the party's General Secretary, took this further in *The Case For Socialism in the Sixties*: 'The scientific revolution is on, but in the capitalist world it is plagued, distorted and confined by monopoly capitalism'.[81] Accusing the Labour government of 'deliberately creating unemployment',[82] and of 'exercising power on behalf of the monopolies',[83] he repeated the argument that automation provided the possibility of abundance, but that under capitalism its potential was thwarted, so that: 'despite the brilliance of its scientists and the skill of its workers, the dead hand of capitalism holds back development'.[84] Though these critiques of the contradictions posed by technological change reflected other left critiques of Wilsonite modernisation, such as those put forward by the New Left, there was a major difference in depth and scope.[85] Apart from the YCL's engagement with modernity, there was little examination of the cultural, democratic or sociological implications of these changes. Rather, the priority remained within the context of labourism: 'the problems posed by the new technical and scientific revolutions place a premium on advanced political action …';[86] 'mass political struggle' was needed 'to make decisive inroads into monopoly capitalism and go beyond that to challenge capitalism and introduce socialism'.[87]

Monopoly capitalism continued to preoccupy the CPGB and was central to the 1968 version of the BRS; the document noted that the main 'state organs' were 'run by the same great monopoly groups who control the wealth of the country and serve their interests'.[88] It identified a shift from monopoly to state monopoly capitalism, in which 'the capitalist state is intertwined with the great banks and monopolies'.[89] The state's role in monopoly capitalism, the BRS argued, was an outcome of the ability of the working class and labour movement in capitalist countries to defend their standards of living, and was facilitated in Britain by Labour governments who sought to 'manage capitalism, rather than take decisive steps to end the power of the monopolies'.[90] The inroads made by monopoly capitalism were becoming extensive, and were being used to break collective bargaining, halt wage increases and undermine the wider democratic process. This conflict between mergers and democracy was important in influencing the party's strategy of developing an 'anti-monopoly' alliance, a 'broad popular alliance around the leadership of the working class, fighting every aspect of the policies of the monopolies'.[91] John Gollan's 'Outlook for 1969', given to the EC, noted the contradictions between democracy and monopolisation,[92] while the main motion at the 1969 congress of the party pointed to the 'tremendous speed-up in the process of monopolisation'.[93]

The party's critique of monopoly capitalism provided it with a holistic and systemic perspective, through which it distinguished itself at the ideological level from the Labour Party. It gave to the CPGB a sense of theoretical superiority and, in contrast to 'right-wing reformism', a revolutionary justification for its existence, while the party's continual talk of 'crisis' provided greater urgency to its arguments.[94] However in practice the nature of its remedies, far from being the basis of a revolutionary alternative to labourism, were based on advocating greater militancy in trade union struggle in order to put pressure on the leadership of the Labour Party. This was crucial in cementing the party's political and industrial strategy: eventually its critique of monopoly capitalism became integrated into what became known from the late 1960s as the alternative economic strategy – an economic and political strategy which brought together sections of the Labour Left and the CP around a set of common themes. This was to be the cornerstone of ideological unity between the Labour Left and the CP, and confirmed a consolidation of, rather than challenge to, 'labourism'. Such an ideological convergence was strengthened by the strategic perspectives that the party had adopted around 'left unity'.

ORGANISING FOR STRUGGLE: THE PRINCIPLE OF LEFT UNITY

The party's strategy of organising broad alliances has been alluded to – it featured in most party documents as a tactical manoeuvre. But from the early 1960s a new emphasis on left unity is apparent in the party's perspective. As we have seen, new opportunities existed for a closer relationship with the Labour Party, with the weakening of the cold war, and left advances in the trade unions. The respect Bert Ramelson was winning through working with the Trade Union Broad Lefts provided new sources of influence, and he sought to maintain a strong 'insider' influence within the industrial advisory committees, which were used to bring the party into regular contact with mainstream trade unionism. These advisory committees were the traditional way in which the CP organised to influence policy, and to decide on which candidates should be supported in all the major union elections, though they had been an area of contention since the Electrical Trades Union (ETU) scandal, when their secrecy was made an issue in the trial.[95] Under Ramelson, from the mid-1960s these committees took on the more central role of helping to direct the new militancy as well as consolidating mainstream appeal. Acting on the outcome of a consultation process among party industrial workers that took place between 1964-65, and an EC decision in March 1965 to 'broaden ... considerably our contact with other trade unionists',[96] Ramelson developed a strong network of advisory committees that put maximum emphasis on alliances with what were regarded as progressive left allies. The new forms of left unity started to develop from 1964, with broad lefts in established unions such as the NUM, which managed to resolve long-standing ideological and political differences between CP members themselves as well as between the CP and others on the left. Another fertile ground for communist influence was DATA/TASS, in which a long established Broad Left was able to consolidate around even longer standing forms of collaboration between the CP and the Labour Party (though the CP's role in this union was 'low key'[97] until the late 1960s, when communists – such as Ken Gill – won positions in the leadership).

In this way the Broad Left strategy helped to consolidate the party's integration into mainstream labourism and to further break down some of the ideological barriers that had divided the party from the Labour Left in the past. It also led to what can be seen as a dual strategy of influencing the mainstream as well as organising at the grassroots. This amounted to a redefinition of the role of the rank and file at the same time as placing greater emphasis on winning leading positions and influencing those in power in the trade union movement. The CP's industrial strategy since the 1920s had consistently practised a series of compromises based on maintaining support at the base while simultaneously pursuing revolutionary objectives, as Fishman has shown. However, while the principles of what Fishman calls 'trade union loyalism' and 'rank and fileism' both feature in this period, there was, significantly, a trend towards closer allegiances to the official leaderships; in this the role of rank and file militancy was redefined by the party as having as its aim, as McIlroy puts it, to 'stimulate official action, not to supersede it':[98]

> Eschewing rank and fileism, the party perceived a need to channel rank and file resistance and provide a bridge between militant struggles from below and the official movement against state intervention ... [99]

The growing role of the state in trade union affairs was to be the focal point for much of the CP's activity, notably in resisting the attack on unofficial strikes. It was during a struggle of this nature – the seaman's strike of 1966 – that Ramelson's success in mobilising action at dock gate meetings (and on the NUS negotiating committees for example) was acknowledged by Prime Minister Wilson, though in a somewhat exaggerated manner. Wilson was not completely inaccurate, however, in holding responsible for the strike a 'tightly knit group of politically motivated men', and the 'whole formidable power of the Communist Party's industrial apparatus', if the informal meetings and close co-operation between Ramelson and the leadership of the NUS is taken into account.[100]

The most successful aspect of the CP's strategy of organising left unity amongst trade unionists was the setting up of the Liaison Committee for the Defence of Trade Unions (LCDTU), which was founded in September 1966 to lobby against the Labour Government's Prices and Incomes Bill. It brought together shop stewards committees and union branches across different industries under communist leadership to pursue CP policy. It followed other lobbying committees that had been formed by the International Socialists and the Socialist Labour League. The LCDTU became a very effective organising vehicle at the grassroots, and it was crucial in delivering victories in a series of struggles particularly in the peak period 1967-68. It was not a rank and fileist organisation opposed to the official leaderships, nor did it see its only constituency as left militants; instead it sought to influence and pressurise the official leaderships, and in fact it became as much an effective lobbier for TUC policy as it was an agitator for a change in direction. Between 1966 and 1969 LCDTU focused its attention on mobilising communist and other left support in opposition to incomes policies and the Donovan Report. This new impetus towards the construction of left unity can be found at a broader political level in the main resolutions of the party congresses between 1965 and 1969. It was the main slogan at the 1965 congress, while subsequent congresses had similar titles – for example 'Left Unity in Action For an Alternative Policy' (1967), 'Monopolies, Left Unity and the Communist Party' (1969).

The discontent with the Wilson government strengthened the feeling in the party that a new left unity could be realised. One of the recurring assertions in this campaign for left unity was the need to 'break the right-wing grip' of the labour movement. This demarcation between left and right, not always clearly defined, was not essentially an antagonism between 'revolutionary' and 'reformist': it was polarised around a specific set of policy areas in the labourist lexicon. 'Right-wing programmes', according to the party, included incomes policies, a 'mixed economy', insufficient militancy in the face of opposing legal restrictions on trade unions, and, later on, support for the common market. The party defined as right-wing those programmes which it regarded as accepting the economic constraints of capitalism, in proposing to bring trade unions into line in order to fit in with the demands of the economy. Left unity on the other hand needed to be built around the nationalisation of the monopolies, free collective bargaining and import controls. The larger world views to which these were often attached by the party – counterposing 'managing capitalism' to a 'Labour government with socialist policies and a new leadership' – often seemed less important than the degree of organisational commitment involved in any particular campaign, and the level of the struggle:

> In the process of launching and sustaining a movement to bring the labour movement to the pursuit of socialist aims, isolating and defeating the right wing, the left will clarify its own thinking as well as that of

others. The experience of struggle will help towards clarity of ideas, just as clarity of perspective helps the immediate struggle. They are interdependent.[101]

Events continued to confirm to the party that new forms of left unity were possible. In a keynote article in *Marxism Today*, Sam Aaronovitch, a leading party economist, identified Labour MPs who were in agreement with party policy on a range of demands. These included the defeat of pay freezes, the imposition of price freezes, the ending of overseas military spending, a reduction in the export of capital, the imposition of import controls, the repeal of anti-trade union legislation, the selling of portfolio assets in order to pay off debts and the nationalisation of monopolies based on planning.[102] This converging policy programme leant substance to the party's political strategy; it was beginning to believe that it could have a real influence in Labour Party debates.

THE PRAGUE SPRING AND AFTER

The Communist Party's condemnation of the Soviet invasion of Czechoslovakia has been seen by many researchers as a defining moment in the development of the Gramscian or Eurocommunist positions in the party. It is certainly true that had the CP not condemned the Czech invasion it would have lost much of the input from the new generation of students, feminists and young communists.

However, the condemnation of the invasion should not be seen as a sudden shift, but as a development made possible by the ideological transitions discussed above. Changes already taking place – the influence of the humanist strand of party intellectuals, the notion of national independent roads to socialism, and the input of the new social forces – meant that the party's strategy already owed less to the Soviet Union than it had in the past. The Soviet Union was still regarded in the party press as a higher stage of society than the capitalist West, and was often used as a favourable contrast to the US. However, it had ceased to be the focal point of the party's ideological and strategic perspectives; moreover, it did not function as the main cause of the divisions and alternative strategies that evolved in the 1970s. Though reaction to the invasion of Czechoslovakia in 1968 was crucial to the later development of Eurocommunism, and of greater autonomy for the CPGB, its role was less important in terms of the evolution of the party's central political strategy. This was because those who opposed the party's critical position on Czechoslovakia, while significant in number, represented factions that were already in decline. The occasion seemed to mark the passing of older party ideologues such as Palme Dutt and Andrew Rothstein, who opposed the majority party position, and to confirm the 'humanist' turn of others like Klugmann. A.L. Morton, for example, praised Czech leader Dubcek's reforms as the 'most positive and exciting communist development for many years'.[103]

The party had welcomed Dubcek's attempt at 'socialism with a human face' as being compatible with their own BRS; in its official response to events, Dubcek's initiative represented 'positive steps taken to tackle the wrongs of the past and (to) strengthen socialist democracy'.[104] Beyond the official response, party intellectuals found inspiration in the Dubcek example, though many went to some lengths to distinguish between the Prague spring and earlier events in Hungary in 1956 (when the party had not criticised the Soviet invasion).[105]

The Prague Spring and reaction to its subsequent suppression had several implications for the party's strategy. Firstly, it confirmed a stronger commitment to an independent road, consistent with the party's political direction and statements over the previous decade. Many of those most opposed to the party's position on Czechoslovakia were from an earlier generation, or were part of marginal factions around Sid French in the Surrey District (the latter were to leave ten years later over the revised version of the *British Road to Socialism*). One of the most vociferous critics of the party's position, Rajani Palme Dutt, the party's leading theoretician from the 1920s to 1950s, urged the Congress of 1969 to reject it decisively, 'so that what I fear in the historical record, when all the facts are known and weighed, will be found to be a blot on our record may be expunged'.[106] Andrew Rothstein, another founding member, also called for a rejection of the motion.[107] Although membership continued to decline after 1968, there is no substantial evidence to suggest that the party's position on Czechoslovakia was a main reason for leaving – in contrast to the experiences of 1956. Indeed the numbers of a later generation who were subsequently influenced to join seem to have compensated for the defectors.

Secondly, the party condemned an 'intervention' (rather than an 'invasion'), and the subsequent discussion on the party's Executive Committee continued to reflect the battered survival of the Soviet 'mantra'. The invasion of Czechoslovakia in August 1968 elicited fairly restrained criticism from the party leadership. Its changing responses to the situation can be gleaned from a set of statements from the Political and Executive Committees between July and September 1968. The PC had thought, prior to the invasion, that 'with mutual trust and confidence on each side it is possible for a solution of outstanding problems to be solved'. At its next meeting, on August 8, it continued to be optimistic about the possibility of avoiding conflict: ongoing talks with the CPSU not only 'confirmed the hope that ... it is possible to find an agreed basis for dealing with outstanding problems', but also that the events 'have reinforced socialist unity'. 'The Bratislava meeting', the PC statement read, 'made clear that while the struggle for socialism and its consolidation in each country is based on well-defined universal principles, there are variations because of specific national features and conditions'.[108]

This, however, was not the view of the CPSU and, following the invasion, the British Communist Party eventually condemned the 'intervention'.[109] Three days after the invasion, John Gollan gave a very cautious response. While critical of the Soviet action, he also reasserted the status of the Soviet Union, and the CPGB's continuing respect for it. 'We completely understand the concern of the Soviet Union about the security of the socialist camp in view of the ruling military danger, the menace of West German militarism ... In taking up our stand we are speaking as true friends of the Soviet Union ... we will never be found in the company of the anti-Soviet forces of this country'. He ended with the statement that 'our present disunity only serves the interests of imperialism'.[110]

This was hardly a positive recognition of 'sovereign' communist parties deciding their own future; it was more, as Thompson records, a question of 'fraternal criticism'.[111] As late as 21 September the leadership of the British party was still hopeful of an agreement, stressing the CPSU's 'readiness to co-operate with Czechoslovakia on the basis of mutual respect, equality, territorial integrity, independence and socialist solidarity'.[112] Thus, although their decision to be critical to some extent put them in line with public opinion and New Left positions, it had severe limitations. Not only did they see the invasion as a blemish rather than a systemic consequence of the Soviet model, they had also been at pains to distinguish between this intervention and the case of Hungary twelve years earlier. The party did continue to publish in *Comment* details of the Czechoslovakian Action Programme, on the basis that 'readers would be interested to know what the programme says'.[113] But the Soviet mantra was evident in the party's ambivalence: critical of misdemeanours but still wanting to see the Soviet Union in a positive light.

Recent evidence suggests that one reason for this ambivalence may have been the need to sustain the party's continuing financial links with the Soviet Union. It has now been confirmed that the party had been receiving money from the Soviet Union since 1958, in the wake of the party's loss of membership in 1956. However, Reuben Falber, the party's Assistant General Secretary during the 1960s and 1970s, who collected the money from representatives of the Soviet Embassy, has said that the amount decreased significantly in 1970 due to the differences between the Soviet Union and the British party over the invasion of Czechoslovakia. 'Because we were in such disagreement with them ... I felt we couldn't go on accepting it'.[114] In the event, despite Falber's request for the money to stop, smaller sums of £12,000 to £15,000 were paid over, for pension purposes, in contrast to the previous usual annual sum of £100,000 (these pension recipients included Palme Dutt). The loyalty to the Soviet Union could thus be said to have continued in a more detached way. The disagreement of prominent figures like Palme Dutt may also have increased the party's caution in its criticism, causing it to fear, perhaps, the possibility of a breakaway (such as did occur later); such a group would also be a rival for Soviet funds.[115]

Thirdly, if we accept that the party's response to the Prague events was consistent with its emerging political direction, then the argument is reinforced that the most decisive strategic tensions within the party were of a more domestic nature; the differences were more about its relationship to the labourist mainstream than its relationship to the Soviet Union. Moreover the impact of arguments over labourism on the growing organising schism in the party is not as easily reducible to the Eurocommunist-Stalinist polarity as some have claimed. Sassoon, for example, in describing the divisions in western communism as a whole, argues that:

> ... in all domestic affairs, those pro-soviet communists were indistinguishable from trade union militants in West European social democratic parties. They all espoused 'workerist' positions, rejected stabilisation policies and urged return to 'hard' wage bargaining.[116]

Callaghan has also argued that pro-soviet and 'economistic' positions were mutually dependent.[117] However the situation was more complex than this: Bert Ramelson, Tony Chater and Ron Bellamy, for example, all leading advocates of 'economistic' positions within the British party, all also condemned the Soviet actions in Prague.[118] Divisions over the Soviet Union and the Prague Spring are therefore on their own inadequate in explaining the significant and specific conflicts over the party's subsequent political strategy. Rather, as the discussion above has suggested, the answers lie in an examination of differences related to labourism, which was crucial to the party's role in industrial militancy, and continued to dominate its politics in the late 1960s and early 1970s.

IN SEARCH OF A STRATEGY?
This chapter has examined the areas of ideological renewal in the CP between 1964-1968, and the ways in which socialist humanism and militant labourism helped shape the new political agenda of the party. Each of these doctrines influenced particular aspects of party life.

Socialist humanism, in the CPGB's own interpretation and application of it, presented a more independent and critical outlook, one in which intellectuals assumed a greater importance and in which the possibilities of human intervention and the role of personal agency brought a new relationship with radical christianity. It also helped to ease a transition to new forms of creative Marxism in the 1970s; and it helped to maintain a strong intellectual influence at a time when faith in the socialist world was crumbling, and a variety of other left and Marxist groups were competing for attention. Thus the 1968 version of *The British Road To Socialism* stressed the importance of a 'democratic advance to socialism',[119] and a commitment to a 'multi-party system' under socialism, with parties 'hostile to socialism (having) the right to maintain their organisation, publications and propaganda and to contest elections'.[120]

On the other hand, militant labourism was crucial in increasing and sustaining the party's influence in the labour movement under the new leadership of Bert Ramelson. This was evident in the party's role in the new militancy after 1968 – which was to intensify during the 1970s; and the party's successes in this field also gave new weight to the strategic importance accorded to the labour movement in the BRS. The emphasis on the labour movement was given a new significance by the party's progress in trade union work, and the new position was reflected in the following statement: 'If the working class is to challenge the power of the monopolists, the autonomy of the trade union movement will have to be defended and every move towards state regulation of the unions rejected'[121]

These two doctrines were the main driving forces behind the party's attempts to renew its political strategy. Thus Callaghan's claim that 'at no time did the party confront the legacy of Leninist and Stalinist politics and its own history of subordination to the Soviet Union'[122] is overly dismissive of changes in the leadership's strategy, and underestimates the extent to which changes were taking place amongst the membership as a whole; deep-seated attitudes in the party were showing signs of change, in the area of culture, the Soviet invasion of Czechoslovakia and in the party's relationship to the Labour Party.[123] It should be noted, however, that the closer relationship to the Labour Party did not prevent stringent criticism of the failures of the 1964 Labour government. In condemning the way in which the government had 'facilitated the growth of monopoly' and was the 'prisoner of the existing state machine',[124] the party proposed its own programme as the basis for left unity, one based on full employment, taking 'full command of the nation's resources', and extending the 'broad popular alliance against monopoly capitalism'.[125]

However, despite these attempts at renewal, the party's fortunes were declining, notably in the arena of electoral politics; its performance in the 1966 election was its worst for decades. Membership was also declining, while sales of the new *Morning Star* – which succeeded the *Daily Worker* in 1966 – were also struggling to hold up. Moreover the BRS itself drew a whole range of criticisms.[126] These came not only from 'dissident' party districts like Surrey and Hants and Dorset, which condemned the party's position on Czechoslovakia and its continuing attention to 'bourgeois' electoralist matters, but also from a range of other critics. For example, Idris Cox, a veteran party leader, described the draft of the new British Road to Socialism as 'most unsatisfactory', 'repetitive' and 'long-winded', 'and most unlikely to make any significant positive impact upon Communist Party members, let alone the labour movement as a whole'.[127] Congress discussion in the pages of *Comment* during 1969 revealed criticism of the programme from many sides, particularly focusing on its lack of theoretical clarity. In fact the BRS relied heavily on rhetoric, notably the insistence on 'struggle' as the key to progress. Not only was this description of its political strategy vague – for example 'in the course of this many sided struggle the labour movement *will find the way* to throw off its right wing leadership';[128] it was also repetitive. There was, for example, not only a 'many sided struggle', but the 'struggle of the labour movement', a 'struggle for living standards', the 'struggle against the right wing within the labour movement' and the 'immediate struggles'. There was little indication of how to proceed other than helping to shift the Labour Party to the left. Moreover, despite the language of 'struggle' which dominated party discourse, changing the Labour Party seemed to depend mainly on courting and cajoling trade union leaders behind the scenes – an activity at which Bert Ramelson excelled.

Moreover, the two doctrines, while each opening up new possibilities, did not relate easily to each other – an indication of future points of contradiction. On the one hand the intellectual renaissance and political pluralism associated with socialist humanism were leading in the direction of a new analytical framework, one which would allow a reconciliation with some of the anti-labourist stances of the New Left, and a greater exploration of ideological and cultural politics, as was to be characteristic of the party's Gramscian approach in the 1970s. On the other hand, the party's growing industrial and organisational influence, associated with militant labourism, was pulling it towards a focus on very specific areas of struggle, which remained rooted within industrial working-class cultures and in the economic sphere, and depended upon very traditional forms of organisation. The political and theoretical differences that these two approaches were developing became increasingly problematic for the party in the subsequent period. These contradictions became particularly apparent in debates over the party's industrial strategy, which is the focus of the next chapter.

Notes

1. See for example G. Hodgson, *Socialism and Parliamentary Democracy*, Spokesman, 1977, pp138-178, for an extended discussion of the politics of the party's programme.
2. George Matthews, the former Assistant General Secretary of the party, has admitted Stalin's knowledge and encouragement of The British Road to Socialism. See 'Stalin's British Road?', *Changes*, 14-27 September 1991, in which Matthews describes the process by which Stalin endorsed the main features of the programme, in consultation with Harry Pollitt, the party's General Secretary, on the latter's visit to the Soviet Union in 1950 for medical treatment. Despite the fact that Pollitt had published *Looking Ahead*, with a chapter entitled 'The British Road to Socialism', in 1947, the party leadership had not discussed the necessity of such a programme at its meetings prior to Stalin's intervention. Matthews, Emile Burns and R.

Palme Dutt prepared a document that incorporated Stalin's recommendations. Matthews concludes the article by saying 'It is clear to me that without the intervention of Stalin nothing like the original British Road to Socialism would have been produced, and it is doubtful whether there would have been a long-term programme at all'.
3. A 'communist vocabulary' was not confined to the CPGB See C. Shore, *Italian Communism ...*, op cit; and J. Jenson and G. Ross, *The View from the Inside*, op cit, for more on the role of 'linguistic rituals' within the PCF. More general accounts of democratic centralism can be found in M. Waller, *Democratic Centralism*, op cit.
4. See A. Westoby, *The Evolution of Communism*, Polity Press, 1989, for a good discussion of the development of Leninism in this period.
5. L. J. Macfarlane, *The British Communist Party: Its Origin and Development until 1929*, Macgibbon and Kee, 1966; S. MacIntyre, *Little Moscows: Communism and Working Class Militancy in Inter-war Britain*, Croom Helm, 1980.
6. J. Fyrth, *Britain, Fascism and the Popular Front*, Lawrence and Wishart, 1985.
7. See K. Morgan, *Against Fascism and War*, Manchester University Press, 1989.
8. G. Hodgson, *Socialism and Parliamentary Democracy*, op cit, p162.
9. Congress Reports, 1961, 1963, 1965; CPGB.
10. B. Hogenkamp, in *Film, Television and the Left*, op cit, p88, cites rare footage of the Party Congress of 1963, which gave one of the final images of the party's old guard. 'It shows a party that was largely dominated by the 'old guard' (Rajani Palme Dutt, Bob Stewart and Willie Gallacher are all shown close-up), inward-looking and still living in the age of austerity instead of affluence'. On the generational changes in the trade unions see J. McIlroy, 'The Communist Party and Industrial Politics', 1964-1979 – paper given to British Trade Unions and Industrial Politics conference at the University of Warwick, September 1997.
11. A. Hutt, *British Trade Unionism*, Lawrence and Wishart, 1962, p209.
12. Mike Power, interview with author; similar views were expressed by Dave Purdy and George Matthews in interviews with author.
13. Ramelson's admirers in this respect included rivals such as Steve Jefferys, the Industrial Organiser of the International Socialists during the 1970s (S. Jefferys, interview with author).
14. V. I. Lenin, 'Left-Wing Communism: An Infantile Disorder', in V. I. Lenin, *On Utopian and Scientific Socialism*, Progress Publishers, Moscow, 1965, p184-189. Lenin's intervention was crucial in persuading doubters like Willie Gallagher of the merits of working with the Labour Party. For a discussion of these issues see W. Kendall, *The Revolutionary Movement in Britain 1900-1921*, Weidenfeld and Nicholson, 1969.
15. Following the Labour Party's ban on individual members holding joint membership, from 1924 he was a communist-only MP. For a discussion of the political contribution of Saklatvala during this period as an MP, see M. Squires, *Saklatvala: A Political Biography*, Lawrence and Wishart, 1990, and J. Callaghan, *Rajani Palme Dutt*, Lawrence and Wishart, 1993.
16. The ban on Communist Party members attending Labour Party meetings as trade union delegates was introduced in 1927.

17. W. Thompson, *The Good Old Cause*, op cit, p134.
18. The party had supported Left candidates for elections in the earlier period, but in the case of Lawrence Daly it was now prepared to do so even when a CP candidate was available.
19. Maoists followed Reg Birch out of the party for these reasons in 1963; while for those like Sid French, Secretary of the Surrey District of the party, the perceived abandonment of Leninism in favour of electoralism was a continual source of criticism (particularly in debates over the party's resolutions at Congress), until he eventually led a breakaway, in 1977, to form the New Communist Party.
20. *The British Road To Socialism*, CPGB, 1951. The need to 'break the right-wing grip' on the Labour Party, challenging 'right-wing domination', 'right-wing leaders', 'right-wing social democracy', and 'right-wing reformism', was frequent in party discourse, in identifying its immediate political objective of shifting the Labour Party in a Left direction. Congress Reports carried in special issues of *Comment*, following the Congress, record this. See for example *Comment*, November 29, 1969.
21. See *Tribune* editorial, 3 December 1965, quoted in W. Thompson, *The Good Old Cause*, op cit, p142.
22. For example, party congresses continued to refer to this, usually at the end of motions in a rallying call for donations.
23. The party's membership declined continually from 34,281 in February 1964 to 30,607 in 1968. There was a small rise, during the most militant periods between 1971 and 1973, from 28,803 to 29,943 (EC Reports, CP/CENT/ORG).
24. The Cultural Committee's distribution of responsibilities according to a statement in 1964 included S. Aaronovitch, Sociology; M. Dobb Economics; E. Hobsbawm, History; A. Kettle and A. Bush, Artist and Society; M. Cornforth, Philosophy; J. D. Bernal, Science; M. Heinemann, 'The Novel'. Cultural Committee File, CP Archive.
25. See for example the work of Maurice Cornforth, a philosophy student of Ludwig Wittgenstein – notably, *Marxism and the Linguistic Philosophy*, Lawrence and Wishart, 1965.
26. This concern was evident as early as 1959, when an unsigned draft report, *Winning Intellectuals to the Party*, was circulated within the Cultural Committee. The author was almost certainly Arnold Kettle. The Cultural Committee minutes of the early 1960s illustrate a broad interest in arts and cultural questions – including the activities of the 'Unity Theatre Company'; a discussion of the third television channel; the merits of working-class realist cinema, including *The Loneliness of the Long Distance Runner*, first shown in 1962; and a *Policy For Leisure*, in 1963, in which the party condemned the 'commercial exploitation of the means of enjoyment', and advocated increased funding for the arts. For a discussion of the party's relationship to the media at this time see B. Hogenkamp, *Film, Television and the Left*, Lawrence and Wishart, 2000. The most significant intellectual initiative at this time was the *Challenge of Marxism* series of public lectures, launched in 1963 as a 'week of discussion and debate, under the auspices of *Marxism Today*'. Its aim was to 'show the contribution of Marxism to the problems of our time in the fields of politics, science and culture and in the battle of ideas'. This was held at the

Marx Memorial library and became the basis of a book under the same title, published by Lawrence and Wishart in 1963. The *Challenge of Marxism* can be seen as a forerunner, in its aims and objectives, to the *Communist University of London*, first held in 1969.

27. See M. Kenny, *The First New Left*, op cit; and 'Communism and the New Left' in G. Andrews et al, *Opening the Books*, op cit, pp195-209.
28. E. P. Thompson, *William Morris: Romantic to Revolutionary*, Lawrence and Wishart, 1955. For Thompson, socialist humanism, and his critics, see M. Kenny, *The First New Left*, op cit, pp69-85; L. Chun, *The British New Left*, op cit, pp29-35; and C. Taylor, 'Marxism and Socialist Humanism', in R. Archer et al, *Out of Apathy: Voices of the New Left 30 Years On*, Verso, 1989.
29. L. Chun, *The British New Left*, op cit, p30.
30. Ibid, p30.
31. E. Thompson, 'Socialist Humanism: An Epistle to the Philistines', in *New Reasoner*, 1, 1957, p107.
32. L. Chun, *The British New Left*, op cit, p33. See E. P. Thompson; 'Socialist Humanism; An Epistle to the Philistines', op cit.
33. See in particular J. P. Sartre, *Being and Nothingness*, Washington Square Press, New York 1966; G. Lukacs, *History and Class Consciousness*, Merlin 1971.
34. His critique of these thinkers was set out in *The Poverty of Theory and Other Essays*, Merlin 1978.
35. A. Kettle, 'How Left is the New Left' *Marxism Today* October 1960, quoted in W. Thompson *The Good Old Cause*, op cit, p122.
36. See James Klugmann, 'Editorial' in *Marxism Today*, June 1969, for reports of these meetings.
37. *Comment*, 20.5.67. See R. Williams et al, *May Day Manifesto*, Penguin, 1967.
38. M. Johnstone, interview with author. 'Rehabilitation' was his word. He appeared on an edition of the BBC programme *Late Night Line-Up*.
39. See N. Wood, *Communism and British Intellectuals*, Gollancz, 1959.
40. *Questions of Ideology and Culture*, CPGB, 1967. The document was reprinted in *Marxism Today* in May 1967 to launch a discussion of its contents.
41. Ibid.
42. The debate reflected what many communists saw as a decisive break from the past. Margaret Cohen, for example, in a discussion contribution in *Marxism Today* (July 1967), wrote: 'In practice many of us have been moving away from old, often deeply established attitudes towards the arts... because life itself has compelled us to do so. I find this statement welcome and refreshing because it registers a clear departure from more old dogmatic positions which I believe have isolated so many of us – above all the attitude that we know all the answers and that there must be a 'line' on everything... Apart from the arrogance of such a standpoint, it is not conducive towards making allies and to winning people to our policies'. Of those critical of the document, John Lewis, a leading party intellectual, while welcoming 'tolerance' and the 'desire to work with all shades of opinion' asked 'whether it is really necessary to repudiate so much... ' (*Marxism Today*, July 1967, p222). More traditional criticisms included Marguerite Morgan, who maintained that the 'socialist countries have a

higher cultural level than the rest of us' and that the document would lead to 'individualist self-expression' (*Marxism Today* September 1967). Most of the published responses however were supportive of the document.
43. QIC, ibid.
44. Ibid.
45. For James Klugmann, the humanist turn seemed to epitomise a personal catharsis. A long-standing party intellectual, his earlier humanist concerns in the 1930s had been overshadowed by his compromised role as a party functionary made most apparent in his book *From Trotsky To Tito* (CPGB, 1951), essentially a defence of Stalinism, which argued that Trotskyites, fascists and social democrats were colluding against the socialist world in supporting the Tito government in Yugoslavia. In addition to his work as editor of *Marxism Today*, his pivotal role in the Communist-Christian dialogue, and his general interest in socialist humanism, many of the younger generation of intellectuals, in interviews with the author, commented on his support for their endeavours.
46. *The Future of Man*, CPGB, 1970, p14.
47. Ibid, p4.
48. Ibid, p9.
49. See for example the interest in the work of Marcuse, notably his *One-Dimensional Man*, Routledge, 1964. Reviews of these works, a mixture of sympathy and condescension, appeared regularly in the party press during this time. Denis Dworkin's *Cultural Marxism in Post-War Britain*, Duke University Press, 1997, discusses the impact of the new interest in Marxism on the university and student sectors. L. Chun, *The British New Left*, op cit, pp110-124, discusses the impact of these ideas on the New Left. See also *Western Marxism A Critical Reader*, New Left Books, 1977, for a critical discussion of these ideas.
50. See D. Sassoon, *One Hundred Years of Socialism*, op cit, p302. Pope John's encyclical of 1963, *Pacem in Terris*, is sympathetic to co-operation with 'false philosophical doctrines' on humanitarian grounds.
51. Canon P. Ostreicher, 'Preface', in J. Klugmann and P. Ostreicher, *What Kind of Revolution?*, Panther Modern Society, 1968.
52. P. Ostreicher, 'Dialogue Between Christianity and Marxism', in *Marxism Today*, April 1967.
53. Ibid.
54. 'Dialogue Between Christianity and Marxism', in *Marxism Today*, September 1967.
55. Ibid, p286.
56. Ibid, p287.
57. Ibid, p288.
58. This included *Comment* and the *Morning Star*, as well as *Marxism Today*.
59. As one example, see the contribution from Stan Cole, a communist fitter, who in response to some suggestions in the party which saw such a dialogue as a 'luxury', argued that in his work as a trade union activist it was 'religious teaching and the practical problems of life that directed my steps along this particular road, seeing Jesus Christ as a man fighting oppression, helping the weak and the poor, healing the sick. Industrially it was trade unionism and politically the Communist Party that, to me, seemed a natural continuity'. *Marxism Today*, February 1970.

60. J. Saville, 'The Ideology of Labourism', in R. Benewick, R. N. Berki, B. Parekh (eds), *Knowledge and Belief in Politics*, p215.
61. T. Nairn, 'The Nature of the Labour Party', *NLR* 27 October/September 1964.
62. 'The sickness of labourism' was the title of his last chapter in *his Parliamentary Socialism: A Study in the Politics of Labour*, Merlin Press, 1972. For studies which also see labourism as synonymous with the conservative drifts of the Labour Party in Parliament see G. Elliott, *Labourism and the English Genius*, Verso, 1993, and D. Coates, *The Labour Party and the Struggle For Socialism*, Cambridge University Press, 1975. For a good critical discussion of these analyses see T. Forrester, *The Labour Party and the Working Class*, Heinemann, 1976.
63. L. Panitch, *Social Democracy and Industrial Militancy*, Cambridge University Press, 1976, p1; G. Foot, *The Labour Party's Political Thought*, Croom Helm, 1985, p357.
64. Who traces the concept to the nineteenth-century world of labour before the formation of the Labour Party.
65. W. Thompson, *The Long Death of British Labourism*, Pluto Press, 1993, p46.
66. Ibid, p6.
67. Ibid, p10.
68. Ibid, p57.
69. For the differences between labourism and European social democracy, see S. Berger, *The British Labour Party and the German Social Democrats*, Clarendon Press, 1994; G. D. H. Cole, *A History of Socialist Thought 1789-1939*, 1968. Many put this distinction down to the more uneven development of Marxism in Britain: See for example R. McKibbin, 'Why Was There No Marxism in Great Britain?' in *EH*, 99, 1984, pp297-331; and K. Willis, 'The Introduction and Critical Reception of Marxist Thought in Britain 1850-1900', in *Historical Journal*, 20, 1977, pp417-59.
70. N. Fishman, *The Communist Party and the Trade Unions*, op cit, p9.
71. Ibid, p12.
72. Willie Thompson, *The Long Death of British Labourism*, op cit, p101.
73. See for example J. McIlroy, 'Notes on the Communist Party and Industrial Politics', op cit.
74. See M. Jenkins, *Bevanism: Labour's High Tide*, pp200-223, for a discussion of communist-Labour relations in the 1950s. Jenkins argues that hostility to Aneurin Bevan and his supporters was a recurrent theme in the party's politics, despite the fact that much of Bevan's union support depended on communist-Labour Left alliances. The party saw the Bevanites as little different from mainstream social democrats and therefore 'as legitimate targets for continuing scepticism and hostility', op cit, p216.
75. V. I. Lenin, *Imperialism the Highest Stage of Capitalism*, Foreign Languages Press, 1975.
76. See in particular P. Baran and P. Sweezy, *Monopoly Capitalism*, Monthly Review Press, 1966.
77. *End Monopoly Rule*, CPGB, 1963.
78. Ibid.
79. Ibid.
80. Ibid.

3. Ideological and Strategic Renewal in the CPGB   103

81. J. Gollan, *The Case For Socialism in the Sixties*, CPGB, 1966, p4.
82. Ibid, p31.
83. Ibid, p37.
84. Ibid, p44.
85. For New Left discussions of modernisation see M. Kenny, *The First New Left*, Lawrence and Wishart, 1995, pp136-139.
86. J. Gollan, *The Case For Socialism in the Sixties*, op cit, p65.
87. Ibid.
88. *The British Road to Socialism*, CPGB, 1968.
89. Ibid, p8.
90. Ibid, p10.
91. Ibid, pp13-14.
92. See the report of this in *Comment*, 25 January 1969.
93. Congress Report, CPGB, *Comment*, 29 November 1969.
94. While the crisis of the British economy in the late 1960s, including the 'devaluation' issue, gave substance to the CP's arguments of crisis, its constant emphasis on the 'crisis of monopoly capitalism' appeared frequently in Congress resolutions (*see Congress Reports* for 1965, 1967, 1969), and was used to supplement the call for 'intensification' of the class struggle.
95. J. McIlroy, *Notes on the Communist Party and Industrial Politics*, op cit, p11.
96. Ibid, p15.
97. Ibid, p34.
98. Ibid, p8.
99. Ibid, p9.
100. Wilson's relevant speeches included the following (House of Commons, 20 June 1966): 'It's difficult for us to appreciate the pressures which are being put on men I know to be realistic and reasonable not only in their executive capacity but in the highly organised strike committees in the individual ports by this tightly knit group of politically motivated men who, as the last General Election showed, utterly failed to secure acceptance of their views by the British electorate, but who are now determined to exercise back-stage pressures, forcing great hardship on the members of the union and their families and endangering the security of the industry and the economic welfare of the nation'. On 29 June 1966 he argued: 'The whole formidable power of the Communist Party's industrial apparatus has for some time been directed towards this end (ie the takeover of the NUS) and the seaman's strike with all its background of justification for industrial action, has provided the ground'. Both taken from Hansard and quoted in P. Foot, 'The Seaman's Struggle' in R. Blackburn and A. Cockburn, *The Incompatibles: Trade Union Militancy and the Consensus*, Penguin, 1967, p190.
101. BRS, 1968, p27.
102. Sam Aaronovitch, 'Forward Or Back? Prospects For the Movement', in *Marxism Today*, January 1967.
103. 'Congress Discussion', in *Comment*, 27 September 1969.
104. *Morning Star*, 27 July 1968; W. Thompson, *The Good Old Cause*, op cit, p155.
105. James Klugmann, for example, argued that the possibility of 'counter-revolution' was the distinguishing feature which continued to justify the

Soviet action in Hungary in 1956 (see *Comment*, 11 October 1969), while he was one of the most strident critics of the invasion from within the party hierarchy, arguing in *Marxism Today* ('Editorial'), October 1968, that the intervention in Prague amounted to 'distortions and grave errors – like bureaucracy, suppression of democratic rights, misuse and abuse of power, unjust arrests and trials'.

106. 'Congress Discussion', *Comment*, 11 October 1969.
107. According to Rothstein, an 'analysis of the class issues involved, national and international, was lamentably absent from EC statements'. *Comment*, 1st November 1969.
108. These statements were all reprinted in *Marxism Today*, September 1968.
109. Noted by Mike Waite in 'Sex'n'Drugs'n'Rock'n'Roll (and Communism)', in G. Andrews et al (eds), *Opening the Books*, op cit, p220.
110. Report of EC meeting of 24 August, in *Comment*, 31 August 1968.
111. W. Thompson, *The Good Old Cause*, op cit, p157.
112. Quoted in 'Editorial', *Marxism Today*, November 1968.
113. *Comment*, 14 September 1968.
114. R. Falber, interview with author. See also Falber's statement in *Changes*, November 16-29, 1991.
115. R. Falber, G. Matthews, interview with author, in F. Beckett, *Enemy Within*, op cit, pp146-148.
116. D. Sassoon, *One Hundred Years*, op cit, p320.
117. J. Callaghan, 'Endgame', in D. S. Bell, *Western European Communists and the Collapse of Communism*, Berg 1993, p172.
118. See *Comment*, October 18 1969, for Ramelson's defence of the EC position and his condemnation of Dutt.
119. *BRS*, 1968, p4.
120. op cit, p31.
121. op cit, p16.
122. J. Callaghan, *The Far Left in British Politics*, op cit, p172.
123. For example the *BRS* stated that the party 'does not seek an exclusive position of leadership'. *BRS* 1968, p6.
124. *BRS*, 1968, p11.
125. Ibid.
126. Both Surrey and Hants and Dorset districts blamed the decline of the party's membership, the drop in *Morning Star* sales, and electoral reversals on its move towards reformism, parliamentarism and critical positions towards Soviet actions (referred to by the Surrey District as a 'serious weakening of our internationalism', 'Congress Discussion' in *Comment*, September 6 1969). See also the Hants and Dorset contribution to 'Congress Discussion' in *Comment*, November 8 1969.
127. 'Congress Discussion', in *Comment*, October 25 1969.
128. *BRS*, 1968, p6. My emphasis.

4. The CPGB's Industrial Strategy 1968–1974

The previous two chapters have described the ways in which the Communist Party sought to renew itself, both in the development of its political ideology and also through attempts to refine its strategy. This attempt at renewal was a response to changes in British culture and politics as well as new developments in the party's relationship to the Soviet Union. A major consequence of these attempts at renewal – under pressure from its quite different constituent groups – was a further departure from Leninism and greater assimilation into the political culture of labourism. Here the party's pragmatism allowed it to strengthen its position as the militant expression of labourism – defined by a commitment to building 'left unity' and opposing 'monopoly capitalism' – while seeking to influence the Labour Party through its key organising roles in directing trade union 'struggle'. It is in this context that this chapter will assess the industrial and economic strategy of the CP, and in doing so will critically assess its implications for the party's subsequent political directions while drawing some preliminary conclusions on the effect of these developments on the wider left and labour movement. It will be evident that the party's increasing influence in the labour movement faced important constraints and was temporary, and that the gains it made through its industrial work did not strengthen its status as an independent political force. Indeed the essential argument here is that this apparent paradox between respective gains and losses in its industrial and political status is the key to understanding subsequent conflicts and schisms between its different groups, and, therefore, the problematic development of its future strategy.

As with other aspects of the party's history there has been very little research into the Communist Party's industrial strategy or its links with the trade union movement in the 1960s and 1970s. Moreover, unlike the other aspects of the party's role, where some documentary evidence is available to support the more general accounts, much of the material of the industrial department, such as minutes of meetings of the industrial advisory committees, has been shredded.[1] Mapping the party's industrial activities is therefore made more difficult by the need to derive information about this work either from the limited documents available on the party's wider political role, such as minutes for Executive or Political Committee meetings, interviews, personal correspondence, and articles in party journals, or from individual union records, in which the activities of communists have been recorded alongside other activists. The first in-depth study of the party's industrial strategy during the 1960s and 1970s, carried out by John McIlroy, has made a major contribution towards understanding the complexities of this period, by bringing much new evidence to light: this will be discussed at some length here.[2]

The lack of systematic or continuous records has meant that much existing research has obscured, misinterpreted or underestimated the party's role in what was a very significant period of industrial conflict. In many studies of labour history during the period, the Communist Party appears only in passing – and some accounts barely mention the party at all.[3] In other accounts, which mention its role in some of the major industrial disputes, its significance has been reduced to the activities of individual Communist Party trade unionists, and the broader spheres of its influence – such as the 'behind the scenes' manoeuvres between communist and trade union activists – are neglected; the complexity of the party's position in appealing at different times to the rank and file as well as officialdom has also been lost. Moreover, as McIlroy and Campbell have argued, an important reason for this is that much of the research takes a 'top-down' approach, which accepts uncritically the position that decisive points in the party's history can be ascertained from 'high politics', in which the 'responses from below' are viewed as 'semi-automatic'. Amongst neglected areas, they argue, are the ways in which 'the CP's trade union interventions were organised … the relationships between union activists and the party and between rank-and-file CP members and the Party's political and industrial leadership'; and the reasons 'why the Party did not grow in what seemed to be promising conditions'.[4] Because of the nature of the party's work and the methods employed by Bert Ramelson, who relied to a large extent on personal contacts and unofficial as well as official alliances, the need to pay attention to issues 'on the ground', including the specific circumstances of particular unions, becomes particularly important.

MILITANT LABOURISM AND THE CONSOLIDATION OF THE NEW STRATEGY

It is also necessary to keep in mind the wider context in which the CP's relationship with the British labour movement and the Labour Party developed, and the impact this had for the CP's industrial strategy during the period 1968-1974. This period arguably comprised the most intense wave of industrial unrest in Britain since the second world war. Certainly in terms of days lost through strike action, numbers of

4. The CPGB's Industrial Strategy 1968–1974

strikes (including many unofficial ones), the new categories of groups who became militant, and the new forms of protest (from sit-ins to go-slows), various different factors combined to make it a very volatile period.[5]

The previous chapter described the origins of the party's new industrial strategy, under the leadership of Bert Ramelson, in which it had found a new role in the trade union movement – one which opened up new channels of influence, notably the possibility of influencing the policy of the Labour Party through winning trade union positions. Later events were to consolidate and strengthen this role and provide new momentum for the party, even if they did not result in increases in membership or success at the polls. While the strategy's success was evident in the election of communists to leading positions within specific unions, the main impact was through its organisational presence and the networks that Ramelson had set up, which, at their highest points, reached the higher echelons of the TUC.

Several trends and dilemmas were evident. Firstly, the CP sought to reassert the primacy of the industrial spheres in its work. This is not evident in the minutes of the key EC and other leading committees where, from the limited material that is available, it appears that the industrial sphere came behind electoral issues and those concerning the international communist movement.[6] These documents, however, almost certainly hide the real importance given to industrial struggles. The industrial department was given greater autonomy from leadership control than other sections of the party, prompting one former Assistant Industrial Organiser to describe it as equivalent to 'a Party within a Party'.[7] As the leading 'industrial comrade', Ramelson's own dominance and ways of working were given preferential treatment, and he himself was one of the first to be consulted within the leadership on key policies. The *Daily Worker* and, after 1966, the *Morning Star*, consistently covered industrial issues far in excess of any other topic, while *Marxism Today*, the party's 'theoretical and discussion journal', under the editorship of James Klugmann was in the habit of consulting Bert Ramelson on questions of industrial strategy.[8] There is also evidence to suggest the development of a schism amongst party members, with those communists working in trade unions becoming separated from the wider political work of the party branches. This schism was another example of the labourist ethos within the party, which was to be important in the later ideological divisions over its strategy.[9]

Secondly, the party had begun to re-negotiate its relationship to the trade union hierarchy. Significantly, this included a shift away from the 'rank-and-fileism' which, according to Fishman, had been central to the party's strategy in the inter-war period. The party continued until the early 1960s to move towards becoming a lobbying or mobilising force behind the TUC.[10] This new relationship to the trade union hierarchy was strengthened both by the election of more prominent left-wing trade union leaders, like Jack Jones and Hugh Scanlon, and by the increased respect the party won across the labour movement for its role in leading resistance to government-imposed legal restraints on trade unions and the imposition of incomes policies. For its own part, the move away from rank-and-fileism was justified in the gains the party was making through its industrial advisories and in organising support for the trade union Broad Lefts: a process made easier by the arrival of a new generation of trade union leaders. Moreover, as has been argued, this strategic change was given further legitimation by the ideology of militant labourism.

The combination of this strategic change with a continuing decline in the number of factory branches – despite attempts to resurrect them[11] – provided an opportunity for others to the party's left, like the International Socialists, to make inroads, and to attempt to fill the vacuum left by the party, particularly in the newer white-collar unions.[12] Having apparently abandoned its claim to a leading 'vanguard' role in the *British Road to Socialism*, major questions surface over the extent of the party's revolutionary objectives, its political raison d'être. While the strategy of constructing Broad Left alliances in the unions enabled the demonstration of aspects of the 'anti-monopoly' alliance in action, unexplained areas of the party's strategy remained. The nature of transition to a socialist society began to rest solely with the party's ability to influence the Labour Party – which some critics in the party saw as a retreat into reformism.[13] Moreover there seemed to be an inherent contradiction in the party's political strategy which was amplified further by its closer involvement in labour movement officialdom. The party existed as an alternative to the Labour Party, yet put increasing faith in the latter's ability to deliver a 'left government of a new type'. In order to sustain support amongst the left it had to be seen to be radical on matters of policy; yet paradoxically its ability to influence policy in a leftward direction was because of its greater access to the labour movement, achieved through pragmatism. Bert Ramelson was clear that the Labour Party had always been the 'vehicle of the working class';[14] now the party's ideology of 'militant labourism' brought it a stronger identification with the political culture and ideals of the mainstream labour movement, notably through the priority given to free collective bargaining and working with and through traditional forms of trade union networks in order to influence Labour Party policy. Preserving its radical edge, on the other hand, was to be achieved by maximising struggles on the wages front and helping to extend these struggles to include wider groups of workers.

By 1968 this strategy was starting to pay dividends, giving the party more influence in the labour movement. Many of its new generation of leading trade unionists, such as John Tocher, George Wake, Dick Etheridge and Cyril Morton (AEU), Mick McGahey, Arthur True and

Sammy Moore (NUM), Lou Lewis (UCATT) and Max Morris (NUT) were taking their places in influential trade union positions, while Ken Gill (AUEW-TASS) became the party's first elected National Official in 1968. Beyond these new positions of influence held by individuals, the party managed to extend its number of delegates to the TUC from the 1960s through into the 1970s. Its greatest source of encouragement, however, was its influence in the Broad Left in the main unions. This was notable after the election of Hugh Scanlon, a former communist, as President of the AEU in 1967, on the basis of communist support; and in general the Broad Left had helped secure additional senior positions in the union hierarchy for left candidates.[15] The election of Jack Jones as leader of the TGWU in 1969 was also helped by Broad Left support. The party, through the Broad Left, also extended its influence to other unions through sympathetic individuals, for example Alan Sapper (ACTT), Ray Buckton (ASLEF) and Ken Cameron (FBU). It is important to remember here that the party's increased representation did not necessarily lead to increased control over mainstream union policy or leadership.

As McIlroy argues, some of these gains had a 'brittle' and 'tenuous' nature, based on delicate personal networks and alliances that had been forged by Ramelson.[16] One aspect of this was the compromise made in not standing party candidates but supporting those within the Broad Left, which meant that the party had to curtail its independent political positions as a sacrifice for the greater good. Indeed, prior to Scanlon's election, Ramelson had to struggle on the CP advisory to win support for his candidature, following previous support for party candidates such as Reg Birch and Claude Berridge.[17] Scanlon's election was a watershed as, though it was not the first time the party had supported non-party candidates for trade union elections, it was the first significant Broad Left victory in the new period of militancy.[18]

The new strategy brought dilemmas, however, as well as benefits. The party's influence increased, but for further advance it remained reliant on its broader allies. This meant that there would be ambiguities over the nature of its advance as an independent political force within the labour movement. Its biggest independent vehicle in the labour movement was the LCDTU, which was under the close control of the party, an 'arm of his [Ramelson's] department, conveyor for CP policies, a means of extending party networks and a pressure point on union leaders'.[19] It was the main organising force behind opposition to attempts made during this period to restrict trade union activity, such as the Donovan Report, *In Place of Strife*, and the Heath government's Industrial Relations Act (IRA). The LCDTU was in the forefront of the major industrial battles of the period, and remained controlled by leading communist trade unionists, chaired initially by Lou Lewis of UCATT and later by Kevin Halpin and – according to McIlroy – it 'took no initiatives without the imprimatur of the Industrial

Department'; it was, effectively, a 'CP franchise'.[20] Yet the successes of the LCDTU, until 1973 when it started to decline, went alongside decreases in membership and long-term decline of workplace and factory branches.[21]

SITUATING THE PARTY WITHIN THE NEW MILITANCY

The industrial militancy which took place in Britain from the late 1960s and extended into the 1970s has been described as the most intense period of industrial activity for fifty years.[22] The period included the opposition to the Labour government's *In Place of Strife* and Donovan Report, the miners strikes of 1972 and 1974, the Pentonville Dockers dispute over the Heath Industrial Relations Bill, and the building workers' strike of 1972, and ended with the splits within the labour movement over the Social Contract, from 1974. The militancy can partly be understood against the background of specific political and economic circumstances – it extended from the end of the consumer boom of the late 1950s, and thus to continuing rises in real wages, to the 'stagflation' and oil crisis of 1973, and ended with the onset of economic recession from 1974. This period, 1968-1974, was characterised in general by the UK's comparative (to other European countries) low rates of growth, its balance of payments crisis (following devaluation by the Wilson Government in 1967) and its falling rates of profit. In industrial relations it marked the growth of a distinctive and widespread shop stewards movement and a significant rise in unofficial strikes. As a result of the greater tensions between unions and government, with the state seeking to control trade union power, it combined to produce what many have seen as the era of 'corporatism'.[23]

All European countries experienced marked increases in militancy and unrest at this time. Sassoon has shown that a distinctive aspect of this new militancy was the number of unofficial strikes and the new forms of protest that were identified with it. The strikes, which had initially arisen in conditions of relative boom as a response to anti-inflationary policies, were followed by more militant opposition to the attempts by governments to impose legal restrictions on trade unions, general deflationary policies, and incomes policies. The experience of these developments opened up new opportunities for trade union activity. In some countries (Sweden, for example), the strongest emphasis was on industrial democracy or workers control; in others, more egalitarian social reforms were wedded to trade union action.[24]

In Britain, where radicalism was more sporadic, and where there were weaker connections between trade unions and social movements, industrial militancy had specific dynamics. In particular it needs to be understood in the context of the deflationary stop-go policies of the Wilson government, which had failed to resolve the balance of payments crisis, resulting ultimately in devaluation. The 1964-1970 Labour government's way of halting this economic decline was to put restraints on incomes, and place further legal impositions on trade unions to prevent unofficial strikes and the corresponding decline in profitability (since incomes provided a much easier government target than prices). This was the purpose of the 1964 National Board for Prices and Incomes and the TUC-Government Agreement of 1965. It was the failure of these two initiatives that led to a statutory pay freeze between 1966 and 1969.[25]

The significance of the Wilson government's attempts to impose incomes policies was long-term and widespread, and shaped the political and industrial conflicts of the period along particular lines. For the Communist Party, Wilson's strategy provided the rationale for extending its industrial influence, with the prospect of fulfilling its overall political strategy of shifting the Labour Party in a leftward direction. At the heart of the opposition to incomes policies was a more general strategy of opposing government intervention in the bargaining process. The issue of incomes policies opened up lines of division between the Labour government and the labour movement that would last for the next decade. The dispute over incomes policies, according to Thompson, represented 'an unprecedented fissure opening up within the body of Labourism between that part of it concerned with the state and all the remainder'.[26]

THE CP AND FREE COLLECTIVE BARGAINING

The Donovan Report, published in 1968, was the first attempt by the Wilson government to limit unofficial strike activity through state intervention. While the primary purpose of Donovan was to seek ways of regulating trade union activity, some of its recommendations had additional objectives, such as to protect workers against unfair dismissal, while it also proposed legislation to make it illegal to prohibit trade union membership in employment contracts. In fact the TUC initially welcomed the proposals on the grounds that they would formalise collective bargaining, noting that the recommendations stopped short of advocating legal interference in strikes, or of imposing strike ballots or 'cooling-off' periods – as followed with later legislation.[27]

The Donovan Report also recommended that a 'Commission on Industrial Relations', made up of top management, unions, and government, be formed to regulate collective bargaining. Leaving aside the clear indications this gave of the corporatist framework that would grow in later years, left critics maintained that, if implemented, Donovan would mean a new system of industrial relations in which power would be centralised at company and factory level, with activities outside this facing legal action. For the veteran communist J.R. Campbell, writing in *Marxism Today*, this would result in trade unions being put in a 'very restrictive straitjacket'. He saw the power of shop floor organisation being diminished at the expense of new powers for top management. The right of shop stewards to participate in negotiations was being threatened: 'Trade Unionists must be clear ... that the factory-wide agreement is aimed to strip the shop stewards in most factories of their existing powers of negotiation'.[28]

Donovan was a relatively tentative move against shop-floor bargaining compared to what followed. *In Place of Strife*, published in 1969, took things much further, with its proposals for compulsory strike ballots and measures clearly aimed at reducing the wave of unofficial strikes that had increased sharply since the mid-1960s. The controversial areas of Barbara Castle's bill were the powers to be given to the Secretary of State to impose a pause for conciliation (effectively a 'cooling-off' period) for up to 28 days on the occasion of an 'unconstitutional strike'. This power would be used when unofficial strikes were perceived as having consequences for the economy – a rather broad and ambiguous criterion whose interpretation seemed to be left to the Secretary of State. Official strikes that were perceived as representing a threat to the economy, or were seen as not having the support of the membership, would need a ballot. Additionally, the Secretary of State would be given powers to intervene in inter-union disputes. Thus the bill was a clear challenge to free collective bargaining.

In Place of Strife met with mass opposition from wide sections of the labour movement. The role of the CPGB was crucial in certain respects. The most important factor was the success it gained in mobilising opposition through the role of the LCDTU in organising the shop stewards in sporadic days of unofficial action, in February and May 1969, leading to calls for a general strike and a special TUC Congress. Through the activities of the LCDTU – its first major initiative – the CP was confirmed as an effective player *both* at grassroots and at a higher, official level, with Ramelson able to win allies on the TUC General Council. *In Place of Strife* was finally withdrawn in June 1969, on the basis that the TUC would agree to take some action against unofficial strikes.

The defeat of *In Place of Strife* certainly seemed to vindicate the party's industrial strategy at this time. Though Ramelson's ability to cajole and persuade his new-found allies was in all likelihood a crucial aspect of the campaign, the party's EC was in no doubt about the reasons for the defeat of *In Place of Strife*, in its assessment of the struggle at the September 1969 EC meeting. The legislation had been brought about, it was argued, by the government's desire to solve its economic problems by 'depressing living standards', 'pushing on with wage restraint' and generally 'solv[ing] the crisis at the expense of the workers'. The eventual defeat of the legislation was due to the 'power and strength of the organised Trade Union Movement'. Moreover, 'our programme of left unity has contributed substantially to the advance and the victories so far registered'. It was the combination of mass struggle and the forging of left unity in the course of that struggle that had led to the significant (even if not complete) victory in compelling the government to drop *In Place of Strife*. The victory, in the EC's interpretation, therefore confirmed the correctness of the party's strategy (they did, however, also note that there were still 'weaknesses' in the TUC General Council's acceptance of unofficial strikes as 'unconstitutional'). The next objective was to increase pressure on the General Council and develop the 'mass movement further'. The 'lessons of the past period' were that left unity was the 'key to advance' and that the Communist Party and the *Morning Star* had played an 'indispensable role ... (in) developing action and unity. It was our challenge that roused the movement, unified the workers and smashed the penal clauses'.[29]

The defeat of *In Place of Strife* had a much wider significance for the relationship between the Labour leadership and an increasingly militant trade union movement. Rank-and-file movements grew in confidence, and there was a wave of new wage demands from public sector employees between 1969 and 1970, and a strike at Fords which would have been unconstitutional had the bill become law. Trade union membership increased by 15 per cent between 1969 and 1970, particularly amongst less organised groups such as teachers, women and ancillary workers. Panitch argues that union leaders 'did not so much lead their members into the wage explosion of 1969-1970 as rush after them in the new militancy'.[30]

The unexpected election of the Conservative government in 1970 brought more challenges; it was a declared intention of Heath to introduce more legislation to deal with union militancy. His Industrial Relations Act (IRA), passed through a guillotine motion in 1971, re-introduced the cooling off period recommended by *In Place of Strife*, as well as compulsory strike ballots, with the added dimension of an Industrial Relations Court. The court would have the power to impose fines on unions if they took part in what was deemed to be 'unfair industrial practice'. Unions were expected to register with a new registrar of Trade Unions and Employer Associations.[31]

The TUC, backed by increasingly effective Ramelson-led industrial advisories, held rallies in January and February 1971, with a Special Congress in March at which unions were advised not to register, and to boycott the Industrial Relations Court. After the Bill became law in August 1971, the TUC's Annual Congress rejected the advice of the platform and voted to tell members to de-register. At the following year's TUC Congress some unions (COHSE, NUPE, Equity and the British Air Line Pilots Association) were expelled, while the Transport and General Workers Union was fined for contempt of court. Other unions, such as the railway workers, went on a 'work-to-rule' over the proposals. The biggest dispute, however, was over the Industrial Relations Court decision to gaol five dockers for an unofficial boycott of road haulage firms, in protest against 'containerisation', whereby unregistered dockers were stripping containers. The subsequent legal action under the new Industrial Relations Act, undertaken by Heaton's, a road haulage firm based in St Helens in Merseyside, led to the imprisonment of the dockers.[32]

The case of the 'Pentonville Five', three of whom were communists, precipitated the most serious antagonism between the unions and the government under the new legislation, with calls for a general strike unless they were released. For the Communist Party it was the high tide of its industrial influence. By July 1972, at an emergency Industrial Aggregate meeting of about sixty of the party's leading trade unionists called by Bert Ramelson, the instructions by the latter to put pressure on the TUC for a general strike were more than rhetoric. One of the key demands was the threat to close down Fleet Street by party print workers. Mike Power, a print worker who attended the meeting, recalls Ramelson instructing the print workers to close Fleet Street by the end of the day as a prelude to the more general stoppage, a general strike by the end of the week. Power described it as 'the apex of the Party's power': 'Bert knew what was achievable that day when he looked around the room'.[33] The LCDTU took swift action to organise solidarity in support of the gaoled dockers. According to McIlroy, 'CP members were instrumental in spreading stoppages to the national newspapers, engineering and building'.[34] The threat of a general strike was real enough to secure the release of the dockers.

The Heath government also saw the first national miners strike since 1926, with Arthur Scargill leading his workers to Saltley Gates in 1972, and there was a seven-week-long postal workers' strike in 1971; all these events, as well as the range of other actions taken against the IRA, made it clear that the main purpose of the IRA, namely to reduce the number of strikes, had failed abysmally. More days were lost to strikes in 1972 than at any time since 1926;[35] it was the most intense period of strike activity that had been seen for fifty years.[36] As Lyddon has argued, the 'Glorious Summer' of militancy saw unprecedented rank-and-file struggles, as well as specific forms of 'secondary' and 'flying' pickets, indicating the extent of solidarity, notably around the builders, dockers and miners struggles.[37] More industrial unrest over the controls on prices, via the Price Commission and pay board, and a limitation of wage increases to 7 per cent, led to more unrest, a further miners strike and the Three-Day Week (from December 1973), which culminated in the defeat of the Tory government in February 1974.[38]

ASSESSING THE PARTY'S IMPACT

The Communist Party played an important organisational role in the industrial struggles of the period. Crucial to its role throughout was sustaining the ideology of militant labourism. The main elements of this were, firstly, the party's defence of free collective bargaining in response to state intervention, driven by the idea that 'a fair day's pay' should be decided by voluntary bargaining processes. (This was at one level an attempt to re-establish the consensus of the 'golden age' of industrial relations that had existed until the 1960s, and which was therefore consistent, as Taylor has shown, with the mainstream approach of British trade unionism in the post-war period, defined by a consistent opposition to state involvement in union activities.[39]) This leads to the second element of this approach, that it depended upon reaching compromises between capital and labour – albeit without the aid of the state – a key feature of mainstream labourism. Its militant approach therefore was limited by these objectives, of 'brokering' capital-labour relations rather than contesting them. Thirdly, the militancy advocated by the Communist Party was constrained by the tactic of putting pressure on trade union hierarchies. This gave a particular meaning to Communist Party militancy. The militancy characteristic of militant labourism was a conditional one, of pressurising those in the leadership as much as organising those in the rank and file. Taylor writes: 'The Party opposes shop floor action in itself. Communists believe militant behaviour is a way of bringing pressure to bear on established union leaders and making them pursue policies that reflect the mood of the rank and file'.[40] Therefore it was the role of shop stewards in organising the Broad Lefts and influencing trade union and TUC leaderships that was the key, rather than organising the rank and file in defiance of leaderships. While the party remained active within rank-and-file movements, such as the builders unions where they helped to form the 'Building Workers' Charter' in alliance with the International Socialists in 1970, in the main their suspicion of rank-and-file movements increased during this period, leading to a denunciation of Trotskyist tactics at the Pilkington Glass strike in 1970.[41] Moreover the party's actions around *In Place of Strife* and the Industrial Relations Act had been organised with this in mind, and the successes of the campaign were regarded by party leaders as vindication of this strategy.

Critics from within the party pointed to the limitations of the strategy. One argument that had first developed in the Party Group, and which was central to the later Gramscian challenge, was that the party's approach was both defensive and 'economistic', in its emphasis on the battle over wages as the pre-condition *in itself* for political advance, with very little indication of how this would connect to wider political and social transformation. Criticisms from outside the party pointed to the conservatism of the party, arguing that its incorporation into the trade union and labour movement hierarchy meant the abandonment of a class position – a viewpoint characteristic of rival groups on the left, notably the International Socialists.[42]

Some sympathisers disputed the charge of economism, claiming that the party helped to politicise industrial struggles in new ways. One example was the Upper Clyde Shipbuilders dispute where, as Foster and Woolfson argue, the sit-in put on the agenda issues of ownership that provided a distinctive challenge to monopoly capitalism. In this case the struggle 'demonstrate[d] in embryo that the organised working class does indeed have the unique ability to unite in alliance against monopoly rule and, in doing so, generate ways to wider social transformation'.[43] This example, however, was an exceptional case of the party directing industrial action towards wider political and social transformation, which did not seem to depend on Labour Party or TUC benevolence. In the subsequent debates over workers control and in the disputes with its Gramscian wing, the party reverted to a defence of militant labourism in order to refute the arguments in favour of extending democracy to the workplace and other social spheres, whilst also defending free collective bargaining.

It would be inaccurate to describe the party's approach as 'economistic' in entirety. Party activists in trade unions adopted pragmatic and creative approaches to the very different conditions faced in different unions, without altering the party's dominant strategy of influencing the Labour Party through trade union pressure.

EXTENDING THE PARTY'S INFLUENCE IN THE UNIONS

The party leadership derived much confidence from its role in this unprecedented period of militancy. For Ramelson, the influence of the party in trade union affairs had never been greater: 'we have more influence now in the labour movement than at any time in the life of our party', he told Robert Taylor in January 1974.[44] The party influence continued at two levels: amongst the rank and file, instigating and organising the militancy; and at the more official level, where increasing respect within the trade union hierarchy was being achieved. In 1972, the TUC ended its ban on communists attending trades councils (which had stood for twenty-two years), and more conciliatory words were used for their work even among moderate trade union leaders. By 1974, 10 per cent of trade union officials were estimated to be in the CP. The party had six members on the NUM Executive (out of a total of 27), four members on the NUR and UPW Executives respectively, two on the UCATT Executive, and 10 members on the 38-strong TGWU Executive. The ASLEF President was a party member, and TASS was in the process of being communist-dominated, with Ken Gill its Secretary Designate. The NUT President, Max Morris, was also a communist, while arguably the party's most influential support was to be found behind Hugh Scanlon in the AUEW.[45]

Figures alone probably do not explain the extent of communist influence, given their behind the scenes organising abilities, the role of advisories in influencing candidate selection and promoting policy, and the tendency for communists to be trusted with key roles.[46] One example of this is the role of the *Morning Star* in the mainstream labour movement. As the only national newspaper to consistently carry sympathetic coverage of trade union issues, it became a vehicle not only of the more militant sections but of the more mainstream viewpoint. It was common practice during this time for *Morning Star* journalists – Mick Costello (the Industrial Editor and later Ramelson's successor as Industrial Organiser in 1978), Alan Brown and Charlie Brewster – to 'ghost-write' articles for leading trade unionists who wanted to preserve anonymity or didn't have time to do it themselves. This illustrated both the extent of access the party had to leading trade union opinion and the greater degrees of reciprocal trust. According to a *Morning Star* journalist who was employed during the peak period of militancy, 'the chances are that an article by a trade unionist in the 1960s and 1970s was ghost-written (by CP industrial organisers) … that was the way it was done'.[47]

Different researchers have drawn different conclusions about the extent of party influence in industrial politics in the 1970s. For Thompson, the lack of a strong independent political presence was reflected in what he saw as a 'marked break' with previous practice: party trade unionists were adopting a more supportive role in aiding workers in struggle, rather than 'instigating' struggle through political conviction and the imposition of party policies.[48] McIlroy, on the other hand, rejects this as: 'plainly mistaken': 'The party sought consistently to mobilise workers to take industrial action against state policies. It did so, however, on the basis of calculated, limited objectives, with caution and finesse, and through a series of interlocking dialogues between its militants on the ground and the Industrial Department which enabled it to select engagements with some prudence'.[49]

Anderson and Davey also argue that the party sought to go beyond a rank-and-file versus official leadership polarisation, and instead: 'concentrated on targeting/moving key people – senior shop stewards, union representatives and officials – these were allowed to operate autonomously from the party in most activities and getting candidates of the left (not necessarily CP members) elected as trade union leaders, executive members and delegates to union conferences'.[50] The picture which emerges is one of pragmatism and low-profile politics; the extent to which the party succeeded in political mobilisation must be doubted, though as the next section argues, it varied according to local union power struggles.

THE LIMITS OF PRAGMATISM: THE PARTY'S INFLUENCE IN THE TRADE UNION BROAD LEFTS

The industrial influence described so far in this chapter should not be seen as indicative of a stronger political strategy. Here the difference between 'influence' and control' is worth commenting on – best illustrated through the party's work on the ground within the Broad Lefts. Extensive recent research by McIlroy suggests that the role of the CPGB in trade union Broad Lefts was uneven. This strategy included supporting the moderate UPW leader Tom Jackson in the aftermath of the 1971 postal strike, despite the strike's defeat and no agreed pay rise; and support for the moderate David Basnett in his election for General Secretary of the General Municipal Workers Union in 1972. The relationship between the party and the Broad Left was also found to vary between different unions: in the National Union of Teachers the CP President Max Morris was regularly at odds with Broad Left policy; while, according to McIlroy, in the Transport and General Workers Union the CP was content to offer almost unconditional support for Jack Jones and his fellow leaders (though recent evidence suggests that even here there were underlying tensions on the ground in the attitude towards Jones).[51]

The point to be emphasised here is that the gains made by the party through stronger union networks did not result in a more coherent strategy. Paradoxically, the party's pragmatism, while crucial in extending party influence, allowed so many different local applications that any sense of strategic unity across the different unions was very difficult to achieve. This is apparent in McIlroy's case study of four trade unions. In the National Union of Mineworkers, for example, the CP was successful in holding together a 'national left coalition' from 1967, when Lawrence Daly (who had left the CP in 1956) defeated right-wing candidate Joe Gormley. In the subsequent alliances (which helped elect leaders like Mick McGahey and Arthur Scargill), the co-operation between Communist and Labour Party members was so close that political differences seemed to be of negligible importance.[52] A formidable alliance of Labour Left and communist trade union leaders was established, which also included Dai Francis, the CP's Welsh NUM General Secretary; Emlyn Williams, a leading figure on the Labour Left; and Jack Dunn, communist leader of the Kent miners.

In the Electricians Union (ETU), according to McIlroy, the situation was entirely different. Here, in the aftermath of the ballot-rigging scandal, there was much distrust of the CP, and its influence at the top was minimal. Its role was limited to a 'caucus' of individuals, devoid of even the rank-and-file role of attempting to change policy and elect representatives, confining itself instead to 'the building of a ginger group dedicated to democratisation and the search for allies across the broad spectrum'.[53] There was no detailed Broad Left programme and in this more hostile climate the CP's influence was much reduced; the union was dominated by a succession of right-wing anti-communist leaders, including the former communist Frank Chapple.[54]

Only in DATA/TASS (renamed AUEW TASS from 1970), where there had been a Broad Left movement since the 1940s, could the CP be described as exercising control rather than influence. In this union a stronger tradition of 'lay-member' democracy existed, which helped facilitate the election of communists to leading positions. Following Ken Gill's election as the first communist national official in 1968 (he

4. The CPGB's Industrial Strategy 1968–1974

became General Secretary of the union from 1974), the CP consolidated its support in the leadership by winning positions through a three-line party whip, by the gradual isolation of previous allies to the left of the CP, and by assimilating previously moderate opponents. While this resulted in a CP-dominated executive, to McIlroy it meant that the CP had put its own constraints on radicalism in controlling the Broad Left, leading to conflicts with the growing left opposition in the International Socialists.[55]

In the AEU, the CP adopted a position of total loyalty to Hugh Scanlon, whose election as President in 1967 came on the back of strong communist support (even in preference to a communist candidate, Reg Birch, a Maoist). Scanlon's election was seen by the party as a model victory for the Broad Left. This close co-operation meant that the AEU Broad Left did not have distinct policies from the union as a whole, and, according to McIlroy, CP activists were assimilated to such an extent that they offered no independent political position: a standpoint which endeared them to the official leadership in the propitious period of the early 1970s, but which made decline all the more severe when the breach took place with Scanlon over the Social Contract (when Scanlon joined Jack Jones in support of the Labour government's wage restraint policies).[56]

The diverse nature of communist activism in the different trade unions has several implications for any estimation of the role of the CP in industrial politics. Firstly, the creative and pragmatic initiatives communists took allowed them to sustain varying degrees of political influence in quite different settings, ranging from being the leading political force to the distrusted opposition. Thus whilst in general communists subscribed to common Broad Left initiatives in seeking to unite with the Labour Left and maintain influence on trade union leaderships, the different political traditions and balances of power within unions required 'complicated transactions' on the part of communists in order to retain any important role.[57] The pragmatism of communist activists, coupled with the versatility of Ramelson, was clearly an asset in the CP's increased influence with trade union leaderships, whilst it maintained – through the LCDTU in particular – a strong voice amongst the rank and file. One implication of this pragmatism for the party was further confirmation of the movement away from democratic centralism. Despite Ramelson's organisational abilities, and with the exception of TASS, after 1968, the complex situations in which the party found itself meant that it was in no position to enforce any centralised discipline or control.

However, this diversity and pragmatism accentuated the problems facing the party in its attempts to project an alternative political strategy. Sharing a similar labourist heritage to its allies on the Broad Left meant depending on trade union and Labour leaderships for recognition. At the same time, the schism between industrial and ideological politics, soon to develop into political differences from the mid-1970s, remained unaddressed, and, if anything, the success of the industrial wing and the autonomy given to Ramelson merely served to reinforce it. Despite continuous election campaigning, the party made no serious breakthroughs at the electoral level, and the industrial department remained the most significant force and public face of the party. Its influence in the unions did not bring significant new recruits to the party and, as party congress credentials continually indicated, much of the party trade union membership was ageing and not being replaced.[58] Factory branches, previously a core site of communist activity, continued to decline, while the party's links with the official mainstream meant that those seeking a more rank-and-fileist agitation were drawn to others on the left, such as the International Socialists.[59] The party was often caught between supporting unofficial disputes and attempting to win influence in the mainstream. The case of Des Warren, one of the 'Shrewsbury Three' building workers gaoled for carrying on unofficial strike action in breach of the Industrial Relations Act, is a case in point. Warren, a communist at the time of his imprisonment, felt let down by the party, claiming that the party was more concerned with maintaining its relations with the trade union hierarchy than fighting for the release of the pickets.[60]

THE CONSOLIDATION OF MILITANT LABOURISM: INDUSTRIAL STRATEGY MEETS POLITICAL STRATEGY

Despite these signs of decline, the party leadership was convinced that the strategy adopted under Ramelson since 1965 was correct, and was crucial to its overall political strategy. This was confirmed by a new statement of its political position, *Time To Change Course: What Britain's Communists Stand For*, written by Jack Woddis, the head of the party's international department. This document was perhaps also a reflection of its desire to refute the argument put forward by critics to its left, as well as dissidents within its own ranks, that it was becoming merely a left-wing pressure group for the Labour Party, and had lost its independent political identity. For fears that the party was having problems with its identity had surfaced despite its role in the new militancy. Even in the aftermath of its decisive intervention in the case of *In Place of Strife*, important questions – such as 'what is specific?' about the party's position and whether the party was 'stressing sufficiently our position' – were heard on leading committees.[61]

Time To Change Course was the first major political statement of the party's position since the revision of the *British Road To Socialism* in 1968, and was an attempt to reiterate the party's independent political position. Woddis saw the industrial advances as further justification of the 'correctness' of the party's strategy, and indicative of what he called a 'new mood abroad'.[62] He identified the 'new forms of struggle' generated by opposition to wage constraint as an indication of the possibilities of constructing an 'anti-monopoly alliance', the fundamental strategic goal of the party's overall strategy. The 'new forms' included direct action, occupations and demonstrations, which reached beyond traditional trade union tactics, and paved the way for more creative forms of struggle. Woddis identified new groups, including the low-paid and public sector workers – civil servants and teachers – that had 'displayed unprecedented militancy in their action for higher pay'.[63] The breadth of issues which the unions had been involved in encompassed Anti-Apartheid, the Vietnam War, and the Common Market, and this was an indication to Woddis of increased politicisation, while the Upper Clyde Shipbuilders work-in, in 1971-2, represented to Woddis a new type of struggle in Britain, which 'showed that the bosses could be defied': 'It revealed the great capacity of the workers to organise to practice operative democracy with themselves taking the major decisions in consultation with their elected shop stewards'.[64] Woddis went so far as to claim that the principle of work-ins and sit-ins 'helped to put over the view that socialism, as society run by the workers, is possible'.[65]

Woddis's arguments, however, confirmed adherence to the ideology of militant labourism in two further ways. Firstly, they reinforced the priority given to free collective bargaining, and opposition to incomes policies and legislation on trade union action.[66] Secondly, the shift to the left in the trade unions confirmed to Woddis that the forces needed to defeat the right-wing leadership were being developed by the party within the Broad Lefts, while the shift to the left in the Labour Party following its conference in 1972, evident in the early drafts of its election manifesto, meant 'a confirmation ... of the correctness of our policy and a success for our work in implementing it'.[67]

It was claimed that this closer working relationship with the Labour and trade union left did not represent a weakening of the party's independent political position. According to Woddis, the party still had a leading role, and he saw this progressing further through turning the different struggles into 'advances to challenge the political power of the ruling class'.[68] This would be achieved, according to Woddis, along the lines of 'an alternative programme' which, based on left unity arising out of 'further rises in the scale and purpose of the mass movement and a strengthening of the Communist Party', would include the ending of all wage restraint, strict price controls, free collective bargaining, and 'new types of nationalisation with measures of workers' control'.[69]

Despite Woddis's optimism over the party's impact, the ideological nature of the party's strategy remained ambiguous. The 'reformism' he condemned did not disguise the fact that the party's key demands themselves remained essentially reformist – such as the strengthening of free collective bargaining – while its leading role was heavily compromised by its need to influence the trade union hierarchy, a task which demanded tact and guile rather than confrontation. Ultimately it needed the respect of the trade union left, and its own objectives were therefore reliant on others' goodwill. Ramelson may have boasted that 'the party can float an idea early in the year and it can become official Labour Party policy in the autumn',[70] but there was no clear reason why people should join the Communist Party on the grounds of political conviction – rather than, for example, the Labour Party. This unresolved dilemma was evident at the 1973 party congress, which broadly reflected a triumphalist mood, due to the conviction that the party had been proved correct in its strategy. In his opening speech General Secretary Gollan argued that over the previous two years, 'as we forecast, class confrontation on an unprecedented scale has taken place'. 'As the Party of Marxism [we are] out to inject consistent socialist theory into the movement. Everything indicates our essential role'. He also asserted the need to 'end the grip of reformism over the British working class'. On the other hand, however, he saw prospects for closer collaboration with the Labour Left, in light of the publication of the 1974 Manifesto. Such gains in the Labour Party and 'a great strengthening of the CP', he said – despite falling membership since 1964 and dwindling electoral performances – 'are two sides of the same coin'.[71]

THE CONSERVATISM OF MILITANT LABOURISM

The leadership's belief in the correctness of the party's political and industrial strategy and its connection with the objectives of the *British Road To Socialism* and other strategic documents did not obscure the very different positions that could be found in the Communist Party in the 1970s, notably between the industrial struggles and student movements. Although these were the most productive areas of the party's work, there is very little evidence of any overlap between the two.

It is important to recognise at the same time that these divisions were beginning to reflect faultlines on the wider left, between on the one hand a second New Left – whose elements included opposition to the Vietnam War, the student and feminist movements, and new interests in Marxism – and on the other a labourism of which the industrial department of the Communist Party was the most militant expression.[72] The second New Left grew independently, owing little to developments in the Communist Party, unlike its predecessor that had grown in the aftermath of 1956. Moreover, it provided a further challenge to the Communist Party's status as the leading force to the left of Labour. Though the second New Left was made up of a disparate range of voices in Britain, it represented in theoretical terms an explicit rejection of the ideologies and strategies associated with labourism. It is not surprising, therefore, given the Communist Party's own 'labourist' leanings, that the party would become an object of its critique, while dissenting voices within it would seek a closer identification with the New Left. Two practical examples illustrate the strategic implications

4. The CPGB's Industrial Strategy 1968-1974

of this predicament: the party's consolidation of militant labourism in response to the arguments of the workers control movement, and its attempts to develop an alternative economic strategy.

The proposals set out by the Institute for Workers Control (IWC) were influential from the late 1960s as the New Left sought to develop alternative forms of working-class democracy. Indeed one observer went so far to argue that 'industrial democracy was to the 1970s what political democracy was to the 1870s'.[73] The interest in workers control reflected technological changes, the changing nature of the workforce, the growth of new social movements and the problems of democratic control and ownership that were features of corporatism. However, while the CPGB had an early commitment to 'industrial democracy' in the aftermath of war, and an early disaffection with nationalisation,[74] it was not until the 1960s that the arguments became a more familiar part of the left's agenda.[75] The main revival in arguments for workers control emerged after the setting up, in 1968, of the Institute for Workers Control, which had grown out of a series of annual workers control conferences that had taken place since 1964, gradually increasing in numbers and influence amongst trade unionists, academics and journalists. The range of issues taken up by the IWC was broad, and included industrial relations legislation, incomes policies, unemployment, productivity and bargaining.[76] The arguments put forward by the IWC and its supporters also raised questions of a 'pre-figurative' politics, in which immediate democratic and popular struggle would help determine the long-term character of an alternative socialist society.[77]

Such arguments, as will be shown in the next chapter, were to be popular with the Gramscians in the party during the re-writing of the BRS in 1976-1977. In the late 1960s, however, the Communist Party remained very sceptical of the IWC and its politics, at pains to point out that 'real' workers control could only be achieved in a socialist society. Crucially, however, the fundamental *strategic* questions that were raised by the IWC were rejected by the party in favour of more traditional forms of struggle – the extension of the power of shop stewards, the intensification of militancy on the wages front and the strengthening of bargaining structures. The party's position was made clear in a debate in the pages of *Marxism Today* in 1968-1969 between Bert Ramelson and Ken Coates and Tony Topham of the newly established IWC, in a discussion which impinged upon the wider theoretical and strategic debates that were beginning to take place on the left. Ramelson started by taking issue with the terminology, warning of the 'glib talk of workers control', a term which 'lacks reality and is incapable of being realised';[78] he preferred 'industrial democracy'. Ramelson saw such arguments as both utopian and 'defeatist', views which would fall victim to the 'traps set by the employers, the Establishment and some right-wing trade union leaders'. Terms like 'participation' and 'consultation' merely produced a 'facade to give the impression that workers' representatives at a number of levels have been party to decision-making'. While consultation could play a 'useful role' in shaping management policy, it was a 'dangerous pipe-dream to believe that the appointment or election of workers representatives ... to ... management would result in workers control so long as the property rights remain vested in the shareholders'.[79]

Ramelson's critique reflected the Communist Party's long-standing suspicion of groups to its left that it perceived as challenging its status, while his comments also reinforced elements of the party's core strategy. Strikes would remain the central way of advancing workers' rights and living standards, to be supplemented, he argued, by building the workplace organisation of shop stewards, and by increasing the information available to the workers through the opening of company records – though he remained sceptical of the 'utopian attitude' of those who advocated a complete 'opening the books' strategy. He cautiously accepted the proposal of workers being elected to boards of nationalised industries, though he did reject similar proposals for the private sector, on the basis that profit-seeking motives could only be challenged in this instance by 'strong trade union organisation and militant action'. Overall, the main contribution to increasing industrial democracy would come through traditional methods; for example 'a big recruitment drive to increase trade union membership'. Ultimately, for Ramelson, the interim measures of the IWC were 'no substitute for political action guided by a revolutionary political party aimed at securing political power for achieving the transformation of society, thus creating the conditions for a vast expansion of industrial democracy and the establishment of genuine workers control'.[80]

Though Ramelson's arguments were couched in radical language, they amounted to a defence of the traditional labourist bargaining strategies that the party had embarked upon under his leadership. It was this that Coates and Topham took issue with in their response, arguing that the existing economic and industrial context meant that the left and the labour movement had a 'simple option': either to 'respond defensively' to the attack by government and employers, or to provide 'positive alternative strategies in which the question of preserving and augmenting trade union powers and controls must figure at the very centre of concern'. The Ramelson strategy was overly defensive, and lacked analysis of the relations of power, or an advanced strategy for challenging 'managerial authority' and the 'powers of capital in the economy'. Workers control was more than a set of interim measures, as Ramelson claimed; it should be seen initially as encompassing a 'dual power' scenario, in which either the workers would take over the economy or the 'old establishment' would reassert its power. Workers control could become then a transitional strategy, in which 'hostile management' was controlled by workers' actions. While this might help to open doors to a new challenge to capital by labour, it was distinct, however, from 'self-management', a future form of socialised economy. Therefore the term 'workers control' had a much stronger meaning than 'industrial democracy', by virtue of its potentially 'hegemonic' force, one which encouraged 'the development of socialist consciousness [as] it challenges all the assumptions made within the system, and conveys a host of new possibilities to every worker who has it'. 'Like the idea of "black power" it brings not only self-respect, but the possibility of hegemonic thinking to a grouping which has tasted too much of subordination'.[81]

This led them to reject Ramelson's excessive reliance on traditional struggles. The wages struggle, they argued, was about 'control within capitalist society – on its own it does not comprehend the full significance of the relationship between ownership, control, the distribution of income and the nature of the product in the market economy'.[82] Workers control would also mean an end to sectionalism, as it would lead to unity between different unions and sections of the workforce. Ultimately, a workers control strategy was needed to go beyond the preservation of rights within a capitalist order, and the 'defensive postures which characterise simple resistance, resistance to incomes policies ... [and] legal restrictions on trade union rights'; a strategy was needed which represented an 'alternative line of advance', which would direct the escalation of resistance and allow it to 'break out' of the constraints of the capitalist system. The big question the IWC was putting forward was how to achieve the 'hegemonic' rule of the working class. It advocated winning hegemony for an alternative economy at the point of production, extending democracy to the economy as part of a prefigurative strategy towards socialism.[83]

The debates over workers control gathered momentum during the 1970s, and the profile of the IWC was raised by a series of disputes and workers' initiatives, such as those at the Upper Clyde Shipbuilders in 1971-72, and at Lucas Aerospace in 1977. And they had some practical influence: the radical Labour Manifesto of 1974 proposed legislation 'for a radical extension of industrial democracy in both the private and public sectors',[84] and this led to the publication of the *Bullock Report* in 1977, though the proposals were never taken seriously by the Labour government.[85]

The IWC debate illustrated some of the strategic weaknesses of the Communist Party, that were to become crucial as the Gramscians developed their critique: how could it prefigure an alternative social and economic system?; how could it develop an effective political strategy?; who would be its allies and how would they coalesce into a political bloc? These questions were discussed by the CPGB in the internal debates that were beginning to take place, but they also impinged on the general strategy of left advance in terms of the expectations of the 1974-1979 Labour governments.

THE CP, THE LABOUR LEFT AND THE ALTERNATIVE ECONOMIC STRATEGY

The Communist Party's continued belief in its own industrial strategy, which led it to officially reject the workers control movement, despite some support from its ranks,[86] was given an added significance in the circumstances surrounding the defeat of the Heath government in 1974. This was a defeat which confirmed the impact of the new militancy: Heath took on the miners and lost; his industrial relations strategy was in ruins, and he lost the ultimate battle of 'who rules Britain'. There is disagreement among historians over the extent of possibility for left advance during this period, though there is general agreement that the British state was undergoing a 'hegemonic crisis', in which popular consent for consensus politics was beginning to break down, and the existing ideological and social norms were being called into doubt.[87] For many on the left at the time there was the hope that the new militancy would lead to big shifts in the balance of power: that for the first time left-led trade unions would be major players in the incoming Labour government, and that Wilson would not be able to retreat to his industrial policies of the past.

The new militancy had been accompanied by radical policy shifts in the Labour Party between 1971 and 1973. These included (at the 1971 Labour Party Conference) commitments to 'nationalisation without compensation'; the 'integration' (effectively abolition) of private schools; an 'end' to private practice within the NHS; public ownership of banking, insurance and building societies, the building industry and North Sea Oil; and opposition to Britain's membership of the 'Common Market'.[88] Revisionist figures such as Shirley Williams became isolated, and the rise of Tony Benn as unofficial leader of the left was confirmed (along with the first instance of the term 'Bennery'), as the latter identified himself with the new radical agendas. It was Benn who argued, in closing the debate on industrial policy at the Labour Party Conference of 1973, that the next period of government would be different from the past: 'the crisis that we inherit when we come to power will be the occasion for fundamental change and not the excuse for postponing it'.[89] It was one of Benn's allies, however – Stuart Holland – who was the most influential in shifting Labour's industrial strategy to the left. As a member of Labour's Industrial Policy Committee, Holland had prepared a 15,000-word document which set out the future Labour government's commitment to planning. The document, entitled *Labour's Programme For Britain* (1972), called for firms to be required to submit details of their projects, finances and general objectives. This was followed by the decision to set up a National Enterprise Board, which would have the power to buy the controlling interests in profitable firms. The same conference also voted to boycott the European Parliament. Taken together, these proposals on paper meant that Labour's 1974 manifesto was its most radical ever.[90]

These proposals brought the Labour Party close to the political positions advocated by the Communist Party, and increased the feeling amongst the party leadership that it was having an impact on mainstream Labour opinion in line with the BRS – which also argued for large-scale nationalisation, redistributive taxation and major public investment programmes. The term 'Alternative Economic Strategy' (AES) has been used to describe these common programmes, and its main features were: advocacy of a major redistribution of wealth; a commitment to substantial nationalisation; support for economic planning; opposition to the Common Market; and support for import controls, price freezes and the expansion of public spending. However, all opportunity for cementing this militant labourist consensus was to end abruptly, long before the TUC finally adopted the AES at its Congress in 1977.[91] Divisions over the Social Contract had the consequence of destroying the militant labourist consensus between the communists and Labour Left, and of deepening differences within the CP itself.

BATTLES FROM WITHIN: DIVISIONS OVER ECONOMIC AND INDUSTRIAL STRATEGY EMERGE

Until 1974, events had done nothing to divert the CP from its strategic objectives. Its strategy remained focused on the immediate objectives of defeating trade union legislation and opposing incomes policies. However, the election of the new Labour government in 1974, and the debates over its programme, began to raise questions within the party over what its own strategy should be, including its relationship with the Labour Left – particularly now that the latter was making inroads within the Labour Party.[92] These strategic questions were given their first significant critical hearing on the party's Economic Committee, which was chaired by Ramelson and composed of leading party trade unionists and party economists, including a younger group around Bill Warren, Pat Devine and Dave Purdy – some of whom had already voiced concerns about labourism from their time in the Party Group.

The focus for the disputes over strategy on the Economic Committee centred on the party's analysis of the causes and consequences of the emerging critical economic condition of Britain. This included above all the causes of inflation and the emerging crisis, which had provided the economic rationale for the party's industrial and political strategy. From the minutes of the Economic Committee Meetings between 1973 and 1975, the dominant view was that wage increases played a minor, if any, part, in the causes of inflation. Instead inflation was the result of a combination of 'external' (world) and 'internal' (British) aspects of a world capitalist crisis. The external factors included the collapse of the international monetary system of fixed exchange rates and the ensuing economic instability between capitalist countries, the sharp increases in world prices of food, raw materials and particularly oil (between 1972 and 1974), and the rise in power of the multinationals, which led to increases in monopoly. The domestic factors included the devaluation of the pound in 1967, a low growth rate, due to under-capacity production, and, it was argued, the lowest rate of investment and the highest interest rates in the western world.[93]

'It is the combination of all these factors added to the general ones', wrote Ramelson, 'which is responsible for the British inflationary rate being higher than in many other countries'. It wasn't that wage demands were leading to price increases but, according to Ramelson, 'by and large, wages have been chasing prices', while money wages had risen more slowly than the rate of productivity and therefore 'could not have been the cause of rising prices'.[94]

This economic analysis clearly impinged on and served to justify the party's political and industrial strategy, which resisted any attempts to impose incomes policies. There was, however, a rival interpretation that was being developed by younger members of the party's Economic Committee (in addition to Warren, Devine and Purdy, it included Mike Prior, an associate of Warren and, like the latter, a member of the Smith Group in the late 1960s). This group located the causes of inflation within a different analytical framework. It was an alternative view (referred to as the 'conflict position' in the Economic Committee minutes), which took as its starting point the change in the balance of forces between capital and labour. According to this position there were three processes that were responsible for the economic conflicts characterising Britain at the time. Firstly, the Keynesian policies of the post-war period, which had led to new economic and social stability until the early 1960s, had reached a situation by the late 1960s in which the state's ability to exercise control over the economy was weakening, resulting in major conflicts over the allocation of resources between workers, capitalists and government over levels of investment and productivity. Secondly, the working class, through trade union bargaining power, had won a greater measure of control over money wages, which had risen at a faster rate than productivity: 'a situation which must inevitably either lower profit margins or cause price rises'.[95] Two main effects of the increase in the bargaining power of the trade unions were apparent, namely that money wages were increasing every year, and governments had to commit themselves to increasing amounts of welfare expenditure. Therefore they rejected the view that arms expenditure, for example, was a more important variable than wage demands in the causes of inflation. Thirdly, it was apparent that these were conflicts which were becoming increasingly fought out over wages. The dual consequences of strong trade unions and 'low productivity growth' had led to inflation, which should now be recognised as the primary economic and social problem of the contemporary class struggle. Inflation was not therefore the outcome of one particular variable.

This led the authors to conclude, controversially, that 'the pressure for increased wage demands put forward by a working class freed from the constraint of endemic unemployment is the only consistent explanation for the emergence of *persistent* (their emphasis) inflation as the major economic problem of modern capitalism'.[96]

This position was clearly at odds with official CP policy, and led to major debates on the Economic Committee. The debate found its way into a prolonged discussion in *Marxism Today* between December 1973 and August 1975, which encapsulated growing differences.[97] It also had clear implications for the argument over the merit of incomes policies, thus raising questions over the party's industrial and economic strategy, making it the first serious critique from within the party itself. Indeed for Purdy and Prior in particular it was to be the basis of an extended critique of economism which became a core element of the Gramscian alternative discussed in the next chapter. Moreover, the differences began to reflect political debates on the wider left at this time over the proposed Social Contract, in which the coalition between the CP and the trade union left, which had been so effective in opposing trade union legislation, began to break down over what the Labour strategy should be in government.

BATTLES FROM WITHOUT: THE SPLIT OVER THE SOCIAL CONTRACT

As we have seen, the position of strength on the left meant that the relationship between the Labour Party and the unions increasingly followed a distinctively radical agenda. Here, the key question for those on the left was how to translate these shifts into a radical industrial policy. The Labour Party had set up its own Liaison Committee, through which it was hoped that agreement with the unions could be reached. The committee included six representatives each from the NEC, PLP and TUC General Council. It was in these meetings that the Social Contract was conceived. Agreement on repeal of the Heath Industrial Relations Act, and the need for price controls, planning, and the redistribution of wealth had been reached already; but a consensus on incomes was more problematic – for recent historical reasons – and, amidst the prevailing economic climate, this was to be the crucial policy area.

Jack Jones had set in motion the idea for a strategy of what he called 'voluntary conciliation and arbitration'.[98] This would be achieved through an agency – later known as ACAS – which would remain independent of government. Jones argued that, to be acceptable to all sides, the strategy must be seen to address the problem of inflation, while at the same time remain opposed to statutory incomes policies. This proposal, which was first officially mooted at the Labour Party NEC in February 1973, was taken to the Liaison Committee, and, in return for commitment to left policies, was agreed formally at the TUC Congress of 1974, following a motion moved by AUEW (TASS). The motion incorporated 'eight points' for radical social change, including the extension of public ownership, a large-scale redistribution of wealth, the control of company profits, and the 'halting of capital exports'. It also supported the setting up of a National Enterprise Board with responsibility for planning agreements. The reference to pay claims was limited to the view that unions would make moderate pay demands in return for these socio-economic reforms.

Thus the Social Contract from its formation incorporated an element of pay restraint. Cuts in pay were not envisaged; the idea was for voluntary restraint in exchange for other radical, social and economic programmes, while also allowing greater support for lower paid workers. In theory this was a qualitatively different agreement from that which underpinned earlier incomes policies. As Graham Taylor wrote four years later:

> Normally, a promise of pay restraint by the TUC would be seen by the establishment as a helpful move towards higher profitability for British industry and towards social harmony via class collaboration. In this case, however, because of the high pitch of militancy throughout the trade union movement the TUC had secured as its quid pro quo nothing less than the dreaded 'Bennery'. Moreover to rub salt in the wound, the TUC was being promised public ownership without any commitment to cut the living standards of the workers.[99]

Stuart Holland saw the Social Contract as a means with which to challenge the 'commanding heights' of the economy, and to enable the transformation of the class structure through the transfer of elements of economic control to the working class:

> It will only be through the negotiated and bargained support of the trade union movement that such critical change will prove to be possible. If it is to be effective, such bargaining and such negotiation must involve a new dimension to the relationship between the Labour Party and the labour movement, backed by new means for widening the effective control of working people over the main strategy for social and economic transformation. This means not only a Social Contract in the sense of agreement as the main strategy for transformation of British capitalism, negotiated between government and the unions at the national level, but also a spearheading of means for working people either to control their own companies outright, or to take part in a process of national bargaining as the contribution which their firms should make both to themselves and to society as a whole.[100]

Holland emphasised the 'wide-reaching dimensions to the social contract'. Moreover he likened the 'pre-agreement' involvement of the working class to Rousseau's social contract, in which the people would enter into negotiations and seek agreement with the legislator on the organisation of society and in the process enhance individual freedom and democracy. Essentially, Holland argued, *'the Social Contract must be a contract for a socialist programme'* (his emphasis).[101]

In its origins, therefore, it was clear that the Social Contract was conceived from a position of left-wing advance, consistent with other policy gains won by the Labour Left, and representing an opening for fundamental shifts in the balance of power towards the working class. For left-wing trade union leaders it was an indication of how to use their recent strength and consolidate the gains of the new militancy.

For the Communist Party, however, and for Bert Ramelson in particular, the Social Contract represented a challenge to the party's industrial and economic strategy since 1965, when it had set out its opposition to incomes policies and all forms of government interference with trade unions. Ramelson was in no doubt about the need to oppose the Social Contract, even if it meant a rift between himself and his allies in the trade unions, notably Jones and Scanlon. The Social Contract, he argued, represented a 'negation' of free collective bargaining, as it involved the imposition of frameworks of wage-bargaining that were defined by others, notably government. Unlike Jack Jones and other left supporters of the Social Contract, he saw no essential difference, in the consequences for workers' living conditions, between statutory and voluntary incomes policies. His argument was that there should be no government involvement in any bargaining arrangements. He saw in the Social Contract the old revisionist politics of 'trying to solve the crisis of capitalism by cutting the workers' living standards',[102] and the betrayal of the rank and file by the leadership. Moreover the Social Contract was 'preparing the ground' for statutory or compulsory incomes policies.[103] Nor did Ramelson accept the view of 'equal sacrifices', with better-paid workers holding back on wage demands to enable the low-paid to pursue increases. This would mean that better-off workers, rather than the bosses, paid for pay rises. Defeating the Social Contract, then, was essential in providing left directions for the Labour Party. The 'alternative policy' Ramelson outlined must start with 'the recognition that the problems stem from the contradictions of capitalism and their solution, therefore, cannot be sought in policies which shy away from measures which interfere with the basic power structures of capitalism as the Social Contract does'.[104] His policy proposals included the end to foreign debt; halt in military expenditure at home and abroad; import controls; price freezes, 'to halt inflation for six months'; the 'state take-over' of monopolies; and the expansion of demand by increases in wages and welfare spending. According to Ramelson, this was 'an alternative policy that could tackle inflation and secure jobs; it is a programme which, while tackling immediate problems, also challenges the power of the monopolies'.[105]

The Social Contract therefore brought to an end the alliance that had existed between Ramelson, Jones and Scanlon. 'Get out of my union', Jones is reported to have said to Ramelson at this time.[106] It also meant the beginning of the demise of the party's influence for, as we have seen, it had maximised its resources into sustaining a close relationship with the same left trade union leaders who were the architects of the contract. This was the signal for the decline in the party's organised militancy. The LCDTU had dwindled to less than 100 delegates by the time of its 1974 Conference, and now had no clear role to play.[107] The dilemmas can be illustrated through the predicaments facing Ken Gill, the party's leading trade unionist in 1974. As the Marx Memorial Lecturer in March of that year, he had used the occasion to vindicate the party's industrial strategy as amounting to a 'consistent Marxist lead in struggle', and had welcomed the 'ideological leadership provided by the Marxists' (i.e. the CP) in the miners strike of that time.[108] By the end of the summer however, Gill found himself at the TUC withdrawing the TASS motion which, in line with CP policy, had been critical of the Social Contract, in order to placate Hugh Scanlon, for the benefit of facilitating the merger of AUEW/TASS. Thus, as McIlroy asks: 'If the CP could not motivate its own leading members, how could it influence those independent of it?'.[109]

Notes
1. Nina Temple, the party's last Secretary, confirmed this to the author; George Matthews, custodian of the party archives, interview with author. The reasons given by both were concerns over security for individuals still active in trade unions.
2. This work stands alone in the depth and range of its investigation into the party's industrial work. Initially this research can be found in J. McIlroy and A. Campbell, 'The Communist Party and Industrial Politics 1964-1975', a conference paper presented to 'British Trade Unions: Workers' Struggles and Economic Performance' held at the University of Warwick 19-20 September 1997. Subsequently John McIlroy has developed and adapted this material for 'Notes on the Communist Party and Industrial Politics' in J. McIlroy, A. Campbell and N. Fishman (eds), *British Trade Unions and Industrial Politics* Volume 2, Ashgate 1999.
3. For example Robert Taylor's *The Trade Union Question in British Politics* (Blackwell 1993), while a useful overview of British trade unionism, carries no discussion of the role the CP played in the important industrial struggles of the 1970s.
4. J. McIlroy and A. Campbell: 'The Communist Party and Industrial Politics 1964-1979', University of Warwick, op cit, pp4-10.
5. For a good discussion of the extent of strike activity and its political impact during this period see J. Kelly, *Trade Unions and Socialist Politics*, Verso 1988, pp104-114.
6. EC minutes show this consistently during the period.
7. Gerry Pocock, former Assistant Industrial Organiser, interview with author.
8. M. Prior interview with author.

4. The CPGB's Industrial Strategy 1968–1974

9. According to Newton, from his interviews with party members, this demarcation was already in place by the early 1960s. See K. Newton, *The Sociology of British Communism*, op cit. However it was not until the later period that it became an issue for the party leadership. At the EC meeting in September 1969, for example, David Bowman, a leading party member in the National Union of Railwaymen, was alarmed about the schism between the trade union and political identities of members, commenting that in his experience communists were accepted on the basis of their work as trade unionists rather than their politics. He also felt that the party was getting too close to the Labour Party. He left the party a year later and went on to become NUR President. See R. Falber, 'handwritten notes of EC Discussion', September 1969.
10. See N. Fishman, *The Communist Party and the Trade Unions 1933-45*, op cit; N. Fishman, 'No Home but the Trade Union Movement: Communist Activists and "Reformist" Leaders 1926-1956', in G. Andrews et al (eds), *Opening the Books*, op cit, pp102-123.
11. Factory branches continued to decline from 1962, despite attempts held at different times to rebuild them, through factory and workplace branch conferences and priorities identified by the EC and PC. This picture can be pieced together from available documents in CP/CENT/IND/1//2/3. Reports of the Factory Branch conference in 1966 can be found at CP/CENT/ORG/3. The factory branch conference in 1976 is at: CP/LON/BRA/1/ and CP/CENT/ORG/3/1. See also J. McIlroy 'Notes on the Communist Party and Industrial Politics', op cit, pp221-222.
12. For evidence of the rise of the IS membership during this period see J. Kelly, *Trade Unions and Socialist Politics*, op cit, p114; J. McIlroy, 'Always Outnumbered; Always Outgunned' in J. McIlroy et al (eds), *British Trade Unions and Industrial Politics*, op cit.
13. This critique came from two quite different sources – the Smith (later Party) Group and the leadership of the Surrey and Hants & Dorset Districts. For a critical contribution of the leading member of the Smith Group see Bill Warren, 'The British Road to Socialism', *New Left Review* 63 Sept-Oct 1970, pp27-41. For a discussion of the origin of the Smith Group see G. Andrews, 'Young Turks and Old Guard: Intellectuals and the Communist Party leadership in the 1970s', in G. Andrews et al (eds) *Opening the Books*, op cit; Mike Prior papers.
14. B. Ramelson interview with L. Panitch, in *Social Democracy and Industrial Militancy*, Cambridge University Press 1976, p57.
15. For example Ken Brett, Bob Wright and Les Dixon: J. McIlroy, 'Notes on the Communist Party and Industrial Politics', op cit, p234.
16. Ibid, pp221, 244.
17. See 'Notes For a Meeting to be Held on 26th September 1966' in Ramelson Papers, CP Archive. The vote in favour of Scanlon was 24-16; J. McIlroy; 'Notes on the Communist Party and Industrial Politics', op cit, p234.
18. The party had previously incurred criticism from within its own ranks for supporting the non-communist Jack Tanner of the AEU during the 1920s and 1930s. For Scanlon's own views on militancy following his election see 'The Role of Militancy', interview with Hugh Scanlon, *New Left Review* 46, 1967.

19. J. McIlroy, 'Notes on the Communist Party and Industrial Politics', op cit, p221. See also J. McIlroy and A. Campbell, 'Organising the Militants: the Liaison Committee for the Defence of Trade Unions 1966-1979', *British Journal of Industrial Relations*, 3, 9, 1 1999.
20. J. McIlroy, 'Notes on the Communist Party and Industrial Politics', op cit, pp244-245.
21. For figures of factory branch membership see CP/CENT/ORG.
22. See D. Lyddon, 'Glorious Summer: 1972; the High Tide of Rank and File Militancy', in J. McIlroy, N. Fishman and A. Campbell (eds), *British Trade Unions and Industrial Politics*, op cit, p326.
23. See for example: K. Middlemass, *Politics in Industrial Society*, Andre Deutsch 1979; T. Benn, *Arguments For Democracy*, Jonathan Cape 1981, pp156-158.
24. D. Sassoon, *One Hundred Years of Socialism*, op cit, pp374-375.
25. According to Sassoon, Britain, unlike other countries, resorted to incomes policies because of its dependence on 'export-led' priorities, while the centralised nature of the trade union movement (based on occupation rather than political affiliation) could be used to impose wage restraint across the board: D. Sassoon, *One Hundred Years of Socialism*, op cit, p367. In Italy and France, where the different union federations were weaker and less cohesive, other anti-inflationary measures such as fiscal or monetary strategies were adopted. See also G. Bedani, *Politics and Ideology in the Italian Workers Movement*, Berg 1995, pp197-208.
26. W. Thompson, *The Long Death of British Labourism*, Pluto Press 1993, p78.
27. For a discussion of the Donovan Report, see K. Coates and T. Topham, *The New Unionism: The Case For Workers' Control*, Penguin 1974, pp208-211; and D. Baines and E. Reid, *Governments and Trade Unions*, Heinemann 1980.
28. J. R. Campbell, 'The Delusions of Donovan', *Marxism Today* 1968. For a critical discussion of the implications of the Donovan Report see also K. Coates and T. Topham, *The New Unionism: The Case For Workers' Control*, Penguin 1974, pp208-211; and D. Baines and E. Reid, *Governments and Trade Unions*, op cit.
29. All these comments can be found in the EC notes of September 1969, under 'Notes For Introductory Speech on Trade Union Resolution', unsigned but Ramelson, CP/CENT/EC/13/20.
30. L. Panitch, *Social Democracy and Industrial Militancy*, op cit, p218.
31. For a fuller discussion of Heath's Industrial Relations Act, see H. Pelling, *A History of British Trade Unionism*, 4th edition, Macmillan 1987, pp283-300.
32. The Pentonville Five case is discussed at length in F. Lindop, 'The Dockers and the 1971 Industrial Relations Act Part 1; Shop stewards and Containerisation', *HSIR* Spring 1998; B. Weekes, M. Mellish, L. Dickens and J. Lloyd, *Industrial Relations and the Limits of Law*, Blackwell 1975; D. Lyddon, 'Glorious Summer; 1972 the High Tide of Rank and File Militancy', op cit.
33. M. Power interview with author.
34. J. McIlroy, op cit, p239. See also CP/LON/IND/2/10, 'Notes of emergency industrial aggregate', 23 July 1972.
35. H. Pelling, *A History of British Trade Unionism*, op cit, p287, cites the figure of 24 million days.

36. See for example J. Cronin, *Labour and Society in Britain 1918-1979*; J. Hinton, *Labour and Socialism; A History of the British Labour Movement 1867-1974*, Wheatsheaf Books 1983, pp195-196; D. Lyddon, 'Glorious Summer: 1972; The High Tide of Rank and File Militancy', op cit, p326.
37. D. Lyddon, 'Glorious Summer', op cit.
38. For Ramelson's critique see *Smash Phase III*, Communist Party pamphlet, CPGB 1973.
39. R.Taylor, *The Fifth Estate: Britain's Unions in the Modern World*, Pan Books 1980.
40. Ibid, p124.
41. J. McIlroy, 'Notes on the Communist Party and Industrial Politics', op cit, pp339-341.
42. See for example D. Hallas, 'The CP, the SWP and the Rank and File Movement', *International Socialism*, 1:95. For a critique of the IS/SWP see J. Bloomfield, 'The Myth of Rank and Fileism', *Comment*, 30 November 1974; G. Roberts, 'The Strategy of Rank and Fileism', *Marxism Today*, December 1976.
43. J. Foster and C. Woolfson, *The Politics of the UCS Work-In*, Lawrence and Wishart 1986, p19. See also W. Thompson and F. Hart, *The UCS Work-In*, Lawrence and Wishart 1972.
44. R. Taylor, 'Reds Under the Bed', *New Society*, 17.1.74.
45. This evidence is cited in a variety of sources – see: J. McIlroy, 'Notes on the Communist Party and Industrial Politics', op cit; R. Taylor, *The Fifth Estate*, op cit, p122. See also J. Lloyd, 'All Together Now', *London Review of Books*, Vol 22 No 20, 19 October 2000.
46. *The Needs of the Hour*, an instruction bulletin issued by Ramelson and distributed to party trade unionists, was also a regular method of sustaining the Party's network of influence.
47. C. Myant interview with author.
48. W. Thompson, *The Good Old Cause*, op cit, p136.
49. J. McIlroy, 'Notes on the Communist Party and Industrial Politics', op cit, p243.
50. P. Anderson and K. Davey, '"Moscow Gold?" The True Story of the Kremlin, British Communism and the Left', *New Statesman and Society*, 7 April 1995.
51. J. McIlroy, 'Notes on the Communist Party and Industrial Politics', op cit, p26. Recent evidence from the Public Records Office, released in January 2001, suggests party shop stewards in the TGWU were split on whether to support Jones in calling off the National Dock Strike for 13 July 1970. 'The Party will not find it easy to reconcile the stewards to Jones policy', according to the Security Service report – in all probability the work of a 'mole'. The *Morning Star* editorial of 15 July was said to be 'the subject of much anxious consideration'. Details can be found at Pro.gov.uk PREM/15.92.
52. J. McIlroy, 'Notes on the Communist Party and Industrial Politics', op cit, pp228-230. See also V. Allen, *The Militancy of British Miners* (1981) for an account of Communist-Labour alliance in the NUM in the 1970s.
53. J. McIlroy, 'Notes on the Communist Party and Industrial Politics', op cit, p231.
54. Ibid, pp230-231.

55. Ibid, pp231-233. For a critique of TASS from the left in this period, see B. Parkin, 'The Broad Left in TASS', *International Socialism* 74, January 1975.
56. J. McIlroy, 'Notes on the Communist Party and Industrial Politics', op cit, pp233-236.
57. Ibid, p236.
58. Congress Reports for 1973, 1975 show an ageing membership of trade union delegates.
59. For details of the Party's declining factory branches nationally see CP/CENT/IND/1/3 and CP/CENT/ORG/3/1. Details of district factory branch activity is mainly confined to London and can be found at CP/LON/BRA/1/8. It is important to bear in mind also that the communist influence was in particular unions with particular strongholds, such as engineering unions in Sheffield and Manchester, Upper Clyde shipbuilding, the Welsh area of the NUM, British Leyland at Birmingham and Fords at Dagenham, and the building industry in London and Birmingham. See J. McIlroy, 'Notes on the Communist Party and Industrial Politics', op cit, p237. In the emerging white-collar unions such as NUPE and the CPSA, the party remained on the periphery, while its activists in the NUT began to be outflanked by the rise of the IS and other Trotskyist groups. See J. McIlroy, 'Always Outnumbered, Always Outgunned: the Trotskyists and the Trade Unionists', in J. McIlroy et al, *British Trade Unions and Industrial Politics*, op cit, pp259-296, for an extended discussion of Trotskyist influence in trade unions in the 1970s.
60. See D. Warren, *The Key to My Cell*, New Park Publications 1982. Warren, the only communist of the three gaoled and who spent two years in prison, argued that the party could have led the resistance but that he received no 'real backing'. 'I wanted to fight but the Party couldn't or wouldn't tell me how and I was thrown back on my own resources' (p149). He wrote a pamphlet which the party refused to publish or review in the *Morning Star*. After leaving the CP he joined the Workers Revolutionary Party.
61. This critique was articulated by critics from different sections of the party. Bill Warren and Mike Prior of the Smith Group (later Party Group) first outlined the lack of theoretical rigour in arguments in circulated documents within the group. See also B. Warren, 'The British Road to Socialism', *New Left Review* 63, September-October 1970. The Surrey and Hants and Dorset Districts submitted regular critiques of the party's political direction – in particular the contrast between its industrialism and its electoralism and the decline of factory branches.
62. J. Woddis, *Time To Change Course: What Britain's Communists Stand For*, CPGB 1973, p119.
63. Ibid.
64. Ibid, p102.
65. Ibid, p103.
66. Ibid, p33. Democracy itself, despite the support for the UCS approach, was also still seen in a narrow context, conceived essentially in class terms. The fight for greater democracy was a class act carried out by the working class in mass struggle.
67. Ibid, p110.
68. Ibid, p121.

69. Ibid, p127.
70. R. Taylor, 'Reds Under the Bed', op cit.
71. J. Gollan, Introductory speech to Congress, reprinted in *Comment*, November 1973.
72. For development of the 'second' new left see: P. Sedgewick, 'The Two New Lefts', in D. Widgery (ed), *The Left in Britain 1956-1968*, Penguin 1976; R. Archer et al (eds), *Out of Apathy: Voices of the New Left Thirty Years On*, Verso 1989; L. Chun, *The British New Left*, op cit, pp60-93.
73. T. Forrester, 'Whatever Happened to Industrial Democracy', *New Society*, 17.7.80. Workers control and related ideas also had a wide influence in other European countries, including Sweden. See D. Sassoon, *One Hundred Years of Socialism*, op cit, pp374-5.
74. K. Morgan, *Against Fascism and War*, op cit, p175.
75. The first New Left in Britain, in contrast to mainstream labourism, had a strong commitment to workers control on the grounds that arguing in its favour provided an important opportunity to break down barriers between political and industrial sections of the labour movement; it would also give the trade unions a broader political role in extending democracy across civil society, and in the furtherance of socialist aims in a practical way. Much of this interest in workers control had developed in the debate over modernisation under the Wilson government, where such initiatives were seen as an attempt to project an alternative view of modernity. They did have some immediate political influence through the submission of a document on democracy and industry which was adopted in a much watered down version by Labour's Home Policy Committee in 1960. See M. Kenny, *The First New Left*, op cit, pp135-136. The undiluted New Left version appeared as 'Anon', 'Missing Signposts', *New Left Review* 12 1961. Lin Chun also identifies workers control as one of the defining features of the New Left in *The British New Left*, op cit, p117. Beyond the New Left, workers control also found support amongst the small British and Irish Communist Organisation (BICO), where it featured regularly in the organisation's journal, *Problems of Communism*, during the mid 1970s. See *What Workers Control is About*, British and Irish Communist Organisation 1977. Prominent Labour figures like Arthur Scargill also supported the movement.
76. Richard Hyman has described the purposes of the IWC as threefold: to make available company information to the workers on the basis that this was part of industrial democracy; to campaign for trade union representation in management decision-making structures though maintaining that the difference between this form of 'participation' and 'control' should be recognised; and thirdly to argue for the 'control bargain', a term used by IWC leaders to describe a counter-offensive to the management's 'productivity bargain', and an attempt to turn the agenda towards challenging areas of managerial authority in the pursuit of an 'equality of status'. See R. Hyman, 'Industrial Conflict and the Political Economy', *Socialist Register*, Merlin Press 1973.
77. See L. Chun for a discussion of the relationship between the New Left and Workers Control in *The British New Left*, op cit, pp122-123.
78. B. Ramelson, 'Workers Control? Possibilities and Limitations', *Marxism Today*, October 1968.

79. Ibid.
80. Ibid.
81. T. Topham and K. Coates, 'Discussion Contribution on Workers' Control', *Marxism Today*, January 1969.
82. Ibid.
83. Such a position can be traced back to Gramsci's early writings where he focused on how the working class could begin to create their own forms of social ownership and organisation, leading to the development of an alternative state structure. A. Gramsci, *Selections From Political Writings 1910-1920*, Lawrence and Wishart 1977, pp65-69.
84. Quoted in T. Forrester, op cit.
85. The Bullock Report had its declared intention as 'putting the relationship between capital and labour on a new footing', through elected representatives to a single-channel system of representation and accountability. However, as Forrester records, in response to the efforts of Prime Minister Callaghan and his minister Edmund Dell, this became watered down in the Industrial Democracy white paper; this put forward 'joint representation committees', in which the workforce would have only one third of the seats on a supervisory board. The Communist Party submitted evidence to the report which reflected Ramelson's earlier misgivings; namely that 'full workers control can only be developed in a socialist society', while it maintained an unwavering emphasis on free collective bargaining as the key element of industrial democracy: 'we ... see the major advance in industrial democracy coming through the further development of collective bargaining, with all major decisions being the subject of mutuality'. Evidence to the Committee of Inquiry on Industrial Democracy, CPGB February 1976, p3.
86. Documents circulated within the Party Group implied support for the IWC.
87. See S. Hall et al, *Policing the Crisis*, op cit.
88. The party played a strong role in the 'No' campaign. Though there was some disquiet amongst some Gramscians, this did not develop into a sustained critique at the time. Material on the party's role in the 'No' campaign can be found in EEC box files in CP Archive.
89. Quoted in D. Howell, *British Social Democracy*, Croom Helm 1976, p299.
90. For a discussion of Labour's policy shifts at this time see M. Hatfield, *The House the Left Built*, The Garden City Press Ltd 1978; D. Howell, *British Social Democracy*, op cit, pp287-234.
91. Following a motion moved by Ken Gill, cited in F. Beckett, *Enemy Within*, op cit, p182.
92. David Howell argues that there was little prospect of Labour's radical programme being translated into policy once in government, because of the tensions between the parliamentary leadership and those of the industrial wing of the labour movement over dealing with the economic crisis. D. Howell, *British Social Democracy*, op cit, pp287-324. Tony Benn's diaries record that Wilson threatened to veto the 1973 manifesto, as an example of the extent of the determination of those on the right to hold on to power. T. Benn, *Against the Tide: Diaries 1973-1976*, Arrow Books 1990, p46.
93. CP/CENT/EC /15.

4. The CPGB's Industrial Strategy 1968–1974

94. B. Ramelson, *The Social Contract: Cure All or Con-Trick*, CPGB 1974, p12.
95. B. Warren and M. Prior, *Advanced Capitalism and Backward Socialism*, Spokesman 1975, p8.
96. Ibid, pp8-9.
97. The contributors to this discussion in *Marxism Today* were: J. Purton, December 1973 and January 1974; P. Sloan, February 1974; Pat Devine, March 1974; L. Finley, May 1974; D. Cobham, July 1974; R. Bellamy, November 1974; M. Dobb, Feb 1975; M. Prior, April 1975; P. Hall, July 1975; B. Ruhemann, August 1975; and a contribution from Soviet Economists, September 1975.
98. J. Jones, 'How to Rebuild Industrial Relations', *New Statesman*, 18 February 1972.
99. G. Taylor, 'The Labour Government 1974-78', *Marxism Today*, October 1978.
100. S. Holland, *The Socialist Challenge*, Quartet Books 1975, p38.
101. Ibid, p40.
102. B. Ramelson, *Cure-All or Con-Trick*, CPGB 1974, p17.
103. Ibid, p22.
104. Ibid, p24.
105. Ibid, pp25-26.
106. Reported in R. Taylor, *The TUC: From the General Strike to the New Unionism*, op cit, p231.
107. J. McIlroy, 'Notes on the Communist Party and Industrial Politics', op cit, p245.
108. The lecture was reprinted as 'Marxism and the Trade Unions', in *Marxism Today*, June 1974.
109. J. McIlroy, 'Notes on the Communist Party and Industrial Politics', op cit, p246.

PART THREE

The Rise and Fall of an Alternative Strategy: 1975–1979

5. From Gramscism to Eurocommunism, 1975–1977

THE EMERGENCE OF BRITISH GRAMSCISM
The previous chapters have explained how the Communist Party attempted to renew its political direction, ideology and overall political identity, during the period 1964-74. Its newer constituencies – students, feminists and young communists in particular – imposed new challenges on the party, and, through a mixture of pragmatic engagement and response to pressure, the party went some way towards accommodating these, but without resolving questions raised for its political strategy. The party's ideological renewal predominantly centred on what has been described as militant labourism; but alternative strands included a re-articulation of socialist humanism on the part of long-standing communist intellectuals, together with early indications of a growing Gramscian perspective that was becoming critical of the party's strategy. These perspectives, moreover, taken alongside critical events in the socialist world, as well as major cultural and social changes in the nature of British society, meant that new faultlines in the debate over Communist Party strategy were appearing. Dilemmas arising from the party's seeming inability to generate an independent political strategy became more apparent than before, on the one hand because of the closer links to the Labour Party, and on the other because of the party's modified relationship to new social movements, over which it was no longer seeking dominance. The Soviet 'mantra', while still in evidence, was no longer the dominant political paradigm that shaped British communist priorities; it had been weakened by the rise of Western communist parties such as the PCI, and by the further evidence of abuses of power within the existing socialist world. At the same time the 'condition of England (or Britain) question' – in particular the changing experiences of class, the impact of non-industrial

5. From Gramscism to Eurocommunism, 1975–1977

struggles, and the significance of economic crisis from 1975 – was becoming central to the party's internal discussions and debates.

This chapter will assess how these new faultlines became consolidated and entrenched as major ideological divisions. The schisms outlined in the previous chapter between the industrial and intellectual sections of the party intensified between 1975 and 1977. Moreover the balance of power between the different sections also fundamentally altered. Those active in the communist universities, student movement and feminist groups began to exert more influence as they took on more prominent positions of leadership within the party. Intellectuals found a further niche in the new political opportunities afforded by a renewed interest in Gramsci and Marxism. Furthermore, the ideology of militant labourism, which had brought greater strength to the industrial wing of the party, and wider recognition of the party as a whole, was on the wane, in the aftermath of the division with the Labour and trade union left over the Social Contract.

The implications of these developments, it will be argued, were long-term and fundamental. The development of Gramscism (which will be used as a generic term to describe the critical positions adopted by the younger intellectuals, feminists and students), together with the older 'humanist' intellectuals provided the intellectual and political rationale for change in the party's identity and strategy. According to its advocates, the party's strategy needed to be based on a different understanding of the dynamics of political change, for example through analysing the relationships between class and social movements; it also needed to reject economism, in favour of Gramsci's concept of hegemony; and – in affinity with the Eurocommunist movement from the mid-1970s – there should be a new focus on democracy as the prefigurative path to socialism. These developments not only challenged the main tenets of militant labourism; they also brought into question some of the more deep-rooted cultural characteristics of the party. Paradoxically they thus accelerated its decline, while simultaneously contributing a new intellectual energy to the British left as a whole.

BRITISH GRAMSCISM AND THE NEW LEFT

The influence of Gramsci's work on the British Left has been widely commented on, with many scholars arguing that his work has been given more extensive attention in Britain than in any other country outside Italy.[1] Certainly the number of publications about Gramsci has grown consistently since 1971 when the core of his work was first published in Britain.[2] However, what concerns us here is the political and strategic impact that his work carried for the CPGB in a particular period. In order to assess this impact we need to understand the specific contexts in which his work came to be adapted by those seeking to transform the party; in the main these were 'young turks' on the Economic Committee, intellectuals, feminists and former YCL and student activists; people from these groups began to take up leading roles in the party, and in wider support networks.

The arrival of Gramsci into British political culture had a varied journey, across, as Forgacs has noted, 'a wide spatial, temporal and cultural gap; on the one side Italy between the wars, on the other post-war Britain; on the one side, the third international and the struggle against fascism; on the other the culture of labourism and the post 1945 welfare state'.[3] Moreover, Gramsci's acceptance into the world of the British left had specific and differentiated applications, recognition of which is crucial for an understanding of Gramsci's impact on the CPGB. The first English translation of his work *The Modern Prince* in 1957 was only published – by Lawrence and Wishart – after pressure from intellectuals in the wake of the exodus over Hungary the previous year.[4] As Forgacs also argues, Gramsci was perceived by some in the party hierarchy as being outside the orthodox communist tradition, and there was only limited, and belated, interest in his work. Indeed the publication of his *Prison Notebooks* by Lawrence and Wishart in 1971 was only made possible by the joint efforts of Stephen Boddington, an intellectual in the Party (Smith) Group, and Roger Simon, the latter contributing a necessary subsidy of £2000 to its publication.[5]

In the meantime, Gramsci had been adopted by the New Left. His work was important for the 'first New Left', notably his ideas on the links between culture and politics, which can be seen in the work of Raymond Williams, Gwyn A. Williams and Edward Thompson. The first New Left, according to Kenny, was thus a vehicle for 'the dissemination of Gramscian ideas', particularly in the relationship between politics and culture;[6] while it was through the first New Left that the 'theoretical and methodological shifts registered by [Gramscism] paved the way for the popularity of concepts such as hegemony, organic intellectuals and the war of position'.[7]

What was significant here, as Forgacs and Kenny emphasise, was that the work of Williams and Thompson had only an indirect effect in mediating Gramsci's ideas. In the absence of in-depth familiarity with Gramsci's work, the work of Williams and Thompson 'provided a framework, an intellectual space, within which Gramsci, or at least a certain side of Gramsci, could be made visible and readable ...'.[8] In particular, it was the cultural emphasis of Gramsci that related closely to that of Williams and Thompson in their work on class and community.[9] These connections are significant for the current discussion. As has been shown, the young communists in the 1960s also provided space for the development of Gramscian ideas rooted in popular culture, while it will be shown that for both an older generation of intellectuals, as well as the newer cohort, the cultural emphases in Gramsci's ideas were crucial to their critique of militant labourism.

Gramsci's work had an even stronger and more directly theoretical influence in the writings of 'second New Left' intellectuals such as Tom

Nairn and Perry Anderson. In their analysis of the British state in the mid-1960s they drew on Gramsci's critique of economism – in particular the failure of the labour movement to go beyond what Gramsci called the 'economic-corporate' condition.[10] Their critique of economism was similar in some ways to that found in the later Gramscism of the CPGB, though, as Forgacs has pointed out, the forum within which they formulated their ideas was a restricted one: 'a relatively isolated assimilation, destined to be circumscribed within an audience of "professional intellectuals" ... It was a relatively disembodied Gramscism in terms of a concrete political project'.[11]

The events of 1968 gave further impetus to the reception of Gramsci's work. In Britain, as elsewhere, Gramsci's ideas helped to provide new thinking within the student and radical movements of the time, though rival interpretations were now on offer, which helped to delineate differences on the wider left. For the growing Trotskyist groups, Gramsci became an inspiration for grassroots militancy and student occupations, with his work and activism in the Turin Factory Councils being used to preserve his legacy within an orthodox Leninist framework.[12] Meanwhile, for communist students and others on the party's Cultural Committee, there was a notable interest in the importance Gramsci gave to winning ideological and cultural *hegemony* as a pre-requisite to taking political power. This was the essential component of a 'war of position' that redefined the revolution as a process, and which demanded a new understanding of the relationship between civil society and the state.[13]

THE INFLUENCE OF GRAMSCI IN THE CP

The assimilation of Gramsci's ideas in the Communist Party became a reference point for critical voices, as they began to see in his ideas ways of justifying particular strategic and ideological directions. Two points need to be made here. Firstly, Gramscism in the CP did not develop as an undiluted theoretical or conceptual framework, but was incorporated in an uneven way, with some aspects of his work emphasised more than others. Secondly, the term 'Gramscian' will be applied here to a range of groups who had different 'claims' on Gramsci, in that Gramsci's work addressed different concerns that carried specific messages for different groups in the party. These included former YCL members who had been inspired by the cultural politics and events of the 1960s; students who found new intellectual energy in Gramsci's work; and feminists who, in embarking on an ideological and organisational challenge to the structures and practices of the party, drew much from Gramsci's critique of economism and the complex ways in which ruling ideologies operate. In addition, the older cohort of intellectuals, of whom James Klugmann was the most prominent, were invigorated by Gramsci's emphasis on culture and the importance of intellectual work.[14]

The political application of Gramsci's ideas by these groups – what can be called 'Gramscism in the CP' – was defined by three main areas, around which my discussion and argument in this chapter will be organised: (a) a critique of the economism of the party's mainstream strategy, and an alternative emphasis on ideology and culture; (b) a redefinition of the meaning of class and its relationship to 'new social forces', and the resulting political implications; and (c) a prefigurative strategy which would facilitate the transition to socialism. Before discussing in more detail the role of British Gramscians in constructing these alternative and challenging political positions, some clarification needs to be made.

In judging the Gramscian influences on the party's ideological and strategic priorities, the focus will inevitably be on those in positions of influence or leadership, or the various 'networks' within the party (such as party committees, the party press, the CUL, the Theory and Ideology Committee), most of which were concentrated in London. It is therefore difficult to assess the extent of Gramscian ideas within the party as a whole, or across the wider membership, or to account thoroughly for regional variations, although the effect on the party's strategy can be assessed to some extent by analysing the vehicles and forums for dissemination and argument. Within the Gramscian wing itself there were also considerable differences over political priorities at different times; for example there were differences over what levels of confrontation with the leadership should be adopted, over the merits of the re-written *British Road to Socialism* in 1977, and over the importance of the inner-party democracy debate in 1979, when Gramscians submitted 'alternative proposals' to the EC's majority report.

The mid-1970s saw Gramscians take on leading positions within the party. Leading student activist Sue Slipman became elected to the party's Executive Committee in 1975 and sat on *Marxism Today*'s editorial board, while Jon Bloomfield, the party's former National Student Organiser, became District Secretary of the party in the West Midlands. As mentioned earlier, another former Student Organiser, Dave Cook, was promoted to become National Organiser of the party in 1975, a leading position in the party, responsible for directing the party's strategy and organisational priorities. This was the biggest sign to date that the Gramscian influence was having an effect on the party. Pete Carter, the leading YCL activist of the previous decade, became one of the few Gramscian trade union leaders, from his base at UCATT, the builders' union, in the West Midlands. Feminists influenced by Gramsci started to have greater influence on the National Women's Advisory, with leading feminists like Beatrix Campbell and Judith Hunt playing more prominent roles; Campbell was a frequent contributor to the party press, and Hunt was a member of the EC and the *British Road to Socialism* working group. Campbell, like other leading Gramscians Bill Warren and Mike Prior, had been a member of the Party Group, which folded in 1970. The extent of Gramscian influence in the party was shaped to some degree by differentiated levels of power in the party. Sue Slipman's membership of the EC in 1975 strengthened the alliance between herself, Martin Jacques, Dave Cook and Pete Carter, enabling more influence within the higher echelons of the leadership, though they remained a minority on the EC. Jacques continued his rise from his early appointment to the EC in 1967, being placed on various leading party committees, co-authoring the *British Road to Socialism* in 1976, and becoming editor of *Marxism Today* in 1977 on the death of James Klugmann. Yet the positions of these leading Gramscians meant that they also faced more constraints in their day to day battles, in having to negotiate with a leadership that, while supportive of their work, remained suspicious of some of its long-term political implications, committed as they were to militant labourism as the organising strategy for advance. Much of the more heretical and critical work came from those who were nearer the margins of the party, for example the organisers of the CUL – notably Alan MacDougall, Ken Spours, Sally Hibbin, Geoff Roberts and Chris Nawrat – or editors of critical journals, like *Eurored, Socialist Europe* and *Red Letters*; while Sarah Benton's brief editorship of the party weekly *Comment* in the late 1970s foreshadowed the heresy of *Marxism Today*, in drawing in a broad range of contributors and confronting some of the more contentious aspects of the party's traditions, such as its Soviet links.

Yet the influence of Gramsci was not limited to a new generation. Long-standing intellectuals such as James Klugmann, Arnold Kettle, Roger Simon and Brian Simon continued to rediscover more independent ideological positions. Eric Hobsbawm, who had previously played very little part in party work, and Monty Johnstone, previously viewed with suspicion by the leadership, took on more prominent positions (in different ways) in helping to shift the party towards a Gramscian outlook. This was apparent not only in their writings, but also through their greater profiles as speakers at party forums: Johnstone on questions of socialist democracy and critiques of the Soviet Union; Hobsbawm in his seminal work *The Forward March of Labour Halted?*, which criticised the economism and sectionalism of the British left, and is discussed more fully in the next chapter.

THE CRITIQUE OF ECONOMISM
In the last chapter we saw how the industrial strategy of the party – defined here as militant labourism – became the focus for criticism by 'young turks' on the Economic Committee. This critical debate, which put the whole basis of the party's political strategy into focus, intensified from 1974 as the Labour government took shape.

George Matthews, along with many others in the leadership, considered the election of the new Labour government as a vindication of the industrial and economic strategy found in *The British Road to Socialism*, which emphasised the mobilisation of workers and the need to pressure trade union leaderships to shift to the left:[15] Heath's calling of an election on the premise of 'Who Governs Britain?' was a direct response to pressure from the miners strike and other industrial struggles, which the Communist Party had helped to organise.

The criticism by the young turks, however, not only rejected this assumption that communist political influence was growing – apart from some policy shifts there was very little evidence of communist influence in Labour's programmes; they also started to question the basis of the strategy itself, in particular the 'economistic' aspects which saw in working-class struggle an easy transition from industrial militancy to political radicalism, mistaking commitment to the principles of free collective bargaining and opposition to all incomes policies for a high stage of political consciousness. Indeed incomes policies were essential to the alternative positions that were beginning to be advanced by the young turks. Dave Purdy went furthest in advocating incomes policies, arguing that they could become the lynchpin of an alternative political strategy, perceiving in the idea of the Social Contract the possibility of socialist transition, along similar lines to Stuart Holland. Not only did he reject the view that wage demands were unrelated to inflation, he denied the further assumption that incomes policies were 'inevitably unfair'. He argued that such a position ignored the constraints faced by unions seeking 'free' collective bargaining under capitalism, and ignored the view that incomes policies could be used as a means of raising low incomes. He also argued that it was an 'exaggeration' to see incomes policies as merely relating to cutting wages, since capitalists often opposed incomes policies as interventions in the 'free' market. Perhaps most significantly, Purdy argued that free collective bargaining, so crucial to the party's industrial, economic and political strategies, often overlooked the powerless and low-paid in favour of better organised and skilled workers. For Purdy this meant that the current pursuit of incomes policies contained 'a strong egalitarian flavour'.[16]

The most developed critique of economism from the young turks was provided by Bill Warren and Mike Prior in their publication *Advanced Capitalism and Backward Socialism*, which addressed the Communist Party in the context of the predicaments of the left as a whole. According to Warren and Prior, the party's industrial strategy, based upon opposing incomes policies and promoting free collective bargaining, was not merely a misreading of the economic causes of inflation but, more significantly, had led to a serious absence of political engagement. Therefore, although the industrial struggles of the early 1970s had come close to direct confrontation with the state, there were important failures that needed to be faced, notably the inability of the left to enhance the industrial struggle so that it could become a stronger political intervention. The disputes may have won sectional gains, but they did not project a political alternative which would involve the working class in helping shape its own future. Thus the working class 'was doomed to defend, never to lead or control'.[17] The left – in which, they argued, the Communist Party played an important part – had missed big opportunities that had developed on two related fronts, namely the crisis in the capitalist economic system, in which its 'ideological supports (had been) shaken', and the growth of newer forms of political struggles, involving a range of groups beyond the traditional working class, and including professional workers, intellectuals, feminists and students. These groups were involved in 'areas of contestation' in 'non-economic' spheres.[18] In such a scenario, the authors argued that democracy could take on a new meaning as the basis for alliances between the working class and these new 'areas of struggle'.

Drawing on Gramsci's concept of hegemony, and its emphasis on intellectual and moral leadership, they argued that it was through democracy that, 'the working class (would) ... develop its own political and cultural hegemony over society'.[19] The failure of the party, along with sections of the wider left, was not to recognise this opportunity. Instead, according to Warren and Prior, the party's position 'quite simply envisages that, as the problems of British capitalism get worse, industrial struggles over wages will escalate ... to the point where an all-out clash with the capitalist state becomes inevitable. This clash will initiate a new, more political phase, the essence of which will be a conscious move towards socialism by the working class'.[20] The defeat of the Heath government over its industrial relations legislation was 'neither the result of an expanding working-class industrial struggle nor the triumph of a genuinely political strategy'.[21] The miners strike which precipitated Heath's downfall was, they maintained, a 'sectional dispute': 'It is quite specious for the left to claim that the election of a Labour government owed anything to a mounting political struggle'.[22] The main problem was that 'economism'– defined here as the view that political consciousness and advances develop automatically from economic crisis and industrial conflict – was the 'dominant theme' in the strategy.[23]

There must be some doubt as to whether the industrial department of the Communist Party, even if it were so inclined, could have had the power and authority to inject the left with the Gramscian strategy that Warren and Prior advocated, given the complexity of its negotiations and precariousness of its alliances with the labour movement mainstream at this time. What is of concern here, however, is the significance of Warren and Prior's arguments for the future of the party's strategy. Their critique of economism has strong similarities with Eric Hobsbawm's analysis, *The Forward March of Labour Halted?*, discussed fully in the next chapter, while Warren and Prior's emphasis on democracy as a way of coalescing the different social groups in a 'hegemonic' alliance was the first indication of the alternative Gramscian position that was to have some impact on the party's political strategy between 1976 and 1977. While Warren and Prior had few allies on the Economic Committee, and were 'constantly at loggerheads' with the 'industrial comrades', they did have some sympathisers from an older generation of intellectuals who were increasingly finding common ground with younger colleagues.[24] The economist Joe Ball empathised with the young turks, though he was more cautious in his criticisms,[25] while Sam Aaronovitch, like Ball another long-standing member of the Economic Committee, was also critical of the economism of the strategy pursued by Bert Ramelson, because the latter 'wanted to hang on to the notion that the workers would come to the revolution ... over the struggle of wages and the economic battle'. 'This', according to Aaronovitch, 'was a ridiculous idea'.[26] A text book which highlighted the different positions was withdrawn from publication by Lawrence and Wishart, one of several instances where the leadership remained suspicious of what it perceived as excessive heresy.[27]

Although debate in the party was limited, as there was no formal mechanism for relaying the Economic Committee discussions to the EC, the conflicts did reach the Party Congress of 1975, when Purdy put forward an amendment to the EC motion on incomes policies. He called for 'a national plan directed towards the elimination of unemployment, the planned growth of incomes, the achievement of control over the balance of payments and the taking over of large enterprises by the state'. He argued that:

> In the context of a challenging programme of this type, a policy for regulating incomes has a completely different significance from the policies which successive governments have operated in the past. The labour movement should declare its willingness to accept voluntary pay restraint as a contribution to the success of the programme and as a way of easing the transition to a socialist economy in which the planned development of incomes would be part of a comprehensive and democratic system of economic planning.[28]

THE FEMINIST CRITIQUE

As discussed in Chapter Two, by the mid-1970s party feminists had seen their influence extended both within the party and on the wider left. This was due in large part to the impact of *Red Rag*, which had started to take on board explicitly feminist issues – a development which can be seen as a measure of feminist success in the party, and which was to be further reinforced by a 'Feminist University' held in 1977 in Bristol, which followed the format of the Communist University of London. While there were still many areas of contention between party feminists, notably over the role of the WLM and the relationship between women and the working class in the party's strategy for socialism, the wider momentum of the Women's Liberation Movement – at its peak during the mid-1970s – meant that the ideological significance of feminism was likely to clash with the party's industrial and economic strategy, which still prioritised the (male) industrial worker, with its core base remaining in engineering, mining and building. Given the party dependency on its role in these traditionally male-dominated sectors, both for its industrial strength and its political influence, the feminist critique of economism went to the heart of the party's strategy.

For many feminists the priorities of trade unionism remained too closely geared to the priorities of the male breadwinner, in pursuit of a 'family wage'; free collective bargaining was often linked to the fight to protect wage differentials, which did not help the cause of the disproportionately large numbers of women in low-paid jobs. *Red Rag* remained very critical of narrow economistic agendas which did not adequately address either the particular experiences of women or the sexual division of labour. To fight on 'the wages front' alone was to accept the economic rationale of the system and the patriarchal relations it depended upon. The fight for better working conditions for women, on the other hand, brought into question a much wider range of existing social relations, as women were involved in a much wider network of private and public spheres of life. A shorter working week, for example, 'gives the grounding for the re-making of sex-typing in working-class homes';[29] this was an argument which went to the heart of the party's strategy, which, it was felt, did not challenge sufficiently the sexual division of labour. Feminist arguments for a 'new economy' resonated strongly with the contemporaneous arguments of the young turks on the Economic Committee, for an incomes policy which was geared towards low-paid workers, and for a wider understanding of inequality, one which included a recognition of different levels of power, and extended beyond the public and private spheres of the home and workplace.

The appeal of Gramscian analysis for feminists in the party was that it enabled the consideration of class inequality in a broader context, and recognised that there were different levels of oppression, and a need to develop alliances and coalitions between traditional class groups and other social movements. While Althusserianism had helped provide, for some, the structural explanation of the reasons for women's oppression, and the link between patriarchal ideology and social formations, Gramscism in the Communist Party provided a political framework within which to articulate feminist ideas.[30]

THE CULTURAL CRITIQUE
Much of the critique of economism was motivated by an increasing concern amongst the Gramscians that it narrowed the space for

political engagement. From the mid-1970s there was an increasing number of instances of dissatisfaction being expressed over the relegation of cultural issues in favour of more traditional political agendas. Moreover the renewed emphasis on culture in this new Gramscian approach went beyond the position adopted by the Cultural Committee in 1967 in *Questions of Ideology and Culture*; the latter, though recognising the plurality of cultural forms and the weaknesses of monolithic views, did not make explicit the political possibilities of cultural politics, leaving the meaning of 'culture' largely synonymous with 'art'. This attempt by the Gramscians to redefine a 'cultural politics' drew on the YCL legacy, and the New Left legacy, but it was now connected to the wider academic and political debates of the mid-1970s. Such connections were made on a regular and increasing basis in the Communist University of London; and within left academia as a whole these debates were flourishing. One example of a cutting-edge site of cultural critique was the Centre for Contemporary Cultural Studies in Birmingham, whose postgraduate students included a number of communists and feminists.[31]

These developments had a considerable impact on the debates on the future strategy of the party, with Gramscians arguing that popular culture was a vital terrain of political struggle. Indeed they succeeded in carrying a proposal in 1976 to split the Cultural Committee into two – an Arts and Leisure Committee and a Theory and Ideology Committee (TIC). This reflected a new emphasis on ideology, in particular one which recognised the *political* significance of culture, following on from the positions adopted by the YCL a decade earlier and now vindicated by the emphasis on the importance of ideas and culture found in Gramsci's writings.[32] In his report to the Executive Committee in May 1976, Martin Jacques developed this position by arguing that in order for the party to play a 'unique' role, it needed to recognise that 'class struggle is not confined to economic struggle ... but is also ideological and cultural ... we have the unique possibility to bring together industrial and cultural workers both within and outside the party and, on this basis, provide cultural leadership both in broad campaigning and in the life and activity of the party itself'.[33]

The emphasis on activity in the cultural sphere, already reflected in different ways in student, CUL and YCL events, took on a more formal importance in the Communist Party's political work under the influence of the Gramscians. As part of this second 'cultural turn', following the YCL initiatives of the 1960s, the party organised a series of cultural-political events. These included the 'Moving Left Show' in 1975, which included a mixture of political and cultural events, and a 'festival of Marxism' in Manchester the same year. In 1977 the party organised its biggest political-cultural initiative when it held the 'People's Jubilee', a left alternative event to the Queen's Jubilee at Alexandra Palace, at which 11,000 people attended and which gained wide press coverage.[34] According to the EC in July, the People's Jubilee was

> ... by far the biggest event we've had in post-war years and its scope was something quite new for us. The political rally at the jubilee was a great expression of the internationalism of our party. It demonstrated our closeness to the struggles of the British people, and showed the relationship of these to the battle for socialism in Britain.[35]

Revealingly, Nigel Tanburn, the organiser of the event, was more specific in his description of its main appeal, and redirected his emphasis away from orthodox politics: 'There was a mistaken tendency, in my view, to present the political rally as the most important aspect of the event'.[36] He emphasised instead the cultural contribution:

> The most important aspect of the People's Jubilee was undoubtedly its cultural content. Not only because such things as music, theatre, film, art and sport formed the bulk of the events in a new and stimulating way, but because there was the implicit recognition of three important things. Firstly, the ability of cultural means of expression to provide effective political communication in a stimulating and enjoyable way was recognised. Secondly, the need for cultural activities to have a place at political events without necessarily having a direct political content was acknowledged. Thirdly, the People's Jubilee was unique in its recognition of the need in this country for a national forum at which the richness and diversity of socialist and progressive culture could be represented, and in its attempt to provide such a forum.[37]

It was the perception of culture as an alternative means of political expression that was crucial, a position that closely followed Dave Cook's earlier interventions; and this approach was also considerably strengthened by the success of communist festivals in Europe – the *Fête de l'Humanité* in France and the *Festa dell'Unità* in Italy. By the mid-1970s these were regularly visited by groups from the British party. Many of the Gramscians favourably contrasted the new cultural face of the party with that of other official spheres of the party's public activity. Thus between 1976 and 1977 there was sustained criticism of the content of the *Morning Star*, which had seen a consistent decline in circulation since 1974.[38] Criticism expressed in the party press included its 'amateurish, sloppy and grossly unattractive' format, and its 'turgid, laboured and tediously repetitive' style;[39] what's more, the subject matter itself was 'boring' and 'narrow',[40] to the extent that it 'prevents the left having access to the paper, other than access approved by the Communist Party'.[41] Moreover this problem was identified with the paper's economistic preoccupations, which continued to reaffirm the official ideology of militant labourism. In the run-up to the 1977 Congress, the criticism of the *Morning Star* resulted in the unusual situation of an amendment being carried in opposition to the EC, which condemned the 'unimaginative' editing of the paper by Tony Chater. This was one of the few occasions when the leadership was defeated in the history of party congresses. Moreover, this was more than just a criticism of the editor; the amendment and subsequent discussion, moved by Jon Bloomfield, illustrated the differences between the Gramscians and those in the mainstream economistic leadership.[42]

POLITICAL AGENCY AND THE LIMITS OF ECONOMISM

Gramscism in the CPGB in the mid-1970s was therefore characterised by a broad conception of politics which increasingly saw itself at odds with the dominant ideology of militant labourism, and therefore highlighted the necessity of reforming the party's strategy. One of the key aspects of the Gramscian influence was the emphasis on political agency. Moreover this emphasis on agency was an important unifying strand in the emerging alliance between different generations of Gramscians in the party at this time.

For the older tradition of intellectuals, Gramsci's work enabled a renewed emphasis on political agency and intellectual freedom, values drawn from an earlier communist tradition but which now had a stronger relevance for the 1970s.[43] For Sam Aaranovitch, a former party organiser who had become one of the leading party economists critical of the economism of the Ramelson strategy, Gramsci provided a 'different kind of thinking about how the transition to socialism would take place', while others, notably Roger Simon and James Klugmann, began openly expressing their enthusiasm for Gramsci's work.[44]

This political unity between generations, largely brought about by Gramsci's work, and strengthened through the CUL in particular, should not, however, obscure important theoretical differences. The most significant of these differences can be found in the responses to the rise of Althusserianism. Many party students in particular had been influenced by Althusser, for his intellectual rigour, new structuralist frameworks and the insight he had brought to an understanding of Marx. Althusser was another 'anti-economistic' Marxist, making him an ally for those in the party seeking an alternative to militant labourism.[45] He enjoyed much influence amongst the new generation of left intellectuals, with communist students at Keele University being particular enthusiasts, while the British Althusserians Paul Hirst and Barry Hindess maintained regularly large – if occasionally bemused – audiences at the CUL in the mid-1970s.[46] While for some the theoretical rigour was important in establishing a more scientific basis for Marxism, for others it was very debilitating in seemingly reducing the need for politics and leading to esoteric cul-de-sacs. In *Marxism Today* in the early 1970s a sharp clash between Althusser and the humanist party intellectual John Lewis crystallised many of the concerns around structure and agency. Though Lewis was criticised for his theoretical shortcomings, the issues raised and subsequent discussion led to what might be called a creative tension within those groups sympathetic to Gramsci.[47] Moreover Althusser himself, along with Poulantzas, had been openly critical of the humanism in Gramsci's work, and aspects of the debates between Lewis and Althusser could be seen as a rehearsal of those in a more public setting between E. P. Thompson and Althusser.[48]

However, in the context of the CP's internal politics, many communist students and feminists saw in Gramsci a greater possibility of developing a feasible political strategy than in Althusser. For Geoff Roberts, Gramsci provided an 'ideological rationalisation' for the development of an alternative political strategy which, by focusing on the need for agency and more autonomous forms of politics, could incorporate the new social movements.[49] Indeed George Bridges, the former YCL leader, was 'never attracted to the Althusserian approach', because of its apparent denial of the role of agency. Some found that Althusser 'did your head in',[50] or was 'a bit like taking acid'.[51] The reason that communists found more political inspiration in the work of Gramsci was the centrality for Gramsci of politics, and of the need to intervene, participate and re-shape history; in addition, the influence of the Italian Communist Party, for whom Gramsci's legacy was crucial, was at this time growing in the CPGB.[52]

REDEFINING CLASS POLITICS

The first chapter of this book argued that the socio-economic and cultural changes evident in British society from the 1960s were beginning to weaken the party's ethos and identity, which had been largely based on the values of the skilled working class. By the mid-1970s these processes had also led to significant changes in the party's social composition, changes which reflected to some degree wider class transformations under way in British society. Within the CP there was much debate about the meaning and significance of these changes.

The most notable evidence of change in the party's class composition was a crisis in the factory branches, the training ground of many of its leading industrial cadres.[53] As McIlroy has noted, this decline 'underlines clearly the party's failure to benefit in terms of membership growth from the role it played in the militancy'.[54] The erosion of the factory branches was further reinforced by the resignation from the party of some of the party's leading industrial organisers, notably Jimmy Reid (who left in 1976);[55] while others, as argued in the previous chapter, had lost positions of influence. The inability of the party to win recruits in white-collar unions provided more evidence that its social composition had not expanded much beyond its traditional core, and was also indicative of its inability to build at grassroots level.[56]

Furthermore, taken alongside the strong link between the Gramscian milieu, intellectuals and the new social movements, these developments, as Thompson notes, had to some degree led to a 'class division operating in the Party'.[57] There was now a clear divide, at a time of consistent membership decline – in terms of the nature of activity, political culture and 'socialising' influences – between the Gramscian groupings and the other sections of the party.[58] The Gramscians were often to be found in the CUL, student forums and unofficial intellectual networks. This did not mean that the different sections did not meet at all, but membership figures suggest that trade union activists had much lower attendance records at branch meetings and were largely absent from the CULs, despite subsidies from the party in order to attract them.[59] Perhaps it is not surprising therefore that a polarity and suspicion was beginning to arise between different groupings. The whole question of class – in relation to the composition of the party, its meaning, and its relationship to other social groupings – was to become the biggest source of conflict in the party, and eventually led to major schisms.[60]

The decline of the skilled working-class base of the party, together with the existence of more clearly polarised groups within the party, became the background to a wide-ranging debate about the whole meaning of class. The rival positions could be characterised as being between 'narrow' or 'broad' class definitions. Concern over the adequacy of the party's interpretation of class had first been raised in an article by Alan Hunt in *Marxism Today* in 1970, which addressed the issue in the context of the wider theoretical debates influenced by the writings of Gramsci, Althusser and Poulantzas.[61] The issue had also been raised at a more directly political level at an EC meeting in January 1971, at the height of a period of militancy;[62] perhaps unsurprisingly, the EC showed little recognition at this discussion of any necessity to rethink its position as set out in the BRS.

However by the mid-1970s the concern over the changes in class structure started having some effect on discussions in the party, and a debate ensued in *Marxism Today* between 1973 and 1974, initiated by Jack Cohen of the party's EC. Cohen recognised that 'the working class is becoming more heterogeneous and fragmented', and noted the arrival of 'new sections' – the white-collar workers and 'technical workers' – who were being integrated into the labour movement. However, although 'they frequently bring with them a refreshing lack of inhibition with regard to the forms of struggle ... they have deeply rooted petit-bourgeois ideas, especially with regard to politics, to socialism and to the struggle to achieve it'.[63] They therefore needed to learn the habits of the traditional 'core' working class, under whose 'leadership' they would fall.[64] Such a position vindicated the existing class analysis of the party, rooted in the mobilisation of the industrial working class, though did little to suggest that the party prioritise the recruitment of the new sections. Moreover subsequent contributions to the discussion criticised Cohen for his understanding of class, in particular his 'lumping together' of different class groups, and claimed that his failure to distinguish their different relationship to the mode of production was a way of masking the decline of the traditional working class itself.[65]

This critique was given a stronger theoretical underpinning at a conference organised by the Communist Party's Sociology Group in 1976, at which the main theme was the need to develop Marxist concepts of class which rejected the perceived economism of much of orthodox Marxism, in which 'political struggles or social ideologies are explained as manifestations or reflections of economic forces'.[66] The participants at this conference included Nicos Poulantzas, who maintained that the working class was defined as 'productive labourers', arguing that the new sections constituted a 'new petit-bourgeois'.[67] The implications of Poulantzas's argument were that the new sections could not be said to occupy the same class position or interests as the traditional working class, a position rejected by Hunt, who set out a 'broader' concept of the working class. Although this broader concept of the working class was not defined by what Hunt called the 'immediate' 'class relations' of production, based on a worker selling his/her labour power, it did embody the political and ideological aspects of the working class through militant practices. The distinction between old and new working-class groups, he argued, recognised the different 'class practices' of different sections of the working class.[68]

The theoretical debates at the conference, which also included feminist and other critiques that saw multiple levels of oppression, based on sexuality, 'race' and gender, which extended beyond the workplace into more 'private' spheres of life, implied that a political strategy had to incorporate these different levels and articulate a variety of different interests.[69] It was the balance between the different interests, and in particular the relationship between the working class and 'new social forces', as well as the meaning of 'working-class' itself, that distinguished the different viewpoints held within the party. Gramscian analysis was well placed to deal with these issues because of its recognition of the inequalities and oppressions that went beyond immediate economic contexts – though it was continually argued that these remained crucial and therefore the need was to construct a bloc of a range of 'historically progressive' groups.[70]

CLASS AND THE POLITICS OF LIBERATION

This analysis had been supported by the impact of social movement activists within the party, at a time when communist students were enjoying their strongest influence in the NUS, and in the Broad Left which dominated student politics at this time. The strategy of communist students had clear connections with Gramscian ideas, notably in the attempt to construct hegemonic alliances, with the aim of fundamentally challenging the existing structure of higher education. There was nothing new in the idea of communists organising broad alliances in the student movement; this was a strategy that had always been part of communist work, from as far back as the 1930s. What was distinctive about this approach was the use and understanding of Gramsci's work, and the attempt to apply his ideas in a particular context. Significantly, it was a strategy which refused to defer to labourism, in terms of prioritising student support for the wider labour movement, or for official Labour candidates (who usually opposed the Broad Left). It was also a strategy in which democracy was seen as a lynchpin around which a broad coalition of groups (including liberals, feminists, students and anti-racist campaigners) would organise in providing alternatives to existing educational policies. This meant that the practice of a Gramscian politics, which went beyond a militant labourist understanding of class, was learned by communist students before other sectors of the party, and it was formative in the development of the wider Gramscian impact on the mainstream strategy of the party.[71]

The impact of feminism in the mid-1970s had a similar effect in putting forward alternatives to the class priorities of militant labourism. As explained in Chapter One, the 'class before gender' approach, which had shaped the party's work amongst women, was a particular area of contention. By the mid-1970s the National Women's Advisory, which included leading Gramscian feminists such as Beatrix Campbell, Sue Slipman and Sally Hibbin, was able to promote some of the key demands of the Women's Liberation Movement, such as abortion on demand, the need for autonomous movements, and the importance of issues such as sexuality and lesbianism. The minutes of the meetings show the growing influence of the Gramscian feminists, and the conflicts with more traditional women leaders, such as Jean Styles or Maggie Bowden, who regarded the WLM with suspicion, on the grounds of its demands for autonomy.[72] Proposals, for example, that the NWA should discuss sexuality and lesbianism brought conflicting views on how significant this was, how it should be discussed in the party press, and whether it should be in the features pages or the Women's Page of the *Morning Star*.[73] The debate in the March 1976 meeting over 'abortion on demand' – a position contrary to the party's policy – was even more contentious, with Jean Styles, the party's Women's Officer, reporting back to Gordon McLennan that it 'was a storming session with real division of opinion'. Here the Gramscian feminists had challenged the party's statement that abortion should be seen 'as a regrettable final stage in birth control and family planning', arguing that the party should adopt the WLM position of abortion on demand. There were divisions between Irene Swan,

Rosemary Small, Gerry Cohen (attending from the EC) and Styles and the Gramscians, with the conflict remaining unresolved at the end of the meeting.[74] Dave Cook, the party's leading Gramscian and by now the party's National Organiser, attended the June 1976 meeting, and supported the feminist position; he also supported a commitment to produce a handbook on 'do's and don'ts on sexist behaviour' for party members.[75] The feminist impact, like that of the students, made an important contribution towards a broadening political perspective; in this case 'the new social forces' could no longer be relegated into a secondary position behind the priorities of class. In making these arguments feminists gave increased support to the Gramscian position in the party.

The Gramscian view that different levels of oppression needed to be recognised and reflected at the strategic political level was further endorsed by the party's belated acknowledgement of gay liberation. Gays and lesbians had received little recognition by the party prior to 1975, other than in its official opposition to discrimination against homosexuals; as with gender and 'race', this issue was subordinated to the prior claims of class analysis. By the mid-1970s, however, there was a distinctive Gay Liberation Movement, one which included several communists. Moreover, the focus on *liberation* was significant, in that it emphasised the autonomous nature of gay and lesbian politics (like that of feminism), and recognised that the causes of oppression could not be confined to traditional class based explanations. It was therefore another challenge to the class basis of militant labourism. As with women's liberation, gay liberation suggested a type of emancipation that was beyond mere economic struggle, and one that could no longer be subordinate to traditional political and economic demands.

The Communist Party's endorsement of gay liberation in 1975, therefore, was both contentious and, to some extent, surprisingly progressive in comparison to its slow adoption by other social movements. To some degree this was a measure of the growing Gramscian influence. Dave Cook, the party's National Organiser, was a prominent advocate; and others, such as Sarah Benton as the chairperson of the National Gay Rights Committee, played an important role in getting the party to adopt more pro-gay liberation positions. The party passed a motion at the 1975 Congress opposing discrimination against gays and lesbians. At its EC meeting of September 1976, however, it went further. It opposed the 'criminalisation' and 'victimisation' of homosexuals, and called for changes in the law to equalise the age of consent with heterosexuals, for the removal of by-laws which prohibited sex between people of the same sex, for stronger definitions of privacy to enable legal compatibility with heterosexuality, and for the outlawing of discrimination in education, employment and housing. The party went further than urging legal reform, however, to challenge deeply held prejudices; it called into question the view that homosexuality should be regarded 'as a mental illness requiring aversion therapy' – a position that some party members had themselves held;[76] advocated 'free sex education and social studies curricula that include free discussion of homosexuality'; and supported the claims of gay parents to be able to adopt children, and committed itself 'to combat existing and anti-gay attitudes wherever they are found, including among the left, in the labour movement and in our own party'. The party concluded its statement by asserting 'the right of people to be openly and actively gay and giv[ing] support and encouragement to Gay comrades to work in the Gay movement'.[77]

The party won wide recognition for its stance. The *Gay Times* described the decision as 'the fullest and most far reaching such policy ever adopted by a non gay organisation': 'it will be greeted with enthusiasm by some, whilst others will feel sad that their own parties have not yet been so forthcoming. However it is greeted, it must for the time being serve as a model for those who would wish their parties to follow suit'.[78]

The party gave immediate practical expression to this aim by setting up a Gay Liberation Committee, an advisory committee to the EC. As with the NWA, the documents suggest that Dave Cook as National Organiser had a pivotal role in writing the founding statement of the advisory, in support of pressure from gays and lesbians within the party itself.[79]

The party's endorsement of gay liberation was further evidence that the Gramscian approach of recognising different levels of oppression was having a real impact on the party's strategy. Indeed, the focus on the 'new social movements' had developed some way beyond Gramsci's own writings, and is more accurately described as a re-application of his ideas in a different context. This did not extend however to the party's relationship with the black movement. The party's failure to recruit amongst black people after the early 1960s, which mirrored the wider failures of other political parties, was partly indicative of significant generational differences. Thus the strong influence the party enjoyed in the anti-colonial movement, which allowed it to maintain West African and West Indian branches in the 1950s (discussed in an earlier chapter), was followed by a decline in membership from the mid-1960s. This was in spite of the party's prolonged involvement in anti-racist campaigns such as the Anti-Apartheid Movement, opposition to the National Front, and organisation of solidarity work in defence of the imprisoned black American communist Angela Davies between 1969 and 1970.[80]

According to Trevor Carter, one of the party's leading black activists, one of the reasons for this failure to recruit or appeal to potential black members was the rigidity of the party hierarchy. Thus party leaders remained in control of the West Indian Advisory Committee – which continued to meet throughout the 1970s; this committee came under the tutelage and direction of leading communists like Jack Woddis, Idris Cox and R. Palme Dutt. Additionally, much of the responsibility for writing party statements and formulating policy was assigned to particular – usually leading white – comrades, notably Kay Beauchamp and Joan Bellamy. While much respected by black party members, some complained of the 'maternalistic' approach of these two, and remained frustrated at the lack of progress by black members inside the party.[81]

While the lack of black faces in the party's public profile, and its inability to win over new generations of black Britons, can partly be attributed to the lack of autonomy and encouragement for black members, more fundamental in terms of the power of the existing black membership was the failure to resolve the 'class versus race' conflict. The party press was generally critical of black power, and the *Caribbean Times*, a paper that was sympathetic to the party's positions and which reached much radical black opinion, endorsed a similar political culture to the *Morning Star*, with its emphasis on traditional industrial issues.[82] The party was more comfortable when issues of 'race' were part of a broader industrial struggle; thus it maintained a good relationship with local community relations councils through the work of individual communists, and organised solidarity in many issues of discrimination against ethnic minority groups in the workplace. In the most prominent dispute, at Grunwick, which reached the national headlines between 1976 and 1978, the party locally played a leading role in defending Asian workers dismissed for attempting to form a union; this was seen as typical of the way in which class struggles could overcome sectional interests.[83]

While some black members remained critical of the party's reductionist or 'workerist' positions on race, there was no strong cohort – as there was with feminists and students – to take the issue further. Rather it was left to individuals such as Trevor Carter, Asquith Gibbes and Vishnu Sharma to make their case. Moreover, the Gramscian strategy seemed to have little purchase for the party's black membership. Indeed, Trevor Carter, the leading black member most closely aligned to the Gramscians, was to describe the development of Gramscism into a Eurocommunist strategy as 'a white boy's business'.[84]

GRAMSCISM MEETS EUROCOMMUNISM: A NEW POLITICAL STRATEGY?

The critique of economism, the wide-ranging debates over the meaning of class, and the arguments over the more central role for new social movements, are indications that the impact of Gramscian ideas was having significant effects on the debate over the party's strategy. It also suggests that Callaghan's argument that Gramscian ideas 'were ... confined to a small minority of (mainly) intellectuals ...' ignores the diversity and extent of the intellectual and educational networks that Gramscians worked within.[85] Thus, not only was Gramsci central to ten of the specialist courses at the Communist University in 1977, but his ideas eventually found their way into mainstream CP educational literature, with day schools and public meetings, as well as the party's press, discussing Gramsci's work. The appointment of Martin Jacques as editor of *Marxism Today* in 1977, and Sarah Benton as editor of *Comment* in 1978, provided additional outlets, while more specialist journals such as *Eurored* and *Red Letters* provided more focused Gramscian perspectives. The rise of the intellectual strata in the party was contemporaneous with the decline in the party's industrial base, the party's traditional bedrock of support. Above all, during the run-up to the Congress of 1977, when the BRS was being re-written, and there was extensive debate in *Comment* and elsewhere over the nature of the party's strategy, Gramscian influence was evident in the argument over the need to develop a broad democratic alliance.

The debate over the *British Road to Socialism*, which began officially in 1976, in preparation for the Congress of 1977, drew on many of the issues referred to above. During the process of re-writing the BRS links were made between the Gramscian perspective and the wider Eurocommunist movement, notably around the objective of formulating a pre-figurative strategy, taken from Gramsci's argument that an aspiring hegemonic bloc should be exercising intellectual and moral leadership prior to taking official political power; indeed it was a 'precondition' for taking power.[86] In the context of the Eurocommunist debates of the time, such a pre-figurative strategy focused on the need to extend democracy to a wide coalition of groups, on the basis that the democratisation of society represented both a challenge to the existing order of capitalist society and the formative conditions for constructing a new socialist society. The link between Gramsci and the Eurocommunist movement was not a direct one, since Gramsci died in fascist Italy, in a quite different era. While many have pointed to the significance of his ideas – for example the contrast between a 'war of position' and a 'war of manoeuvre', and the notion of revolution as a process – it is difficult to make a direct connection between his thoughts and Eurocommunist politics. Rather it is necessary to understand the way in which his ideas helped to influence the strategy adopted by the PCI, and subsequently, and in very different circumstances, that of other parties, including the much smaller Communist Party in Britain. Moreover any discussion of the links between Gramscian ideas and Eurocommunism must also include a recognition of the role of Gramsci's successor as PCI leader, Palmiro Togliatti, who was an early critic of the Soviet Union, and an advocate in 1956 of the idea of 'polycentrism' – the acceptance of different roads to socialism in different countries.[87] Moreover Togliatti's emphasis on democracy went further than mere 'popular frontism' – the maximisation of the broadest anti-fascist alliances – crucial though this was. For Togliatti, democracy had to be extended to a range of social institutions; it had to permeate into the economic and social spheres as part of a long-term strategy for socialism. This position, influenced by Gramsci's concept of the 'war of position', became commonly referred to by the PCI in the 1970s as 'structural reformism'.[88]

There is little evidence that Togliatti's ideas were of much *strategic* influence on the British Communist Party until the mid-1970s (he died in 1964); prior to this he was celebrated as an important communist leader who had played a key role in the defeat of fascism and had led the PCI in the immediate post-war years. By the mid-1970s however, his ideas were important in providing an example of a non-Soviet socialist strategy, in which democracy could be part of a revolutionary strategy in the conditions of Western Europe. Also important was Berlinguer's strategic concept of the 'historic compromise', which was formulated in 1973 as an attempt to interpret the significance for communists in the West of the success and subsequent defeat of the democratic socialist government of Allende in Chile, as well as the electoral victories and municipal policies of the PCI in major Italian cities and regions.[89] Gramscians in the British Communist Party now had concrete inspirational examples of what a communist strategy might include, even if there was little comfort to be had from the party's own electoral and political fortunes.[90]

EUROCOMMUNISM AND THE CENTRALITY OF DEMOCRACY

The peak period of Eurocommunism, between the years 1975-1979, saw the best electoral performance by the PCI, the development of the 'Union of the Left' in France between the socialists and communists, and a brief rise in support for the PCE in the aftermath of the defeat of the Franco regime in Spain. These developments led to joint statements by the PCI, PCF and PCE, even though there were differences of circumstances and perspective for all three parties. What united them was the emphasis on democracy, and in particular the rejection of classical Leninism, and the need to construct broad democratic alliances in the direction of socialism.[91] While the British party was in a very different situation, with no electoral base and a small, declining membership, at a strategic and philosophical level the Gramscians saw the relative success of their European partners as an inspiration for addressing their own predicament. Such issues came to shape discussion in party journals; in particular in *Eurored*, an explicitly Eurocommunist journal, there was discussion of the fortunes of the Eurocommunist parties, including their strategic dilemmas, and of the ideas of thinkers like Balibar;[92] and *Socialist Europe* became the focus for critical discussions of 'existing socialist' countries.[93] These discussions also fed into the party's public debates, to the extent that many British Gramscians started to identify themselves as 'Eurocommunist', though in Britain the term was used with varying degrees of confidence:[94] Martin Jacques and Monty Johnstone, for example, both preferred not to use it, because of its lack of clarity.[95] The greatest identification with the term from the Eurocommunist wing was by George Bridges, the former YCL activist. In the mid-1970s Bridges was a leading activist in one of the strongest Eurocommunist districts of the party – Lewisham, in South London. In an article clearly identifying the significance of Eurocommunism for the CPGB, Bridges argued that it provided the possibility of developing a different strategic role for the party. It could become a 'generaliser, unifier and strategist': 'It must aim to be hegemonic (in the sense of winning consent for its position) within the new historic bloc. Its leadership role is won through its ability successfully to pose realistic tasks which advance the revolutionary process. It has to reflect within its ranks the progressive elements of the new bloc'.[96]

However the notion that Eurocommunism could provide the basis for a transformation of the party was not a widely held standpoint. Although more extended discussions did take place in *Eurored*, and the journal – for a limited time and with a small readership – continued to follow the fortunes of other Eurocommunist parties, there was a lack of in-depth analysis of what a Eurocommunist strategy might mean for the British Communist Party.[97]

Nevertheless Eurocommunism became an important generic term in the mid- to late-1970s, referring to an alternative *democratic* strategy. It began to be used in a positive way by communists across Europe, who sought an alternative idea of socialism, based around the extension of democracy. This extension of democracy could open up the possibilities of alliances, and could also offer a transformative challenge to advanced capitalist societies – from which socialism could result. Significantly, this led to a rejection of the concept of the 'dictatorship of the proletariat', which had formerly been seen as the means whereby the working class would take state power.

This was confirmation of a direction that had long been established in the ideas of Togliatti. For Togliatti – drawing on the theoretical insights of Gramsci – 'hegemony' had become the accepted way to describe the operation of power structures within advanced capitalist societies, and also the basis of an alternative strategy. For the PCE's Santiago Carrillo, the eradication of the term 'the dictatorship of the proletariat' was a necessary condition for the success of any alternative and deeper democratic ideal. He argued that 'the dictatorship of the proletariat has been implanted with a one-party system, as a general rule, and has undergone serious bureaucratic distortions and even very grave processes of degeneration'.[98] The rejection of the concept of the dictatorship of the proletariat was a crucial part of the shift in Eurocommunist thinking to a concept of revolution through democracy; this was linked to other new ideas on the nature of socialist transition, in which parliamentary democracy and multi-party pluralism were key components. Berlinguer of the PCI answered his Leninist critics thus: 'We see parliament as an essential institution in Italian political life and not only for today, but also in the phase of transition to socialism and in building socialism itself'.[99] In France the PCF rejected the dictatorship of the proletariat at its 22nd Congress in 1976, adopting instead the alternative slogan, 'democracy to the fullest'.[100]

Debate in the British party focused on the nature of pluralism, and the right of other political parties to oppose and replace communist government. The party leadership felt the need to clarify its position in November 1976, issuing a statement which explicitly rejected the term 'dictatorship of the proletariat': 'We consider the word "dictatorship" completely inappropriate as a description of the socialist society we want to build'. This decisive break with the remnants of Leninism was further manifest in the argument that ... 'it has become historically associated with the concept of achieving socialism through armed insurrection'. The term 'proletariat' was also applied in a way that implied 'a dictatorship over the rest of the population, which again is not our intention'.[101]

REVOLUTIONARY DEMOCRATS AND THE NEW BRITISH ROAD TO SOCIALISM

The biggest opportunity for Eurocommunists to influence the party's strategy came with the re-writing of the BRS in 1976-1977, a process which engaged the party from top to bottom. The debate was initiated in 1976, and culminated in the Congress of 1977. The party's decision to allow a Granada film crew to produce a fly-on-the-wall documentary of the events leading up to and including the Congress, and its invitation to others on the left to contribute to the discussions, gave the party's strategy a higher public profile than in the past. This decision was also influenced by the leadership's desire to project a more open image, in order to consolidate the more independent stance it had taken since the mid-1960s. However, while this new emphasis on democracy was welcome, for the party leadership – unlike for the Gramscians – it did not mean a decisive break with what had gone before. This meant that a division grew between those Gramscians who wanted to transform the strategic direction of the party, and those in the leadership who were more cautious in their endorsement of change.

Rival interpretations of the significance of democracy to the new strategy reflected the contending positions. For the Gramscians, the new emphasis on democracy meant a fundamental break with the past, with democracy becoming the lynchpin for alliances between the working class and new social movements. For the leadership, who welcomed the new emphasis on democracy, the new strategy was in essence a modification of what went before, a continuation of an evolving strategy.[102] In addition, a minority in the party, led by Sid French of the Surrey District, opposed the re-writing of the BRS as unnecessary revisionism, which they saw as symptomatic of a mistaken rejection of key Leninist tenets.

The main point of contention centred on the replacement of the concept of the 'broad popular alliance' with that of the 'broad democratic alliance'. It was the political and conceptual significance of this change that marked the respective positions. The broad popular alliance had been an 'anti-monopoly alliance', in which the party would organise all those oppressed by the monopolies in a direct challenge to capitalism. The broad democratic alliance, as argued by the Gramscians, indicated that different levels of oppression were not reducible to class and could be challenged by democratic struggles involving new social forces. Moreover, the broad democratic alliance closely paralleled similar concepts within other Eurocommunist parties: including the alliance of the 'forces of culture and labour' (PCE); the 'new historic bloc' (PCI); and the 'Union of French people' (PCF). For the mainstream leadership, however, while the extension of democracy was an important illustration of the renewal of the party's appeal, the battle to halt oppression was modelled on industrial struggle, and working-class action would bring together the interests of different social forces. Moreover, for many in the leadership there was much suspicion over the 'broad' concept of class, which they saw as endangering the hegemony of the core traditional workers on whom the party's main hopes still rested.[103]

For the remaining Leninists the change was seen as fundamental, as for the Gramscians, but with the opposite effect. For them this change meant that the party had abandoned in theory what it had long abandoned in practice, namely its Leninist heritage; the party had now accepted what the Leninists conceived of as the bourgeois premises of parliamentary democracy, in its advocacy of pluralism and the right of parties hostile to socialism to participate in a future socialist system. Immediately prior to the 1977 Congress, Sid French, who had also opposed the turn towards renewal begun in the 1960s, led 700 or so members out of the party to form the New Communist Party.[104]

For Gramscians like Jon Bloomfield, however, the key political faultlines were now between what he called the 'revolutionary democrats' and the mainstream leadership. He argued that while there were areas of agreement over the rejection of Leninism and the importance of involving parties and movements beyond the CPGB, there were also substantial differences in interpretation, in terms of the meaning of democracy and its radical potential to transform the state. The differences included different analyses of the way in which the 'ruling class ruled'. For Bloomfield, the leadership failed to grasp 'the real roots and strength of ruling-class hegemony', or why 'the fierce class battles of the early 1970s did not bring an upsurge in left politics'. He also reiterated the critique of economism, inasmuch as it expected political change to follow on in an uncomplicated way from trade union struggles. The leadership maintained a narrow concept of democracy, he argued, and it was too culturally conservative, for example in failing to grasp the political significance of the Communist Universities or the

5. From Gramscism to Eurocommunism, 1975–1977 165

People's Jubilee. This had led to a strategic stalemate, and a lack of clear political leadership: 'Unless we give a clear political dimension to our branches and advisories we will remain a ginger group and our programme stays unrealisable'.[105]

The draft version of the BRS had been drawn up by a group which was evenly split between Gramscian and traditionalist influences, and this compromise pervaded the content of the programme.[106] The responsibility for writing it fell to George Matthews and Martin Jacques, who were representatives of the two positions. These two main writers have contrasting recollections of the process, with Jacques describing the clashes over the role of democracy, ideology and the role of new social movements as amounting to a 'Mexican stand-off', while Matthews denies major differences in substance.[107] Some of the behind-the-scenes differences in the BRS Commission were recorded in the Granada programme *Decision British Communism*, which gave an illuminating insight into the extent of the deliberations and machinations that took place at party congresses.[108]

The attempt to reconcile the different Gramscian and traditionalist views meant that the final draft of the BRS contained contradictory positions. It carried the 'traditionalist' reference to deepening economic and political crisis,[109] but also pointed in greater depth than before to the particular oppression of women, black people and trade unionists, and it also recognised environmental damage to a greater extent. Its discussion of culture focused on the way in which capitalism commercialised and distorted cultural forms, rather than on advancing the political directions offered by a cultural politics.[110] It accepted the Gramscian idea of revolution as process, however, and the strategic concept of a 'broad democratic alliance' ran through the document. This represented an advance in the important sense that a *democratic alliance* resonated more with the idea of a prefigurative *strategy*, linked to the future socialist alternative, rather than the more *tactical* 'broad popular alliance', which had the more limited objective of mobilising opposition to capitalism. The document accepted the 'broad' definition of the working class, though reference to its 'leading role' left the precise nature of the relationship between this group and the new social forces unresolved. It also committed the party to political pluralism by arguing that other political parties had the right to co-exist in a socialist society. The area most indicative of the differences between the Gramscian position and that of the leadership was the passage on the way in which the ruling class rules in a capitalist society. In the first version, the Gramscian influence of Jacques is apparent in a long passage on the way in which ruling groups rule by consent, arguing that 'class struggle is not simply economic or even economic and political. It is also ideological and cultural'.[111] In the final draft however this is watered down and accompanied by more orthodox explanations which focus on 'capitalist domination'.[112]

A year-long debate in the pages of *Comment* brought out the range of differing opinions. Another Gramscian, the feminist Beatrix Campbell, welcomed Bloomfield's clarification of the 'revolutionary democratic position', though she argued that the document as it stood prevented the adoption of this position, because of its failure to understand either the dynamics of state power, or the strategy a socialist movement would need to adopt in order to take power.[113] Alan Hunt, in endorsing the revolutionary democratic position, rejected the pragmatism of the traditionalists for its 'administrative' rather than 'political' leadership, and argued that the new BRS should represent a move away from the 'dogmatic' stance on the economy, the belief in 'perpetual economic crisis' and 'sectarian attitudes'.[114] Pat Devine, one of the young turks on the Economic Committee, while agreeing that the final draft of the BRS was an advance, felt that the draft did not escape the party's 'chronic economism', so that the Broad Democratic Alliance ... 'co-exists uneasily with the perspective of transforming the Labour Party by remote control', and the party appeared inescapably as 'a ginger group, rather than as a party with a central role to play in the building of a broad democratic alliance'. He went on to argue that more attention should be paid to the 'qualitative changes which increase democratic control over the aspect of life involved', rather than 'quantitative demands for more'.[115]

Other criticisms focused on the 'tokenistic' references to the Women's Liberation Movement, which prevented the document from fully endorsing the main ideals of the WLM, including the need for autonomous women's groups, and a recognition of the 'social conditioning of women'.[116] 'Insularity' was a frequent criticism made by the Gramscians. To take one example, according to George Bridges the draft was 'deafeningly silent' on European issues, and it ignored (our) 'responsibility to understand and develop solidarity with the communist and democratic movements of Western Europe in a way which in the past has been reserved for "third world" struggles'.[117]

THE RETURN OF THE SOVIET MANTRA

The party leaders took a pragmatic view of the final draft of the BRS; they accepted some change of emphasis, without any recognition of Eurocommunist influence or, indeed, of Eurocommunism as a distinctive movement. 'We do not consider the term "Eurocommunism" is a useful or accurate one', General Secretary Gordon McLennan told the party's 35th Congress in 1977.[118] Indeed he regarded use of the term as one 'intended to create differences in the communist movement':[119] 'The term itself never appeared in the BRS. Nor was any critical attention given to the existing socialist countries other than distinguishing the "British Road" from the Soviet model as more appropriate for British conditions'.

The persistence of the Soviet mantra was a further underlying reason for the party leadership's pragmatism. Three examples from 1976-1977 confirm that the Soviet links, while no longer the defining feature of the party's perspective, continued to play a part in its political decline. The first example is an article and corresponding series of speeches by outgoing General Secretary John Gollan, by then in serious ill-health, on the twentieth anniversary of Khrushchev's secret speech at the 20th Congress of the CPSU in 1956. Gollan's article for *Marxism Today* was an attempt to assess the long-term implications for the future of communism. He argued that the 20th Congress had 'acted as a catalyst in carrying forward vital developments already emerging in the Soviet Union', and that 'subsequent developments had been profoundly progressive'. 'The two decades since the Congress have demonstrated the superiority of the socialist economic system over the capitalist system', he went on.[120]

The contrast between Gollan's interpretation of 1956 and the Eurocommunist position could not have been stronger. Where for Gollan 1956 was a 'great political turning-point', because of its effect in removing the 'temporary deformation' and renewing the socialist system, for the Eurocommunists it illustrated the necessity to construct a model of socialism that was not only distinct from, but rejected, key tenets of 'existing socialism'. For Georgio Napolitano of the PCI leadership, the moment of 1956 ('I cannot get away from that moment') was crucial in recognising the need to develop an alternative model of socialism based on 'revolution as process', through the 'deepening of democracy'.[121]

The second area of contention was the PC's withdrawal of an invitation to the Soviet dissident Zhores Medvedev to speak at a Communist University event in 1977. The PC's intervention (after Medvedev had agreed to speak) was on the official grounds that Medvedev was 'not currently engaged on scientific work', though this did not impress the Gramscians on the CUL organising group, who organised a petition for CUL participants to sign, while letters appeared from New Left critics and left Labour MPs in the *Morning Star*, complaining of a 'serious infringement of the standards of open-minded discussion ... by higher communist organisers'.[122]

Thirdly, the Soviet mantra was apparent at the same 1977 Congress which had endorsed the new edition of the BRS. Another motion confirmed the party's lingering admiration of the Soviet Union. The motion, noting the 60th anniversary of the Soviet Revolution read:

> On this 60th anniversary of the October Revolution this Congress of the Communist Party of Great Britain ... places on record the great debt owed to the USSR and the CPSU for the great example and inspiration not only of the October Revolution but by the triumphs of socialism over 60 years both in peace and war.[123]

The motion went on to describe the USSR as the 'mightiest country in the socialist family', and declared the party's intention of 'strengthening its bonds with the USSR and all socialist countries and their Communist Parties and to resist Cold War denigration of both the theory and practice of socialism'.[124]

Despite the efforts of the more vociferous Gramscians, who attempted to oppose the motion, it was carried overwhelmingly.[125] It therefore poses the question of the extent of Gramscian influence on the mainstream party. There seems little doubt that the party's Soviet links remained, for the bulk of the membership – though not for the Gramscians – a source of admiration and inspiration, even when the Soviet approach ceased to have any strategic input as a model. At the same time, though it remained a strong source of identity to many communists, it is clear that for others, including the 'humanist' intellectuals of an earlier generation, this was declining.

The full extent of the party's Soviet connections only came to light in 1991, when it was revealed that the party had continued to have financial links with the Soviet Union right up until 1979. As we saw in chapter three, Reuben Falber, who as Assistant General Secretary to John Gollan and Gordon McLennan had a key administrative role during the period under investigation, admitted to being the recipient of money from 1958 until 1979, which he laundered through the party's finances, often represented in the accounts as contributions to the party's 'fighting fund'. The initial sums donated were as high as £100,000, but these dwindled, on Falber's recollection, to £10,000 by the end. He argued that the payments were reduced following the party's more critical stance after the Soviet invasion of Czechoslovakia in 1968, and were only used subsequently to pay 'pension' money to veteran communists.[126] Receipt of the money clearly denied the party's claim to independence at the level of financial support, and reflected considerable deceit by some in the leadership, who had maintained that the party was sustaining its own campaigns. On the other hand only four people are thought to have known of the money, and by the 1970s, with the change in the party's composition and identity and the stronger Gramscian influence, it can be argued that the party's strategy was not fundamentally affected.[127] Indeed the major disputes over political direction, as discussed above, were over the questions of class, the role of the labour movement and the meaning of democracy. Moreover, there is also evidence of Soviet disquiet over the critical direction of the party, which suggests that the actual significance of the Soviet Union was less than it would have wished.[128] What these three examples illustrate is the tension between the party's pragmatic endorsement of new directions and its inability to wholly come to terms with its Soviet past.

A HOLLOW VICTORY?

The decisive majority in favour of the new BRS was seen to be a partial triumph for the Gramscian-Eurocommunists, primarily because of the

5. From Gramscism to Eurocommunism, 1975–1977

acceptance of the 'broad democratic alliance'. However, there was a mixed reception from the Gramscian-Eurocommunists themselves. Many, including Dave Cook, took the positive view that the new strategy could be carried out in everyday political practice. For others, however, there was less enthusiasm. Dave Purdy and Mike Prior rejected the document outright, regarding it as 'shoddy tinkering';[129] they argued that it 'fails to follow through the implications of the strategy it lays down. The crying need is for long, detailed and polemical arguments which can be considered and balanced'.[130] This was not long in coming, as the two had completed *Out of the Ghetto*, a sustained critique of the economism of the British left (including the Communist Party), and an elaboration of their earlier arguments.[131] This had been distributed in draft form at the CUL and at the Congress, to the annoyance of party leaders who called them in for an explanation.[132] *Out of the Ghetto* became their swansong, for both were to leave the party in the next couple of years. For others the new BRS seemed to be overtaken by other – arguably more fruitful – developments. In particular Martin Jacques became editor of *Marxism Today* on the death of James Klugmann in 1977, making it clear from the outset that the journal was to be open to the left as a whole; and Sarah Benton became editor of *Comment* in 1978, with a similar open approach; both journals went on to provide new spaces for the kinds of cultural politics that had previously been debated.

However the impact of the rise of Gramscism and Eurocommunism was mixed. On the one hand, as will be argued in the next chapter, these developments made a major contribution to new forms of cultural and social movement politics. A new generation of intellectuals emerged, bringing more theoretical rigour and strategic thinking. On the other hand, Gramscian influence had had only partial effect on the party itself. The Gramscians had not won over the leadership, but had rather extracted concessions with significant degrees of compromise. The Gramscians had mobilised around the CUL and other intellectual spaces, and had set out what an alternative strategy might be, but they had not 'hegemonised' the industrial department as the route to influencing the wider labour movement. Instead they had opened up underlying schisms – over the centrality of class struggle, the relative importance of culture, and the extent to which the labour movement needed modernising. The leadership, meanwhile, having achieved the cautious modification of its strategy without major splits, remained suspicious of attempts to transform the party further. An ageing leadership, labourist ethos, and the continuance of the Soviet mantra, did not co-exist easily with the Gramscian agenda. And, as the next chapter will demonstrate, the advance of the Gramscians had the effect of bringing out the party's deeply rooted contradictions, rather than of transforming its practice.

Notes

1. D. Forgacs, 'Gramsci and the British Left', *New Left Review* 176, July-August 1989, pp70-88; S. Hall, 'Gramsci and Us', *Marxism Today*, June 1987.
2. The Lawrence and Wishart edition of Gramsci's *Prison Notebooks* was published at this time.
3. D. Forgacs, 'Gramsci and the British Left', op cit, p72.
4. Ibid, pp72-73. He points out that the first attempt to publish it in early 1956 had been rejected by the party's Political Committee, because it was thought to be too heretical.
5. D. Forgacs, 'Gramsci and the British Left', op cit, p83; Kevin Morgan, oral communication with author, based on interview with R. Simon.
6. M. Kenny, *The First New Left*, Lawrence and Wishart 1995, p6. Forgacs uses the term 'broker' to describe the New Left's role, op cit, p74.
7. M. Kenny, *The First New Left*, op cit, p209. Gwyn A. Williams in an early article on the significance of Gramsci for the British left noted that it was no coincidence that the interest in Gramsci should parallel critical discussions on the nature of the 'establishment', the 'exhaustion of the Labour movement's ethic', and the emergence of 'managerialism' and 'affluence'; these issues increased the significance, as Williams saw it, of the role of 'active consent' and 'hegemony' as set out by Gramsci. See G. Williams, 'The Concept of "Egemonia" in the Thought of Antonio Gramsci; Some Notes on Interpretation', *Journal of the History of Ideas*, XXI 4 October-December 1960, p596.
8. D. Forgacs, 'Gramsci and the British Left', op cit, p74; see also Kenny, *The First New Left*, op cit, p209.
9. Both Kenny (pp5-6 and 114-115) and Chun (p55, pp111-14) discuss the influence of Gramsci on the first new left.
10. See T. Nairn, 'The British Political Elite', *NLR* 23 Jan-Feb 1964; 'The English working Class', *NLR* 24 March-April 1964; 'The Anatomy of the Labour Party', *NLR* 27-28 Sept-Oct and Nov-Dec 1964; P. Anderson, 'Origins of the Present Crisis', *NLR* 23, Jan-Feb 1964.
11. D. Forgacs, 'Gramsci and the British Left', op cit, p76. See also M. Kenny, *The First New Left*, op cit, p137.
12. These differences were accentuated with the development of Eurocommunism (see below). The rival interpretations of Gramsci were later drawn out further by an article by Perry Anderson, Editor of *New Left Review*. See P. Anderson, 'The Antinomies of Antonio Gramsci', *New Left Review* 100, November 1976-January 1977.
13. For Gramsci's concept of hegemony see A. Gramsci, *Selections From Prison Notebooks*, Lawrence and Wishart 1971, pp12-13, 55-60, 104-6, 206-8, 228-9, 238-9, 261-4. M. Jacques's 'Notes on Intellectuals', first given to a Cultural Committee meeting on 'The Role of Intellectuals Today' in 1969, and published in *Marxism Today* October 1971, was the first published account of Gramsci's work from a leading communist student.
14. Interviews with S. Aaronovitch, M. Jacques.
15. G. Matthews, *Marxism Today*, February 1975.
16. D. Purdy, 'Some Thoughts on the Party's Policy Towards Prices, Wages and Incomes', *Marxism Today*, August 1974.
17. B. Warren and M. Prior, *Advanced Capitalism and Backward Socialism*,

Spokesman 1975, p3.
18. Ibid, p13.
19. B. Warren and M. Prior, *Advanced Capitalism and Backward Socialism*, op cit, p26.
20. B. Warren and M. Prior, *Advanced Capitalism and Backward Socialism*, op cit, p1.
21. Ibid, p3.
22. Ibid, p3.
23. For Gramsci's critique of economism see *Selections From Prison Notebooks*, op cit, pp158-168.
24. D. Purdy, M. Prior, G. Matthews, J. Ball, interviews with author.
25. J. Ball, interview with author.
26. S. Aaronovitch, interview with author.
27. D. Purdy, J. Ball, interviews with author.
28. CP Congress Report CP Archive.
29. A. Wise, *Red Rag*, No 3 1973.
30. Juliet Mitchell's classic feminist text *Women's Estate* (Penguin 1971) was heavily influenced by Althusser's work on ideology. For further discussion of the impact of Althusser on feminism see A. Assiter, *Althusser and Feminism*, Pluto Press 1990.
31. For an interesting discussion of feminist activism at the CCCS see C. Brunsdon, 'A Thief in the Night; Stories of Feminism in the 1970s at CCCS', in S. Hall, *Critical Dialogues in Cultural Studies*, Routledge 1996, pp276-286.
32. The remit of the new 'Theory and Ideology Committee', was to 'encourage and promote the development of Marxist thought and study ... To be responsible for the activity and development of specialist groups'. TIC Box CP Archives.
33. M. Jacques, 'Culture, Class Struggle and the Communist Party', report to EC 8/9 May 1976, reported in *Comment* 26 May 1976. The proposal for splitting the Cultural Committee into two was made in this report.
34. This included, in addition to the main broadsheet papers such as *The Guardian* and *The Times Higher Education Supplement*, and left newspapers and journals, BBC TV and Radio, the *Sun*, *Daily Mirror*, *Daily Express*, *Melody Maker*, *New Musical Express*, *Time Out*, *Spare Rib*, *Stage* and the *Listener*. The event, unusually, made a profit of £2,609.80 for the party. Reported in CUL Organisers' Reports. CUL Box CP Archive.
35. Gordon McLennan's report to EC July 1977, reported in *Comment* 23.7.77.
36. N. Tanburn, 'After the Show', *Comment* 23 July 1977.
37. Ibid.
38. According to a report to the EC (May 8/9 1976) by Tony Chater, *Morning Star* editor, the paper had lost 'about 4,300 copies between Feb 1974 and January 1976'. Reported in *Comment* 15 May 1976.
39. J. Saltley, *Comment*, letters, 18 September 1976.
40. D. Green, *Comment*, letters, 26 June 1976.
41. S. Iliffe, *Comment*, letters, 12 June 1976.
42. 1977 Congress Report, *Comment*, December 1977; Jon Bloomfield interview with author.

43. This would confirm Michael Kenny's argument in *The First New Left* that much of the writings of Thompson and others who left in 1956 drew on the humanism found in the party prior to 1956. M. Kenny, 'Communism and the New Left', op cit, p196.
44. S. Aaronovitch, interview with author.
45. See L. Althusser and E. Balibar for their critique of economism, *Reading Capital*, New Left Books 1970.
46. Althusser was also 'phenomenally popular' amongst the Cambridge left according to Jude Bloomfield, a communist student at Cambridge in the early 1970s. One of the reasons for Althusserian influence at Keele was that Ronnie Frankenberg, Keith Tribe and Athar Hussein, leading Althusserians, were all academics based at the university at this time. Sue Slipman, Jude Bloomfield, interviews with author. Willie Thompson remembers attending one of the Hirst lectures and not understanding a word. Alan MacDougall described the Althusserian discussions as 'real cutting edge stuff'. Interviews with author.
47. See J. Lewis, 'The Althusser Case Parts I and II', *Marxism Today*, January and February 1972; and L. Althusser, 'Reply to John Lewis', Parts I and II (Self-Criticism), *Marxism Today*, October and November 1972. For a defence of Althusser in this debate see the contribution from G. Lock, *Marxism Today*, June 1972.
48. See in particular the chapter 'Contradiction and Over Determination' in *For Marx*, NLB 1962; and *Reading Capital*, NLB 1970. Forgacs, op cit, p75, also makes this point. See E. P. Thompson, *The Poverty of Theory and Other Essays*, Merlin 1978, for his critique of Althusser.
49. Geoff Roberts interview with author. Jude Bloomfield, Jackie Heywood, Joanna De Groot and Ken Spours were amongst other feminists and students who expressed similar views in interviews with the author.
50. S. Slipman interview with author.
51. C. Nawrat interview with author. Sally Hibbin, later to be a notable film director, was another Gramscian less impressed with the Althusserian approach to culture. As she put it: 'You don't read films, you watch them'. Interview with author.
52. The Party Education Department organised regular exchanges with the PCI during the mid 1970s, which included party schools and visits to the Festa dell'unita. The Lewisham branch in London had links with the PCI and the PCF during 1976-79 and was twinned with Antibbes, a PCF-controlled borough. Details of the Lewisham CP can be found in the archives of the London District of the CPGB at CP/LON/BRA; G. Bridges, G. Browning, M. Johnstone, interviews with author.
53. J. McIlroy, 'Notes on the Communist Party and Industrial Politics', op cit, p222. He shows that the workplace membership declined from 265 to 116 between 1964 and 1979. This does not tell the whole story, however, as many were not functioning; out of 43 workplace branches in London in 1975 only 16 were meeting regularly. McIlroy, op cit; CP/LON/BRA/1/19.
54. Ibid.
55. Others who left at this time included Bernard Panter and John Tocher.
56. The party's trade union composition for 1975/76 can be found through limited workplace data for 1976 at CENT/IND/1/2, regular PC state-

ments (CP/CENT/PC/13/22) and Congress Credentials Reports for the 1975 Congress – 1975 CP/CENT/CONG/19/07.
57. W.Thompson, *The Good Old Cause*, op cit, p167.
58. From 34,281 in 1964 to 25,293 by 1977. EC Reports CP archive.
59. CUL Organisers reports show this. Under the influence and organisation of Pete Carter, NUM members and other trade unionists did attend CUL 1976. CUL Boxes. However this seemed short-lived and the CUL remained student dominated. CUL Boxes CP Archive.
60. Some caution should be observed in analysing the class alignment within the party. There were some trade union activists and leaders – such as Pete Carter in UCATT, and Jack Adams and Roger Murray (BL Shop Stewards based in Birmingham) – who adhered to Gramscian positions, and many middle-class intellectuals who held on to a more orthodox position.
61. A. Hunt, 'Class Structure in Britain Today', *Marxism Today*, June 1970.
62. See G. Cohen, *Comment*, 20.1.71.
63. J. Cohen, 'Some Thoughts on the Working Class Today', *Marxism Today*, October 1973.
64. Ibid.
65. See for example M. Bleaney's response in 'Discussion', *Marxism Today*, February 1974.
66. The conference led to a publication of the book *Class and Class Structure*, Lawrence and Wishart 1977. The quote is from A. Hunt's introduction to the book, p7.
67. N. Poulantzas in A. Hunt (ed), *Class and Class Structure*, op cit.
68. Ibid
69. See for example Jean Gardiner's contribution in Hunt (ed), *Class and Class Structure*, op cit, pp155-164.
70. For Gramsci's work on the construction of a 'social-political bloc', see *Selections From Prison Notebooks*, op cit, pp202-5; and for a good discussion of its meaning see W. L. Adamson, *Hegemony and Revolution*, University of California Press 1980, pp176-179.
71. For a discussion of the influence of Gramsci's ideas on communist student politics, see K. Spours, 'Students, Education and the State', *Marxism Today*, November 1977.
72. Minutes of the NWA meetings can be found at CP/CENT/WOM/3.
73. One suggestion from the 'traditionalists' was to invite a 'Party psychologist' to contribute an article. For the discussion of these views see NWA minutes at 13/9/74 CP/CENT/WOM/3/5.
74. 'The discussion got very heated', Styles told Gordon McLennan in a letter. 'It was obvious that we were not going to get very far by further argument so I proposed that we adjourn the discussion to the next meeting and ask you or a member of the PC to attend'. She went on, 'I bit my tongue on a number of things which were said – I'll tell you about these verbally. Also some problems connected with the WLM – these I think can be overcome, but some points are a bit dicey'. NWA minutes 10/10/75 in CP/CENT/WOM/3/5.
75. NWA 11/6/76 in CP/CENT/WOM/3/5.
76. This view persisted amongst some members who argued that acknowledging rights of homosexuals fell short of endorsing the 'liberation' of

'gayness'. John Hoffman, a member of the Resolutions Committee (RC) at the 1975 Congress, wrote to Gordon McLennan complaining that the new EC statement endorsed policy that had not been agreed at the Congress. His point was that the RC, while opposed to discrimination against homosexuals: 'do not accept either the concept of "Gayness" nor the analysis of homosexuality put forward by members of the Gay Liberation Movement. The RC took the view that to describe homosexuals as "Gays" was to trivialise their problems and to accept the analysis of a homosexual who found "liberation" and fulfilment in this particular form of relationship, was not scientifically justified'. He argued that the 'omission of ... "Gay rights" and use of "Gay Liberation" ... was therefore deliberate: in the RC's view, neither the concept of "Gayness" nor the concept of "Gay liberation" were acceptable'. J. Hoffman letter to G. McLennan 29.9.76. Elizabeth Wilson and Angela Weir had a different experience of more progressive communist attitudes in bringing up their daughter as a lesbian couple. Interviews with author.

77. EC Minutes and correspondence September 1976 CP Archive.
78. *Gay Times*, October 1976.
79. EC minutes and correspondence September 1976 and January 1977 CP Archive.
80. Though the main anti-racist movement, the Anti-Nazi League, owed more to Trotskysim, as did 'Rock Against Racism', set up by the Socialist Workers Party.
81. T. Carter, interview with author. According to Marika Sherwood, these attitudes were already well-entrenched in the party's hierarchy during the late 1950s and early 1960s, when Claudia Jones, a prominent black American communist, was in Britain. For a discussion of Jones's 'deteriorating' relationship with the party leadership see M. Sherwood, *Claudia Jones: A Life in Exile*, op cit, pp77-82.
82. The analysis provided by J. Williamson in the early days of the movement – 'The Meaning of Black Power', *Comment*, 11 November 1967 – was indicative of some of the suspicions the party continued to hold towards the concept of black power. According to Williamson, Black Power's most serious flaw was 'its failure to understand the class basis of oppression'. It was also 'wrong' in two further ways, 'going it alone' and an 'anti-white' attitude.
83. See J. Dromey and G. Taylor, *Grunwick: the Workers' Story*, Lawrence and Wishart 1978, which covered the dispute from a CP perspective. Dromey was close to the party at this time though he was not actually a member. The book's concluding paragraph summed up the optimism the party continued to hold for the unifying nature of traditional class politics: 'Above all, the course of the strike illustrated with a vividness rarely seen before how a section of workers totally unorganised, totally ignorant of trade unionism, totally insecure in a foreign land, can yet develop – in response to autocratic treatment – such militancy, attract in a few months such solidarity, that all the forces of the state, the media, the police, the courts, employers' organisations, racial prejudice and women's inequality can be swept aside by the freshness and dynamism of determined struggle' (p199).
84. T. Carter, interview with author.

5. From Gramscism to Eurocommunism, 1975–1977

85. J. Callaghan, *The Far Left in British Politics*, Basil Blackwell 1987, p179.
86. A. Gramsci, *Selections From Prison Notebooks*, Lawrence and Wishart, op cit, pp12-13, 161-2.
87. As far as the links with Eurocommunism are concerned, Togliatti's emphasis on 'progressive democracy', initially formed during the aftermath of fascism in Italy in 1944-46, the period in which the PCI became a mass party, was crucial in the process of opposing capitalism as well as forming the basis of the future socialist society. According to Togliatti: 'the working class and the advanced masses, in order to reach socialism – that is in order to develop democracy to its extreme limit which is precisely that of socialism – must discover a new path, for instance, from those which had been chosen by the working class and the labouring masses of the Soviet Union'. 'La nostra lotta per la democrazia e il socialismo', *Il Partito*, Rome 1973, p56, quoted in D. Sassoon, *The Strategy of the Italian Communist Party*, Frances Pinter 1981, p35 (the best account of the role of Togliatti in directing the strategy of the PCI). In an article in the magazine *Nuovi Argomenti* in 1956, Togliatti argued that the Soviet Union was 'limited and partially suffocated by the intervention of bureaucratic and authoritarian methods of leadership and violations of legality'. In P. Togliatti, *On Gramsci and Other Writings*, Lawrence and Wishart 1979, p129. His concept of 'Polycentrism' is also discussed here, on p141.
88. 'Structural reformism' was the term used to describe the strategy through which the working class and its allies would come to power through the gradual democratisation of dominant institutions and the challenges to the monopolies from the strengthening of public control over the economy. For further discussion of Togliatti's concept of structural reformism, see C. Boggs, *The Socialist Tradition*, op cit, p112.
89. Berlinguer, fearing that in Italy there would be a coup in response to an elected socialist government, as in Chile, argued: 'We are concerned that if the ruling social groups count on smashing the democratic framework, on splitting the country in two and unleashing reactionary violence, this must spur us on ourselves to embrace ever more solidly the cause of the defence of freedom and democratic progress, to avoid the vertical division of the country and to work with even greater resolve, intelligence and patience to isolate the reactionary groups and seek every possible form of agreement and convergence among all the popular forces'. E. Berlinguer, 'Lessons From Chile', *Marxism Today*, February 1975.
90. For an account of one of the PCI's strongholds in local government, see M. Jaggi, R. Muller and S. Schmid, *Red Bologna*, Writers and Readers 1977.
91. The most vivid example of the centrality of democracy for the Eurocommunist parties is probably to be found in the Rome declaration of November 1975, signed jointly by the PCI and the PCF. This endorsed the 'lay nature and democratic functioning of the state', 'the plurality of political parties ... the right to existence and activity of opposition parties ... the free formation of majorities and minorities and the possibility of their alternating democratically'; 'the existence, guarantee and development of democratic institutions fully representative of popular sovereignty and the free exercise of direct, proportional universal suffrage'. Quoted in M. J. Bull and P. Heywood, *West European Communist Parties After the*

Revolutions of 1989, St Martin's Press, pxviii. The Berlin Conference of European Communist Parties held in 1976 was also important in resisting attempts by the USSR to impose more pro-Soviet loyalty on the Western CPs. See J. Barth Urban, *Moscow and the Italian Communist Party*, Cornell University 1986.
92. *Eurored*, which was set up in 1976, emerged from the West European Committee.
93. *Socialist Europe*, edited by Geoff Roberts, arose in 1977 from the Committee for the Study of European Socialist Countries, set up, according to Monty Johnstone, one of its leading members, for 'ideological reasons' (interview with author). Chaired by Dennis Ogden, it met every three or four months to discuss latest developments in the socialist countries.
94. The term, first used by the journalist F. Barbieri in an article for *Il Giornale Nuovo* (26 June 1975), was one that was imposed from without, by opponents who saw it as a pernicious attempt by communists to exert power by different means. The anti-communist tone is evident in Barbieri's statement that: 'A Eurocommunist Europe would definitely mean the Sovietisation of Europe'. See G. Schwab, *Eurocommunism: The Ideological and Political Theoretical Foundations*, Greenwood Press 1978. Moreover, even those to whom the term was most applied had some reservations. Santiago Carrillo, the leader of the PCE, for example, put the word in quotes and described it as one 'not coined by the communists and its scientific value may be doubted. (However) ... it has acquired a meaning among the public and, in general terms, serves to designate one of the current communist trends'. S. Carrillo, *Eurocommunism and the State*, Lawrence and Wishart 1977, p8. For the origins of Eurocommunism, see also: P. Elliott and P. Schlosenger, 'On the Stratification of Political Knowledge: Studying Eurocommunism as an Unfolding Ideology', *Sociological Review* Vol 27 February 1979; and D. Sassoon, *One Hundred Years*, op cit.
95. Interviews with author. This reluctance reflected pragmatic rather than political reasons. Johnstone, for example, 'never used the term specifically, although I identified myself with it'.
96. G. Bridges, 'Western European Communist Strategy', in S. Hibbin (ed), *Politics, Ideology and the State*, Lawrence and Wishart 1978, pp129-130.
97. David Fernbach's article 'Eurocommunism and the Ethical Ideal' made strong connections between socialist humanism, new social movements and the strategic predicaments of the CPGB, but this was not published until 1980, by which time the Gramscian-Eurocommunist influence was beginning to fade. D. Fernbach, 'Eurocommunism and the Ethical Ideal', in M. Prior (ed), *The Popular and the Political*, 1980. Indeed, it was not until the 1980s that its strongest Eurocommunist identity was evident, when it was described variously as a 'Eurocommunist' party, or controlled by 'Eurocommunists'. By this time the 'Eurocommunist moment' itself had long disappeared, with the decline in the respective electoral fortunes of the main parties.
98. S.Carrillo, *Eurocommunism and the State*, op cit, p155.
99. E. Berlinguer, 'Lessons From Chile', *Marxism Today*, February 1974.
100. Quoted in G. Bridges, 'Western European Communist strategy', op cit.
101. 'Statement on Dictatorship of the Proletariat', CP, 14 November 1976.

102. See for example James Klugmann's article, 'The BRS: A Brief History Since 1945', in *Comment*, 5 February 1977.
103. W. Thompson, *The Good Old Cause*, op cit, p172.
104. Most of those who departed were from the Surrey, Sussex and Hants and Dorset districts.
105. J. Bloomfield, Congress Discussion, *Comment*, 9 July 1977.
106. The exact composition of the group was John Gollan, George Matthews, Dave Priscott (representing the mainstream leadership), and the Gramscians Martin Jacques, Pete Carter and Judith Hunt.
107. M. Jacques and G. Matthews, interviews with author. Willie Thompson also records the division in *The Good Old Cause*, op cit, p172.
108. This was a series of three programmes shown by Granada TV in late 1977. The programme illustrates the different political priorities of the Gramscian and leadership positions on the BRS commission.
109. *BRS*, CPGB 1977, pp6-7.
110. 'Culture is commercialised and people are denied the opportunity to develop their talents and abilities to the full. Human relationships are distorted and sex exploited for profit by newspapers, advertisers and big business'. *BRS*, op cit, p2.
111. M. Jacques, 'How Capitalist Rule is Maintained', chapter 1 (draft) *BRS*, 1976, p3. D. Forgacs points out this disparity in 'Gramsci and the British Left', op cit, p81. See also Jon Bloomfield, *Comment* Congress Discussion, op cit.
112. Capitalist 'domination' was mainly said to be apparent in state ownership and control of the mass media. *BRS*, op cit, pp4-5. D. Forgacs points out this disparity in 'Gramsci and the British Left', op cit, p81; see also Jon Bloomfield, *Comment*, 'Congress Discussion, op cit.
113. B. Campbell, *Comment* Congress Discussion, 3 September 1977.
114. A. Hunt, *Comment* Congress Discussion, 3 September 1977. See also G. Roberts, 'Contribution to British Road Discussion', in *Morning Star*, 1 June 1977, for similar critique.
115. P. Devine, *Comment* Congress Discussion, 29 October 1977.
116. Lewisham Borough Communist Party, *Comment* Congress Discussion, 3 September 1977. Many feminists were unhappy with the party's lukewarm response. See also Josie Green, *Comment*, 3 September 1977.
117. G. Bridges, *Comment*, Congress Discussion, 29 October 1977. The journal *Eurored* had given tentative sympathy to a pro-Common Market position.
118. Reported in *Comment*, 26 November 1977.
119. G. McLennan, interview with Peter Avis, *Morning Star*, 4 July 1977.
120. J. Gollan, '"Socialist Democracy – Some Problems". The 20th Congress of the Communist Party of the Soviet Union in Retrospect', *Marxism Today*, January 1976.
121. G. Napolitano/E. Hobsbawm, *The Italian Road To Socialism*, Lawrence Hill and Company 1977, p30. For British Eurocommunists, most of the dissenting positions on the Soviet Union were to be found in *Socialist Europe*, which carried interviews with leading Soviet dissidents and opened a debate on the 'crisis' of Soviet ideology.
122. See correspondence between Reuben Falber and Sally Hibbin, CUL Organiser, in CUL files, CP archive: Letter of complaint in the *Morning*

Star 13 July 1977 from Labour MPs and members of the Bertrand Russell Peace Foundation; and letter from M. Rabstein (course organiser) to G. McLennan, 15 July 1977. CUL Box 2. According to Rabstein, 'The fact that he (Medvedev) could not speak in the Soviet Union about his work is neither his fault nor that of CUL organisers; we know where the fault lies. The fact that he could not speak at CUL is neither his fault nor that of the CUL organisers: I fear where the fault lies'.

123. Congress Report, *Comment*, November 1977. The Granada Programmes *Decision British Communism* show how the attempts by younger Eurocommunists to prevent the Congress adopting the motion were thwarted by Irene Brennan, Chair of the Congress Resolutions Committee.
124. Ibid.
125. The Granada *Decision British Communism* programme showed an attempt by Geoff Roberts to 'refer back' the Soviet anniversary motion.
126. For Falber's admission see *Changes*, 16-29 November 1991. R. Falber, interview with author.
127. *Changes*, op cit.
128. See letter to James Klugmann from 'Soviet citizen' Yuri Levin, complaining that the Soviet Union prevented circulation of the January 1976 edition of *Marxism Today*. In CP/IND/KLUG/12/08.
129. D. Purdy, Congress Discussion, *Comment*, 9 July 1977.
130. M. Prior, Congress Discussion, *Comment*, 9 July 1977.
131. M. Prior and D. Purdy, *Out of the Ghetto*, Spokesman 1979.
132. Theoretically they were in breach of party rules for publishing and distributing unauthorised documents; they were not however officially disciplined.

6. The CP in Decline

GRAMSCISM PUT ON HOLD
Those Gramscians who were worried that the degree of compromise in the BRS amounted to an excessive deference to militant labourism had their fears confirmed by the events of 1977-79. This period was characterised by the reassertion of control by the party leadership, in face of the increasing momentum of decline – in membership, industrial and political influence, unity and independent identity. This chapter will describe how the conflict between the Gramscian perspectives and the dominant ones of militant labourism accelerated the party's decline; and how this was brought sharply into focus by an intervention by one of the party's most prestigious intellectuals, Eric Hobsbawm, in 'The Forward March of Labour Halted?', a debate initiated in the pages of *Marxism Today*, but one which involved left thinkers beyond the Communist Party.

The conflict between the leadership's priority of emphasising its core industrial influence and the Gramscian concern with modernising the party amplified schisms which had been developing since the 1960s. The differing responses to the breakaway to form the New Communist Party were another example of conflicting positions over the future direction of the party, while the Gramscian influence continued to increase in various spheres of the party's work.[1] At the ideological level, Sarah Benton, after her appointment as editor of the party's weekly *Comment* in 1978, was one source of new energy. Benton, who had joined the party in the late 1960s as a consequence of being impressed by its attempts to find a dialogue with feminism and move away from Stalinism,[2] adopted from the outset a more critical and open editorial approach. This included a more direct confrontation with the party's Stalinist past and more critical attention to the party's traditional ethos, thereby risking confrontation with the party leadership. She also attempted to position the party as part of a wider left, inviting contributions from those beyond the party's ranks, hitherto unprecedented for the party's weekly.[3] Thus *Comment*, under Benton's brief editorship, adopted a heretical and critical stance before the later position taken by *Marxism Today* under Martin Jacques's editorship. Jacques, who was appointed editor as successor to James Klugmann, following the latter's illness and subsequent death in 1977, was initially more restrained in his approach, which reflected his more senior position in the party.[4] Nevertheless, in the editorial of the September 1978 issue he argued that the journal, which had previously had a low circulation and very little exposure beyond the party, 'must appeal to the wider left', and would include a broader range of contributors and themes.[5] The most important early examples of this were Eric Hobsbawm's 'Forward March of Labour Halted?', in September 1978 (discussed below), and Stuart Hall's 'Moving Right Show', published in January 1979.[6] Hall's contribution marked a shift in the trajectory of the Gramscian position in the party: Gramsci's ideas now became the context for understanding the rise of the new right and the predicaments of the left. His analysis of 'Thatcherism' as a hegemonic project with deep roots in working-class fears and aspirations (and as such needing serious attention from the left) stimulated a long-running discussion in the pages of *Marxism Today* over the subsequent decade. As far as the Communist Party was concerned, this helped to further delineate rival positions between the Gramscian and traditionalist constituencies, as they argued over the extent of the crisis on the left. Beyond the Communist Party the debate provided the stimulus for a long-term assessment of left prospects, as well as wide-ranging discussions of the peculiarities of Thatcherism.

There was still sufficient optimism within Gramscian circles for the CUL of 1977-78 to record its biggest attendances to date; and for the organising group, in particular Geoff Roberts and Chris Nawrat, it provided a further opportunity to wage the party's battles over strategy in a public forum. Yet CUL was an isolated example of the party's presence, and in the higher echelons of the party tougher battles were on the horizon.[7] At the more direct strategic level, party National Organiser Dave Cook and leading party economist Pat Devine – both sympathetic to Gramsci's ideas – sought to initiate a transformation of the party's democratic structure in a major challenge to party tradition. The 1977 Congress had agreed to set up a new commission on inner-party democracy, the first for twenty years, to report with proposals to the 1979 Congress. Cook, Devine and four other Gramscian members of the Commission saw this as an opportunity to democratise and modernise the party's structures. Cook argued in *Marxism Today*, during the process of the Commission's deliberations, that the party must change its mode of work and needed to express its new commitment to democracy in its own practice: 'If ever the maxim "once the political line is decided organisation decides all" needed replacing by "involvement decides all" it is now'.[8] This provoked a response from the leadership, who were not willing to compromise on inner-party democracy. Dave Priscott, Yorkshire District Secretary, in an argument typical of this position, feared that the proposals of Cook and his allies would 'amount to the liquidation of the party as an effective revolutionary force'.[9] This response indicated the unease of the party leadership towards challenges to the existing structures of the party, which they considered a direct challenge to their authority.

These differences over the future organisation of the party were reflected on the commission itself, where the six Gramscian members, outnumbered by those loyal to the leadership, were forced to submit 'alternative proposals' as well as signing the majority report.[10] It is possible to discern an alternative, more fluid, concept of the party in the alternative proposals, one aimed at allowing dissenting voices from the party grassroots to be heard at a more formal level; this would offer a challenge to the grip of the leadership, which hitherto had been extremely well entrenched. For the authors it was seen as a further attempt to strengthen the 'pre-figurative' link between the democratic organisation of the party and the future socialist society.[11] The proposals advocated the abolition of the 'recommended list' for Congress leadership elections, and the election of the leadership by secret ballot.[12] It condemned that part of the party's heritage which was imbued with the 'anti-democratic, distorting practices which have come to be known as Stalinism'. It criticised the 'anonymous' and 'monolithic' impression of the leadership, and 'the pretence of a leadership that is never wrong'. It accepted the basic premise of democratic centralism, namely that the party should unite around collective leadership once a decision had been reached, but argued for the recognition of 'different trends and positions' in the party, and the open discussion of political differences – a view which the leadership and opponents interpreted as the endorsement of factionalism.[13]

This critique reflected to some degree a broader concern within the European communist movement at this time over the inadequacy of the organisational framework that had been inherited from an earlier, very different set of circumstances. For example the prominent French intellectual Louis Althusser argued in a series of articles in the French newspaper *Le Monde* that the PCF's organisational structure needed rescuing from what he perceived as its Stalinist heritage. He emphasised the need to create space for freedom of expression, and argued for an end to the recommended list system and the 'filtering of candidates' for party elections; he also argued for a 'truly sovereign' party Congress. He argued that discussion and disagreement would make a positive contribution to the democratic renewal of the party: 'If the party is alive its unity will be contradictory ... but will also be open and fertile'.[14] Althusser, along with other French intellectuals like Balibar, defended the concept of democratic centralism. Their criticism was against what they saw as an abuse of it.

The critique put forward in the British CP was similarly not a renunciation of democratic centralism per se, but rather the leadership's interpretation of it. Moreover the critique not only challenged the party's leadership, but was also an attempt to accommodate, in an organisational form, the politics and practices of the new social movements – first taken up by young communists, students and feminists, and discussed in the first part of this study.[15] Thus the party leadership's fear at the 1979 Congress was that 'loose pluralism' would result from the alternative proposals; and they echoed a concern first expressed twenty years earlier, that the party's class culture, as the organising principle of its identity, would be further eroded.[16] The defeat of the alternative proposals was testament to a change in the balance of power between the leadership and the Gramscians: in the debates on the BRS the latter had extracted concessions from the leadership, but in the case of inner-party democracy the suggested reforms went beyond what the leadership – and indeed the membership at large (for whom the party remained a strong source of identity) – considered safe for the party's existence.

FROM RENEWAL TO INERTIA: THE LEADERSHIP FIGHTS BACK

The attempt to change the party's own constitution was therefore a modernising step too far for the leadership. Those in the leadership who were uneasy at the scale of the changes in the BRS, but who could accept it as a reasonable compromise, took exception to the critique of the party's own practices and culture. This suggests that new ideas that could help win support for a party struggling to keep its members and expand influence could always find support amongst the leadership, for pragmatic reasons; but that ideas which challenged the very nature of the party's organisation were likely to be met with greater suspicion and concern. This was particularly germane for a party leadership which by 1979 had clocked up more than ninety years of full-time service between its three leading members – Gordon McLennan, Bert Ramelson and Reuben Falber.[17] In the case of Falber, custodian of the party's funds, more serious issues concerning the party's future may have been at stake.[18]

The leadership started to reassert itself as defender of tradition and orthodoxy. This manifested itself in the conflicts that started to occur with the Gramscians. Dave Cook, the most prominent Gramscian, and leading advocate of the 'alternative proposals', had his position as National Organiser redefined to relieve him of the more political roles, and was later relegated to the position of National Election Agent. He spent most of 1979 in this reduced role, organising the party's sixtieth anniversary celebrations and the annual card issue. Sarah Benton's heretical period as editor of *Comment* had brought continuing conflict over editorial control, and the leadership's practice of discussing and taking decisions over the content of the journal without involving the editor led to her eventual resignation, citing as reasons 'bureaucratic inertia' and 'lack of collective political discussion'.[19] And in a second notable intervention by the party leadership into a Communist

University event, Monty Johnstone was prevented from giving a keynote speech at the 1979 CUL. Johnstone was also at the centre of another controversy, when the London District Secretary Gerry Cohen threatened to resign if Johnstone was made the party's delegate to the Bulgarian Communist Party Congress.[20] Martin Jacques, despite being made editor of *Marxism Today* two years earlier, was not re-elected to the Political Committee in 1979. The defeat of the alternative proposals at the 1979 Congress confirmed the extent of this backlash, and provided evidence of a realignment between the leadership and those committed to more traditional communist politics, for whom party loyalty was a strong virtue and internal discussion an unnecessary diversion. Some commentators have attributed this defeat of the Gramscians, at least in part, to a tactical mistake by Cook and his allies, arguing that they chose the wrong issue at the wrong time; furthermore some Gramscians felt less strongly about organisational questions, and saw them as a diversion from the more directly political questions.[21]

THE FORWARD MARCH OF LABOUR HALTED

Whatever the reasons for it, the backlash helped polarise the broader political differences between the leadership and the Gramscians. These were fuelled further by the debate on the Forward March of Labour Halted, which was initiated by Eric Hobsbawm.

The Forward March of Labour Halted was first presented as the Marx Memorial Lecture in 1978, and subsequently published in *Marxism Today*; it then became the title of a book which also included respondents to Hobsbawm.[22] Until this intervention Hobsbawm – one of the country's most distinguished historians – had not played a leading role in the party's political and strategic work. For example he was not a member of official party committees – though he had remained a member of the party's History Group and was a regular speaker at CUL. He had authority and status as a leading historian, and belonged to a generation that had lived through fascism and the different crises in communist history; and he was one of those who had remained in the party in 1956. His analysis now opened up debates beyond the Communist Party, and, together with other contributions to *Marxism Today* in the 1980s, helped to create the basis for a renewal of the New Left.

The 'Forward March' debate is pivotal to any understanding of the different perspectives in the party on its role and relationship to the labour movement. It served to further crystallise the contending political positions between, on the one hand, those who wanted to retain a strong commitment to traditional industrial politics, and, on the other, the Gramscians, who saw a greater need for alliances between different social groups. Moreover this debate has a wider relevance for the long-term future of the British left and broader developments in British society. These developments included the break-up of the post-war

Keynesian consensus from 1976 as economic crisis deepened, and the intensification of conflict from 1977 over the Social Contract, which was to culminate in the 'winter of discontent' in 1978 and the election of the first Thatcher government.

Hobsbawm's main argument was that the dynamics that had originally driven the labour movement, such as the development of class consciousness, instances of fundamental class solidarity, and the political and electoral advances of the working class, had come to a halt thirty years before – around the late 1940s and 1950s. Since this time the labour movement had endured several periods of profound crisis, and Hobsbawm analysed the features of these crises in some depth.

He argued that the changing structure of British capitalism had brought about a long-term decline in manual occupations as a percentage of the workforce, despite the fact that 'proletarianisation' was increasing in other sectors, notably in the growth of white-collar employees. The development of technology had produced new groups of professionals and technicians, as well as replacing labour with machines in many cases.[23] Hobsbawm argued that this decline of manual occupations had had a major industrial and political significance both for class and political identity (in terms of political and voting alignment), and for the ability to organise collectively in bargaining and other forms of action. This was affecting the mass trade unionism that had its origins in the new unionism of the 1880s, when craft unionism had become radicalised and integrated together with the 'general' unions, and had reached its peak by the 1930s. Also affected was what Hobsbawm termed 'a common style of proletarian life'; he argued that the convergence between work and leisure, around such developments as mass cinema, football, the council flat and the fish and chip shop, had helped to consolidate a strong class identity; thus changing patterns of work and leisure had very broad political and cultural implications.[24]

Furthermore the workforce was becoming increasingly feminised, with the rise in married women's employment and the decline of male-dominated manual sectors.[25] And mass immigration since the 1950s had also brought new challenges for the labour movement's perception of who it represented. Hobsbawm noted in both these cases the rise of 'sectionalism' within the working class. Although he acknowledged that sectionalism had occurred previously – between, for example, craft unions and less skilled workers – he argued that there were qualitative and more fundamental differences in these more recent instances of sectionalism that occurred since the 1950s. Moreover this sectionalism was to be found in the very nature of some strike actions, including some disputes that had been classified as expressions of class struggle. The reason for this, according to Hobsbawm, was that the working class was now less homogeneous than ever before:

We now see a growing division of workers into sections and groups, each pursuing its own economic interest irrespective of the rest. What is new here is that their ability to do so is no longer related to traditional criteria such as their technical qualifications and standing or, as it were, the social ladder. The new strength of the group lies not in the amount of loss they can cause to the employer, but in the inconvenience they can cause to the public, that is to other workers by power blackouts or whatever. This is a natural consequence of a state monopoly capitalist system in which the basic target of pressure is not the bank account of private employers, but, directly or indirectly, the political will of the government. In the nature of things such sectional forms of struggle not only create potential friction between groups of workers, but risk weakening the hold of the labour movement as a whole. The sense of class solidarity may be further weakened by the fact that the real income of a family may no longer actually depend on a worker's own job alone.[26]

Moreover, Hobsbawm argued that trade union economism was another significant reason for the decline in class consciousness. Recent trade union militancy, he argued, was 'almost entirely economist militancy', with most struggles being fought as 'pure wage strikes'.[27] He also argued that this 'straightforward economist trade union consciousness' might at times 'actually set workers against each other rather than establish wider patterns of solidarity'.[28] Although he noted the 'recovery and impetus' of the 1960s, a lack of leadership on the left had meant that opportunities were missed; he saw this as all the more regrettable considering the world crisis that capitalism had entered into. He ended his argument with an appeal to the whole labour movement:

> If the labour and socialist movement is to recover its soul, its dynamism and its historical initiative we, as Marxists, must do what Marx would certainly have done: to recognise the novel situation in which we find ourselves, to analyse it, realistically and concretely, to analyse the reasons, historical and otherwise, for the failures as well as the successes of the labour movement and to formulate not only what we would want to do, but what can be done. We should have done this even while we were waiting for British capitalism to enter its period of dramatic crisis. We cannot afford not to do it now that it has.[29]

Hobsbawm's analysis gave greater impetus to the simmering debates in the party – on the differing interpretations of class, the question of the economistic and sectional nature of militant labourism, the significance of new social movements, and how to respond or 'intervene' in the crisis of capitalism. His analysis was sympathetic to the Gramscian position, and his intervention at this time provided stronger authority and legitimacy to the arguments of the newer Gramscian generation.

He could not be dismissed as a young turk. He highlighted in a deeper historical analysis the complexity of the British class structure, discussion of which by Alan Hunt and other members of the party's Sociology Group had been an early sign of the development of contending political positions. His critique of economism followed that of the young turks on the Economic Committee, while coinciding with the publication of *Out of the Ghetto* by Mike Prior and Dave Purdy.[30] For Purdy and Prior, similar trends to those identified by Hobsbawm meant that the Communist Party alone would not be able to deliver the political leadership that was needed, because of its size, its organisational structure and its adherence to economism and sectionalism, as well as its inability to completely distance itself from Moscow. In strident and forthright language they argued that the left could only 'renew' itself if it recognised a greater role for social movements, adopted a broader definition of politics beyond parliament and trade unions, constructed a socialist incomes policy, and recognised the way in which different levels of power had become more widely diffused within civil society. It was an analysis which incorporated their critique of the preceding decade, but it suggested a strategy which they felt to be no longer realisable within the Communist Party.[31]

THE DEBATE OPENS UP

Hobsbawm's analysis, like that of Purdy and Prior, situated the dilemma of the Communist Party within the predicaments of the wider left:[32] though Hobsbawm was addressing the left and labour movement in general, his views had clear implications for the role of the Communist Party. The party, in a position of leadership in the labour movement in the 1970s, had gone along with much of the labourist orthodoxy. Since it had drawn on the skilled sectors of the working class for its moral and political leadership, the decline of these sectors would have particular implications for the party.

Party critics of Hobsbawm focused on his claims about economism and sectionalism. Thus Ken Gill, by this time the party's senior trade union official, in a rapidly declining industrial section, disagreed with Hobsbawm's conclusions.[33] Gill rejected the view that the trade unions followed narrow economistic agendas which limited their objectives to the 'wages struggle' alone. He pointed to the 'breadth' of working-class struggle, evident in, for example, workplace occupations, the equal pay battles and the boycott of South African goods by workers. This, he said, showed a 'maturity' of working-class action and it was therefore inaccurate to see the main industrial struggles as bereft of political radicalism. Moreover he argued that the Communist Party's demand for the restoration of free collective bargaining was 'profoundly political'.[34] As far as the Communist Party's role was concerned, Gill argued that it was the acceptance of the Social Contract by the Labour leadership that was the root cause of the current dilemmas, and this was a mistake the Communist Party would not have made. Gill's arguments can be seen as a reinforcement of the position Bert Ramelson and the Industrial Department had taken at the time, namely that the main 'lessons of 1970-1974' should be the further development of a 'militant wage movement', along the lines of the militant labourist strategy that Ramelson had pursued since the mid-1960s.[35]

Kevin Halpin, another key figure in the party's industrial work, from his role as leader of the Liaison Committee for the Defence of Trade Unions (LCDTU) during its most militant period, also took exception to Hobsbawm's argument. His view reflected the attitudes of many industrial activists towards the Gramscian wing of the party in the mid-1970s, namely that they were too involved with the theoretical work of the party, and not enough with its activism – particularly industrial activism. Halpin maintained that the party must address 'the imbalance which favoured the theorists', which led to 'the limited participation in the discussion of the theories and policies of our movement of those who are in the thick of carrying them forward in the labour movement'.[36] His political objections were similar to Gill's, namely that the 1970-1974 period of class struggle had indicated what could have been done had the Labour Party not adopted the Social Contract, and TUC not failed to give leadership. Moreover, he argued that the events of this period justified the correctness of the party's industrial politics:

> [The] shrinking of the working class in traditional industries does not present any major change in the direction of our work ... The discussion frequently presents a picture of thousands of communists searching for a factory gate with leaflets and papers to put across our policy. The opposite is the case – thousands of factories, pits, sites and depots are crying out for our policy and no one is there to put the case.[37]

THE CONSOLIDATION OF DIVISION

The debate initiated by Hobsbawm amplified differences over industrial policy within the party. Pete Carter, one of the few Gramscians among leading party industrial workers, agreed with Hobsbawm's analysis, warning against the 'ever-growing dangers of sectionalism within the working class'.[38] The key question for Carter was: 'why are we no further forward in winning political advances?'. Though drawing a clear line between his position and that of Hobsbawm, he was also critical of the traditionalists:

> One despairs when Gill says that the restoration of the wages movement is the key area of struggle, without any concrete suggestions as to how it is related to either the political struggle of the left or other areas of struggle like what is the relationship between the fight for wages and the

struggle over investment policy, the problems of workers' control, or whether products are socially useful or not.[39]

The differences continued to spill over into the pages of the wider party press during 1978.[40] In the context of the broad democratic alliance, the Gramscians argued that the trade unions needed to broaden their focus and engage with new social movements, to forge unity between different social groups; meanwhile the traditionalists were pursuing a more orthodox class position. In a key debate between contending exponents of the two positions, Dave Cook argued that the industrial advisory committees needed to 'interact' more with the wider political work of the party at branch level. (This of course was an old critique, but it had been given new impetus by the new democratic focus of the party's strategy.) Mick Costello (who had succeeded Bert Ramelson as Industrial Organiser in 1978) retaliated by arguing that the unions remained the primary vehicle of the party's politics, and the economy was the key area of struggle.[41] This dispute, which reflected other underlying tensions at different levels of the party,[42] was reinforced in Costello's report to the EC in early 1979, just before the wave of militancy that has subsequently been described as the 'Winter of Discontent'. While admitting that 'de-industrialisation' was taking place, Costello's response was to argue for an extension of free collective bargaining and the promotion of workplace bargaining.[43]

These quite different views of class politics impinged on many areas of the Communist Party's work, both in actual political and industrial struggles[44] and in its organising committees.[45] And the debate initiated by Hobsbawm also had a wider significance for the British left, as was demonstrated by similarities between party and non-party contribututors in debates over the future of the labour movement. Thus it is possible to discern in the contributions to *Marxism Today* two broad strands, of 'traditionalist' and 'modernising' opinion. Amongst the 'modernisers' who agreed with Hobsbawm's analysis that the left and labour movement had been held back by economism were the Labour MP Stan Newens, Bob Wright of the AUEW, Jack Jones of the TGWU and Raymond Williams, a 'first' New Left intellectual. The 'traditionalists' seeking a continuity of industrial and class struggles included Bernard Dix, the leader of NUPE (whom Hobsbawm had criticised for 'sectionalism'), Steve Jeffereys, the former industrial organiser of the International Socialists, and the socialist feminist Hilary Wainwright. Meanwhile Tony Benn, who was emerging as the unofficial leader of the left at this time, was more ambivalent. His concept of 'corporatism', used to explain the ways in which Labour governments had acted to incorporate different interest groups (notably trade unions and management), appealed in different ways to both positions within the Communist Party. On the one hand it resonated with the Gramscian critique of economism (in particular the over-emphasis on free collective bargaining), and its argument for the need to extend the political struggles to the new social movements. On the other hand, Benn also argued that 'wage control' was a crucial element of the corporatist strategy, thereby effectively ruling out any form of incomes policy.[46] Benn was to break more decisively with the *Marxism Today* analysis in the early 1980s, the period in which he sought the deputy leadership of the Labour Party.[47]

More substantive indications of consolidated, long-term and irreversible divisions between the two positions within the party itself can be derived from the political direction of the *Morning Star* under Tony Chater's editorship. Following the decision of the 1977 congress to criticise the political and cultural content of the *Morning Star* as being narrowly economistic, there was little evidence of any change in direction; indeed any analysis of its content at this time would reveal a strengthening of labourist positions. The difference in the late 1970s between the *Morning Star*'s political outlook and that of *Comment* and *Marxism Today* gives a clear indication of the ideological disputes between the Gramscians and those committed to militant labourism. Moreover the refusal of Tony Chater to change the content of the *Morning Star* in light of the congress motion, and the reluctance of the party leadership to take action, was the beginning of a long-running breach between the party and its daily paper. It was to reach its climax in 1985 when the party, having sided with the Gramscians in what was by then a swiftly declining organisation, lost control of it.

By 1978-79 it was becoming apparent that the different positions could not be reconciled within one political party. Whereas in 1977 the leadership had compromised with the Gramscians in the re-writing of *The British Road to Socialism*, had appointed Martin Jacques as editor of *Marxism Today*, and remained supportive of the creativity of their efforts in attempting to renew the party, by 1979 the position had changed. Fears over the scale of the party's decline led to a new suspicion of the political significance of Gramscian arguments for the future of the party.

THE DECLINE OF THE PARTY'S INDUSTRIAL BASE

The party's industrial base, which had still been able to play a key organising role in the mid-1970s, was much weaker towards the end of the decade. The demise of its industrial core inevitably had major repercussions for the party. Above all, it highlighted the strategic vulnerability at the heart of the party's militant labourism, namely its dependence both on strengthening the party's links with official trade unionism and, at the same time, providing a critique of its limitations. In a period of labour movement strength, as in the early 1970s, it was possible to do this, on the basis of the alliance with Jones and Scanlon, and the party's role in helping to mobilise and direct the militancy. In the less propitious period of the late 1970s, in the aftermath of the

Social Contract and in the context of the growth of the socio-economic forces outlined by Hobsbawm, it was much more difficult. As McIlroy argues:

> As the tenuous nature of the gains of the upturn since 1968 became apparent, so did criticism that the industrial leadership had leant too much, and too unsuccessfully, on establishing its bona fides with union leaders – and allowing CP trade unionists too long a leash – at the expense of sustained work amongst the rank and file.[48]

This argument was most forcefully put by critics from the left who felt the party had become excessively incorporated into the official structures of the labour movement. There is much evidence to suggest that by the late 1970s the IS/SWP had taken over the leadership of the rank and file of many unions from the CP, ending a process that had begun a decade earlier when the CP embarked on its labourist position.[49] There is also evidence that the party started to put less emphasis on workplace and factory branch activity in its period of influence within the trade union hierarchy between 1968 and 1975. McIlroy has shown that there was a political shift in the party's attitude towards workplace organisation in these years, exemplified by the absence of such initiatives in Congress resolutions.[50] It was only in 1975, when the party's industrial work had started to wane, that there was an attempt to retrieve the situation with a conference on workplace organisation, though this brought a minimal return.[51] By 1978, representation had deteriorated to 26 factory branches, a strong sign that the party could no longer sustain an industrial base, despite its maintaining of some influence within the trade union hierarchy. McIlroy argues that 'the picture suggested was not a national community of political branches but rather a shallower, personalised network of trade union militants – individuals or handfuls – largely concerned with industrial issues, sometimes with limited attachment to the CP'.[52]

Very specific political conclusions can be drawn from the evidence of this industrial decline. As Thompson argues, such a predicament could be seen to be inevitable given the 'party's tacit abandonment of its independent trade union role in the early 1960s and cultivation thereafter of a united broad left'.[53] In other words, as soon as the party's ability to organise mass united action became weakened, its political justification for existing was brought into question. The contrasting priorities of the different political sections of the party were by now contributing in more visible ways to the overall decline of the party's independent political strategy. The remaining and declining industrial activists, backed by the *Morning Star*, became increasingly focused on trade union work, notably through a continuation of opposition to the Social Contract and involvement in the onset of the 'Winter of Discontent'; thus they maintained a militant labourist trajectory similar to that which had sustained the struggles of the early 1970s, when the party had been at the centre of the new militancy.[54] Meanwhile the Gramscians and other intellectual networks were not able to draw the industrial comrades in any numbers to their debates, despite the fact that their underlying arguments for the renewal of the party depended upon a new relationship between intellectuals and industrial workers. This might explain why Martin Jacques and Dave Cook, for example, sought a more pragmatic strategy than other more radical Eurocommunists, and why they were criticised for not challenging the party leadership more directly.[55]

Party membership declined dramatically between 1975 and 1979. The party lost approximately 28 per cent of its overall membership – falling from 28,519 members in June 1975 to 20,599 in June 1979.[56] In percentage terms this was as big a decline as had taken place in the aftermath of 1956.[57] Moreover, this decline was not limited to its trade union sections, which might have been expected given the party's declining influence in this sphere. Nor can it be explained adequately in terms of the impact of the breakaway associated with the formation of the New Communist Party, whose official membership was only about 700.[58] All sections of the party suffered a decline.

THE YCL'S DOWNTURN

The YCL was also in decline. It had begun to go through similar ideological divisions to those which were now shaking the party itself at an earlier period. A conservative backlash had occurred after the 1960s generation of YCL activists had graduated to the party proper, which had led to continuous conflict between rival groups. At the YCL Congress of 1979, under Nina Temple's leadership, and with the modernising group in the majority, the delegates went further than the party was prepared to go and voted to reject democratic centralism. However this made no difference to the organisation's health. Although the YCL had maintained a public presence, not only within mainstream organisations and youth campaigns such as the school students campaign, anti-racism and the early campaigns against the unemployment of the late 1970s, but also amongst the broader cultural-political movements, such as punk rock, it could not reverse the steady decline. Despite attempts to identify with the punk movement, such as a change in the format and style of *Challenge*, to give it an anti-authoritarian image, and some limited recruitment amongst punks who played in bands, the YCL did not succeed in making major inroads.[59] Additionally, the wider disaffection with politics amongst young people in Britain – partly epitomised by movements such as punk – caused problems for the YCL as for other political movements.[60]

In fact the YCL's decline was more rapid than that of the party, and it is noticeable that its downturn was severest at precisely the time the Gramscian-Eurocommunist influence was at its peak. The programme on which they had fought, *Our Future*, continued the theme initiated a decade earlier on the 'culture as politics' approach, and this only served to amplify the divisions – and in a more confrontational and direct way than in the main party.[61] Critics of *Our Future* focused on what they perceived to be the abandonment of class in favour of a looser pluralism of new social movements – a similar critique of Gramscism to that deployed by critics in the main party. This approach, it was felt, would amount to the 'liquidation' of the YCL itself.[62]

The YCL Congress of 1979, therefore, far from being the birth of a new political direction, was the YCL's 'last call' as a national political force. By the early 1980s its work was sporadic and uneven, with little appeal to new generations, and, in contrast to the successes of the 'cultural turn' of the 1960s, it was unable to adapt itself to the new youth movements and subcultures.

THE STUDENT DEMISE

Similarly, the party's membership amongst students started to decline, after the peak period of the early to mid 1970s. Party students were unable to maintain their strategic influence in the politics of the NUS, or to sustain the successes of intellectual forums such as CUL. Party student membership was in continuous decline after its peak of almost a thousand in 1973. By 1978 it stood at 585.[63] As noted in Chapter Two, the students were the fastest growing section of the party in the early to mid 1970s, providing a significant intellectual forum for the advance of the Gramscian strategy in the party. The main strategic contribution made by communist students had been the Broad Left, in which the communists co-existed with, and in many cases gave ideological leadership to, a broader left bloc of independents and left Labour students. By the late 1970s, however, this alliance had started to decline, eventually coming to an end in 1979 when it was succeeded by the Left Alliance. This was a similarly broad coalition, but it did not rely on the roles of the Labour and Communist *Parties*, giving greater emphasis to *individuals* in the independent left, and with a more prominent role for Liberals. The Left Alliance thus had a looser ideological and organisational base; it also faced new electoral challenges from Labour students, who began to challenge independent left hegemony within the NUS, a process that gathered pace during the 1980s.[64]

Of those who had played a leading part in communist student politics, some, like Jon Bloomfield, had graduated to full-time party work, but others began to move away from the party, disillusioned by the slow pace of change. It will be remembered that communist students in the Broad Left had been used to the concept of broad democratic alliances and pluralism, based on the positive endorsement of new social forces, some while before the party cautiously took these on board in the BRS. Therefore, while the party's shift in this document was welcomed by students – who sought, for example, to apply the new strategy to the question of the 'democratisation of higher education' – for many student activists it was too little too late, and they sought new avenues elsewhere.[65]

The most notable departure was that of Sue Slipman, NUS President during 1977-1978 and a member of the party Executive Committee from 1975. Slipman had grown increasingly critical of the party's inability to reform itself, adopting a much more critical position than other Gramscian members of the EC. She has described her approach on the EC at this time as 'a bit kamikaze': that is, her criticisms were becoming such that they did not hold out the possibility of change; nor was she prepared to exercise caution in her criticism. Having been consistently critical of the economism of the party's approach,[66] by 1979 she felt that the party was unreformable. The new 'British Road' was insufficiently pluralist, in her view, and she felt that democratic centralism itself needed to be overhauled. The party's conservatism meant that it was beyond reform: 'It was quite clear to me that there was to be no break from the past. The past was where people were embedded'. Moreover she felt isolated on the EC. Those closest to her – Dave Cook, Martin Jacques and the YCL General Secretary Tom Bell – were much more cautious, holding on to the idea that positions could be won. Cook, she said, had been 'very courageous' and had 'come out fighting with the minority report'; Jacques was 'very equivocal about where he was …'; and Bell was 'rather nervous and worried' about open criticism. Essentially, she felt that their 'private' beliefs did not become public criticisms to the degree that she felt was necessary. Slipman only stayed in the party until 1979 out of loyalty to Cook in his attempt to democratise the party. Following the defeat of the Minority Report on Inner Party Democracy she left the party, by this time already clear that she was no longer a communist. Her decision to join the Social Democratic Party in 1981 rather than the Labour Party (as some of her contemporaries chose to do at this time) was fuelled by the need for a critique of 'labourism'.[67]

In addition to the loss of some of its leading student activists, the Communist University of London showed signs of decline from 1978, when its numbers had peaked. Only 517 people attended CUL 11 in 1979, a 50 per cent decrease on the previous year.[68] Many reasons were given for this decline. Minutes of review meetings and organisers' reports suggest that the CUL had exhausted its potential. Jon Bloomfield, who had played a key role as National Student Organiser in its peak years, attributed its decline to the 'changing nature of CUL'. He pointed to the decline of the specialist courses which had been crucial to the 'ability to generate capable Marxists in the academic fields'. Without them the CUL had become a 'general Marxist jamboree with no thread or theme'. Other reasons given included the 'ageing' of the 1968 generation, and the failure to involve more recent generations of undergraduates. There was also a feeling amongst some of 'déjà vu', with people meeting the same people and hearing similar arguments. Some critics complained that the organisers of CUL had not been ruthless enough in broadening its political base, and extending an arm to a broader range of groups, beyond the Marxist tradition.[69] It had moved from a 'model shop of Marxism ... to a supermarket in which a range of differing approaches to Marxism were offered to the growing number of participants', as the organiser's notes had put it for CUL 11.[70]

ANOTHER EXODUS OF INTELLECTUALS?

The decline of CUL, however, has to be seen in the wider context of the decline of the party. Eurocommunism itself was on the wane after 1979, following the defeat of the PCI's 'historic compromise', splits in the PCE and the challenge to the PCF from Mitterrand's Socialists in France. These developments had repercussions in the CPGB, in the sense that the main external source of inspiration for the Eurocommunists was now in doubt. Moreover, the decline of the party's leading intellectual forum – CUL, which finally ended in 1981, after another poor year in 1980[71] – and of the YCL and student organisations, was supplemented by the departure of some of its most critical and heretical intellectuals. Dave Purdy and Mike Prior were perhaps the most notable of the Gramscian intellectuals who left the party at the end of the 1970s. Purdy had begun to feel a mood of 'deep despair' during the Winter of Discontent, and he 'began to have serious doubts that the party could be won for the cause of enlightenment'. He made the decision that 'if IPD (Inner Party Democracy) won I would stay, if lost I would leave'.[72] He therefore left the party in December 1979 and joined the Labour Party in 1980. Mike Prior, who had been an ally of Purdy's and a constant critic of the party, also left at a similar time, disillusioned with the party's inability to change.[73]

The radical group of Eurocommunists who had come together at the CULs of 1977-78 – Geoff Roberts, Chris Nawrat, Alan McDougall and Ken Spours – had also departed from party activity by the late 1970s. This group, together with others from the Lewisham borough of the party, including George Bridges and Genia Browning, had, like Prior and Purdy and Slipman, been openly critical of the party. Their criticisms also focused at times on Dave Cook and Martin Jacques – in effect, the leading Gramscians – for not challenging the party leadership more openly. For Nawrat, who 'quit' politics, after 1979, with the rise of Thatcherism, there had been 'lost opportunities' through the failure of the leading Gramscians (Cook and Jacques) to confront the party leadership. His colleagues, Roberts, Spours and MacDougall, similarly disheartened by events, nevertheless redirected their energies towards a broader 'new left' journal, which they saw as the best way of sustaining their politics[74] – *Politics and Power*. This journal was published by Routledge, and included on its editorial board Gramscian and Eurocommunist activists, and wider New Left and feminist thinkers beyond the party, many of whom had come together at the CUL.[75] It was to be a 'Eurocommunist' *New Left Review* according to its founders, and had the objective of 'bringing together intellectuals of various theoretical and political experiences who have shown an interest in creating new dimensions within the British Marxist tradition'.[76]

The departure of such significant intellectuals, who had been the backbone of much of the Gramscian input over the preceding decade, together with the erosion of the party's industrial base and its weakening political influence in the labour movement, combined to catapult the party into rapid and serious decline, a predicament characterised by the increasingly inward-looking context in which it debated its future. The Broad Democratic Alliance, or 'BDA' as it became known, seemed destined to become a relic of party jargon along with all the other terminology, such as 'progressive forces'[77] – and was caricatured openly by Sarah Benton in her time as editor of *Comment*. One attempt to widen the appeal of the BDA, as part of a broader political and cultural strategy of the left, was a Lawrence and Wishart book based on papers from the last ever Communist University of London, with chapters on gay cultural politics, feminism and the importance of anti-racism; Dave Cook was given the task of explaining why the BRS contained a strategy which could unite these popular currents. The low sales of the book provided another indication that the broad democratic alliance was not reaching the people it was principally addressing.[78] These developments were testament to the inability of the party to incorporate 'new social forces'. The 'broad democratic alliance' depended necessarily on an extension of communist influence if it was to have any effect, while it also needed to hold onto its leading social movement activists and intellectuals. Its failure to do so is important in understanding the party's demise at this time.[79] The decline of the party included therefore what could be described as a 'second exodus' of leading intellectuals (following the departure of John Saville, Edward Thompson and others who left in 1956 to set up the first New Left). For both the Gramscians of the 1970s and their predecessors it was the party's failure to change and modernise its organisation that was crucial.[80]

The 'internalised' nature of the party at this time in some ways paralleled that of the Labour Party, as it too moved into a period of decline. Despite the rise in influence of left activists, and some policy shifts, there was no long-term transformation of the Labour Party at this time, nor much evidence of anything similar to the 'Gramscian' approach adopted by dissidents within the CP. If anything, as Thompson has suggested, these developments reflect the wider decline of labourism – a culture to which the Communist Party remained to a large extent committed.

Notes

1. Rival contributions in Congress Discussion in *Comment*, 9 July 1977, show Gramscians such as Jon Bloomfield welcoming the departure of French and his allies, whom he saw as representing the 'sectarian' traditions of the party, while the leadership regretted their departure.
2. S. Benton, interview with author.
3. Benton's more controversial contributions as *Comment* Editor included a front cover depicting Stalin's murdered millions. This provoked a response from the party's EC in January 1979 which described it as a 'crude representation of the Party's policy and its publication was an error of judgement', reported in *Comment*, 3 February 1979.
4. M. Jacques, interview with author.
5. Editorial, *Marxism Today*, September 1978.
6. *Marxism Today*, January 1979,
7. This group also included Ken Spours and Alan MacDougall. The group wanted a more confrontational approach to the leadership. They had organised opposition to the party's motion at the 1977 congress commemorating the 60th anniversary of the Soviet Union. The Granada documentary shows them manoeuvring behind the scenes at the congress. G. Roberts, C. Nawrat, A. MacDougall, K. Spours, interviews with author.
8. *Marxism Today*, December 1978.
9. *Marxism Today*, February 1979. See also M. Costello, *Marxism Today*, June 1979.
10. The six were Joanne Richards, Pat Devine, Maria Loftus, Dave Cook, Veronica Luker and Josie Green. The submission of 'alternative proposals' was itself an unusual precedent and indicated both the extent of disagreement and the caution over the need to represent the contending views.
11. See the section 'For the Open Argument of Politics' in *Alternative Proposals to Report of Commission on Inner Party Democracy*, CPGB 1979, pp48-50.
12. The 'recommended list' was a list of candidates recommended for election to the new EC, made by the outgoing EC and inevitably adhered to by Congress delegates. Thus it was a main method of ensuring a self-perpetuating leadership. The list could be amended at Congress by the Election Preparation Committee, but it was quite difficult to persuade them to make changes. The only occasions on which any deviance from the list occurred were the 1929 election to include Wal Hannington, and in the North West District election in 1985 by which time the split in the party was at its most severe. See W. Thompson, *The Good Old Cause*, op cit, pp45, 193.
13. 'Alternative Proposals', op cit; D. Priscott, *Marxism Today*, February 1979, op cit.
14. This 'openness and fertility' that he referred to contrasted with what he saw as the 'cementing' of party unity at any price around a party leadership which controlled 'not only men [sic] but also the truth'. The leadership of the PCF condemned Althusser's intervention as 'factional activity'. All quoted in M. Waller, *Democratic Centralism*, Manchester University Press 1981, p130. Jensen and Ross in their ethnographic study of the Eurocommunist branch of the PCF during 1978 also found critiques of 'centralism' paramount. J. Jensen and G. Ross, *The View From the*

Inside, University of California Press 1984, p21. In Italy, the 'Manifesto Group' had split with the PCI over similar critiques of centralism though this occurred much earlier, in 1968. See R. Lumley, *States of Emergency* (Verso 1990) for further discussion of this group.

15. This objective of the alternative proposals is supported by a range of wider evidence which includes the 'Congress Discussion' in the pages of *Comment* in September-October 1979; see also D. Cook, *Marxism Today*, December 1978; also P. Devine, interview with author.
16. This phrase was used frequently in the debates at congress by those in the leadership such as Dave Priscott and Irene Swann. See Congress Reports 1979 CP Archive; and W. Thompson, *The Good Old Cause*, op cit, pp176-177. The majority report was accepted overwhelmingly at Congress with some minor amendments by the EC.
17. This defensiveness was evident in the tone of much of the leadership's response to the alternative proposals. See for example Bert Ramelson in *Comment*, 18 August 1979, for his dismissal of what he saw as the 'verbal gymnastics and double talk' of the proposals.
18. According to Monty Johnstone, it was felt by Dave Cook subsequently that Falber's role as Chair was influenced by his knowledge of the funds from Moscow, though there is no empirical evidence available to demonstrate this fact. Falber himself denied such a connection. Monty Johnstone, Reuben Falber, interviews with author.
19. S. Benton, Resignation letter to EC, 6 November 1980, CP Archive EC Box.
20. CP/IND/MATH/02/05. The London district reflected some of the most critical traditionalist currents at this time. The leadership's backdown over Cohen's threat led to some Gramscians accusing the leadership of emotional blackmail. See letter from Brian Nicholls in *Comment*, 21.7.79.
21. Geoff Roberts, for example, regarded the challenge to the leadership over inner-party democracy as a 'big mistake' and a 'diversion' from the main political challenge. Jude Bloomfield also thought that more time should have been spent 'consolidating the positions around the British Road' and that intervening around inner party democracy was 'unwise because ... it underestimated the difficult and delicate task of transforming the party'. Interviews with the author.
22. *Marxism Today*, September 1978. It appeared in book form as *The Forward March of Labour Halted?*, edited by M. Jacques and F. Mulhearn (Verso 1981), and including contributions from critics and supporters alike.
23. E. Hobsbawm in M. Jacques and F. Mulhearn (eds), *The Forward March of Labour Halted?*, Verso 1981, pp8-9.
24. Ibid, pp7-8.
25. '... the organised working class a hundred years ago [was] almost entirely masculine ... except in the textile industry', E. Hobsbawm, 'Forward March of Labour Halted?', op cit, p9.
26. Ibid, p14.
27. Ibid, p18.
28. Ibid.
29. Ibid, p19.
30. According to Prior, this was their 'swansong'. It appeared in its completed version in 1979, published by Spokesman, and precipitated their departure.

31. M. Prior and D. Purdy, *Out of the Ghetto*, Spokesman 1979. Much of their work was drawn from discussions in the Smith and Party Groups, from the alternative economic analysis, and the work of Bill Warren, who had died in 1976.
32. Though there is no evidence of any formal collaboration between them.
33. Gill was General Secretary of AUEW (TASS) and a member of the TUC General Council at the time of publication of 'The Forward March of Labour Halted?'.
34. Gill, op cit, p22.
35. Gill, op cit, p22.
36. K. Halpin, reply to Hobsbawm, 'Forward March of Labour Halted?', op cit, p33.
37. Ibid, p37.
38. P. Carter, reply to Hobsbawm, 'Forward March of Labour Halted?', op cit, p25.
39. Carter, reply, op cit, p26.
40. Sarah Benton introduced a 'rethinking left' debate on similar issues in *Comment* during 1978-1979, while *Marxism Today* debated the issues for two years after Hobsbawm's original analysis.
41. Formerly the *Morning Star's* Industrial Editor he joined the Industrial Department in 1977 and took over as organiser when Bert Ramelson retired in 1978.
42. D. Cook, 'The British Road To Socialism and the Communist Party', *Marxism Today*, December 1978; M. Costello, 'The Working Class and the Broad Democratic Alliance', *Marxism Today*, June 1979. See for example the contributions by Sam Aaronovitch, 'The Working Class and the Broad Democratic Alliance', *Marxism Today*, September 1979, representing the Gramscian position; and Lawrence Harris, *Marxism Today*, December 1979, representing the traditional class analysis.
43. M. Costello, 'Development of Work in Industry: notes for Political Committee', 15.2.79, CP/CENT/PC/14/32; J. McIlroy, 'Notes on the Communist Party and Industrial Politics', op cit, pp224-225.
44. One noticeable example of this was the Grunwick dispute, in which the Communist Party played a significant role, through the Brent Trades Council – in what proved to be one of the last major industrial struggles of the decade. Beneath the unity, however, quite different views of class struggle were held by different members of the Trades Council, cutting across party politics. According to Graham Taylor, a party activist involved in the dispute, there were big disagreements in the Brent Communist Party over what Grunwick meant for the future of class politics. Interview with author. See also: J. Dromey and G. Taylor, *Grunwick: the Workers' Story*, Lawrence and Wishart 1978.
45. This was also true of the Industrial Relations Committee, an advisory committee that had been set up in 1976. While the leadership's position was dominant on this group, there were also critical voices, similar to those on the party's Economic Committee, who were less convinced that the party's analysis of class forces, based on free collective bargaining and wage militancy, added up to a political strategy. As Andy Fairclough put it: 'The wages struggle is only one way and an increasingly less important way, of defending the interests of workers and by itself it does not really

advance the struggle at a time when important developments mean qualitative changes are possible in the British labour movement'. See the contributions of Andy Fairclough, Frank Carr, Paolo Garonna and Roger Seifert, Industrial Relations Group minutes, 23.10.76, Mike Power Papers.
46. T. Benn interview with E. Hobsbawm in Jacques/Mulhearn, op cit, pp75-99. For his discussion of corporatism see also *Arguments For Democracy*, Jonathan Cape 1981.
47. F. Beckett, *Enemy Within*, op cit, p200.
48. J. McIlroy, 'Notes on the Communist Party and Industrial Politics', op cit, p221.
49. Criticisms of the party's industrial strategy from the left include S. Jeffereys, 'The Challenge of the Rank and File', *International Socialism*, March 1975; D. Hallas, 'The CP, the SWP and the Rank and File movement', *International Socialism*, February 1977; for an overview of Trotskyism in British trade unions see J. McIlroy, 'Always Outnumbered, Always Outgunned; the Trotskyists and the Trade Unions', in J. McIlroy, N. Fishman and A. Campbell, *British Trade Unions and Industrial Politics*, Ashgate 1999, pp259-296.
50. Ibid.
51. Only 91 representatives attended. McIlroy, 'Notes on the Communist Party and Industrial Politics', op cit, p222; CP/CENT/PC/13/22.
52. Ibid, p222.
53. W. Thompson, *The Good Old Cause*, op cit, p176.
54. See S. Aaronovitch for a critique of the limitations of this strategy, in 'The Working Class and the Broad Democratic Alliance', *Marxism Today*, September 1979. The opposition to the Social Contract remained the main focus of industrial and political work. See K. Halpin, 'The Contract Must Die by July', *Morning Star*, 17 June 1977.
55. 'The CUL wasn't the Party', M. Jacques, interview with author.
56. Source: Communist Party Congress Reports, 1975, 1977, 1979.
57. The party's membership fell by 33, 095 in 1956, to 24,670 in 1958, amounting to a similar percentage figure. CP/CENT/ORG.
58. Though many left in the aftermath of this.
59. Mike Waite, 'Young People and Politics', op cit, pp149-150, found some conflicting views on the party's appeal to punks.
60. P. Cohen, in 'Losing the Generation Game' (in J. Curran (ed), *The Future of the Left*, Polity Press/New Socialist 1984, pp100-121) gives a good outline of the schism between young people and the left from the late 1970s.
61. *Our Future*, YCL 1979.
62. M. Waite, 'Young People and Politics', op cit, quotes Kenny Coyle, a 'traditionalist' YCL activist, as representing this position.
63. As of May 1978, student box CP Archive.
64. The CP Archive contains documents which chart the transition from Broad Left to Left Alliance.
65. These ideas were explored in J. Bloomfield, 'A Democratic Strategy for Post-School Education', *Marxism Today*, October 1976; K. Spours, 'Students, Education and the State', *Marxism Today*, November 1977; A. Pearmain, *Towards An Educated Democracy: A Strategy For the Democratisation of Post-School Education*, Education Office, Manchester

University Union 1977. Many of these issues were also discussed in 'Rethinking Our Strategy: A New Look at the Strategy for the Democratisation of Post-School Education', a communist student summer school held in Manchester in July 1978.

66. 'Workerist codswallop', as she put it. Interview with author.
67. S. Slipman, interview with author. She remained on the Editorial Board of *Marxism Today* until she joined the SDP, at which point Martin Jacques 'requested that I leave the editorial board'. She says that she would not have left but for this request and 'wrote him a pretty stiff private letter'.
68. CUL 11 Organiser's Notes, September 1979, CUL Box CP Archive.
69. Jon Bloomfield's handwritten notes summarised contributions from the CUL 11 organising group meeting on the future of CUL; undated but September 1979.
70. CUL 11 Organiser's Notes, CUL Box, CP Archive.
71. Initially for a 'year off' to reflect on its role; insufficient enthusiasm meant that it did not reappear. Organiser's notes, CUL Meetings, CP Archive.
72. D. Purdy, interview with author.
73. M. Prior, interview with author.
74. C. Nawrat, G. Roberts, K. Spours, A. MacDougall, interviews with author.
75. The other board members were Beatrix Campbell, Fran Bennett, Anne Showstack Sassoon, Alan Hunt, Paul Hirst and Barry Hindess.
76. *Politics and Power* founding statement. Routledge published four issues but the journal ceased following internal divisions on the editorial board.
77. This appeared as a quiz, 'The Correct Guide to Communese' in the Christmas edition of *Comment* in 1978.
78. The book was *Silver Linings*, edited by G. Bridges and R. Brunt, 1981. While it was based on sessions from the recent CULs, its focus was clearly on extending the influence of the 'BDA'.
79. The publication of *Beyond the Fragments*, in 1979 (Merlin Press), by three leading feminists – Sheila Rowbotham, Lynne Segal and Hilary Wainwright – arrived at a similar conclusion, in arguing that the left needed to change its ways of organising and learn from the experiences of new social movements if it was to recover its political direction.
80. W. Thompson, *The Long Death of British Labourism*, Pluto Press 1993, pp91-123.

PART FOUR

The Final Battle

7. The Death of Militant Labourism and the Crisis of Class Politics

THE BATTLE COMMENCES
The last chapter examined the pace of the decline of the Communist Party. The exodus of intellectuals on the one hand and labour movement activists on the other, as well as the rapid decline of its various sections, meant the party was in its poorest shape for years, with little indication of how it might retrieve its fortunes. Taken alongside the wider predicament of the left at this time, some general trends can be distinguished. The militant labourist ideology which had sustained the party's industrial work and which justified its political role, in alliance with the Labour Left, was in deep crisis. This was not only apparent in the decline of the party's own industrial base but was reflected in shifting voting allegiances amongst the working class towards the Conservative governments from 1979. The strikes of 1978, during the 'Winter of Discontent', suggested a very different political environment from that of the earlier part of the decade; the unions were beginning to lose the good will of the British electorate. The Communist Party, having lost its main allies, and now having a reduced influence, was unable to provide much in the form of leadership.

The election of a government that was explicitly anti-union, and which clearly saw one of its main priorities as the restraining of union power, was a new test. Yet the solutions of the past, namely mass campaigning, the organisation of industrial militants, picketing, and other militant forms of action, were no longer obvious options. Moreover, this industrial dilemma was really part of a wider political dilemma. How significant for the left was the decline in labourism and how serious was the rise of a 'new right'? What, in any case, was one to make of the Thatcher government: was it be judged as the usual form of Tory government, or was it something of a qualitatively different ideological formation, as Stuart Hall had suggested in 'The Great Moving Right

Show'? The different responses to this question were to widen the divisions within the party, as well as to provide new faultlines on the left as a whole. These faultlines were mainly related to the crisis of labourism.

In the Labour Party, bigger divisions were emerging over this crisis of labourism, and the crisis of class politics it represented. There were very different responses. Some, like the Militant Tendency, who upheld a very orthodox (and, as many argued, chauvinistic) view of class, made gains in certain districts, notably Merseyside. Others, on the right of the party, dismayed at what they saw as a retreat into class dogma and left sectarianism, broke away to form the Social Democratic Party, an organisation which was itself partly distinguished by its class composition as much as its politics.[1] In a different reaction to the crisis of labourism, Ken Livingstone and others in the GLC developed innovative forms of 'participatory democracy', drawing inspiration from the experiences of the new social movements, and from local strategies pursued by the PCI. These movements were themselves disruptive of traditional discourses of class as found in the politics of 'real labour', as the ousted candidate for Bermondsey declared himself while opposing the candidacy of Peter Tatchell in the 1983 by-election.[2]

As far as the Communist Party was concerned, class had been the cement which had held it together, and it could no longer sustain itself in the face of this polarisation between those trying to hold on to its traditional core in a declining culture and the Gramscians seeking a new type of politics. Predictably, it was an article in *Marxism Today* that was the signal for the party's biggest and final division, when Tony Lane, a sociologist and industrial relations academic, wrote a piece critical of the shop stewards movement, in September 1982.

In discussing the changing role of trade unionism within the context of a 'profound transformation of the industrial landscape', Lane suggested that some sections of the trade union movement, including shop stewards, were becoming noticeably distanced from their members. One example of this was increasing sectionalism of the kind that Hobsbawm had earlier described. Another, more contentious, suggestion by Lane, towards the end of the article, was that a 'new working-class elite' was emerging in some areas, one that was cut off from the rank and file, and was in some cases sustained by 'the expense account syndrome' and the 'franchise of perks and fiddles'; Lane also argued that some stewards had been motivated by careerism, and had sometimes changed sides to become personnel managers or industrial relations directors.[3]

Lane's criticism was not overly different from Hobsbawm's. However the climate had changed in four years, and the declining influence of the party's militant trade union sections meant that it was in no mood to accept criticisms of its own practice from one of the party's own journals. The contrast between the reaction in the party to Tony Lane's article on shop stewards and that of Hobsbawm's earlier

7. The Death of Militant Labourism

intervention on 'The Forward March of Labour Halted' is revealing. The reason for the difference was the direct implication of Lane's argument for the day-to-day work of the party.

The first response to Lane's piece came from Mick Costello, who was now the party's Industrial Organiser, having succeeded Bert Ramelson in 1978. According to Francis Beckett's account, based on interviews with Costello, on the day of publication of Lane's article Costello met Tony Chater, the editor of the *Morning Star*, at a local Wimpy Bar, to discuss how they should respond. The following day the *Morning Star* published an interview with Costello, in his capacity as Industrial Organiser, in which he described the Lane article as 'one which undermines the self-confidence of the working class in its representation and organisation'. It was a 'gross slander on the labour movement', he wrote.[4] *The Daily Mirror* also picked up the story (which was widely assumed to have been passed on by Costello to contacts he had on the paper), and this was subsequently used by Costello and his supporters to show how the anti-socialist press would exploit criticism made by party members and its publications.

This was the main point of criticism. The way in which the attack on Lane was made – in the pages of the party's daily paper – was crucial in polarising opinion, the more so considering the different readerships of the *Star* and *Marxism Today*. It is quite likely that many ordinary members who objected did not read the Lane article; however, Costello's critique clearly attracted significant support from ordinary members, as well as from trade union leaders.

Ken Gill, the party's leading trade unionist, in a letter to Gordon McLennan, was 'shocked' at the content 'but more upset at the decision to print it'. He went on to argue that the 'analysis was not only anti-union, (but) of poor and shallow quality. I hope you can do something radical to protect the party from such damaging displays of ideological incompetence in the future. Working people do not need a Communist Party to protect and fight for their interests if this is an example of party judgement'.[5] Kevin Halpin, also a senior party trade unionist, argued that 'the attack on shop stewards as quoted in the *Daily Mirror* (was) a 'disgrace'. He said that the *Daily Mirror* article was 'raised by the individuals in my shop very strongly and by my party branch even more strongly at lunchtime ... The conclusion that I draw is that comrade Martin Jacques is not a fit person to be the editor (of *Marxism Today*) and I shall so move'.[6]

Derek Robinson, also calling for Martin Jacques's dismissal (for 'exceeding his authority and act(ing) contrary to the principles of the *British Road to Socialism*'), objected to the 'patronising attitude of many academics': 'We are not a bunch of illiterates who cannot handle all relevant matters'.[7] Other leading trade union leaders critical of Lane and Jacques included Malcolm Pitt of the NUM, Mike Hicks of the Printworkers and Tom Durkin, Chair of Brent Trades Council, who claimed the article was 'written mainly by academics for academics; more and more from petty bourgeois, social democratic and Eurocommunist political and ideological positions ... It is in MTD that real elitism can be found and the views of proletarians rarely presented'.[8]

In the days and weeks following, many districts and branches also wrote in to complain, many having passed motions and presumably aware of the split developing within the PC and EC. The London District Secretariat passed a motion calling on the EC to disassociate itself from the Lane article.[9] East Midlands District Committee sent a letter to the EC protesting at 'the thinly veiled and cynical attack on the trade unions (which) has given ammunition to opponents of the labour movement'. It also called on the EC to 'either change the editor of *Marxism Today* or at least warn him as to his future conduct':

> We also call on the EC to take measures aimed at restoring *Marxism Today* as the theoretical and discussion journal of the Communist Party which it no longer is. It has, in our opinion, become a vehicle for propagating the views of one body of opinion inside and outside the Communist Party, rather than a forum for communists and other Marxists who subscribe to the general approach of our party.[10]

South Essex District also sent a letter of support of Mick Costello's position as outlined in the *Morning Star*.[11]

Amongst union branches, Acton Rail Branch in their letter referred to the 'latest outrage to our class', while Chiswick Bus Factory Branch expressed their 'full support for Mick Costello' and called for the September issue of *MT* to be withdrawn from circulation, further sales of the issue to be cancelled and the editor to be replaced forthwith.[12] UCATT TUC delegate Bill Jones claimed in his letter that 'nobody at all' in his delegation agreed with Lane's points.[13]

Other prominent party individuals hostile to Lane and Jacques included two *MT* editorial board members, John Foster (who wanted a 'disclaimer' to go in MT[14]) and Mike Seifert, who expressed his 'strong objection to Lane's article' and 'longstanding concern at the editor's administrative methods'.[15] Maggie Bowden, the National Women's Organiser, also protested at Lane's article.

For Costello and Chater themselves, the task was to get the EC and PC behind them and to attempt to win the leadership – perhaps in a similar way as in the inner party democracy debate – to the view that Jacques was no longer fit to edit *Marxism Today*, and that the opposition from rank and file party members and trade unionists illustrated where the party's priorities should lie.

In his letter to Gordon McLennan, Costello argued that Lane's article was 'a contribution to the current Tory attack on trade unions and the shop stewards in particular'. Claiming that he had been contacted by the *Daily Telegraph* and that his response was an attempt to 'minimise the damage being done', he went on to write: 'The healthy anger at the appearance of this article in our journal from many comrades who have contacted me is very encouraging, but I think more must be done, to show, beyond any doubt, where our leadership stands on this'. He went on to propose that the PC 'censures or reprimands the editor of the journal'; that the next issue should carry an insert from the party leader reasserting the 'fight against Tebbit, incomes policy and slanders against the shop stewards movement'; and, finally, that there should be 'no distribution of this issue [of *MT*] at the (forthcoming) TUC'. He ended by saying: 'Gordon, these are I think minimal urgent steps that are required'.[16]

On 30 August Tony Chater circulated a motion to the EC calling on it to 'issue a public statement to the press repudiating the general lines of the article by Tony Lane and the anti-trade union slanders it contained'. It continued:

> The EC censures the editor of *MT* for publishing this article (and) instructs the PC to present to the November meeting clear proposals which will guarantee strict and effective political control over *Marxism Today*, in order that from now on the party's theoretical journal unambiguously assists the Communist Party to win the ideological battle within the party and the left generally and in that way plays its part in underpinning the mass political campaigning of the party for its policies and the *British Road to Socialism*.[17]

Clearly Costello and Chater were making their big move to 'win the ideological battle', having chosen a battleground close to the heart of militant labourism. The battle was to take place on the PC on 1 September, where attempts would be made to censure or remove Martin Jacques and win the leadership; while a special PC was set for September 7, with the EC meeting, which would ratify decisions taken, fixed for 11-12 September.

Martin Jacques's response was to demand support from the party leadership. Gordon McLennan was away on the day of Costello's statement, but Jacques wrote a note to Ian McKay who was standing in. In it he described Costello's attack as 'outrageous':

> At no stage was I consulted. The first I knew about it was when I read the paper this morning at home. As a member of the EC and PC I must assume this statement was made in a purely personal capacity – and the interpretation put on the article, with which I totally disagree, belongs simply to Mick Costello. In these circumstances I think it is essential that we as a party leadership make it clear that Mick Costello's statement was completely of his own volition – nothing more than an individual and personal statement. That such action was premature and provocative, that we disassociate ourselves from it.[18]

The leadership was clearly being pressured from both positions. 'Democratic centralism' was also used – this time by the Gramscians – to condemn Costello's intervention. In a letter to McLennan, on the day of the first PC following the Lane article and Costello's response, Jacques argued that the failure to consult with either himself or other members of the PC was 'a very serious breach of the normal and necessary code of democratic conduct which should operate, and in my view always has operated, with regard to the actions of PC comrades and leading officers of the party'. He also argued that the statement was a 'gross distortion and caricature of what the article actually is and says. It is absurd to regard the article as in any way unsympathetic to the trade union movement. On the contrary it is written from a totally partisan, pro-trade union position'. He ended by writing: 'Great harm has been done to *Marxism Today* and the Communist Party by Mick Costello's statement. In these circumstances it is essential that the Executive Committee makes clear that the statement was a personal one and that it does not endorse the views expressed in it'.[19]

With the PC containing leading members from both sides, the battle for the centre which still controlled the leadership became tense in the build-up to the crucial meetings. Dave Cook, long-time ally of Jacques and one of the defeated advocates of the Inner Party Democracy reforms, wrote to McLennan on the eve of the PC. 'Mick has got it *all* wrong' wrote Cook:

> Precisely because the attack by the ruling class is so major, it is vital that communists are uncompromising in a fraternal way in criticism of abuses etc. I just want to urge you to be totally opposed to any moves to knife Martin and *Marxism Today* on this issue. The whole thing stinks as a set-up job. A lot of people will be devastated if the PC/EC goes for M. Today and does not criticise Mick's attack. It would be the best possible gift that could be given to the hardliners at the District Congress.

He ended: 'Gordon, sorry to write like this. This is not an official letter to the EC. It's just a note in haste. But desperately worried alarm bells have started to ring in my head'.[20]

Some in the leadership had already come out against Costello. George Matthews, for example, had been in touch with the *Morning Star* shortly after the statement, urging them to allow Tony Lane a 'right of reply'. His complaint was that Chater ruled out a right of reply on the grounds that the PC had not sanctioned one, a position Matthews regarded as 'surely extraordinary': 'I hope that the Political Committee will make clear that it does not support such an attitude, that Tony Lane was unable to speak to Tony Chater and will be given immediate and adequate space for a reply and that other letters on the question, whatever their point of view, will be heard'. He hoped that the EC would 'disassociate itself in clear terms from the statement by Mick Costello'.[21]

In the event a fully attended PC on 1 September was divided narrowly in support of Jacques, rejecting Kevin Halpin's motion to dismiss him, and voting against a motion not to sell *MT* at the TUC by 8-6.[22] The *Morning Star* was defeated. This was the signal for the last chapter of the CP, one that was to be dominated by the divisions between Gramscian-Eurocommunists now in close alliance with the leadership, and 'traditionalists' or 'hardliners' – in this case those who remained committed to militant labourism.[23] A few months after the EC vote, Costello resigned from his job as the party's Industrial Organiser, citing family reasons, only to reappear as the *Morning Star's* industrial correspondent shortly afterwards, ensuring that the two camps would now be sharply divided. From this point on, the party was split in two; the leadership and Gramscian-Eurocommunists were in control of the party and the Costello/Chater group controlled the *Morning Star*, and, with it, a notable list of trade union leaders, and contact with a declining trade union base. Neither side could be described as ultimate victors in this battle. The party was deprived of its daily paper and with it, what was left of its trade union base; and the 'hardliners' were now detached from the party, its political machine and its resources. There was a long struggle as the leadership attempted to win back the paper, through organising shareholders meetings of the People's Press Printing Society (PPPS), which controlled the *Star*. However, the highly centralised control structure of the PPPS, put in place to ensure party control over what was in theory a non-party organisation, meant that it was impossible to win back the paper through mobilising the shareholders. These battles were bitterly fought and further debilitated the party.

Further and rapid decline was inevitable. It was a decline that was driven by the crisis of labourism, and with it the decline of a particular form of class politics.

THE SOVIET MANTRA LIVES ON

Before discussing the wider significance of the crisis of class politics, we need to address the question of the party's relationship to the Soviet Union, and to ask whether and to what extent this remained a factor in the party's divisions. Certainly the media and to some extent party figures now presented the growing dispute as one between 'euros' and 'tankies'. Indeed, if we look closely at the anger which followed from the Tony Lane article, the Soviet Union appears regularly – and revealingly – as a contributory factor. In the same issue of *Marxism Today* as Lane's piece there was an article by Soviet dissident Roy Medvedev, complaining about the lack of direct rights in the Soviet Union, as well as an advert for a book on the KGB. Many of the letters critical of Lane included the Medvedev piece in their attack. The letter from the East

Midlands District Committee, for example, complained that articles on the Soviet Union were 'always written by dissidents, severe critics of the Soviet Union or outright opponents ... what joy anti-soviet warriors must get from such an article'. Chiswick Bus Factory Branch also referred to the 'slanderous article directed at ... the CPSU'; while Derek Robinson talked of the 'anti-Soviet' nature of the Medvedev piece. There is evidence that the CPSU was very unhappy with the article. In the meantime the Soviet Union was continuing to buy 12,000 copies of the *Morning Star* every day – this was a substantial contribution to its revenue, particularly in the context of the decline in its circulation, which increased as the split in the party developed and criticism over its content multiplied. Costello was also thought to be in close contact with the Soviet embassy, and some have suggested this was the real reason for his anger.

However, it should also be noted that the *Morning Star* retained some critical positions in respect of Poland and Afghanistan, while the state of the labour movement was by far its main pre-occupation (as it was for others on the left). Moreover the emergence of Gorbachev in 1985, with his own critical view of the Soviet Union and the need for *Glasnost* and *Perestroika*, was also supported by the *Morning Star*. Therefore, we can say that conflicting positions on the Soviet Union were evident in the arguments that ensued, and they often reflected other deep-rooted differences. However, these were not the decisive points of rupture within the CP, which had its origins in the increasing crisis of militant labourism, and the type of class politics it espoused.

DIVIDED WE STAND

The cementing of division and the acceleration of decline in the CP came at a particularly unfortunate time, coinciding with the last great industrial dispute of the twentieth century, namely the miners strike of 1984-85. The division meant that the Communist Party, for the first time in a major dispute, was unable to give strong leadership, a fact borne out by the criticism it received from others on the left, including some in the leadership of the NUM itself; the party returned the criticism, in its analysis of the problems of Arthur Scargill's tactics. Following Costello's decision to go to the *Morning Star*, the war in the party intensified in the run-up to the National Congress and the Peoples Press Printing Society shareholder meetings. These were to become the two principal battlefields for the party from the mid to late 1980s. The first round of battle was at the PPPS AGM in 1983, when the party failed to get its nominated candidates – Dave Priscott and Bert Pearce – elected to the Management Committee. Continual criticism of the party from the paper, including a statement that 'powerful outside influences' were trying to influence the PPPS elections, further polarised debate. This rather disingenuous description of the party leadership only led to worsened relations. The party Congress of 1983

7. The Death of Militant Labourism

took place, as Thompson describes it, 'amid commotion and mutual hatreds unsurpassed at any time in the CP's history and far exceeding those of 1929 or 1957'.[24]

The party leadership won the day at the Congress, with Chater and *Star* deputy editor David Whitfield losing their seats on the EC (though some *Morning Star* supporters remained on it). From this time on, the party went into a spiral of decline and recrimination, expulsions, conflicts (occasionally violent), investigations, and accusations and counter-accusations. The PPPS managed to keep Chater at the helm – partly through support from non-party members in the labour movement – while the party reasserted its control, often through disciplinary measures, over its districts and branches. As some have pointed out, there was an irony here: the leadership was using Democratic Centralism to its full capacities in dealing with dissidents, while the traditional 'hardliners' acted in a more legalistic way, arguing for the right to dissent.

There was a major struggle in the London District, whose District Committee, under the leadership of Bill Dunn, had opposed the national leadership. Following his sudden death in 1984, the party took the opportunity to reassert its authority. At the District Congress in 1984, chaired by printworker and supporter of the *Morning Star* Mike Hicks, Gordon McLennan instructed delegates that they would not be able to elect a new District Committee until investigations into some of the branches and delegates' credentials were completed. After Hicks refused to go along with this, McLennan left the meeting, with the words: 'All those who support the Communist Party of Great Britain will now leave the hall with me'.[25] After his supporters followed him out, the party reconvened the LDC, suspended 21 members, and re-established whole branches.[26]

At the party's EC in January 1985, Chater, Whitfield, Hicks and others were expelled from membership. Meanwhile, two other notable communists were expelled from different sections of the party – Ken Gill (not without a little irony, as he was about to become the first ever communist President of the TUC), and John Foster, the labour historian and member of *MT*'s Editorial Board. The 1985 Congress ratified the EC decisions, ensuring that the division with the *Morning Star* would be permanent – which had also been made clear by the further refusal of the PPPS to endorse party candidates for the Management Committee.

NO PRIVATE DRAMA

This was all taking place against the backdrop of the miners strike, the last major strike of the industry, and one which brought together traditional trade union forms of struggle. The dynamics which had split the party were now reflected in wider politics, and became encapsulated by the strike: the NUM leadership under Scargill reflected the classic militant labourist position (though without the pragmatism of Ramelson), in its belief that mass picketing would inspire other groups to engage in struggle and this would shift the labour movement and Labour Party to the left. Indeed, as Thompson pointed out, the strike represented the 'climax of militant labourism in Britain'.[27] It was also the last major industrial struggle that the Communist Party would give its organisational weight to, though it was in no position to provide any national leadership. While a number of leading NUM figures were sympathetic to the party leadership and Eurocommunist group, particularly in the Welsh and Scottish coalfields,[28] the party was unable to provide anything other than criticism of the Scargill strategy. This included a failure to support the call for a membership ballot, which might have unified different sectors of the NUM and won more public support. Without the resources of its daily paper to help provide alternatives to the militant labourist strategy of Scargill, it was left to *Marxism Today*, *Focus* (the new name for the fortnightly which had replaced *Comment*) and party meetings to make the case; a disparate range of forums which didn't have the force or the link to be an effective disseminator of party opinion. This did not prevent the party being a controversial voice in the dispute however.

The reason for this is that the miners strike became the active symbol of the debate about class on the British left. It embodied the crisis, the contrasting languages, loyalties and illusions of a much wider debate. For Raphael Samuel, the strike was symptomatic of the divisions on the left, which had been pushed onto the defensive and was doubtful of its own role. 'The miners strike', he wrote, 'serve(d) as a displaced object of the left's discomfort with itself, of a Communist Party which is no longer certain what it exists for, of a Labour Party which is no longer sure what it believes in, of a New Left which has lost its taste for the streets'.[29]

With the Women Against Pit Closures movement, and the growth of other women's support groups, as well as the involvement of gays and lesbians in supporting the miners, both individually and in groups, those on the Gramscian wing could talk of the growing importance of diverse social movements and groups in labour movement struggles. Scargill's strategy, on the other hand, drew admiration from the *Morning Star* group, though not without some criticism.[30] Yet, in their fight for very survival the miners embodied a language and discourse of class that was in crisis. The miners strike was symbolic of the end of a particular era of industrial socialism, based on shared understandings of class and community, whose leading political expression was militant labourism. The issues it raised were indicative of wider dilemmas that were now at the forefront of the concerns of left intellectuals, as they attempted to make sense of the left's descent into crisis.

CRISIS OF CLASS: THE WIDER CONTEXT
The discussion on the crisis of class politics started before the miners strike and continued long after it had finished. It is important to situate the debate in the Communist Party within this wider context, as

many of the assumptions, tensions, arguments, hopes and fears were symptomatic of what was going on within other left parties and movements. Moreover, the changes in the working class – including changes in identification and culture – that were dividing communists were having multiple reverberations beyond the party; they were an issue of debate amongst intellectuals and academics.[31]

The debate over class on the left was a debate that in many ways had followed on from Eric Hobsbawm's 'Forward March of Labour Halted' theme – one which had included sociologists, journalists and commentators as well as historians. Essentially, the key issues were: the relationship between class and party politics; the nature and meaning of 'the working class', including whether there was any longer a 'distinctive working-class culture'; the ways in which social and political alliances were constructed; political and class identities; the disparity between 'activists' and 'the working class'; and the changing nature of party composition, including the relationship between the working class, intellectuals and new social movements or 'social forces'. Overriding these different, though related issues, was the one major dilemma: whither the left in the era of Thatcherism? These questions were made even more difficult, as many pointed out, because of the illusions and misconceptions about the meaning of class. 'Class politics', wrote Eric Hobsbawm in 1985, in a rare intervention into the party's troubles, 'is just a label to stick on one kind of politics (the good one) to distinguish it from brand x (the bad one).'[32]

Jeremy Seabrook, as early as 1978, in his book *What Went Wrong?*, had written of the breakdown in working-class community, cultures and organisations, including the 'sense of hurt, bewilderment and violence in working-class areas', the 'erosion of working-class identity' and the 'pain and disappointment' of working-class people with politics, notably the Labour Party.[33] The breakdown of traditional working-class culture and its replacement by materialism and values of self-interest amounted to 'an assault on working-class identity'. He wrote of:

> ... the vast temples of commodities which dominate every town and city in the country ... Things are beyond blame; but people are not, all sorts of people; spongers, scroungers, immigrants, Asians, thugs, vandals, muggers, child molesters, extremists, wreckers, even trade unionists.[34]

These values had also permeated trade unions according to Seabrook, and, in a comment on their sectionalism and economism that was similar to the conclusions drawn by Hobsbawm writing in the same period, he argued that 'the anger and militancy of recent years, are not necessarily the radical phenomenon which the left makes them out to be'.[35] More worrying, for Seabrook, was the distance between the

Labour Party and the working class, as well as the distance between the new generation of activists and the people they claimed to represent:

> The kind of human being which the Labour Party served is disappearing and will never reappear in that form again ... Within the space of a generation the old working class has become an anachronism, a vestigial reminder of the way the majority of the population once lived. And those activists are increasingly isolated from the working class they still aim to serve.[36]

In 1985, in a book jointly written with Trevor Blackwell, Seabrook was still writing of a 'deep uncertainty about the changing shape and nature of the working class – its dissolution and remoulding'.[37] He now began to talk of a 'post-industrial working class', one that had been 'reconstructed'. Crucially, this reconstruction appeared 'to have rendered the language of class archaic and unilluminating'.[38] Mrs Thatcher had understood this 'sea-change' in the working class and was particularly adept in being able to ...

> detach large sections of the working class from an allegiance which had become enfeebled to organised labour and its movement. She could accomplish this the more convincingly because capitalism itself had been transformed from satanic mill to shopping mall, from an irrational and inhuman system which inflicted suffering and deprivation into a sagacious and beneficent means of distributing the good things in life.[39]

Thatcher had broken the historic link between the working class and the Labour Party, and given expression to the remaking of the 'common life' of the working class. This was in contrast to the Labour Party, which remained conservative and defensive, unable to remake its own political identity in light of the restructuring that was taking place. Moreover, Blackwell and Seabrook argued, the divisions between right and left in the Labour Party that were occurring (and I would add here those in the CP) needed to be understood 'as a displaced discussion about the working class':

> It is especially incumbent upon the left to recognise the nature of these changes [i.e. to the working class], following as they do upon the decay of traditional industries and established patterns of working and living; after all the left has so accurately located these very structural changes within the international division of labour ... Compared with the convoluted and quicksilver movements of capital, socialist analysis of the working class has remained rudimentary and static.[40]

In the final section of the book, entitled 'Moving beyond Labourism with the Working Class', they argued that the 'transformation' of the

7. The Death of Militant Labourism

working class 'has brought to an end one set of possibilities for radical change borne within a tradition of labourism. This moment is irretrievable, and as a result, the elaboration of a new politics becomes at the same time the more difficult and the more imperative'.[41]

It is apparent from Seabrook's argument that he saw the Labour Party's problem as lying in its inability to find an appropriate language or political discourse which could relate to a reconstructed working class. This dilemma, I have suggested, was similar to the one faced by the Communist Party. It is therefore unsurprising that the left as a whole was split in its responses to these debates, divisions which became deep-rooted, and with long-term implications for the future of left politics.

Another notable contributor to the debate in the mid-1980s was the social historian Gareth Stedman Jones. In an article first published for *New Socialist*, Stedman Jones also argued that the roots of the problem lay in an inability to construct a relevant political discourse.[42] He was also critical of those who found simple 'quasi-automatic correlates' from 'objective' sociological analyses of class change. In other words, a rise in affluence amongst the working class should not in itself carry an obvious political message for the direction of party priorities:

> Changes in the social realm necessarily form a large part of the raw material out of which different political languages and practices may be forged or reforged. But such changes are not bearers of essential political meaning in themselves. They are only endowed with particular political meanings as far as they are effectively articulated through specific forms of political discourse and practice.[43]

Stedman Jones also criticised the notion of a 'Forward March' that had been halted, describing this as an 'optical illusion' which prevented a recognition of the 'discontinuous conjunctions which enabled [the Labour Party] to achieve particular and specific forms of success at rather widely separated points of time'; there had been no 'continuous evolutionary movement which at a certain point mysteriously went into reverse'.[44]

Stedman Jones argued that particular 'political meanings' attached to class that had been crucial in Labour's success in the past had now lost their force. Thus the social and political alliance between the 'organised working class' and the 'professional middle class', which had been fundamental to Labour's success, had now broken down. This alliance between professionals and the working class had been established since the 1940s, and was reflected in such movements as CND and Anti-Apartheid. These were 'social alliances ... brought into being and re-created by the construction and periodic reconstruction of a common political discourse'.[45] This common political discourse had started to break down, Stedman Jones argued, in the aftermath of the

Social Contract and the 'winter of discontent' in the late 1970s. Thatcherism, the rise of the Bennite left and the SDP were all manifestations of the same problem: the disjuncture between the working class and their traditional political representatives. Working-class affluence, combined with the radicalisation of the professions, had produced different social forces. According to Stedman Jones:

> The Labour Party will never be able to make a credible appeal to either of its former constituencies unless it attempts to ally them in a new way by taking account of the profound changes wrought by the welfare state, the mixed economy and national decline, both upon the forms of consciousness and the relative material situation of each.[46]

The traditional role of trade unions – namely 'channelling political allegiance and political mobilisation', as well as acting as a 'lifeline ... against employers and the state'[47] – had in the past provided 'the larger loyalties and values which held the labour movement together'.[48] In recent years, with the growth of the welfare state and changes in work patterns, social and economic conditions had been transformed. As a consequence, the nature of 'political consciousness' itself was changing, and it was now driven by 'new forms of social and political discontent, not shaped primarily by the workplace'.[49]

The possibility of creating a political discourse capable of continuing to unite these different groups was being prevented by 'an enduring major premise of Labour Party thinking' – the perception that its constituency was divided between 'a homogeneous, proletarian estate where sectional political interest is accomplished by trade unions', and 'a heteroclite aggregate of idealists, notables or entryists, to be honoured, promoted or circumvented'.[50] Stedman Jones ends by arguing that the 'division between mental and manual labour' was becoming a 'disastrous social distinction' between the different sections of the party.

This argument was similar in many ways to Seabrook's. Neither was arguing that there had been a diminution of the importance of class, but rather that it was in the process of reconstruction; and expression needed to be found for this in a new political discourse – one that went beyond that of labourism. This resonated also with the debates in the Communist Party over 'broad' and 'narrow' definitions of class, and the particular political discourses and identities that shaped them. In an article in *Marxism Today* in May 1984, the sociologist Greg McLennan (son of party leader Gordon McLennan) made a similar argument – that underlying the crisis in Labour's vote amongst the working class, and the corresponding rise of Thatcherism, 'was the very idea of a politics based upon assumptions about the working class'.[51] McLennan wrote of the effect of structural changes in the nature of the working class for its political alignment. He distinguished three positions on the link between class and political commitment on the left. There was the 'reformist' view that the Labour Party would always look after the interests of the working class, a position no longer sustainable because of Thatcher's inroads into the working-class vote. Then there was the – also rejected – traditional 'class conflict' position, which argued that working-class interests could be 'galvanised' by appropriate political leadership and struggle (though he doesn't use the term, this is the position that could be described as militant labourist). Thirdly there was the position represented by Tony Benn, after the 1983 election defeat, that working-class interests could be 'expressed politically in terms of socialism itself', as he put it; or, in Benn's words, that there had been a qualitative rise in socialist consciousness amongst the working class, even if its support quantitatively was in decline.

McLennan argued that none of these positions were any longer sustainable, and that a new political discourse which addressed the changes within the British class system must become more pluralist, to include new 'coalitions of non-class interests'.[52]

> Pluralism is not intrinsically a matter of cross-class alliances; but the extent to which alliances can be forged in and across the diversity of working-class life, or connected to more narrow class questions, is a political issue of some subtlety, not a fact about the 'interests' supposed to exist in the social structure itself.[53]

Sociologist John Westergaard – whose research findings had continually shown the persistence of inequality in Britain, and were used by Marxists to point out to generations of social democratic or conservative thinkers that the 'affluent society' had not led to reduced inequality between classes – was also concerned about the lack of an effective political discourse on the left. Pointing to the Swedish Social Democrats' ability to maintain and modernise their political appeal despite changes to the class structure, Westergaard argued that Labour would have to do more than appeal to 'intuitive class loyalties', or rely on the 'parochial allegiances which have characterised it hitherto'. In particular, it would need to free itself by showing that the 'aims of socialists fit in with majority interests'.[54]

The decay of labourism was becoming apparent in many sectors of British society as the 1980s progressed. The magazine *New Society*, which, under Paul Barker's editorship, was seeking to document this declining culture, included a series of articles by David Selbourne, a writer and academic from the left who was becoming disenchanted with what he saw as a widening gap between left perceptions about the working class and actual working-class realities. In a journey into different communities in Britain, he found the decay of labourism endemic in a range of institutions, and in social and economic predicaments. In NHS waiting rooms, in mining communities, amongst second-generation minority ethnic communities and the unemployed – and in Militant's Liverpool – he found that the left was losing the argument.[55]

Selbourne found that many of the assumptions the left held about the working class were becoming redundant when measured against working-class experience. It was the confusions of class politics that were at the root of the problem, and in particular the growing disjuncture between the organised politics of the left and labour movement and experiences of the working class. This had given rise to a whole series of misconceptions and illusions about 'levels of consciousness', in which sectional interests were mistaken for class consciousness, and incorrect interpretations were made about the radicalism of various struggles, with class identities being imposed on people (the 'human-as-worker'), so that they obscured other allegiances:

> The 'crisis of the working-class movement' is as much the crisis of intellectual failure to grasp its true nature as the crisis of 'the movement itself'. To impute to 'the working class' and its alleged defects of 'consciousness', responsibility for the failure of the socialist project (and its projectors) is to deepen every illusion. Indeed to see fundamentally middle-class concepts of the working class and the 'proletariat' as the organising principles of socialist theory and practice is to have been at odds from the beginning with the self-identification of 'working' people themselves, whether as citizens, appropriators, consumers or individuals.[56]

FEMINISM AND THE CRISIS OF CLASS

Beatrix Campbell – a leading feminist activist in the CP, whose conflicts with the party leadership over the previous decade had led to a sustained critique of the culture and politics of militant labourism – also journeyed into the Labour heartlands, and came up with some different conclusions from Seabrook and the others. In retracing the steps of George Orwell half a century earlier, she also found a crisis in working-class communities – despair, anxiety and above all poverty and unemployment. 'The very fact of unemployment', she wrote, 'cuts the wageless off from the resources of the waged working class and the labour movement'.[57] The labour movement on the other hand, 'bewitched by the enemy, bothered and bewildered by the "passivity" of the people, waits like Micawber for something to turn up'.[58]

Yet she also found resistance, hope, innovation and activity amongst these communities, in particular from the women. According to Campbell, this factor had been missing from other accounts, including Orwell's; other writers had failed to give attention to the way in which these communities had been gendered. Most had also accepted, to an excessive degree, the arguments about contemporary working-class affluence, and were influenced by a nostalgia for a lost and more authentic working class from the past. They were also defeatist. Campbell also argued that the activities of women 'on the move' in their communities were at odds with the prevailing economistic, passive culture of labourism: 'Most importantly, the radicals within the working class I met were mostly women; they were the most reflective and imaginative, it was they who affirmed egalitarianism, it is they who are being transformed by their own experience of change. The men's movement seems not to have noticed'.[59]

Writing before the miners strike, Campbell was later vindicated by the activities of the Women Against Pit Closures groups and other women's campaign groups during the strike. Significantly, her perspective developed out of her earlier critique of economism and the way in which the labour movement organised its politics. Thus the crisis should be seen as one derived from the 'historic compromise between the men's movement and capital'.[60] These arguments had first been developed in the Party Group, subsequently in the group around *Red Rag*, and then on the party's National Women's Advisory. However, they were also influenced by a dispute with the *Morning Star* over an article she had written in *The Guardian*, which immediately followed the Tony Lane case. Her criticisms of 'male chauvinism' in the labour movement brought a counter-attack from Barbara Switzer in the *Morning Star*, which accused Campbell of undermining labour movement morale in a similar way to Lane.[61] Campbell was furious at this attack and demanded a 'right of reply'. After this was turned down she organised a petition at the TUC (on the basis that she was a trade union journalist) and managed to get a large number of prominent signatories, including Arthur Scargill and Michael Meacher of the Labour and trade union left.

Campbell's critique, moreover, offered another dimension to the Communist Party's attempts to find a role for itself in the aftermath of labourism. Her feminism and general belief in the beneficial impact of new social movements, as well as her positive view of 'consumerist culture' amongst the working class (one she shared with other writers around *Marxism Today*), meant that she didn't have the pessimism of others. Other initiatives from outside the traditional labour movement gave strength to her case. For example the peace campaign of women at Greenham Common, which began in October 1982, gave a new dimension to struggle and had implications for the politics of the left. Also significant at this time were the politics of the Greater London Council under the leadership of Ken Livingstone: this gave some indication of what a politics no longer centred on the male working class might look like. For the Communist Party, however, such a politics was a long way off; it would mean in essence a rejection of the class culture on which it had been founded.[62]

FROM CLASS POLITICS TO NEW TIMES

The first chapter of this book argued that class was the central component of the Communist Party's essence as a political organisation. This was apparent not only in its particular social composition, with skilled sections of the working class its core, but also in its broader outlook, the culture it exuded and its organisational practices. Class was the main point of its appeal to new members, and (as Raphael Samuel noted) it was the 'class feeling', 'proletarian morality' and behavioural practices that justified and sustained its work. In Nina Fishman's words, the ability of the party to root itself in 'Life Itself', namely the day to day industrial struggles, gave it a legitimacy within sections of the class as a whole. In this sense it fitted well with a 'Fordist' emphasis on bureaucracy, discipline and hierarchy, and provided a strong core to its various components. That this in turn brought many contradictions and conflicts does not alter the fact that class was crucial to the party's being and allowed it to function, as a small but influential political organisation.

It follows that the erosion of this class core would have disastrous consequences for the party. Following the end of the miners strike, the Communist Party barely functioned as a national political organisation. The party ceased to play a large part in the struggles of the late 1980s – it was often outflanked by the SWP in white-collar union disputes for example – while it played no more than a supporting role in the Poll Tax opposition at the end of the decade. The party remained stronger in Scotland, where it continued to exert some influence in the unions and locally, but this was not sufficient to enable any sort of recovery for the party as a whole. An attempt to reassert the primacy of class politics was made by a group of critics who had remained in the party, in the form of a pamphlet.[63] According to the authors, who were a distinguished group of academics, the Gramscian-Eurocommunist leadership had 'substituted' new social forces and movements for 'class politics'. By this time, however, their argument that the recent period had seen 'an intensification of class struggle', and that therefore the need was to reassert the 'primacy of class' in political strategy, had few sympathetic ears in the party, despite receiving some attention in the press.

By far the biggest contribution the party made from the mid to late 1980s was in the pages of *Marxism Today*. Indeed, it is an irony that as the party declined, the influence of its 'theoretical and discussion journal' was never greater. Popular with the broadsheets, which often used extracts from the magazine, it now attracted some of the best writers and journalists on the left, and was gaining a reputation for the quality of its writing. Its editorial board was opened to include non-party members, including Stuart Hall and David Edgar. From its analysis of Thatcherism it moved into other areas, focusing notably on culture and identity, and for a while including cultural critic Suzanne Moore in its editorial team, while projecting an image of what some liked to call 'designer socialism'. Its iconoclasm was now one of its main features, as it played on the disparity between its approach and that of other sections of the British left; though there was a serious underlying message, that the left had to change its attitude to popular culture, and

7. The Death of Militant Labourism

seek a new life for itself at the heart of social and cultural innovation. The magazine was not afraid to carry interviews with opponents, Edwina Currie and Michael Heseltine being perhaps the most prominent.

The magazine also organised several large gatherings of left audiences. *Moving Left* in 1982 was the first such national initiative, followed by *Left Alive* in 1984; *Left Unlimited*, in 1986, was the largest of these events and was extremely ambitious in its range of speakers. (Some of the inspiration for this came from *le feste dell'Unità* organised by the PCI in Italy.[64]) There was a *Women Alive* event held in 1986, and an event the following year to mark the fiftieth anniversary of Gramsci's death. Local *Marxism Today* initiatives took place in different parts of the country under the direction of Mark Perryman, the magazine's marketing guru.

Though *MT* now had a much easier time in the party, the opposition having been defeated[65] and its status enhanced by the decline of the party in other areas, it was not totally autonomous. It still depended on party funding for its existence and was unable to pay contributors who wrote for it. Moreover, it was supported by a crucial network of discussion groups, almost all of which were run by party members. In many cases the party branch and *Marxism Today* discussion group involved the same people. The magazine continued to court controversy: in 1987, an article by Eric Hobsbawm advocated 'tactical voting' as the only viable way of defeating Thatcherism. This was against party policy, which remained committed to supporting the Labour candidate where no communist was involved – a policy which was an anachronistic hangover from more propitious times, given that the party was in no condition to fight elections with any seriousness.[66] No serious disciplinary action was taken against Jacques for this offence however. (Stuart Weir, editor of *New Socialist* during its most productive period, when it complemented debates in *MT* and often included similar contributors, was not so fortunate, losing his position after a similar proposal.)

The influence of *Marxism Today* was such that when the party decided to consider a new version of the *British Road to Socialism*, many of the members of the commission were established *MT* writers, including (in addition to Martin Jacques) Charlie Leadbeater and Beatrix Campbell. The decision of the committee to work towards what became known as the *Manifesto For New Times* was a direct outcome of a major discussion that had started in the magazine's pages from 1988 (and is the subject of the next chapter).

The influence of *MT* was also apparent in the decision to break with precedent and ask Martin Jacques to give the main political speech at the Congress of 1989. By the time this Congress started however, events in Eastern Europe were moving rapidly, a process for which Mikhail Gorbachev paved the way. Communist Parties everywhere were beginning to rethink their futures, and to face the realisation that it was no longer possible to sustain a communist identity in public political life, however much that identity was modernised. Ironically, the weekend of the 1989 British Party Congress coincided with the reappearance in Czechoslovakian public life of Alexander Dubcek, the leader of the Prague Spring – and thus an early mentor of many delegates present. (Dubcek had been banished to obscurity following the 'normalisation' which followed the Soviet invasion in 1968.) In his speech, Jacques called for a 'no holds barred discussion' on the future of the party.

The party by this time was effectively over, and, while there was a better prospect in Scotland for a continuation of the communist tradition,[67] the only question which remained for the organisation was the nature of its successor. A long discussion in what remained of the party now took place, with three proposals on offer: to retain the Communist Party, but with a reformed structure and ideology; to disband the party and replace it with a 'loose association'; or, finally, what became known as the 'twin-track' approach – to transform the party (including a name change), while encouraging the formation of networks and groups. At a Special Party Congress in 1990, the party, under its new leader Nina Temple, opted for the latter option and set up the constitutional congress to effect the changes, leading to the foundation of the Democratic Left.

During the process of discussion, however, things had moved rapidly in the Soviet Union. A coup in August 1990 removed Gorbachev from power and on his release the decline of the Soviet Union began to accelerate. In a bizarre mini replica of this episode the offices of the British Communist Party were also occupied in August of the same year, by a group called 'The Leninist', who accused the party leadership of selling off the party's archives and thus its historical legacy, an event which attracted some media interest and a marketing opportunity for *Marxism Today*.[68] Meanwhile revelations about the continued receipt of 'Moscow Gold' well into the 1970s led to the resignation of Martin Jacques, Beatrix Campbell and others. Events in Moscow seemed to confirm that the party was over. Yet, its influence was not quite exhausted. The underlying dynamics which had driven the party in its last thirty years, namely modernising political discourses and movements attached to the socio-economic political and cultural landscape in Britain, were to have one final legacy for the British left.

Notes
1. See R. Samuel, 'The SDP and the New Middle Class', in *Island Stories: Theatres of Memory*, Volume II, Verso 1998, pp256-271.
2. The candidate was John O'Grady.
3. T. Lane, 'The Unions; Caught on the Ebb Tide', *Marxism Today*, September 1982.
4. *Morning Star*, 26 August 1982.

7. The Death of Militant Labourism 221

5. K. Gill, letter to Gordon McLennan (undated). All letters and references to the Tony Lane episode can be found in CP/CENT/PC/15/30.
6. K. Halpin, letter to G. McLennan, 27.8.82.
7. D. Robinson, letter to G. McLennan (no date).
8. T. Durkin, letter to Martin Jacques, 4.9.82.
9. Letter to EC, 6.9.82.
10. Letter to EC, 7.9.82.
11. Letter to EC (no date).
12. Both letters sent to EC, 6.9.82.
13. Letter to Martin Jacques (no date). He signs the letter 'Yours (I hope) in unity'.
14. Letter, 17.9.82.
15. Letter, 9.9.82.
16. M. Costello, letter to G. McLennan, 26.8.82.
17. T. Chater, EC motion, 30.8.82.
18. M. Jacques, letter to I. McKay, 26.8.82.
19. M. Jacques, letter to G. McLennan, 1.9.82.
20. D. Cook, letter to G. McLennan. No date, but eve of PC and probably 31.8.82.
21. G. Matthews, letter to G. McLennan, 31.8.82.
22. The eight in support of Jacques were: Pete Carter, Ian McKay, Gordon McLennan, Gerry Pocock, Nina Temple, Martin Jacques, Vishnu Sharma and Ron Halverson; the six opposed were Jack Ashton, Tony Chater, Gerry Cohen, Mick Costello, Tess Gill and Kevin Halpin.
23. It is worth noting that the party, up until the impact of the Tony Lane article in *Marxism Today*, had not been seen as having major divisions. This is apparent in some of the wider press response. See for example *New Society* (16.9.82): 'Though the Conservatives run them close no political group is less given to public feuding than the Communist Party'; the *Financial Times* (diary), 17.9.82, spoke of the 'unprecedented public rebuke of Costello'; and *The Times*, 17.9.82, in the words of its labour correspondent Donald McIntryre, noted the 'growing tendency towards dissent in the party'.
24. W. Thompson, *The Good Old Cause*, op cit, p189.
25. F. Beckett, *The Enemy Within*, op cit, p201.
26. W. Thompson, *The Good Old Cause*, op cit, p193.
27. W. Thompson, *The Long Death of British Labourism*, op cit, p134.
28. These included George Bolton in Scotland and Alan Baker in Wales. Hywel Francis, miners' historian and a leading member of the Communist Party in Wales, presented the alternative position of the Wales NUM, one critical of Scargill, in *Marxism Today*. See in particular H. Francis, 'NUM United: A Team in Disarray', *Marxism Today*, April 1985.
29. *New Socialist*, April 1985.
30. According to Francis Beckett, Bert Ramelson was not overly impressed with many aspects of Scargill's strategy. F. Beckett, *The Enemy Within*, op cit, p205.
31. Ernesto Laclau's and Chantal Mouffe's *Hegemony and Socialist Strategy*, a post-Marxist attempt to find a politics not dependent on the emancipatory project of the working class was published in 1984 (Verso); this book stimulated a long debate which addressed similar concerns about the crisis of class politics within the field of discourse theory and cultural studies.

32. E. Hobsbawm, 'The Retreat Into Extremism', *Marxism Today*, April 1985.
33. J. Seabrook, *What Went Wrong? Working People and the Ideals of the Labour Movement*, Gollancz 1978.
34. Ibid, p13.
35. Ibid, p245.
36. Ibid, pp143-144.
37. T. Blackwell and J. Seabrook, *A World Still to Win*, Faber and Faber, 1985, p17.
38. Ibid, p30.
39. Ibid, p150.
40. Ibid, pp165-166.
41. Ibid, p185.
42. It first appeared as 'Why the Labour Party is in a Mess' in *New Socialist*, Jan-Feb 1982, reappearing as a chapter entitled 'Why is the Labour Party in a Mess?' in *Languages of Class*, Cambridge University Press 1983, pp239-256.
43. G. Stedman Jones, *Languages of Class*, op cit, pp241-242.
44. Ibid, p243.
45. Ibid, p250.
46. Ibid, p254.
47. Ibid, p255.
48. Ibid, p255.
49. Ibid.
50. Ibid, p256.
51. G. McLennan, 'Class Conundrum', in *Marxism Today*, May 1984.
52. Ibid. He also notes in passing that 'most socialists know (of the inadequacy of the existing explanations) but they have been reluctant to risk ... openly saying so'.
53. Ibid.
54. J. Westergaard, 'The Once and Future Class', in J. Curran, *The Future of the Left*, op cit, p88.
55. The essays were published as D. Selbourne, *Left Behind: Journeys into British Politics*, Cape 1987.
56. D. Selbourne, *Against Socialist Illusion: A Radical Argument*, Macmillan 1985, p70.
57. B. Campbell, *Wigan Pier Revisited: Poverty and Politics in the 80s*, Virago 1984, p18.
58. Ibid, p19.
59. Ibid, p233.
60. Ibid, p229.
61. See CP/IND/MATH/06/13 for coverage of this dispute.
62. Campbell interviewed Livingstone for the magazine *City Limits* (on which she was then a journalist) in July 1983, and for *Marxism Today* in May 1985. Her article 'Town Hall Feminism' in *New Socialist*, November 1984, also discusses the GLC's women's committee.
63. Ben Fine, Lawrence Harris, Marjorie Mayo, Angela Weir and Elizabeth Wilson, *Class Politics: An Answer to its Critics*, Leftover Pamphlets, London 1985.
64. Though these were much larger events often stretching over a month or so.
65. More expulsions were confirmed at the 1985 and 1987 Congresses.

66. Though this didn't prevent the election of John Peck to Nottingham City Council, following years of local campaigning. He subsequently joined the Green Party in 1990.
67. W. Thompson, *The Good Old Cause*, op cit, pp206-207.
68. 'This is what they really don't like', said Chris Granlund, then deputy editor, holding up a copy of the latest *Marxism Today*, emblazoned with images of that issue's theme, 'Sexual Desire' (speaking to a Sky news reporter in an interview outside the occupied building in St John Street, London EC1). Most of *Marxism Today*'s marketing initiatives were the brainchild of Mark Perryman, a political-cultural entrepreneur who later founded the Signs of the Times network, and Philosophy Football, the alternative football T-shirt company.

8. New Times and After

THE EVOLUTION OF THE NEW TIMES PROJECT
Much has been written in recent years about the links between the arguments and ideas expressed in *Marxism Today* and the political project associated with New Labour under the leadership of Tony Blair. At a very general level there were commonalities – in the need to break with what in this book has been called 'militant labourism'. Above all, there was a shared argument that the left, from the late 1970s onwards, was out of kilter with the grain of cultural and social change and needed to refound itself in the context of the modern and far-reaching changes that had taken place, notably globalisation. Two of *Marxism Today*'s leading writers in its very last years – Charlie Leadbeater and Geoff Mulgan – have gone on to become leading thinkers and policy advisers within the governments of New Labour, while some other figures – for example David Triesman, John Reid, Kim Howells and Peter Mandelson – passed through the CP in an earlier period, on their way to more propitious careers, though without playing a major role in the CP's own ideological fortunes.

However the extent of these links, which have been made by both 'right' and 'left' critics of *Marxism Today*, are often misrepresented; and the argument that New Times paved the way for New Labour does not stand up – either in terms of any historical scrutiny of the development of the New Times analysis, or of the intellectual influences behind it, the concept of politics which underpinned it, or the scope of its critique of contemporary capitalist societies. The terrain which *Marxism Today* and New Labour shared, a political discourse around 'modernisation' and 'modernity', also reveals stark differences over their meanings.

The origins of the New Times analysis lie in the last years of the CPGB. The previous chapter described the collapse of the party's base as an effective political organisation, but noted the paradox that *Marxism Today*'s influence had never been greater than at this time: it remained an important site of debate for the wider left even as the CP's rapid decline gathered momentum. Perhaps the extent of *MT* influence on future left politics was not immediately clear to many involved in the party at the time however – partly because few expected the party to fold so quickly, and still saw the possibility of renewal. Indeed there was continued criticism of *Marxism Today* from some Eurocommunists close to the party leadership, though *MT*'s relationship to the party after 1985 had in some ways been made easier by the loss of the *Morning Star* and the expulsions of traditionalists. Resolutions critical of the magazine were carried at the Congresses of 1985 and 1987, including criticism of the magazine's failure to carry more contributions from party members, or a broader coverage of issues. *MT*'s editor Martin Jacques still had to provide strenuous political justifications for the direction of *MT*, made more problematic by the debts the magazine was incurring, which the party had to write off. Thus in December 1987, a month after the critical Congress motions had been passed by those who wanted *MT* to be more closely linked to the (now) Eurocommunist leadership, losses of £43,000 were revealed, mainly incurred as a result of the big 'Left Unlimited' event held a year earlier.[1]

MT's autonomy during this time owed a lot to the democratic centralist structures of the party and the 'special relationship' between Gordon McLennan and Martin Jacques. Jacques's view was that the CP was in decline and that it had not learned from – and was now incapable of learning from – the example of *MT*, notably in its ability to reach out to the 'whole of the left', by attracting 'the best writers' and by 'setting the terms of political debate'. In doing so, *MT* did not attempt to give a political 'position'– clearly something that he was worried would occur with a closer relationship to the CP leadership – but an 'approach' or 'orientation'. This approach to politics, he argued, meant that it must remain autonomous and must not return to being an instrument of the party. As Herbert Pimlott notes, this view brought into doubt *MT*'s role as the 'discussion journal of the CP', a description which had adorned its masthead since its inception in 1957. *MT*, in any case, Jacques argued, was no longer a 'journal' but a 'magazine', a difference of some cultural and political significance.[2]

Maintaining *MT*'s 'relative autonomy' was therefore a political battle, one which required a knowledge of the structures and organisational habits of an ageing party.

And in these struggles, the extent of *MT*'s financial dependence on the party – without party support it would have folded – always made forms of compromise inevitable. There was, however, a general point of agreement between Jacques and some of his party critics, namely the need to develop a more focused analysis and strategy for the future of the left. Thatcherism having been dissected at great length, now was the time to set out what the left needed to learn from it. With *MT* now able to draw on a range of thinkers across the broad left spectrum, including academics, journalists and cultural critics, a wide-ranging analysis of the future of the left was conceivable. This development would also be able to address the CP's own immediate predicaments of finding a successor to its *British Road to Socialism*, which had been due in 1989.

In May 1988 the *Marxism Today* editorial board had organised an in-depth seminar[3] which had led to a special 'New Times' edition of *Marxism Today* in October 1988, and the *Manifesto For New Times* became the CP's new – albeit temporary – political document to replace the BRS in 1989.

MARXISM TODAY'S NEW TIMES

The special 'New Times' issue of *Marxism Today* which appeared in October 1988 was followed by a series of articles on the same theme in subsequent issues until September 1989. It included a spectrum of *MT* writers who had been writing for the magazine in previous years. It made for an impressive New Left line-up and included a mixture of historians, sociologists, cultural theorists, economists and political scientists, as well as leading journalists such as Neal Ascherson.[4] It was a measure of the reputation *Marxism Today* had gained that it could call on such a diverse range.

The New Times analysis was driven by the sense that fundamental changes – of an epochal nature – were taking place in Britain and the world. Though they were not on the scale of the shift from feudalism to capitalism, nevertheless they were 'as fundamental and far-reaching as ... the transition in the closing stages of the 19th century from the "entrepreneurial" to the advanced or organised stage within capitalism'. It was a 'qualitative change which has shifted the centre of gravity of the society and the culture markedly and decisively in a new direction'.[5]

The core of the New Times analysis centred on the concept of post-Fordism. Although this had been discussed at some length elsewhere on the left, including in *New Left Review*, the concept was given a new political interpretation by *MT*. Influenced by Gramsci's work on the significance of 'Americanism and Fordism', where he identified social, cultural and political modes derived from changes in the organisation of work, *MT* also saw significant political implications from what were perceived as major changes in work patterns. The Fordist type of production in the early part of the century had transformed different industrial sectors – not only car manufacturing but food processing, furniture, clothes and ship-building; these forms of mass production generated (and depended upon) mass consumption of 'standardised', and readily available products. A 'Fordist' infrastructure also developed which included provision of housing, roads and transport. The protection of national markets, and the pursuit of Keynesian demand management and universal welfare systems, helped to provide stability for new forms of production, including the costs of the workforce. The consequence was not only particular forms of production and consumption, dependent upon 'the semi-skilled worker and collective bargaining ... a managed national market and centralised organisation',[6] but a society amenable to particular forms of politics, based on a mass party, a centralised state structure, certain trends in architecture and mass participation in sport. These developments could be found in Soviet as well as social democratic societies; thus 'Fordism' – from the 1920s until the 1960s in particular – 'was at the centre of modernism'.[7]

Post-fordism should therefore be seen as representing a new form of work, while also signalling significant political and cultural shifts. In place of the Fordist 'economies of scale', post-fordist economies, led in Britain by retailing, technological innovation and new production methods based on 'flexible specialisation', were able to minimise costs, develop niche marketing, tailor products more to choice and respond more quickly to demand and consumer trends. 'Just-in-case' production was being replaced by 'Just-in-time' production, where the 'emphasis has shifted from the manufacturer's economies of scale to the retailer's economies of scope'.[8]

Globalisation had allowed post-fordist economies to expand, while in making the movement of money, people, goods and services easier, it also had strong political and cultural implications. It was no longer possible to conceive politics solely within the confines of the nation state; conventional party politics, economic policy and the authority of the state itself were now being undermined. Locally, the changing nature of the city, and the expansion and transformation of other localities by changes in technology and work, particularly in satellite and other communications technology, also carried significance for a new sense of place, as well as the compression of time and space.[9]

For *MT*, post-fordism and globalisation implied therefore not only a new form of work, but the need for a new form of politics for the future. The decline of mass parties was accompanied by a growth of 'identity politics', notably around sex, gender and 'race', which meant 'new political subjects' were being created. New social divisions (as well as a proliferation of older ones) were reflected in a 'two-thirds one-third society', while significant changes in lifestyle politics, notably through the rise in consumption, were leading to a new politics of the 'self', new opportunities for pleasure and leisure, and more individual freedoms.[10]

Postmodernism reflected many of these more ambiguous, fluid and multiple identities. Political and social identities of the past, shaped by the Fordist era, were more rigid, universal and homogeneous. Moreover, they existed within specific ideological boundaries, driven by science, the belief in progress, and the pursuit of particular definitions of emancipation, freedom and equality. Some of the certainties which underpinned these older ideologies had now broken down, under the pressures of the onset of globalisation, the impact of non-western cultures and the growth of more complex, hetereogeneous social structures. At a more immediate political level, developments in Eastern Europe, notably since the mid-1980s and the arrival of Gorbachev in the Kremlin, were threatening to bring to an end the bipolar political settlement that had existed for the previous fifty years.

The culmination of these changes – including the fall of the Berlin Wall in 1989 and then the Soviet Union itself in 1991 – only gave further strength to the predictions of New Times theorists who had already talked of a 'new Europe'.[11]

FROM BRITISH GRAMSCISM TO NEW TIMES: A NEW POLITICAL TRAJECTORY

The New Times analysis as set out in *Marxism Today* drew much discussion from the British left and beyond. Some of the critics pointed to the way in which *MT* apparently 'celebrated' New Times. Others criticised the way in which post-fordism was now accepted as a universal shift. Others argued that *MT* had accepted too much of the common sense of the Thatcherite era; for example, it took the decline of manufacturing industry as 'given', thus overlooking the need to rebuild it. Others saw *MT* as giving excessive space to identity politics at the cost of more traditional, class-based politics, while some saw in the New Times project a 'new orthodoxy', which was too dismissive of rival positions.

In their defence, Hall and Jacques argued that the New Times analysis was never intended to be a 'position';[12] and they accepted that 'it would be quite wrong to see the world in purely post-fordist terms'.[13] They argued that there was a 'fine line' between on the one hand 'exaggerating' the new and overlooking the 'unevennness and ambiguities that characterise the processes of change', and on the other analysing the 'points of rupture', and giving full recognition to 'changes and how they transform the world in which the left has to operate'. Nor was New Times 'a finished piece of work, comprehensive in scope and already complete, an analysis which covers all the ground and has either to be rejected or swallowed whole'. On the contrary, 'New Times' was, by definition, 'work in progress'.[14]

The essential message of New Times was a political one addressed to the left. Hall and Jacques argued that it was the left's 'failure to move with the times' that was at the heart of its problems and which needed addressing. As a result of this failure, the right – in the form of Thatcherism – had made the new terrain its own; Thatcherism was able to give political expression to the New Times and 'appropriate' them for its own project of 'regressive modernisation'. New Times was therefore a 'project to prise Thatcherism and that world apart':

> the ambition of the 'New Times' project is not only to make sense of the new world – to appreciate the tendencies and limits of post-Fordism, to unravel the emergent postmodern culture, to understand the new identities and political subjects in society – but also to provide the parameters for a new politics of the left, a politics beyond Thatcherism, which can give a progressive shape and inflexion to New Times.[15]

The reference to Thatcherism was crucial; it serves as a reminder that, though the New Times project was conceived between 1988 and 1989, it followed on from and in many ways developed out of earlier arguments in the magazine over the previous decade. Above all, this included the analysis of Thatcherism, and the work of Stuart Hall in analysing the 'qualitative' shift to the right (the 'moving right show') that had been taking place in British politics since the mid 1970s, which could not be explained by traditional left analyses. The connection between these accounts of Thatcherism and New Times was the argument that Thatcherism had 'a much stronger sense of the epochal changes' that were taking place, notably the end of the post-war consensus and the shift to a more 'fragmented and variegated society'. Consequently Thatcherism was able to impose its own interpretation of the significance of the new epoch, which it characterised as signalling the death of socialism, the centrality of the market and the drive towards a new entrepreneurialism. However – and despite some of the criticisms of *MT* – this should not be taken to suggest that Thatcherism and New Times were inevitably compatible or that the interpretations or conclusions of Thatcherism were accepted. According to Hall and Jacques, it was 'becoming clear that Thatcherism's conception of New Times is partial and inadequate, its guiding ideas are just not up to the task':

> It will not succeed in its long-term aim of hegemonising New Times for itself because they are much bigger, more profound, more epochal than it is. For while part of Thatcherism has been modernising, another part has always been regressive, organised around a view of Britain which is essentially backward-looking. From the perspective of New Times, Thatcherism increasingly appears as a weighty and powerful anachronism.[16]

Therefore it was not a question of following Thatcherism or accepting its main political and economic arguments. On the contrary the left, if it was to succeed long-term, needed to appropriate New Times for itself, 'give it its own inflexion', and construct a new project for Britain. One of the dangers, beside that of underestimating the scale of change, was for the left to be insufficiently radical or hegemonic in its own way, resulting in little more than a 'slightly cleaned up, humanised version of the radical Right': 'Such would be the inevitable consequence of two things; a pragmatic adjustment by the Left to the collapse of its various previous versions and a failure to generate its own new historic project'.[17]

New Times also drew on the arguments employed by Eric Hobsbawm in his 'Forward March of Labour Halted'. Hobsbawm's main argument was that the historical advances of the labour movement had come to a halt with changes in manufacturing industry, a weakening class and political identity and a growing rupture between the culture of the labour movement and the British people. The New Times analysis pointed to similar processes, though from a variety of different approaches. Sociologists such as John Urry, for example, in writing of the 'end of organised capitalism', talked of the problems facing the left if it clung to its traditional notions of collectivism.[18] The cultural studies theorist Dick Hebdige wrote of the need for the left to address the 'severance between modernity and progress':

> If the engagement with theories of postmodernity and postmodernism is to be fruitful – dialectical rather than defensive – then it has to be acknowledged from the start that such theories pose a challenge to the Left's ambition to 'change the world' because they question the belief in rationality and progress which direct and underpin the Left(s) project.[19]

One of Hebdige's main arguments was that the big collective identity of the left, built around the idea of mass struggle, was breaking down, and that there were new 'emancipation narratives', such as black political identities, and those of youth movements and popular cultural initiatives. This idea of identity politics, perhaps the most contentious argument developed within New Times, because of its challenge to the supremacy of class as the main organising identity of the left, found expression in different contributions to the debate, notably in areas related to popular culture. The New Times initiated a new social subject, which the left must now address. For Stuart Hall:

> New Times are both 'out there', changing our conditions of life, and 'in here', working on us. In part it is 'us' who are being 're-made'. But such a conceptual shift presents particular problems for the left. The conventional culture and discourses of the left, with its stress on 'objective contradictions', 'impersonal structures' and processes that work 'behind men's (sic) backs', have disabled us from confronting the subject dimension in politics in any coherent way.

These arguments also resonated with earlier concerns of the magazine over previous years. In addition to the debates about popular culture, these included discussions on the experience of the GLC. Thus Beatrix Campbell, amongst others, pointed to the way in which the GLC's pluralist politics encouraged in a positive way new political and social identities, through the opening up of the spheres of civil society in London. Earlier feminist arguments over 'the personal is political' also fitted with the new analysis. As many pointed out, however, there was a tension between, for example, the 'empowering' nature of consumption and the pressures of global capitalism; and there was a debate to be had about the extent of individuality that might be compatible with a renewed socialist politics; such arguments continued and grew in subsequent years.

THE MANIFESTO FOR NEW TIMES

As well as giving new life to the magazine, the arguments developed in *Marxism Today* initiated a wide-ranging and long-term debate – not only on the left but also within academia. As far as the Communist Party was concerned, *Marxism Today* also provided the solution – in its twilight years – to the dilemma of how to replace the *British Road to Socialism*, and its contributors played a central role in the Commission appointed by the EC in March 1988 with the remit of working towards the 1989 Congress. The Commission consisted of the foremost Communist Party contributors to *MT* – Martin Jacques, Beatrix Campbell and Charlie Leadbeater – together with many of those who had been instrumental in winning the party leadership to Eurocommunist positions and keeping the traditionalists isolated. These included Nina Temple, soon to be the party's new leader.[20] *Facing Up to the Future*, a discussion document produced and distributed with the September 1988 edition of *Marxism Today*, cemented the link between the magazine and the new strategic direction of the CP. The conclusions of the document also resulted in the resignation from its drafting group of Monty Johnstone, Marian Darke and Bill Innes, who, while members of the Eurocommunist wing, could not accept the document's 'failure to recognise the centrality of the class struggle in capitalist Britain today'.[21]

Generally, however, *Facing up to the Future* was well-received in the party and by the wider media, and *The Manifesto For New Times* (MFNT) was published in 1989 for discussion in the lead-up to the congress of that year, and was subsequently amended in light of the discussion. The Manifesto opens with a glimpse of what a socialist Britain might look like. It would be one which had left behind 'a capitalist society marked by authoritarianism, exploitation, vast inequalities in wealth and power, and the despoliation of nature',[22] replacing it with a society based on a 'socialist humanism' and 'socialist citizenship'. It would be one 'founded upon a sustainable, socialised economy', which would 'serve people's needs rather than the imperative of profit or the demands of central planners'. It would develop 'to sustain the social and ecological environment with healthy, safe workplaces; cities and towns built around people's needs rather than cars or capital; forms of production, trade and consumption which do not foul our air, sea and land'. Meanwhile, the role for the market would be 'to encourage flexibility, diversity and dynamism, with democratic planning setting the strategic aims of economic development. What matters is the social interests which determine how the tools of market and plan are to be used'.[23]

However, the Manifesto went on to argue that:

> ... for the socialist transformation of society to succeed, the concentrations of power that prevail in a capitalist economy would have to be broken down, and the key sectors of the economy held in social ownership. But power would not be reconcentrated in the hands of the state.

Social ownership would take diverse forms and be complemented by decentralised democratic control.

Indeed democratic decision-making would be extended to businesses, including 'international regulations covering large and transnational businesses'. The MFNT also gave much space to environmental policy and constitutional change, as well as oppressions in the private sphere, whereby 'existing power relationships in the home and in our culture need to be disamantled and democratised just as much as power in the public politics of institutions and in economic organisations and activities'.[24]

As far as communist Eastern Europe was concerned – at the time of publication in sharp and rapid decline – the October revolution of 1917 had 'produced a tarnished socialism ... in which the individual and civil society have been subordinated to the state and the party'. The Manifesto rejected the models of 'the authoritarian Eastern European socialist states, which are riven with inefficiency, corruption, inequality, centralised control, repression and environmental despoilation'.[25]

Subsequent chapters outlined the meaning of New Times, adopting the same concepts as those employed in *MT*, though it also identified a series of 'settlements', which it defined as 'Sites of Struggle'. These settlements were industrial, economic, social, gender, racial, environmental, regional, national, party political and international, and they had 'set basic parameters' within each sphere. This had served to contain most of the various struggles, contestations and conflicts of the previous period – at least until the 1970s – 'within manageable limits'.[26] From the 1970s, however, these 'interlocking, contested settlements began to break apart, provoking a tumultuous economic, social and political crisis at the end of the decade'.[27] This crisis had two consequences: a political vacuum, which the left and labour movement had failed to fill; and thus, relatedly, the growth of Thatcherism and a new capitalist 'regime of accumulation', based on new production methods in global markets. This had started to 'reorganise the British economy'.[28]

Unsurprisingly, much space is given in the MFNT to Thatcherism and its hegemonic role in 'transforming British society, with a conservative modernisation, a renovation of capitalism for the new times'.[29] Moreover, the failure of the left to understand the nature of Thatcherism and the demands of new times featured strongly, and reflected very closely the analysis of *MT* in recent years. Much of MFNT, however, is given over to setting out what a future left strategy should encompass, and advocating a realignment of the left.

THE PHILOSOPHY OF THE MANIFESTO
Underlying these political priorities was a philosophical shift in the overall outlook of the CPGB. Notably, the MFNT marked a distinctive break with militant labourism, because of a recognition of its

inability to offer a solution to Britain's social and economic crisis, its narrow conception of politics, and limited political constituencies. Because of its labourist culture, the labour movement was 'unable to come to terms with the decline of the old constituencies among the male, manufacturing class, and the emergence of new social movements and aspirations'.[30] In addition, the MFNT was critical of union structures that had not been sufficiently open to accommodate or seek a dialogue with new social movements. Moreover, the unions had lost the common purpose and social role assigned to them in the earlier part of the post-war consensus; in the 1970s they had become increasingly distrusted, 'as unrepresentative, sectional interests, acting for their members against the interests of society as a whole'.[31] Thus in the future they needed to find a new role in society. Not only did this build on Hobsbawm's 'Forward March' analysis, it also presented in a stark and openly critical way some of the arguments presented by Tony Lane in his controversial *MT* article six years earlier. This time, however, the party representatives of militant labourism had all but vanished, in many cases along with their branch and union members.

Unsurprisingly, there was a strong Gramscian component in the new document. This featured in different ways: in the analysis of Thatcherism as a hegemonic, rather than electoral, phenomenon; the emphasis on different levels of power and the way in which these operated within a political project; in the deployment of Gramsci's work on 'Americanism and Fordism' in explaining the new post-fordist epoch; and in the greater attention given to civil society, rather than the state, and for political solutions based on the relative autonomy of the political sphere. Perhaps foremost among these influences was the broader concept of the political (what the MFNT called 'A Deeper Shade of Politics'[32]), an expansion of the realm of politics so that political alternatives needed to be rooted in society and social change rather than mere institutions: 'A central part of political realignment in the 1990s would be to establish a new conversation between the left and society'.[33]

The Gramscian emphasis clearly marked the final official break with Leninism.[34] Influences of classical Marxism remained strong, however (though references to Marxism were usually accompanied by the term 'creative'), notably in the analysis of capitalism as a dynamic, progressive, but ultimately crisis-ridden and exploitative system. The critique of capitalism was also extended, to include the 'enterprise culture' that had developed under Thatcherism. 'Struggle', a long-standing communist by-word, remained within the document's vocabulary, and indeed was pluralised to accommodate a whole variety of new struggles, each needing a common ideological home. There was still also reference to class politics. Here, however, there was a shift of emphasis, though it did not amount to the abandonment of a class position, as many have claimed. Rather, class 'remained central to British politics', and was reflected in the 'enormous gulf between the increasingly concentrated, wealthy and internationalised ruling class, which exerts strategic control over financial and industrial capital, and the majority of the working people who have to sell their labour to live – whether by hand or brain, skilled or unskilled, black or white, men or women'.[35] The document also noted that the 'character of class' had changed as capitalism had developed, and was continuing to change under Thatcherism, in a 'new phase of capitalist restructuring'.[36]

The critique of capitalism included a strong environmentalist strand, which called for a new environmental settlement between companies, parties, international regulatory bodies, movements, consumers and the local and central states. 'The general commitment to progressive environmental development' should 'set society's priorities'. This would be done by seeking a new settlement between 'industrial modernisation and environmental protection', as well as a 'sea-change in individual attitudes and behaviour'.[37] This new red-green emphasis was distinctive, but it also enabled some in the party to reconnect with earlier traditions of British Marxism, incorporated in ideas of socialist humanism. To some extent this was an attempt to re-energise the humanist currents that had won people to the party in the 1930s in opposition to fascism, had sustained a new internationalism in support of third world liberation movements, and had led to involvement in the peace movement, and the sort of campaigns that were linked to the Communist-Christian dialogue around third world poverty in the late 1960s.

There was also greater attention given to the role of social movements, influenced by the involvement of the party in the WLM, anti-racist struggles and the student movement. A greater stress on autonomy and the politics of the personal were at the heart of this approach; it meant that at the core of the realignment of the left must be 'a new division of labour between social movements and political parties in mobilising people, expressing aspirations, challenging power and enacting change'.[38] Indeed the focus on new kinds of struggle was indicative of the belief, which had its origins in the feminist and Gramscian strands in the party over the previous decade, that movements were often better able to engage, recruit and mobilise people into political action, by virtue of the fact that they 'stem directly from the changes that people confront in their everyday lives'.[39]

NEW TIMES AND THE NEW LEFT

The New Times analysis came too late to save the party. Politically and intellectually, however, it represented a distinctive analysis of contemporary British society, one which had implications for the development of a 'post-labourist' left – which indeed is what it became. As well as encompassing strong components of the Gramscian and feminist positions that had been developed in the Communist Party over the previous two decades, it also resonated with earlier traditions of the

New Left. Indeed it could be argued that it represented another phase of the New Left, perhaps a third and final phase.

In some ways of course British Gramscism had always reflected aspects of the New Left – for example, in its concern with social movements, the moment of 1968 and the new interest in Marxism. A closer comparison between the ideas associated with New Times and the writings of New Left intellectuals also suggests a stronger continuity with earlier New Left ideas. Generally, the fundamental objective of the New Times analysis, namely to analyse the social, economic and cultural forces which were driving the modernisation of Britain, had always been a concern of the New Left in Britain, from Raymond Williams's *The Long Revolution* to Perry Anderson's *The Peculiarities of the English*. Now the emphasis was on pursuing a radical engagement with modernity rather than the 'regressive modernisation' epitomised by Thatcherism. It should be noted, however, that the extent of decline within the left now surpassed that of the previous lows (the events of 1956, and the disappointments of the 1964-1970 Wilson governments) that had formed the backdrop to British New Left renewal.

One important similarity with the New Left was a commitment to socialist humanism. The humanism of the first New Left, initially partly formed as a critique of the Stalinism of the CPGB at the time, nevertheless found its way into the intellectual life of the party from the late 1960s (in the Communist-Christian dialogue); it was also manifest in the party's support for the Prague Spring, and New Times identified socialist humanism as a key principle of the socialism of the future. Furthermore, the more theoreticist second New Left, under the inspiration of Perry Anderson, Robin Blackburn and others, provided the context for an important debate in the Communist Party between the humanists (notably John Lewis) and Louis Althusser, while the Institute For Workers Control debates – as we have seen – also found their way into the Communist Party's renewed strategy. Another common theme was the New Times critique of the British constitution, for its deferential traditions, archaic languages and procedures, and antiquated institutions – this was heavily influenced by second New Left writers such as Anderson and Tom Nairn. Others on the left drew on these ideas too, notably those who set up the pressure group Charter 88.

New Times critics also followed earlier traditions in their concern with culture, defined by Lin Chun as 'the cultural is political' approach. This concern with culture had been evident in the politics of the YCL in the 1960s, the theories underpinning the CUL, the 'People's Jubilee' in 1977 and the strategy pursued by students in the Broad Left in the same decade. The increasing importance of Cultural Studies in the 1980s also had a significant impact on *Marxism Today*'s analysis, influenced to a large degree by Stuart Hall, who, from the late

1970s, had been arguing that the left needed to construct a new relationship with the forces of mainstream culture, and, since 1972, had been Director of the Centre for Contemporary Cultural Studies in Birmingham.[40] More cultural studies academics, including Ros Brunt, Dick Hebdige and Frank Mort, filled the pages of the magazine during the 1980s and their ideas were strongly reflected in MFNT.

Yet its cultural critique had a different perspective from that either of the New Left tradition or of earlier communist positions, and was of a different order. It saw more positive consequences deriving from consumerism and popular culture than its predecessors, as was evident in its emphasis on identity politics and the way it drew on the discipline of cultural studies. It was also informed by the unsettling feminist critique of traditional work-family lifestyles. Workers had taken on a variety of identities, as consumers, as partners, as individuals. Although it did not have an uncritical view of capitalist consumerism, it saw major improvements in living standards as providing greater choice and mobility – not merely apathy and complacency, as others, including E.P. Thompson, had argued previously. In the extended emphasis on culture, which had been a feature of *Marxism Today* since the mid 1980s in particular,[41] it perceived a massive divide between the culture of the (labourist) left and that of the people it claimed to represent. The left, it argued, had failed to come to terms with the extent of 'the long revolution'. According to Stuart Hall, while negative aspects of the new consumerism were evident, there were positive, even emancipatory, sides to the cultural changes which the left needed to address:

> A labour movement which cannot identify with what is concrete and material in those popular aspirations, and expropriate them from their identification with the private market and private appropriation, will look, increasingly, as if it's trapped nostalgically in ancient cultural modes, failing to imagine socialism in twentieth century terms and images, and increasingly out of touch with where people are at'.[42]

New Times authors argued that the left had become disconnected from society, and was now more out of step with popular aspirations and cultural shifts than at any time in the past.

The radical and pluralist politics of the Greater London Council provided a ray of hope, however – and one consistent with the traditions of the New Left – in an otherwise depressing period. *Marxism Today*'s endorsement of the GLC gave some political substance to what an alternative post-labourist new left politics might look like, with a more vibrant civil society and a recognition in the policies as well as the outlook of its leader that 'identity' was now to be seen as a crucial marker of political engagement.

The concern with culture and identity was also a source of criticism from those who accused *MT* of 'cultural populism',[43] or a concern with 'shallow and superficial trivia',[44] while for Lin Chun such a shift meant the 'death' rather than the renewal of the New Left.[45] It is certainly the case that *Marxism Today* took iconoclastic approaches that at times pushed at the boundaries of left and right. And its discussions of identity, as well as its new interest in individualism, cannot easily be reconciled with New Left positions.

Charlie Leadbeater's argument, for example, that the left's failure of the 1980s was 'its lack of a vision of an individually based collectivism', was a different perspective, one which was more critical of the collective traditions of the left. He argued that the left needed a 'socialist', 'progressive' or 'democratic' 'individualism' (he used all three terms), to be achieved by expanding the sphere of individual responsibility, while at the same time renewing a culture of social responsibility and collective provision.[46] His argument was driven by the view that Thatcherism had created a society which was 'merely a meeting place for a plethora of individual wills, an arena for individual satisfaction, a set of opportunities for individual achievement, advancement and enjoyment'. This type of individualism, he argued, 'fosters the myth that people can and should be self-sufficient'.[47] The left, in response, needed to develop a 'powerful and coherent critique of Thatcherite individualism',[48] based around renewing collective cultures, through a 'new agenda of collective action', while also encouraging 'universal individual rights, social individuality, diversity and plurality'.[49]

More debatable links with the traditions of the New Left were evident in some of the ensuing discussions around 'post-Marxism' and 'postmodernism', which seemed to question the future of the left itself. Yet the purpose of the New Times position – evident in the way it had evolved in *Marxism Today* and the way it was positioned in the MFNT – was quite clear: only through a critical engagement with the latest, distinctive, moment of capitalism, a positive identification with new social movements, and a constantly evolving cultural critique, was the left likely to renew itself.

NEW TIMES AND NEW LABOUR
Those that have made links between New Labour and the New Times tradition have often ignored the new left trajectory and influences behind New Times. Instead they have focused on the role in New Labour thinking of two prominent *Marxism Today* writers of the later years – Geoff Mulgan and Charlie Leadbeater.

Marxism Today/New Times and New Labour are in fact similar in one important sense – their emphasis on the need to modernise, and to break away from labourism. However, even here some qualifications are needed. Firstly, recognition of the need for a break with labourism long predated the New Times debates. It was recognised under the leadership of Neil Kinnock; and many of the reforms he carried out as Labour Party leader from 1983 to 1992, including those he made to the party structures, were essential for the later development of New Labour. Thus there had been a much earlier dialogue between Kinnock and Hobsbawm (dubbed by Kinnock 'his favourite Marxist'); indeed – as was discussed in previous chapters – Hobsbawm's concern over the crisis of labourism had been evident in *Marxism Today* from the late 1970s, and his arguments had formed an important part of Communist Party discussion. A lot of hope was invested in the general election of 1992, when the Labour Party under Kinnock – which could by no means at that time be described as New Labour – was expected to do better than it did. The defeat in this election, in the words of Hobsbawm, was the 'saddest and most desperate in my political experience', not least because one consequence for the Labour Party was the dismantlement – not renewal – of the relationship between Labour and its traditional social alliances of trade unions, public sector and intellectuals.[50]

Nevertheless Tony Blair's agenda of modernisation made him the '*Marxism Today*' party leadership candidate in 1994,[51] for his belief that traditional labourist solutions were no longer applicable, and that the left needed to reconnect with society and modernise its political appeal. This might also explain why some groups and individuals close to *Marxism Today* subsequently became close to New Labour, such as Democratic Left, the successor to the Communist Party and its successor organisations,[52] and the think tank Demos.[53]

Anthony Giddens, the intellectual most associated with the 'third way' ideas which underpinned the Blair agenda, has acknowledged the influence of the New Times analysis. He has gone so far as to say that:

> The objective of third way politics, as I would see it, is to carry through the political implications of new times, recognising that this means that the established positions and policies of the left have to be profoundly revised.[54]

At a general level this may sound a reasonable assessment, and it is one which many commentators, looking for the intellectual provenance of New Labour, have taken as accurate.[55] Yet, if we investigate the arguments and political assumptions of the third way and compare it to the New Times project, there are very significant differences. They start with a common question, namely to find what is distinctive about a modern left politics in an era characterised by the decline and influence of the industrial working class and the challenge of globalisation. However their conclusions differ, partly because of the nature of their critique of existing society, and partly because of the different meanings they attach to the left – they have different perceptions of the left's identity as a movement, as well as of the ideas and principles which should define the left's identity.

Firstly, where the New Times analysis is rooted in a 'systemic' critique of the post-fordist era of capitalism, in which inequalities are endemic to the organisation of the economy, the third way argues that inequality is not a product of structural factors, but is related to lack of integration into the benefits of the market economy. Third-way 'egalitarianism' – defined by Giddens as the one core left value to remain relevant – does not any longer depend on redistribution of wealth, but is achieved through the expansion of meritocratic life chances. 'Equality of opportunity', Giddens argues, 'typically creates higher rather than lower inequalities of outcome'.[56] His conception of meritocracy, however, differs markedly from Michael Young's earlier definition;[57] while his notion of equality has little conceptual connection with previous traditions of the left, either in Tawney's scheme or Crosland's.[58] It is a view of equality that is consistent with a liberal worldview, that is it accepts the logic of the market economy, as a prequisite to greater equality.

Secondly, there is the question of globalisation – central to the third way worldview as it was for New Times. For New Times, however, while globalisation was the new terrain for politics, from which there was no retreat, the task of the left was to put across a view of globalisation that contrasted sharply with the neo-liberal agenda, which was based on the extension of corporate power. In the alternative position, 'sustainable development' was to be central, the role of regulatory institutions crucial, and opposition to third world poverty and debt a priority. For the third way, in Anthony Giddens's scheme, there is little distinction between neo-liberal and other versions of globalisation; indeed, while mention is made of 'global ecological management', the 'regulation of corporate power', 'control of warfare' and the 'fostering of transnational democracy',[59] there is little indication of the changes needed for this to come about, and globalisation and neo-liberalism at times appear inseparable. As far as the position of the third world is concerned, Giddens insists that 'most problems that inhibit the economic development of the impoverished countries don't come from the global economy itself, or from self-seeking behaviour on the part of the richer nations, they lie mainly in the societies themselves'.[60]

Thirdly, the New Times analysis maintained a critique of class divisions, which it saw as endemic in the economic system – while also giving emphasis to other social divisions, such as those based on 'race', gender and sexual orientation. Opposition to these inequalities would be driven by the left in alliance with new social movements. The Third Way, on the other hand, sees inequality as being derived from lack of 'inclusion', and people's opportunities as largely independent of the structural features of the economic system. The emphasis is on strengthening communities, pro-active welfare to work schemes and social capital – though it is committed to extending equal opportunities and promotes anti-discrimination legislation.

Leadbeater is the ex-New Times theorist most committed to widening the sphere of individual freedom, seen as made possible by globalisation, while Mulgan is the person most identified with reconnecting the individual to forms of collective responsibility. However, these positions avoid any idea of collective action to eradicate inequalities, instead focusing on forms of interconnectedness derived from the networks and organisational forms of the knowledge economy.[61] As far as the social costs of individualism are concerned, their solution proposes the strengthening of traditional social institutions, notably the family. This included, on Mulgan's part, an early appreciation of Etzioni's communitarianism; and while he was at Demos, rebalancing 'rights and responsibilities' (an important concern also for Giddens) remained at the core of his thinking.

The differences between the New Times analysis and the third way are substantial, and reflect significant ideological divergences, while being underpinned by contrasting concepts of politics. New Times, in line with earlier New Left traditions, remains committed to ideological struggle, and the role of new social movements was to be crucial. The third way on the other hand prefers looser ideological ties and draws on think tanks and policy networks for its base. The key social groups appear as 'social' and 'civic entrepreneurs' (Bill Gates 'who made his money from nothing'[62] is a particular favourite for third way thinkers), while intellectuals are either too removed to play a key role in politics or insufficiently practical; in short, a suspicion of 'big ideas' dominates – despite the grandiose aspirations attributed to the third way by its own proponents. The difficulty of defining third way politics is not made any easier by its claims to be both distinct from both left and right, while also continuing the tradition of social democracy. The lack of any historical ancestry is also significant, and means that its attempt to distinguish itself as a third way between 'statist' social democracy and market liberalism, while neatly setting up a role for itself, tries to square too many circles.

Its failure to acknowledge the value of any rival non-statist traditions of social democracy – for example those in Scandinavia, or of the new left – also contributes to its fragile intellectual status, and even earlier 'third way' social democratic traditions have largely been ignored.[63] Thus the British SDP gets no attention at all, in spite of its striking similarities; indeed, the SDP's attempt to 'break the mould' between left and right, its appeal to new social constituencies, and its pro-European agendas – not to mention its obsession with 'modernisation' – makes it by far the closest intellectual precursor to New Labour.

For all these reasons the conclusion has to be that the New Left traditions of New Times and the agenda of the third way are ideologically opposed rather than complementary. It is not the case, as Giddens claims, that the third way is a natural development from the New Times analysis, despite the presence of two of *MT*'s most prominent thinkers as leading 'third way theorists'. How, then, do we explain the Mulgan and Leadbeater position? Alan Finlayson has argued that *Marxism Today* has two distinct political legacies. Those that have taken the New Labour route he describes as 'the Demos tendency', one defined by a 'technological futurist' position which has substituted technological change for political struggle. What Mulgan and Leadbeater have maintained from their New Times days, according to Finlayson, was their concern with the sociological, economic and technological transformations inherent in New Times. However, while they have kept the sociological and technological analyses, they have moved away from seeing politics as the site of conflict and contestation. They accept uncritically the logic of the market, and in their research see social trends rather than social conflict as the driving force of change. 'The result', according to Finlayson, 'is to accept economic developments as non-political, even natural phenomena. This blunts analysis and conflicts with aspirations for social change'.[64]

Leadbeater, in particular, in *Living on Thin Air* and *Up the Down Escalator: Why the Global Pessimists Are Wrong*, remains optimistic about the capacity of technology (notably the knowledge economy) and globalisation to deliver goods; he derides critics (who range from *Daily Mail* conservatives to anti-global capitalists) as 'global pessimists'. The progressive direction of capitalism carries all before it. Social conflicts will not outlast the onward march of global progress, and divisions of power – at the core of the New Times analysis – are not a central political problem.

The other *Marxism Today* tendency, according to Finlayson, is defined by its commitment to Gramscian politics, and is most clearly represented by Stuart Hall. This is a position which has retained a critique of capitalism, while seeking a critical engagement with the dislocation of traditional social allegiances and the identification of new social subjects. In Finlayson's summary of this position: 'the challenge for the left was to analyse the social forces and develop new strategies beyond a simple appeal to class allegiance that could generate a wide enough constituency for a hegemonic project of socialist renewal'.[65] For Hall, New Times demanded a political response, one which would mean the expansion of politics into new spaces along Gramscian lines, but would also recognise the adversarial nature of politics, in which ideology and conflict would remain inevitable features.[66] The task of constructing a modernising project depended on an alternative philosophy to the neo-liberal agenda.

This position resonates closely with the British Gramscian tradition within the CP over the previous two decades, which developed into the New Times analysis. It was re-emphasised immediately prior to the 1997 election which brought New Labour to power, and later in a more formulated way in the one-off special issue of *Marxism Today* which appeared in 1998.[67] Here, Hall and Hobsbawm, amongst many others, took issue with the New Labour project for not addressing questions of power, for not mobilising radical opinion and for remaining, to all intents and purposes, committed to a neo-liberal agenda. As Hobsbawm wrote later:

> We could not accept the alternative of 'New Labour', which accepted the logic as well as the practical results of Thatcherism and deliberately abandoned everything that might remind the decisive middle class voters of workers, trade unions, publicly owned industries, social justice, equality, let alone socialism. We wanted a reformed Labour, not Thatcher in trousers'.[68]

It was the commitment to the New Left which most marks out the *MT* legacy from the third way. This has also been apparent in other critiques of the third way from former *Marxism Today* writers, including Beatrix Campbell, who has put forward an incisive feminist critique of the communitarianism behind the Mulgan and Demos agenda, arguing that the resort to communitarianism was a central component of a third way 'between liberal individualism and statist socialism', whose origins lay in conservative debates in the US.[69] At the heart of Campbell's analysis was a critique of the failure of the third way in its communitarian forms to deal with questions of power, and its failure to recognise that the 'imaginary unity of community or family ... is no less fissured by power and subordination than class, nation and empire'.[70]

After the ending of the Communist Party and the closure of *Marxism Today*, these critiques were made in more fragmented and occasional contributions, without an obvious political home. To some they represented voices in the wilderness, left behind by the new directions of modern politics, constrained by the ideological baggage of the past.[71] Yet, the mistake third way advocates have made is in not being able to distinguish labourism from other left traditions. The argument that the New Left – and indeed most variants of European social democracy – are now a relic of history is not borne out by developments beyond Britain and within Europe in recent years. Indeed, New Left political parties (including some former communist parties[72]) who modernised their structures at an earlier moment have survived, even prospered, in electoral coalitions. The anti-global capitalist movement in the early part of the twenty-first century draws on significant 'New Left' influences, notably in its focus on systemic critiques of contemporary capitalism, its support for pacifism, and above all its notion of the expansion of politics; while it contains a fluid mix of ideas, the nature and scope of its critique clearly refutes 'end of ideology' arguments characteristic of third way debates.

Moreover, the third way – with its origins in US debates – has always had a more difficult journey in the rest of Europe, where other

8. New Times and after

social democratic traditions remain important. One of the consequences of the crisis in the Blair project at the time of the second Gulf War in 2003, and the divisions the war highlighted between the UK and the rest of Europe, was a widespread belief that the third way had lost its direction, and that the renewal of European social democracy would be founded on a new relationship between parties and movements.

Notes

1. Herbert Pimlott has a good discussion of these concerns in 'From the Margins to the Mainstream', op cit, pp72-73.
2. M. Jacques, 'Report on *Marxism Today*' to EC 1987, summarised in H. Pimlott, 'From the Margins to the Mainstream', op cit.
3. 'What triggered it off', according to Stuart Hall and Martin Jacques in their introduction to *New Times*, 'was a sense around MT of the need to move on, to develop the magazine's political project beyond the analysis of Thatcherism and the crisis of the left. Above all, it represented the felt need to address the future of the left more directly, from a position rooted in an analysis of present and emergent tendencies in our society'. S. Hall and M. Jacques (eds), *New Times*, Lawrence and Wishart 1989, p11.
4. The full line-up was: Robin Murray, Fred Steward, Dick Hebdige, John Urry, Goran Therborn, Stuart Hall, Sarah Benton, Charlie Leadbeater, Rosalind Brunt, Frank Mort, David Held, David Marquand, Neal Ascherson, Gareth Stedman Jones, Martin Jacques, Tom Nairn, Gwyn A. Williams, Geoff Mulgan, Beatrix Campbell. The playwright David Edgar contributed a short story, while critical pieces from Paul Hirst and Michael Rustin, published in *New Statesman and Society* and *New Left Review* respectively were also included in the Lawrence and Wishart edition. Of the above, Brunt, Steward, Jacques, Leadbeater and Campbell were members of the CP.
5. Hall and Jacques (eds), *New Times*, op cit, p12.
6. R. Murray, 'Fordism and Post-Fordism', in Hall and Jacques (eds), *New Times*, op cit, p41.
7. Ibid.
8. Ibid, p43.
9. G. Mulgan, 'The Changing Shape of the City', in S. Hall and M. Jacques (eds), *New Times*, op cit, pp262-278.
10. R. Brunt, 'The Politics of Identity', pp150-159; C. Leadbeater, 'Power to the Person', pp137-149; G. Therborn, 'The Two-Thirds, One-Third Society', pp103-115; all in S. Hall and M. Jacques (eds), *New Times*, op cit.
11. Obviously the *New Times* project was written at the time of the changes in Eastern Europe, though the overriding trend of the changes was apparent in the writing on this. See, for example, N. Ascherson, 'Eastern Europe on the Move', in S. Hall and M. Jacques (eds), *New Times*, op cit, pp222-229.
12. Hall and Jacques (eds), *New Times*, op cit, p11.
13. Ibid, p13.
14. Ibid.
15. Hall and Jacques (eds), *New Times*, op cit, p15.
16. Ibid, p17.

17. Ibid, p16.
18. J. Urry, 'The End of Organised Capitalism', in S. Hall and M. Jacques (eds), *New Times*, op cit, pp94-102.
19. D. Hebdige, 'After the Masses', in S. Hall and M. Jacques (eds), *New Times*, op cit, pp77-78.
20. The members of the Commission were: Beatrix Campbell, Marion Darke, Tricia Davis, David Green, Joanna de Groot, Ron Halverson, Steve Hart, Martin Jacques, Charlie Leadbeater, Bert Pearce, Jeff Rodrigues, Mhairi Stewart and Nina Temple.
21. Their statement was published in *Marxism Today*, October 1988.
22. MFNT, p2.
23. MFNT, p3.
24. Ibid.
25. Ibid.
26. Ibid, pp4-5.
27. Ibid, p6.
28. Ibid.
29. Ibid, p10.
30. Ibid, p18.
31. Ibid, p19.
32. Ibid, p17.
33. Ibid, p17.
34. Though rather bizarrely the term 'Marxist-Leninism' remained.
35. Ibid, p9.
36. Ibid.
37. Ibid, p21.
38. Ibid, p18.
39. Ibid, p14.
40. Hall had been at the CCCS since 1964. His predecessor as Director was Richard Hoggart. Hall left CCCS for the Open University in 1979.
41. This also included changes to the 'magazine's' style and format, as well as its appraisal of trends in consumption, sport, fashion, sexuality and soap operas. It even became part of the consumption cycle itself, offering 'MT credit cards', mugs T-shirts and a passion for 'designer socialism'.
42. S. Hall, 'The Culture Gap', *Marxism Today*, January 1984.
43. For this critique see J. McGuigan, *Cultural Populism*, Routledge 1992.
44. As John Saville of the 'first New Left' put it in *'Marxism Today*, An Anatomy', *Socialist Register*, Merlin Press 1990.
45. According to Chun this was because of its 'failure to assess ... culture in its comprehensive perspective and to acknowledge the need for a renewal of moral concern and utopian thought'. L. Chun, *The British New Left*, op cit, p194.
46. C. Leadbeater, 'Power to the Person', in S. Hall and M. Jacques, *New Times*, op cit, p138.
47. Ibid, p143.
48. Ibid, p144.
49. Ibid, p145.
50. E. Hobsbawm, *Interesting Times*, Allen Lane, London 2002, p276.
51. As Hall described it in an interview with Jacques. See 'Cultural Revolutions' in the *New Statesman* 5.12.97.

52. Democratic Left was set up in 1991, initially as a 'twin-track' political party and network, though it had difficulty recruiting members even amongst the Gramscian-Eurocommunist generation. Willie Thompson was the only member of the MT editorial board who joined, and the only prominent Eurocommunists who did so were its two leading members, Nina Temple, and Mike Power. Its membership declined from an initial figure of 1,500 (out of the 7000 who remained in the CPGB at the time of dissolution), to under 700 by the time it folded in 2000 to become the 'New Times Network', named after its newspaper which folded shortly afterwards. It increasingly identified itself with a New Labour agenda – a decision which ensured a split with some of its affiliated groups, notably the red-green network. Some Gramscians joined the Labour Party while others, such as Dave Cook and Pat Devine, became involved in 'Red-Green' organisations, retaining a commitment to 'democratic communism'. See D. Cook and P. Devine, 'Life in Death', *New Statesman and Society*, 6.9.91. The New Times Network later became the New Politics Network.
53. Set up in 1993 by Martin Jacques as an independent concern it became closer to New Labour, following the appointment of its Director and former MT writer Geoff Mulgan to the Downing Street Policy Unit, while Charlie Leadbeater, one of the key authors of New Times and a former communist, also became a key figure in New Labour circles.
54. A. Giddens, *The Third Way and its Critics*, Polity 2000, p28.
55. See for example Jonathan Freedland, *The Guardian*, 9.9.98.
56. A. Giddens, *The Third Way and its Critics*, op cit, p86.
57. In *The Rise of the Meritocracy* (Penguin Books, Harmondsworth 1965) Young feared a society driven by expertise. In Blair's and Giddens's use of the term, meritocracy reflects a society based on equal life chances and social mobility.
58. Tawney and Crosland are frequently cited as the classic egalitarian thinkers in the Labour Party. While Tawney's belief in 'equal worth' was based on reducing economic inequality between rich and poor as well as resting on a set of ethics incompatible with 'acquisitive capitalism', even Crosland's more modest theory of 'equal opportunity' was one which demanded redistribution of wealth. See R. H. Tawney, *Equality;* and *The Acquisitive Society*; and C.A.R. Crosland, *The Future of Socialism* (Jonathan Cape 1980). New Labour, despite an early reference in the Borrie Report (The Commission on Social Justice) to 'endowment egalitarianism to be attained across the life cycle', has based its egalitarian theory on a weak liberal notion of 'equal opportunity', which does not go much beyond 'inclusion' in market society. The Borrie Report, set up by John Smith, was an early casualty of Blair's political shift.
59. A. Giddens, *The Third Way and its Critics*, op cit, p124.
60. Ibid, p129.
61. G. Mulgan, *Connexity*, Chatto and Windus, London 1997.
62. A. Giddens, *The Third Way and its Critics*, op cit, p96.
63. A. Giddens, in *The Third Way and its Critics*, op cit, responds to some of these.
64. A. Finlayson, *Making Sense of New Labour*, Lawrence and Wishart 2003.
65. Ibid.
66. This point was also made by Chantal Mouffe in 'The Radical Centre; A

Politics Without Adversary', *Soundings* Issue 9 Summer 1998.
67. The earliest critique of Blair from the New Times camp was Stuart Hall, 'Parties on the Verge of a Nervous Breakdown', *Soundings* Issue 1, Autumn 1995, pp19-34. See also 'New Labour's Double Shuffle', *Soundings* 24.
68. E. Hobsbawm, *Interesting Times*, op cit, p276.
69. B. Campbell, 'Old Fogeys and Angry Young Men', *Soundings* Volume 1, Autumn 1995, pp47-64.
70. Ibid, p51.
71. John Lloyd, *New Statesman*, Sep 1998.
72. The Swedish Left party (VPK) is probably the best example of this. As a 'New Left' party it developed from the old Swedish Communist Party which had already modernised its party structures, and won over the types of new electoral and social constituencies that the CPGB had failed to reach in anticipation of major changes in the class structure. Helped by an electoral system which meant it was in alliance with social democrats and Greens, the change of name in 1990 did not mean a significant shift in its politics or identity. See D. Apter, 'The Swedish Left party: Eco-Communism or Communist Echo?', *Parliamentary Affairs*, Vol 44 No 1 January 1991; and L. Lewin, *A Century of Swedish Politics*, Cambridge University Press 1988. In Italy the break up of the PCI led to a three-way split; the largest of these, Democratici di Sinistra (Democrats of the Left) and Rifondazione comunista ('Refounded Communists) both maintain some New Left influences, as evidenced by their participation in the European Social Forum in Florence in November 2002.

Bibliography

Abrams, M., 'Class and Politics', *Encounter* 17, 1961.
Abrams, M., P. Rose and R. Hinden, *Must Labour Lose?*, Harmondsworth, Penguin, 1960.
Adamson, W., *Hegemony and Revolution*, Berkeley, University of California Press, 1980.
Adi, H., 'West Africans and the Communist Party in the 1950s', in G. Andrews et al (eds), *Opening the Books*, London, Pluto Press, 1995.
Adi, H., *West Africans in Britain*, London, Lawrence and Wishart, 1998.
Althusser, L., *For Marx*, London, New Left Books, 1962.
Althusser, L., *Essays On Ideology*, London, Verso, 1976.
Althusser, L., 'What Must Change in the Party', *New Left Review* 109, May-June, 1978.
Althusser, L., and E. Balibar, *Reading Capital*, London, New Left Books, 1970.
Amis, M., *Koba The Dread*, London, Jonathan Cape, 2002.
Anderson, P., 'Origins of the Present Crisis', *New Left Review* 23, Jan-Feb, 1964. Anderson, P., *Considerations on Western Marxism*, London, New Left Books, 1976. Anderson, P., 'The Antinomies of Antonio Gramsci', *New Left Review* 100, Nov 1976-Jan 1977.
Anderson, P., 'Communist Party History', in R. Samuel (ed), *People's History and Socialist Theory*, London, Routledge and Kegan Paul, 1983.
Anderson, P. and P. Camiller (eds), *Mapping the West European Left*, London, Verso, 1994.
Anderson, P., and K. Davey, '"Moscow Gold"? The True Story of the Kremlin, British Communism and the Left', *New Statesman and Society*, 7.4.95.
Andrews, G., R. Cockett, A. Hooper, and M. Williams (eds), *New Left, New Right and Beyond*, London, Macmillan, 1999.
Andrews, G., N. Fishman, and K. Morgan (eds), *Opening the Books*, London, Pluto Press, 1995.
Andrews, G., H. Kean, and J. Thompson (eds), *Ruskin College: Contesting Knowledge, Dissenting Politics*, London, Lawrence and Wishart, 1999.
Archer, R., D. Bubeck, H. Glock (ed), *Out of Apathy: Voices of the New Left*, London, Verso, 1989.
Aron, R., *The Opium of the Intellectuals*, London, Secker, 1957.
Assiter, A., *Althusser and Feminism*, London, Pluto Press, 1990.
Baines, D., and E. Reid, *Governments and Trade Unions*, London, Heinemann, 1980.
Beckett, F., *Enemy Within: The Rise and Fall of the British Communist Party*, London, John Murray, 1995.
Bedani, G., *Politics and Ideology in the Italian Workers Movement*, Oxford, Berg, 1995.

Beer, S., *Britain Against Itself; The Political Contradictions of Collectivism*, New York, WW Norton, 1982.
Bell, D. S., *Western European Communists and the Collapse of Communism*, Oxford, Berg, 1993.
Benn, T., 'Forward March of Labour Halted', in M. Jacques and F. Mulhearn, *The Forward March of Labour Halted?*, London, Verso, 1981.
Benn, T., *Arguments For Democracy*, Harmondsworth, Penguin, 1982.
Benn, T., *Against the Tide: Diaries 1973-1976*, London, Arrow, 1990.
Benton, S., 'The Decline of the Party', in S. Hall and M. Jacques (eds), *New Times*, London, Lawrence and Wishart, 1989.
Berger, S., *The British Labour Party and the German Social Democrats*, Oxford, Clarendon Press, 1994.
Berlinguer, E., 'Lessons From Chile', *Marxism Today*, February, 1973.
Blackburn, R., and A. Cockburn, *The Incompatibles: Trade Union Militancy and the Consensus*, Harmondsworth, Penguin, 1967.
Blackwell, T., and J. Seabrook, *A World Still To Win*, Faber and Faber, 1985.
Blair, T., *The Third Way*, London, Fabian Society, 1998.
Bloomfield, J., *Class, Hegemony and Party*, London, Lawrence and Wishart, 1977.
Boggs, C. and D. Plotke, *The Politics of Eurocommunism*, London, Macmillan, 1980. Boggs, C., *The Socialist Tradition: From Crisis to Decline*, London, Routledge, 1995.
Boucher, D., *Idealism and Revolution*, London, Edward Arnold, 1978.
Branson, N., *History of the Communist Party of Great Britain 1927-41*, London, Lawrence and Wishart, 1985.
Branson, N., *History of the Communist Party of Great Britain 1941-51*, London, Lawrence and Wishart, 1997.
Bridges, G., 'Western European Communist Strategy', in S. Hibbin (ed), *Politics, Ideology and the State*, London, Lawrence and Wishart, 1978.
Bridges, G., and R. Brunt, *Silver Linings*, London, Lawrence and Wishart, 1981.
Brown, M., R. Martin, F. Rosengarten and G. Snedeker (eds), *New Studies in the Politics and Culture of US Communism*, New York, Monthly Review Press, 1993.
Bruley, S., 'Women and Communism, a Case Study of the Lancashire Weavers', in G. Andrews et al, *Opening the Books*, London, Pluto Press, 1995.
Brunsdon, C., 'A Thief in the Night; Stories of Feminism in the 1970s', in S. Hall, *Critical Dialogues in Cultural Studies*, London, Routledge, 1996.
Brym, R. J., *Intellectuals and Politics*, London, Allen and Unwin, 1980.
Buci-Glucksmann, C., *Gramsci and the State*, London, Lawrence and Wishart, 1980.
Bull, M. J., 'The West European Communist Movement, Past, Present and Future', in M. Bull and P. Heywood, *Western European Communist Parties After the Revolutions of 1989*, London, St. Martins Press, 1994.
Bull, M., and P. Heywood (eds), *West European Communist Parties After the Revolutions of 1989*, London, St. Martin's Press, 1994.
Callaghan, J., *The Far Left in British Politics*, Oxford, Blackwell, 1987.
Callaghan, J., 'The British Road to Eurocommunism', in M. Waller et al (eds), *Communist Parties in Western Europe*, Oxford, Blackwell, 1988.
Callaghan, J., *Rajani Palme Dutt: A Study in British Stalinism*, London, Lawrence and Wishart, 1993.

Callaghan, J., '"Endgame", The Communist Party of Great Britain', in D. Bell (ed), *Western European Communists and the Collapse of Communism*, 1993.
Campbell, B., *Wigan Pier Revisited: Poverty and Politics in the '80s*, Virago, 1984.
Carrillo, S., *Eurocommunism and the State*, London, Lawrence and Wishart, 1977.
Carter, T., *Shattering Illusions*, London, Lawrence and Wishart, 1986.
Caute, D., *Communism and French Intellectuals, 1914-1960*, London, Andre Deutsch, 1964.
Chun, L., *The British New Left*, Edinburgh, Edinburgh University Press, 1992.
Claudin, F., *Eurocommunism and Socialism*, London, New Left Books, 1978.
Coates, D., *The Labour Party and the Struggle For Socialism*, Cambridge, Cambridge University Press, 1975.
Coates, K., and T. Topham, *The New Unionism: The Case For Workers Control*, Harmondsworth, Penguin, 1974.
Cockburn, A., and R. Blackburn, *Student Power*, Harmondsworth, Penguin, 1969.
Cockett, R., 'The New Right and the 1960s, The Dialectics of Liberation', in G. Andrews et al (eds), *New Left, New Right and Beyond*, London, MacMillan, 1999.
Cohen, P., 'Losing the Generation Game', in J. Curran (ed), *The Future of the Left*, Cambridge, Polity Press/New Socialist, 1984.
Cohen, P., *Children of the Revolution*, London, Lawrence and Wishart, 1998.
Cook, D., 'Rocky Road Blues, The Communist Party and the Broad Democratic Alliance', in G. Bridges and R. Brunt, *Silver Linings*.
Coopey, R., S. Fielding, and N. Tiratsoo, *The Wilson Governments 1964-1970*, London, Pinter, 1995.
Coote, A., and B. Campbell, *Sweet Freedom*, London, Pan Books, 1982.
Critcher, C., S. Hall, T. Jefferson, J. Clarke, and B. Roberts, *Policing the Crisis; Mugging, the State and Law and Order*, London, Macmillan, 1978.
Croft, A., *Weapon in the Struggle*, London, Pluto Press, 1998.
Croft, A., '"Authors Take Sides"; Writers and the Communist Party, 1920-1956', in G. Andrews et al (eds), *Opening the Books*.
Crosland, C.A.R., *The Future of Socialism*, London, Cape, 1956.
Croucher, R., *We Refuse to Starve in Silence*, London, Lawrence and Wishart, 1987.
Curran, J. (ed), *The Future of the Left*, Cambridge, Polity Press/New Socialist, 1984.
Davey, K., *English Imaginaries*, London, Lawrence and Wishart, 1999.
Dromey, J., and G. Taylor, *Grunwick; The Workers Story*, London, Lawrence and Wishart, 1978.
Drucker, H., *Doctrine and Ethos in the Labour Party*, London, George Allen and Unwin, 1979.
Dworkin, D., *Cultural Marxism in Postwar Britain*, Duke University Press, 1997.
Eley, G., 'From Cultures of Militancy to the Politics of Culture, Writing the History of British Communism', review article in *Science and Society* Vol 61 No 1, Spring 1997.
Elliott, G., *Labourism and the English Genius*, London, Verso, 1993.

Excell, A., 'Morris Motors in the 1940s', *History Workshop Journal* 9, Spring 1980.
Favretto, I., 'Structural Reformism. The Socialist Management of Capitalism; the British Labour Party and the Italian Socialist Party, 1956-64', unpublished PhD thesis, University of London, 1998.
Fernbach, D.E., 'Eurocommunism and the Ethical Ideal', in M. Prior (ed), *The Popular and the Political*, London, Routledge and Kegan Paul, 1981.
Fine, B., L. Harris, M. Mayo, A. Weir and E. Wilson, *Class Politics, An Answer to its Critics*, 1984.
Firestone, S., *The Dialectic of Sex: The Case For a Feminist Revolution*, London, Paladin, 1971.
Fishman, N., 'The British Road Is Resurfaced for New Times', in M. Bull and M. Heywood (eds), *Western European Communist Parties after the Revolutions of 1989*, London, Macmillan, 1994.
Fishman, N., *The British Communist Party and the Trade Unions, 1933-1945*, New York, Scolar Press, 1995
Fishman, N., 'No Home But the Trade Union Movement; Communist Activists and Reformist Leaders, 1926-1956', in G. Andrews et al (eds), *Opening the Books*, London, Pluto Press, 1995.
Foot, G., *The Labour Party's Political Thought*, London, Croom Helm, 1985.
Foot, P., 'The Seaman's Struggle', in R. Blackburn and A. Cockburn, *The Incompatibles Trade Union Militancy and the Consensus*, Harmondsworth, Penguin, 1967.
Forgacs, D., 'Gramsci and the British', *New Left Review*, 176, July/August 1989. Forrester, T., *The Labour Party and the Working Class*, London, Heinemann, 1976.
Foster, J., and C. Woolfson, *The Politics of the UCS Work-in*, London, Lawrence and Wishart, 1986.
Furet, F., *The Passing of an Illusion: the Idea of Communism in the Twentieth Century*, Chicago, The University of Chicago Press, 1999.
Giddens, A., *The Third Way and its Critics*, Cambridge, Polity, 2000.
Giddens, A. (ed), *The Global Third Way Debate*, Polity, 2001.
Giddens, A., *Where Now for New Labour?*, Fabian Society/Polity, 2002.
Gieben, B., and S. Hall (eds), *Modernity and its Futures*, Cambridge, Polity/OU, 1992.
Goldthorpe, J., and D. Lockwood, 'Affluence and the British Working Class', *Sociological Review* 11, 1963.
Gouldner, A., *The Origins of Marxism and the Intellectuals*, Oxford, OUP, 1985.
Gramsci, A., *Selections From Prison Notebooks*, London, Lawrence and Wishart, 1971.
Green, J., *All Dressed Up; The Sixties and the Counterculture*, London, Jonathan Cape, 1998.
Hall, S., 'A Sense of Classlessness', *Universities and Left Review*, Vol I No 5, 1958. Hall, S., and J. Jefferson (eds), *Resistance Through Rituals*, London, Hutchinson/CCCS, 1976.
Hall, S., 'The Great Moving Right Show', *Marxism Today*, December, 1978.
Hall, S., 'The Crisis of Labourism', in J. Curran (ed), *The Future of the Left*, Cambridge, Polity Press/*New Socialist*, 1984.
Hall, S., *Critical Dialogues in Cultural Studies*, London, Routledge, 1996.

Hall, S., and M. Jacques (eds), *The Politics of Thatcherism*, London, Lawrence and Wishart, 1983.
Hallas, D., 'The CP, SWP and the Rank and File Movement', *International Socialism*, February 1977.
Harrison, R.,'The Forward March of Labour Halted', in M. Jacques and F. Mulhearn (eds), *The Forward March of Labour Halted*, London, Verso, 1981.
Haseler, S., *The Gaitskellites*, London, Macmillan, 1969.
M. Hatfield, *The House the Left Built*, The Garden City Press Ltd, 1978.
D. Hebdige, *Subculture: The Meaning of Style*, London, Methuen and Co, 1979.
M. Heinemann, 'Left Review, New Writing and the Broad Alliance Against Fascism', in E. Timms and P. Collier (eds), *Visions and Blueprints; Avant-Garde Culture and Radical Politics in Early Twentieth-Century Europe*, Manchester, Manchester University Press, 1998.
Hellman, J., *Journeys Among Women: Feminism in Five Italian Cities*, Cambridge, Polity Press, 1987.
Hellman, S., *Italian Communism in Transition: The Rise and Fall of the Historic Compromise in Turin 1975-1980*, Oxford, OUP, 1988.
Hibbin, S., *Politics, Ideology and the State*, Lawrence and Wishart, 1978.
B. Hindess, *The Decline of Working-Class Politics*, London, Paladin, 1971.
Hinton, J., *The First Shop Stewards Movement*, London, Allen and Unwin, 1973.
Hinton, J., *Labour and Socialism*, London, Wheatsheaf, 1983.
Hobsbawm, E., *Labouring Men: Studies in the History of Labour*, London, Weidenfeld and Nicholson, 1972.
Hobsbawm, E., *Revolutionaries*, London, Meridian, 1973.
Hobsbawm, E., 'Intellectuals and the Labour Movement', *Marxism Today* July, 1979.
Hobsbawm, E., 'The Forward March of Labour Halted?', in M. Jacques and F. Mulhearn (eds), *The Forward March of Labour Halted?*, London, Verso, 1981.
Hobsbawm, E., *The Age of Extremes*, London, Michael Joseph, 1983.
Hobsbawm, E. J., 'Intellectuals and Communism', in F. Mount (ed), *Communism*, Harvill, 1992.
Hodgson, G., *Socialism and Parliamentary Democracy*, Leicester, Spokesman, 1977.
Hogenkamp, B., *Deadly Parallels: Film and the Left in Britain 1929-1939*, London, Lawrence and Wishart, 1986.
Hogenkamp, B., *Film, Television and the Left 1950-1970*, London, Lawrence and Wishart, 2000.
Hoggart, R., *The Uses of Literacy*, London, Chatto and Windus, 1957.
Holland, S., *The Socialist Challenge*, London, Quartet Books, 1975.
Hooper, A., 'A Politics Adequate to the Age', in G. Andrews et al (eds), *New Left, New Right and Beyond*, London, Macmillan, 1999ell, *British Social Democracy*, London, Croom Helm, 1976.
Hunt, A., 'Class Structure in Britain Today', *Marxism Today*, June 1970.
Hunt, A. (ed), *Class and Class Structure*, London, Lawrence and Wishart, 1977.
Hutt, A., *British Trade Unionism*, London, Lawrence and Wishart, 1962.
Hyde, D., *I Believed*, London, William Heinemann Ltd, 1950.

Hyman, R., 'Industrial Conflict and the Political Economy', *Socialist Register*, London, Merlin Press, 1974.
Hyman, R., 'Workers Control and Revolutionary Theory', *Socialist Register*, London, Merlin Press 1974.
Isserman, M., *If I Had a Hammer*, New York, Basic Books, 1987.
Jacks, D., *Student Politics and Higher Education*, London, Lawrence and Wishart, 1975.
Jaggi, M., R. Muller, and S. Schmid, *Red Bologna*, Writers and Readers, 1977.
Jameson, F., 'Periodising the 60s', in S. Sayers (ed), *The Sixties Without Apology*, University of Minnesota Press, 1984.
Jenkins, M., *Bevanism: Labour's High Tide*, Leicester, Spokesman, 1979.
Jensen, J., and G. Ross, *The View From the Inside*, Berkeley, University of California Press, 1984.
Johnson, R.W., *The Long March of the French Left*, London, Macmillan, 1981.
Jones, J., *Union Man: An Autobiography*, London, Collins, 1986.
Kaplan, J., and L. Shapiro (eds), *Red Diapers: Growing up in the Communist Left*, Urbana and Chicago, University of Illinois Press, 1998.
Kelly, J., *Trade Unions and Socialist Politics*, London, Verso, 1988.
Kendall, W., *The Revolutionary Left in Britain*, London, Weidenfeld and Nicholson, 1969.
Kenny, M., 'Communism and the New Left', in G. Andrews et al (eds), *Opening the Books*.
Kenny, M., *The First New Left*, London, Lawrence and Wishart, 1995.
King, F., and G. Matthews (eds), *About Turn: The British Communist Party and the Second World War*, London, Lawrence and Wishart, 1990.
Klugmann, J., *History of the Communist Party of Great Britain Vol I 1919-1924*, London, Lawrence and Wishart 1968.
Klugmann, J., *History of the Communist Party of Great Britain Vol II 1925-26*, London, Lawrence and Wishart, 1969.
Klugmann, J., and P. Oestreicher, *What Kind of Revolution?*, London, Panther Modern Society, 1968.
Labour Party, *Labour's Programme*, 1973.
Labour Party, *Labour's Programme*, 1976.
Laclau, E., and C. Mouffe, *Hegemony and Socialist Strategy*, Verso, 1984.
Lenin, V.I., *On Utopian and Scientific Socialism*, Moscow, Progress Publishers, 1965.
Lenin, V.I., *Imperialism; the Highest Stage of Capitalism*, Peking, Foreign Language Press, 1975.
Lenin, V.I., *What is to be Done?* Peking, Foreign Language Press, 1978.
Lloyd, J., 'All Together Now', *London Review of Books* Vol 22 No 20, 19 October 2000.
Lockwood, D., 'Sources of Variation in Working-Class Images of Society', in *Sociological Review* Vol 14 No 3, November 1996, pp 249-267.
Lumley, R., *States of Emergency: Cultures of Revolt in Italy from 1968-1978*, London, Verso, 1990.
Lyddon, D., '"Glorious Summer": 1972, The High Tide of Rank and File Militancy', in
MacDougall, I., *Militant Miners*, London, Polygon, 1981.
MacLeod, A., *The Death of Uncle Joe*, London, Merlin, 1997.
MacFarlane, L.J., *The British Communist Party; Its Origins and Development*

Until 1929, London, MacGibbon and Kee, 1966.
Marx, K., *Selected Writings*, Oxford, OUP, 1985.
Mandel, E., 'The Lessons of May, 1968', *New Left Review* 52, November-December, 1968.
Marcuse, H., *One-Dimensional Man*, London, Routledge, 1964
Marwick, A., *The Sixties*, Oxford, OUP, 1998.
McEwen, M., *The Greening of a Red*, London, Pluto Press.
McEwen, M., 'The Day the Party Had to Stop', *Socialist Register 1976*, London, Merlin Press, 1976.
MacIntyre, S., *Little Moscows: Communism and Working Class Militancy in Inter-War Britain*, London, Croom Helm, 1980.
MacIntyre, S., *A Proletarian Science*, London, Lawrence and Wishart, 1986.
McIlroy, J., 'Always Outnumbered, Always Outgunned; the Trotskyists and the Trade Unions', in J. McIlroy et al (eds), *British Trade Unions and Industrial Politics Volume Two; The High Tide of Trade Unionism 1964-79*, London, Ashgate Press, 1999.
McIlroy, J., 'Notes on the Communist Party and Industrial Politics', in J. McIlroy,
N. Fishman, and A. Campbell, *British Trade Unions and Industrial Politics Volume Two: The High Tide of Trade Unionism 1964-1979*, London, Ashgate, 1999.
McIlroy, J., and A. Campbell, 'The Communist Party and Industrial Politics, 1964-1975', paper given to 'British Trade Unions, Workers' Struggles and Economic Performance, 1940-1979' conference, University of Warwick, 19-20 September, 1997.
McIlroy, J., and A. Campbell, 'Organising the Militants; the Liaison Committee for the Defence of Trade Unions, 1966-1979', *British Journal of Industrial Relations* 39, 1, 1999.
McIlroy, J., et al (eds), *British Trade Unions and Industrial Politics*, Vol II, London, Ashgate, 1999.
McIlroy, J., N. Fishman and A. Campbell (eds), *British Trade Unions and Industrial Politics*, Volume 2, London, Ashgate, 1999.
McInnes, N., *The Communist Parties of Western Europe*, Oxford, OUP, 1975.
McKibbon, R., 'Why Was There No Marxism in Great Britain?', EH 99, 1984.
Middlemass, K., *Politics in Industrial Society*, London, Andre Deutsch, 1979.
Miliband, R., *Parliamentary Socialism*, London, Allen and Unwin, 1961.
Millett, K., *Sexual Politics*, New York, Doubleday, 1970.
Minkin, L., *The Labour Party Conference*, London, Allen Lane, 1978.
Minkin, L., *The Contentious Alliance: Trade Unions and the Labour Party*, Edinburgh, Edinburgh University Press, 1991.
Mitchell, A., *Behind the Crisis in British Stalinism*, London, New Park, 1984.
Mitchell, J., *Women's Estate*, Harmondsworth, Penguin, 1971.
Mitchell, J., *Women: The Longest Revolution*, London, Virago, 1984.
Morgan, K., *Against Fascism and War*, Manchester, Manchester University Press, 1989.
Morgan, K., *Harry Pollitt*, Manchester, Manchester University Press, 1993.
Morgan, K., 'The Communist Party and the Daily Worker, 1930-1956', in G. Andrews et al (eds), *Opening the Books*.
Morgan, K., 'Introduction', in G. Andrews et al (eds), *Opening the Books*, London, Pluto Press, 1995.

Morgan, K., 'Archival Report, The Archives of the British Communist Party', in *Twentieth Century British History* Vol 7. No 3, OUP, 1996.
Morgan, K., 'King Street Blues', in A. Croft (ed), *Weapon in the Struggle*, London, Pluto Press, 1998.
Mungham, G., and G. Pearson, *Working Class Youth Cultures*, London, Routledge and Kegan Paul, 1976.
Nairn, T., 'The British Political Elite', *New Left Review* 23.Jan-Feb, 1964.
Nairn, T., 'The Nature of the Labour Party', *New Left Review* 27, October/September, 1964.
Napolitano, G., and E. Hobsbawm, *The Italian Road to Socialism*, London, Lawrence Hill and Company, 1977.
Newton, K., *The Sociology of British Communism*, London, Allen Lane, 1969.
Panitch, L., *Social Democracy and Industrial Militancy*, Cambridge, Cambridge University Press, 1976.
Panitch, L., and C. Leys, *The End of Parliamentary Socialism*, London, Verso, 1997.
Parkin, B., 'The Broad Left in TASS', *International Socialism* No 74, January, 1975.
Parkin, F., *Middle-Class Radicals*, Manchester, Manchester University Press, 1968.
Parsons, S., 'Communism in the Professions; the Organisation of the British Communist Party Among Professional Workers, 1933-1956', unpublished PhD thesis, University of Warwick, 1990.
Parsons, S., 'British Communist Party School Teachers in the 1940s and 1950s', in *Science and Society* Vol 61 No 1, Spring 1997.
Pelling, H., *The British Communist Party: A Historical Profile*, London, A. and C. Black, 1958.
Pelling, H., *A History of British Trade Unionism*, 4th edition, London, Macmillan, 1987.
Pimlott, H., 'From the Margins to the Mainstream; A Study of the Transformation of *Marxism Today*', unpublished PhD thesis, University of London 2000.
Prior, M. (ed), *The Popular and the Political*, London, Routledge and Kegan Paul, 1981.
Prior, M., and D. Purdy, *Out of the Ghetto*, Leicester, Spokesman, 1979.
Rowbotham, S., *Promise of a Dream*, Allen Lane, Harmondsworth, The Penguin Press, 2000.
Rowbotham, S., L. Segal, and H. Wainwright, *Beyond the Fragments*, London, Merlin, 1979.
Samuel, R., 'The Lost World of British Communism', Part One, *New Left Review* 154, 1985.
Samuel, R., 'The Lost World of British Communism', Part Two, *New Left Review* 156, March-April 1986.
Samuel, R., 'The Lost World of British Communism', Part Three, *New Left Review* 165, 1987.
Samuel, R., 'Born Again Socialism', in R. Archer et al (eds), *Out of Apathy*.
Samuel, R., *Island Stories: Theatres of Memory Volume II*, Verso, 1998.
Sassoon, D. (ed), *The Italian Communists Speak For Themselves*, Leicester, Spokesman, 1978.
Sassoon, D., *The Strategy of the Italian Communist Party*, London, Frances Pinter, 1981.
Sassoon, D., *One Hundred Years of Socialism*, London, I. B. Tauris, 1996.

Saville, J., 'The Ideology of Labourism', in R. Benewick, R. N. Berki, B. Parekh (eds), *Knowledge and Belief in Politics*.
Saville, J., 'Marxism Today, An Anatomy', *Socialist Register*, London, Merlin Press, 1990.
Sedgewick, P., 'The Two New Lefts', in D. Widgery (ed), *The Left in Britain*, Harmondsworth, Penguin, 1976.
Selbourne, D., *Against Socialist Illusion*, London, Macmillan, 1985.
Selbourne, D., *Left Behind: Journeys Into British Politics*, Cape, 1987.
Selbourne, D., *Death of the Dark Hero*, London, Cape, 1990.
Seyd, P., *The Rise and Fall of the Labour Left*, London, Macmillan, 1987.
Seyd P., and P. Whiteley, *Labour's Grassroots: The Politics of Party Membership*, Oxford, Clarendon Press, 1992.
Shaw, E., *The Labour Party Since 1945*, Oxford, Blackwell, 1996.
Sherwood, M., *Claudia Jones: A Life in Exile*, London, Lawrence and Wishart, 1999. Shore, C., *Italian Communism, The Retreat from Leninism*, London, Pluto Press, 1990 Showstack Sassoon, A., *Gramsci's Politics*, London, Hutchinson, 1987.
Simon, R., *Gramsci's Political Thought*, London, Lawrence and Wishart, 1982.
Squires, M., *Saklatvala: A Political Biography*, London, Lawrence and Wishart, 1990.
Srebrnik, H., *London Jews and British Communism*, Vallentine Cunningham, 1994.
Srebrnik, H., 'Sidestepping the Contradictions: the Communist Party, Jewish Communism and Zionism, 1935-48', in G. Andrews et al (eds), *Opening the Books*, London, Pluto Press, 1995.
Stedman Jones, G., *Languages of Class*, Cambridge, Cambridge University Press, 1983.
Steele, T., *The Emergence of Cultural Studies*, London, Lawrence and Wishart, 1997.
Taylor, R., 'Reds Under the Bed', *New Society* 17.1.74.
Taylor, R., *The Fifth Estate, Britain's Unions in the Modern World*, London, Pan Books, 1980.
Taylor, R., *The Trade Union Question in British Politics: Government and Unions Since 1945*, Oxford, OU Press, 1993.
Taylor, R., *The TUC; From the General Strike to the New Unionism*.
Temple, N., 'Transforming Political Culture on the Left', *Renewal* Volume 8 No 2, Spring 2000.
Thompson, E.P., *Out of Apathy*, London, New Left Books, 1960.
Thompson, E. P., *The Making of the English Working Class*, London, Victor Gollancz, 1963.
Thompson, P., 'Labour's Gannex Conscience? Politics and Popular Attitudes in the Permissive Society', in R. Coopey, S. Fielding and N. Tiratsoo (eds); *The Wilson Governments 1964-1970*, London, Pinter, 1993.
Thompson, W., *The Good Old Cause*, London, Pluto Press, 1992.
Thompson, W., *The Long Death of British Labourism*, London, Pluto Press, 1993.
Thompson, W., *The Left in History*, London, Pluto Press, 1997.
Thompson, W., *The Communist Movement Since 1945*, Oxford, Blackwell, 1998. Thompson, W., and F. Hart, *The UCS Work-In*, London, Lawrence and Wishart, 1972.
Tiersky, R., *French Communism 1920-1972*, Columbia University Press, 1974.

Tiersky, R., *Ordinary Stalinism: Democratic Centralism and the Question of Communist Democratic Development*, London, George Allen and Unwin, 1985.

Togliatti, P., *On Gramsci and Other Writings* (ed D. Sassoon), London, Lawrence and Wishart, 1979.

Touraine, A., *The Return of the Actor*, Minneapolis, University of Minnesota Press, 1988.

Trory, E., *Between the Wars: Memoirs of a Communist Organiser* Crabtree Press, 1974.

TUC, *The Development of the Social Contract*, 1975.

TUC, *TUC Report*, 1978.

M. Waite, 'Young People and Formal Political Activity; a Case Study; Young People and Communist Politics in Britain, 1920-1991', unpublished M. Phil thesis, University of Lancaster, 1992.

Waite, M., 'Sex, Drugs and Rock'n'Roll (and communism)', in G. Andrews et al (eds), *Opening the Books*, London, Pluto Press, 1995.

Waller, M., *Democratic Centralism*, Manchester, Manchester University Press, 1981.

Waller, M., and M. Fennema, *Communist Parties in Western Europe: Decline or Adaptation?*, Oxford, Basil Blackwell, 1988.

Warren, B., 'The British Road to Socialism', *New Left Review* 63, September-October, 1970, pp 27-41.

Warren, B., 'Capitalist Planning and the State', *New Left Review* 72, March-April, 1972.

Warren, B., 'Imperialism and Capitalist Industrialisation', *New Left Review* 1, September-October, 1973.

Warren, B., 'Recession and Its Consequences', *New Left Review* 87/88, September-December, 1974 (double issue).

Warren, B., and M. Prior, *Advanced Capitalism and Backward Socialism*, Leicester, Spokesman, 1975.

Warren, D., *The Key To My Cell*, London, New Park Publications, 1982.

Watters, F., *Being Frank: The Memoirs of Frank Watters*, Askew Printing, 1992.

Westoby, A., *The Evolution of Communism*, Cambridge, Polity Press, 1989.

Widgery, D., *The Left in Britain 1956-68*, Harmondsworth, Penguin, 1976.

Williams, D., 'The British Communist Party's (CPGB) Structure: Professionals and Devotees', in *Challenge to Britain*, Common Cause Bulletin 130, 1974.

Williams, G., 'The Concept of "Egemonia" in the Thought of Antonio Gramsci; Some Notes on Interpretation', *Journal of the History of Ideas* xxi October-December, 1960.

Williams R., *Culture and Society*, London, Chatto and Windus, 1958.

Williams, R., *The Long Revolution*, Harmondsworth, Penguin, 1965.

Williams, R., *May Day Manifesto*, Harmondsworth, Penguin, 1968.

Williams, R., *Towards 2000*, London, Chatto and Windus, 1983.

Wood, N., *Communism and British Intellectuals*, Victor Gollancz, 1959.

Articles in journals published by the Communist Party

Aaronovitch, S., 'Forward Or Back, Prospects For the Movement', *Marxism Today*, January, 1967.

Bibliography

Aaronovitch, S., 'The Working Class and the Broad Democratic Alliance', *Marxism Today*, September, 1979.
Ainley, T., 'Questions of Ideology and Culture', *Comment* 27, May 1967.
Althusser, L., 'Reply to John Lewis', Parts I and II, *Marxism Today*, October and November 1972.
Bellamy, J., 'Racialism', *Comment* 10, July 1976.
Bloomfield, J., 'A Democratic Strategy for Post-School Education', *Marxism Today*, October, 1976.
Bloomfield, J., 'The Student Movement Today', *Comment* 7, February, 1976.
Bloomfield, J., 'The Myth of Rank and Filism', *Comment* 30, November, 1974.
Bowman, D., 'Is Workers Control Possible?', *Comment* 7, October, 1967.
Bowman, D., 'The Trade Unions and Left Progressive Unity', *Comment* 12, October, 1968.
Bridges, G., 'British Youth in Revolt', *Marxism Today*, August, 1969.
Campbell, G.R., 'Trade Unions and Incomes Policy', *Comment* 14, January, 1967.
Campbell, G.R., 'The Movement and the Commission, Delusions About Donovan', *Marxism Today*, September 1968.
Cohen, J., 'A Communist Looks at the New Left Manifesto', *Comment* 20, May, 1967.
Cohen, J., 'Some Thoughts on the Working Class Today', *Marxism Today*, October, 1973.
Cook, J., 'The British Road to Socialism and the Communist Party', *Marxism Today* December, 1978.
Costello, M., 'The Working Class and the Broad Democratic Alliance', *Marxism Today* June, 1979.
Davies, B., 'The Future For Youth', *Comment* 3.October, 1970.
Devine, P., 'Inflation and Marxist Theory', *Marxism Today* March, 1974.
Egelnick, G., 'Non-Manual Workers in the Sixties', *Marxism Today*, August 1964.
Gollan, J., 'Socialist Democracy, Some Problems', *Marxism Today*, January, 1976.
Halpin, K., 'The Contract Must Die by July', *Morning Star*, 17 June, 1977.
Hobsbawm, E., 'The Retreat Into Extremism', *Marxism Today*, April 1985.
Jacques, M., 'Notes on the Concept of Intellectuals', *Marxism Today*, October 1971.
Jacques, M., 'Trends in Youth Culture, Some Aspects', *Marxism Today*, September 1973.
Jacques, M., 'Universities and Capitalism', *Marxism Today*, July 1975.
Jacques, M., 'Culture, Class Struggle and the Communist Party', *Comment* 29, May 1976.
Kerrigan, P., 'The Factories Will Be Decisive', *Comment* 18, January 1969.
Kettle, A., 'How Left is the New Left?', *Marxism Today*, October 1960.
Klugmann, J., 'Dialogue Between Christianity and Marxism', *Marxism Today* September 1967.
Klugmann, J., 'The British Road to Socialism; A Brief History Since 1945', *Comment* 5, February 1977.
McLennan, G., 'Interview with J. Klugmann', *Marxism Today*, March 1977.
McLennan, G., 'Interview with Peter Avis', *Morning Star* 4, July 1977.
Matthews, B., 'Britain and the Socialist Revolution', *Comment* 15, January 1972.

Matthews, G., 'The Crisis and the Left', *Comment* 20, March 1976.
Moss, J., 'Should Marijuana Be Legalised?', *Comment* 3, June 1967.
Pearce, B., 'The Strategy For Socialist Revolution in Britain', *Marxism Today*, January 1971.
Purdy, D., 'Some Thoughts on the Party's Policies Towards Prices, Wages and Incomes', *Marxism Today*, August 1974.
Priscott, D., 'The British Road to Socialism and the Communist Party', *Marxism Today*, February 1979.
Purdy, D., 'British Capitalism Since the War', (Parts I and II) *Marxism Today*, September and October 1976.
Ramelson, B., 'Workers Control? Possibilities and Limitations', *Marxism Today*, October 1968, pp296-303.
Ramelson, B., 'Trade Union Militancy', *Comment* 8, July 1967.
Ramelson, B., 'Union Card or Director's Car?', *Morning Star* 3, February 1977.
Reid, B., 'The Drug Scene Today', *Comment* 7, February 1970.
Roberts, G., 'The Strategy of Rank and Fileism', *Marxism Today*, December 1976.
Spours, K., 'Students, Education and the State', *Marxism Today*, November 1977.
Steward, F., 'Lucas Aerospace; the Politics of the Corporate Plan', *Marxism Today*, March 1979.
Tanburn, N., 'After the Show', *Comment* 23, July 1977.
Taylor, G., 'The Labour Government 1974-1978', *Marxism Today*, October 1978.
Topham, T., and K. Coates, 'Discussion Contribution on Workers' Control, *Marxism Today*, January 1969.
Williamson, J., 'The Meaning of Black Power', *Comment* 11, November 1967.
Woddis, J., 'The Anti-Monopoly Alliance', *Comment*, May 1976.
Woddis, J., 'A Communist-Christian discussion in Essex', *Comment* 10, March 1967.

Official party pamphlets
CPGB, *About Marxism: A Communist Party Introductory Course*, 1974.
CPGB, *Report of Commission on Inner Party Democracy*, 1956.
CPGB, *Report of the Commission on Party Organisation*, 1965.
CPGB (Cultural Committee), *Questions of Ideology and Culture*, 1967.
CPGB, *The Role of Communist Party Branches*, 1974.
CPGB, *Report of Commission On Inner Party Democracy, with Alternative Proposals: Comments of the Executive Committee*, 1979.
CPGB, *The British Road to Socialism* (1968 edition).
CPGB, *The British Road to Socialism* (1977 edition).
CPGB, EEC Study Group, *The Common Market: Let's Get Out*, 1980.
Cook, D., *Students*, CPGB, 1973.
Cook, D., *A Knife at the Throat of Us All*, CPGB, 1978.
Gollan, J., *The Case For Socialism in the Sixties*, CPGB, 1966.
Halpin, K., *The Case For the Trade Unions*, CPGB, 1979.
Klugmann, J., *The Future of Man*, CPGB, 1969.
Pollitt, H., *Looking Ahead*, CPGB, 1947.
Ramelson, B., *Smash Phase III*, CPGB, 1973.
Ramelson, B., *Social Contract: Cure All or Con-Trick?*, CPGB, 1974.

Ramelson, B., *Bury the Social Contract*, CPGB, 1977.
Small, R., *Women: the Road to Equality and Socialism*, CPGB, 1972.
Woddis, J., *Time to Change Course*, CPGB, 1973.

APPENDIX
Material from Communist Party Archive
Communist University of London files (1969-1981)
National Student Committee files (1964-1979)
Executive Committee (EC) files, 1964-1979)
Political Committee files (PC), 1964-1979)
Cultural Committee files (1964-1975)
Theory and Ideology Committee (TIC), 1976-1980
Bert Ramelson papers
National Women's Advisory file
Race Relations Committee
West Indian Advisory Committee
Gay and Lesbian Advisory Committee
Communist Party Congress Documents

Communist Party journals consulted
Challenge (YCL)
Cogito (YCL)
Comment
Daily Worker (1964-1966)
Eurored
Labour Monthly
Marxism Today
Morning Star (from 1966)
New Times
Red Letters
Red Rag
Socialist Europe

Non-CP journals
Broad Left Journal
History Workshop Journal
International Socialism
New Left Review
Politics and Power
Socialist Worker
Tribune

Personal correspondence
Personal papers and correspondence of the following were consulted:
Mike Prior (including material related to the Smith Group and the Party Group)
Mike Power
Joe Ball
B. Ramelson (held in the National Museum of Labour History, Manchester)

Index

Aaronovitch, Sam 92, 99, 103, 152, 170, 198, 199
Adams, Jack 173
Adi, Hakim 19, 25, 29, 42, 45
Ainley, Ted 75
Alternative Economic Strategy (AES) 86, 126-132
Althusser, Louis 51, 59, 61, 66, 78, 152, 153, 154, 171, 181, 196, 235
Althusserian, 59, 68, 81, 149, 152
Amis, Martin 12-13, 14, 18
Anderson, Paul 117, 135
Anderson, Perry 78, 143, 170, 235
Anti-Americanism 21, 27
Anti-Apartheid movement 121, 158, 213
Archer, Robin 100, 137
Ascherson, Neal 226, 243
Ashton, Jack 221
Assiter, Alison 171
Avis, Peter 177

Bain, Dougie 47
Baker, Alan 221
Ball, Joe 148, 171
Barker, Paul 215
Beatles, The 34
Beckett, Francis 19, 69, 138, 199, 203, 221
Bell, Tom 193
Bellamy, Ron 55, 95
Benn, Tony 126, 138, 188-189, 199, 215
Bennett, Fran 200
Benton, Sarah 44, 157, 160, 179, 182, 195, 196, 197, 243
Berger, Stefan 102
Berlinguer, Enrico 162-163, 175, 176
Bernal, J.D. 99
Berridge, Claud 109
Bevan, Aneurin 102
Birch, Reg 99, 109, 119
Blackburn, Robin 70, 103, 235
Blackwell, Trevor 212, 222
Blair, Tony 224, 238, 243
Bleaney, Michael 173
Bloomfield, Jon 71, 135, 144, 152, 164-165, 177, 192, 199
Bloomfield, Jude 71, 172
Bolton, George 221
Bowden, Maggie 204
Bowman, David 133
Branson, Noreen 42, 45
Brennan, Irene 178

Brett, Ken 133
Brewster, Charlie 117
Bridges, George 37, 39, 40, 47, 48, 153, 166, 176, 177, 194, 200
British Road to Socialism 17, 18, 32, 74, 77, 84, 88, 93, 95-97, 99, 103, 104, 120, 122, 127, 133, 144, 160, 165, 166, 177, 179, 182, 189, 192, 193, 195, 198, 225
Broad Democratic Alliance 160, 195
Broad Left (Students) 16, 51, 52, 56-58, 155-156, 192
Broad Left (Unions) 86, 89-90, 108, 109, 115, 117-120
Brooks, Gladys 62, 67, 72
Brown, Alan 117
Browning, Genia 49, 172, 194
Bruley, Sue 24, 29, 45
Brunt, Ros 200, 243
Buckton, Ray 109
Bullock Report 138, 175
Burns, Emile 97
Bush, Alan 99

Callaghan, Jim 138
Callaghan, John 69, 98, 104, 159, 175
Cameron, Ken 109
Campaign for Nuclear Disarmament (CND) 30, 33, 213
Campbell, Alan 106, 132, 134, 199
Campbell, Beatrix 62, 63, 65, 68, 71, 72, 144, 156, 166, 177, 200, 216-217, 219, 220, 222, 231, 242
Campbell, J.R. 26, 75, 111, 134
Carr, Frank 199
Carrillo, Santiago 162, 176
Carritt, Bill 70
Carter, Pete 37, 39, 40, 144, 173, 187-188
Carter, Trevor 25, 30, 42, 45, 153, 158-159, 171, 174
Castle, Barbara 112
Challenge 28, 34, 35, 36, 38, 39, 191
Changes 97
Charter 88 235
Chater, Tony 95, 189, 205, 206, 209, 221
Chun, Lin 43, 78, 100, 101, 137, 235, 245
Coates, David 102
Coates, Ken 123-125, 134, 138
Cockburn, Alexander 70, 103
Cockett, Richard 21, 40
Cogito 37, 38
Cohen, Gerry 67, 157, 173, 221

Index

Cohen, Jack 154, 173
Cohen, Margaret 100
Cohen, Phil 19, 71
Cole, G.D.H. 102
Cole, Stan 101
Comment 48, 72, 94, 97, 99, 101, 177, 178, 179, 195, 196, 198
Communist-Christian Dialogue 17, 81-83, 101, 234, 235
Communist University of London (CUL) 16, 51, 52, 54, 56, 59, 79, 150, 164, 167, 177, 178, 182, 189, 193-194, 199, 200
Cook, Dave 14, 39, 40, 52, 56-59, 71, 144, 145, 154, 157, 158, 169, 180, 188, 191, 193, 194, 195, 197, 198, 206, 221
Coote, Anna 71
Cornforth, Maurice 43, 77, 99
Costello, Mick 188, 203-207, 208, 221
Cox, Idris 96
Croft, Andy 19, 27, 42, 43
Crosland, Tony 69, 87, 239, 245
Croucher, Richard 41
Cultural Committee 55, 70, 78, 80, 99, 143

Daily Worker 13, 27, 28, 32, 45, 61, 96, 107
Daly, Lawrence 118
Darke, Marian 231
Davey, Kevin 47-48, 117, 135
Davies, Barney 32, 37
Dell, Edmund 138
Democratic Centralism 17, 29, 181, 193, 206, 209
Democratic Left 238
Demos 238, 241, 242
Devine, Pat 127-128, 166, 177, 180, 196
Dictatorship of the Proletariat 162-163
Dix, Bernard 188
Dixon, Les 133
Donovan Report 91, 109, 110, 111-112
Doyle, Mikki 62
Dromey, Jack 174, 198
Drugs (and YCL) 37
Dubcek, Alexander 14, 92-93, 220
Dunn, Bill 209
Dunn, Jack 118
Durkin, Tom 203, 221
Durrans, Brian 70
Dutt, Rajani Palme 13, 92, 94
Dworkin, Denis 101

Economic Committee 75, 127-129, 145, 148, 149, 198
Edgar, David 218, 243
Eley, Geoff 41, 42
Elliott, Gregory 102
Engels, Frederick 51, 55, 61, 68
ETU Scandal 30-31, 75, 89
Etzioni, Amitai 240
Eurocommunism 15, 16, 17, 18, 52, 92, 95, 141, 159-169, 191, 194, 195
Eurored 161, 176
Executive Committee 67, 68, 93, 106, 107, 150, 154, 157, 204, 205, 206, 209

Exell, Arthur 43

Facing up to the Future 231
Fairclough, Andy 199
Falber, Reuben 56, 67, 70, 94, 104, 133, 168, 177, 178, 182, 197
Feminism 14, 21, 28, 59-64, 141, 148-149, 155-157, 182
Fernbach, David 176
Filling, Brian 53
Fine, Ben 222
Finlayson, Alan 241, 245
Firestone, Shulamith 63, 71
Fishman, Nina 19, 23, 41, 85, 90, 102, 107, 132, 133, 134, 199, 218
Foot, Geoffrey 84, 102
Foot, Paul 103
Forgacs, David 142, 170, 172
Forrester, Tom 137
Forward March of Labour Halted 32, 145, 147, 179, 183-189, 197
Foster, John 115-116, 135, 204, 209
Francis, Dai 118
Frankenberg, Ronnie 172
French, Sid 93, 99, 163, 164, 196
French Communist Party (PCF) 15-16, 161, 163, 164, 175
Furet, Francis 18
Fyrth, Jim 43, 98

Gallacher, Willie 26
Gardiner, Jean 173
Gay Liberation Movement 157-158, 174, 195
Gibbes, Asquith 159
Giddens, Anthony 238-239, 240, 245
Gieben, Bram 40
Gill, Ken 90, 109, 116, 118, 132, 138, 186-187, 203, 209, 221, 240
Gill, Tess 221
Goldthorpe, John 46
Gollan, John 26, 32, 37, 56, 70, 88, 94, 103, 122, 167, 177
Goodwin, Phil 53, 70
Gorbachev, Mikhail 219, 220, 227
Gramsci, Antonio 13, 40, 43-44, 51, 58, 59, 138, 141, 142, 143, 147, 153, 154, 159-160, 170
Gramscians 14, 16, 18, 22, 40, 51, 65, 73, 81, 92, 97, 115, 116, 123, 129, 142, 144, 149, 155, 159, 161, 165, 167, 168, 169, 183, 185-186, 191, 194, 195, 197, 206, 210, 233, 241
Gramscism (British) 17, 140-153, 179-182, 228-230, 235
Granlund, Chris 223
Green, David 171
Green, Jonathan 21, 40, 41
Green, Josie 177, 196
Greenham Common Women's Peace Camp 217
de Groot, Joanna 41, 72, 172
Grunwick 159, 174, 198

Hall, Stuart 21, 40, 44, 46, 47, 59, 138, 170, 180, 201, 218, 228, 235-236, 241, 243, 244
Hallas, Duncan 135

Halpin, Kevin 109, 187, 198, 199, 221
Halveson, Ron 221
Hannington, Wal 196
Harding, Neil 44
Harris, Lawrence 198, 222
Heath, Edward 114, 126, 129, 146, 147
Hebdige, Dick 236, 243
Heinemann, Margot 42, 99
Held, David 243
Heywood, Jackie 37, 38, 39, 47, 48, 172
Hibbin, Sally 71, 145, 156, 172, 177
Hicks, Mike 203, 209
Hindess, Barry 59, 152
Hinton, James 41
Hirst, Paul 59, 152
Hobsbawm, Eric 18, 23, 26, 32, 41, 42, 43, 69, 99, 145, 147, 177, 179, 180, 183-188, 197, 199, 202, 211, 219, 222, 229, 233, 241-242, 244, 246
Hodgson, Geoff 97, 98
Hoffman, John 174
Hogenkamp, Bert 43, 98
Hoggart, Richard 26, 42, 47, 244
Holland, Stuart 126, 130-131, 139, 146
Horner, Arthur 26
Howell, David 138
Howells, Kim 224
Hunt, Alan 46, 53, 154, 166, 177, 186, 200
Hunt, Judith 144
Hussain, Athar 172
Hutt, Alan 46, 98
Hyde, Douglas 27, 43
Hyman, Richard 137

Iliffe, Steve 171, 172
Independent Labour Party 77
Inner Party Democracy (IPD) 18, 180-182, 193, 194, 206
Innes, Bill 231
In Place of Strife 112-113, 115
Institute For Workers Control 123-125, 235
International Marxist Group 71
International Socialists 115, 190
Italian Communist Party (PCI) 13, 15, 82, 140, 153, 160, 175, 246

Jacks, Digby 54, 56, 70
Jacques, Martin 41, 44, 47, 49, 53, 54, 57, 69, 70, 145, 150, 160, 161-162, 165, 169, 170, 171, 177, 179-180, 191, 193, 194, 197, 199, 203, 205-206, 219, 220, 225, 228, 231, 243
Jameson, Fredric 21, 40
Jefferys, Steve 199
Jenkins, Mark 102
Jensen, Jane 98, 196
Johnstone, Monty 47, 79, 100, 145, 172, 183, 231
Jones, Claudia 30, 45, 174
Jones, Jack 75, 108, 118, 119, 129, 131, 132, 139, 189
Jouhl, Avtar 45

Kay, Jackie 71

Kelly, John 132, 133
Kendall, Walter 41, 98
Kenny, Michael 42, 43, 78, 100, 103, 137, 142, 170, 172
Kerrigan, Peter 75
Kettle, Arnold 77, 79, 99, 100, 145
Keyworth, Florence 62
Khrushchev, Nikita 12, 28, 30, 167
Kinks, The 35
Kinnock, Neil 237
Klugmann, James 28, 77, 79, 81, 82, 92, 100, 101, 103, 107, 143, 145, 152, 178, 179
Kornhauser, W. 41
Kuya, Dorothy 45

Laclau, Ernesto 221
Lane, Tony 202-207, 220, 233
Leadbeater, Charles 219, 224, 231, 238, 239-240, 241, 243
Left Book Club 24
Left Unity 77, 89-92, 105
Lenin, V.I. 14, 29, 44, 51, 55, 76, 102
Leninism 17, 73, 74, 86, 105
Lennon, John 14
Lewis, John 100, 153, 172, 235
Lewis, Lou 109
Liaison Committee for the Defence of Trade Unions (LCDTU) 91, 109-110, 112, 114, 119
Link 68
Livingstone, Ken 202, 217, 272
Lloyd, John 246
Lockwood, David 31, 46
Loftus, Maria 196
Lucas Aerospace 125
Lukacs, George 78, 100
Lyddon, Dave 114, 134, 135

MacDougall, Alan 145, 172, 194, 196
MacFarlane, L.J. 41, 98
Macleod, Alison 13, 19, 42
Marcuse, Herbert 69, 101
Marwick, Arthur 21, 40, 69
Marx, Karl 51, 55, 61, 78, 81, 83, 172
Marxism 23, 26, 29, 51, 52, 55, 58, 68, 78, 79, 82, 95, 141, 155, 193
Marxism Today 46, 48, 49, 55, 72, 80, 81, 82, 92, 99, 100, 101, 104, 111, 123, 129, 137, 139, 145, 154, 170, 173, 175, 183, 188, 189, 196, 197, 198, 200, 202-207, 214, 217, 220, 224, 226-231, 236, 238, 241, 244
Marxist-Leninist 38, 62
Matthews, George 46, 97-98, 104, 132, 145, 165, 170, 171, 182, 207
May Day Manifesto 61, 79, 100
Mayo, Marjorie 222
McGahey, Mick 108, 118
McIlroy, John 90, 98, 102, 103, 106, 109, 117, 118, 119, 132, 133, 134, 136, 139, 153, 172, 190, 199
McKay, Ian 205, 221
McKibbin, Ross 102
McLennan, Gordon 26, 156, 166, 171, 174, 177,

178, 182, 204, 206, 207, 209, 221
McLennan, Gregor 214-215, 222
Meacher, Michael 217
Medvedev, Roy 207-208
Medvedev, Zhores 167
Michels, Robert 44
Middlemass, Keith 134
Miliband, Ralph 83
militant labourism 16-17, 73, 83-86, 96, 106-110, 114-132, 179, 201, 205
Militant Tendency 202
miners strike (1926) 24
miners strike (1984-1985) 208-210
Mitchell, Juliet 71, 171
Moore, Sammy 109
Moore, Suzanne 218
Morgan, Kevin 28, 41, 43, 45, 74, 170
Morning Star 28, 32, 48, 55, 60, 61, 63, 64, 65, 96, 101, 103, 107, 113, 116-117, 151, 152, 156, 159, 167, 171, 177, 190, 198, 199, 203, 207, 208, 220
Morris, Max 109, 116
Morris, William 17, 78
Mort, Frank 236
Morton, A.L. 92
Morton, Cyril 108
Mouffe, Chantal 221, 245
Mulgan, Geoff 224, 237, 240-241, 242
Mulhearn, Francis 197
Murray, Robin 243
Murray, Roger 173

Nairn, Tom 83, 102, 143, 170, 235
Napolitano, Giorgio 167, 177
National Council for Labour Colleges 26
National Students Committee 14, 54, 69
National Union of Seamen 90
National Union of Students 51, 55
National Women's Advisory Committee 16, 24, 61, 64, 66, 144, 217
Nawrat, Chris 19, 145, 172, 180, 194, 200
New Communist Party 99, 179, 191
New Labour 237-243
New Left 12, 17, 18, 31, 32, 33, 35, 55, 61, 79, 88, 94, 97, 122-123, 141, 150, 167, 170, 183, 195, 234-235, 236, 242
New Left Review 78, 133, 170, 195, 226
New Reasoner 78
New Socialist 213, 221
New Times 18, 224-243
Manifesto For New Times 231-234
Newton, Kenneth 23, 31, 39, 41, 46, 49, 133
Nicholls, Brian 197
Nicholson, Fergus 52, 54, 56-57

Orwell, George 216
Ostreicher, Paul 82, 101

Palme Dutt, Rajani 28, 45, 97-98
Panitch, Leo 84, 102, 133, 134
Parkin, Frank 39, 46, 49
Parsons, Steve 41
Party Group 63-65, 72, 115, 127, 198

Pearce, Bert 55, 208, 244
Peck, John 223
Pentonville Five 110, 114
People's Jubilee 151, 164, 235
People's Press Printing Society 207, 208
Perryman, Mark 219, 223
Pimlott, Herbert 225, 243
Pitt, Malcolm 203
Plebs League 26
Pocock, Gerry 132, 221
Political Committee 93, 106, 167, 173, 204, 205, 206, 207
Politics and Power 194, 200
Pollitt, Harry 26, 28, 97
Popular Front 24
post-fordism 226-227
Poulantzas, Nicos 154, 155, 173
Power, Mike 48, 98, 114, 134, 199, 245
Prague Spring 14, 38, 92-95, 220
Prior, Mike 54, 70, 72, 128-129, 132, 133, 136, 139, 144, 146-148, 169, 170, 176, 178, 186, 194, 197, 198
Priscott, Dave 177, 180, 196, 208
Purdy, Dave 98, 127-129, 146, 148, 169, 170, 178, 186, 194, 198

Questions of Ideology and Culture 55, 79-81, 100, 150

Rabstein, Martin 178
Radical Student Alliance 53, 54, 69
Ramelson, Bert 15, 16, 48, 75, 89, 90, 95, 96, 98, 106, 132, 133, 135, 137, 139, 152, 182, 187, 188, 197, 203, 209, 221
Red Rag 16, 37, 66-69, 72, 148, 217
Reid, Betty 70
Reid, Jimmy 31, 32, 153
Reid, John 224,
Revolutionary Socialist Student Federation 54
Richards, Joanne 196
Roberts, Geoff 135, 145, 153, 172, 176, 178, 180, 194, 196, 200
Robeson branch 30
Robinson, Derek 203, 208, 221
Ross, George 98, 196
Rothstein, Andrew 55, 92, 104
Rowbotham, Sheila 71, 200
Rustin, Michael 243

Saklatvala, Shapurji 76, 98
Saltley, John 171
Samuel, Raphael 12, 23, 25, 27, 29, 41, 42, 43, 44, 46, 59, 210, 218, 220
Sapper, Alan 109
Sartre, Jean-Paul 78, 100
Sassoon, Donald 40, 63, 69, 71, 101, 104, 110, 134, 136
Saville, John 12, 26, 78, 83, 102, 195, 244
Scanlon, Hugh 75, 108, 109, 116, 119, 131, 132, 133, 189
Scargill, Arthur 114, 118, 208, 209, 210, 211
Seabrook, Jeremy 211-213
Segal, Lynne 200

Seifert, Roger 199
Selbourne, David 18, 215-216, 222
Sharma, Vishnu 159, 221
Sherwood, Marika 45, 175
Shore, Cris 98
Showstack Sassoon, Anne 59, 71, 200
Simon, Brian 55, 70, 75, 77, 80, 145
Simon, Roger 49, 142, 145, 152
Skidelsky, Robert 18
Slipman, Sue 41, 57, 68, 70, 71, 72, 144, 145, 156, 193, 194, 200
Small, Rosemary 64, 68, 157
Smith Group 63, 128, 198
Social Contract 110, 127, 129-132, 141, 146, 187, 190
Socialist Europe 161, 176
socialist humanism 17, 73, 77-83, 235
Socialist Workers Party 190, 218
Soviet Mantra 15, 140, 166-169, 207-208
Soviet Union 12, 13, 14, 15, 17, 18, 22, 30, 38, 78, 86, 92, 94, 95, 105, 145, 160, 167, 207, 220
Spanish Civil War 26
Spanish Communist Party (PCE) 16, 161, 164
Spours, Ken 59, 71, 145, 172, 194, 196
Squires, Mike 98
Srebrnik, Henry 19, 24, 25, 42
Stalin, Joseph 12, 30, 98
Stalinism 13, 17, 38, 101, 179, 181
Stedman Jones, Gareth 213-214
Steward, Fred 243
Swann, Irene 197
Styles, Jean 156, 173

Tanburn, Nigel 151, 171
Tanner, Jack 133
Tarrow, Sydney 50, 69
Tatchell, Peter 202
Tawney, R.H. 239, 245
Taylor, Charles 100
Taylor, Graham 130, 139, 174, 198
Taylor, Robert 115, 116, 132, 135, 137, 139
Temple, Nina 132, 191, 221, 231, 244, 245
Thatcherism 194, 201, 211, 218, 225, 228-229, 232, 233-234
Theory and Ideology Committee 144, 171
Therborn, Goran 243
Third Way 238-243
Thompson, E.P. 12, 26, 78, 100, 142, 172, 195, 236
Thompson, Willie 19, 25, 42, 46, 68, 69, 72, 76, 84, 85, 99, 102, 103, 110, 134, 173, 177, 190, 195, 197, 200, 210, 221, 223
Tiersky, Ronald 45
Time to Change Course 120-121
Tocher, John 108
Togliatti, Palmiro 82, 160-161, 175
Topham, Tony 123-125, 134, 138
Touraine, Alain 40, 69
Townshend, Pete 34
Trend is Communism (The) 34-35
Tribe, Keith 172
Tribune 77, 99
Triesman, David 224
Trory, Ernie 43
True, Arthur 108
TUC 107, 111-114, 129, 187

Upper Clyde Shipbuilders Dispute 115-116, 125
Urry, John 243, 244

Wainwright, Hilary 188, 200
Waite, Mike 32, 36, 43, 45, 48, 104, 199
Wake, George 108
Waller, Michael 29, 45, 196
Warren, Bill 63, 127-129, 133, 136, 139, 144, 146-148, 170, 173, 198
Warren, Des 120, 136
Watters, Frank 71
Weir, Angela 174, 222
Weir, Stuart 219
West African branch 24, 29, 30, 158
Westergaard, John 215
West Indian Advisory Committee 30, 45
West Indian branch 30, 45, 158
Westoby, Adam 44, 98
Whitfield, David 209
Who, The 34
Williams, Emlyn 118
Williams, Gwyn. A. 142, 170
Williams, Raymond 47, 142, 188, 235
Williams, Shirley 126
Wilson, Elizabeth 174, 222
Wilson, Harold 84, 88, 90, 91, 103, 110
Wise, Audrey 171
Wittgenstein, Ludwig 99
Woddis, Jack 43, 120-121, 136
Women Against Pit Closures 210
Women's Liberation Movement 60, 61, 62, 63, 64, 66, 148-149, 156, 166
Wood, Neal 28, 43, 69, 100
Woolfson, Charles 115-116, 135
Wright, Bob 133

Young Communist League 16, 30, 31, 32-40, 51, 52, 57, 62, 64, 67, 141, 150, 191-192, 194, 199
Young, Michael 239, 245